International Trade and Human Rights

SIE *Studies in International Economics* includes works dealing with the theory, empirical analysis, and evaluation of international policies and institutions, in the area of international macroeconomics and finance, international trade theory and policy, as well as international legal and political economy.

Alan V. Deardorff and Robert M. Stern, Editors
Constituent Interests and U.S. Trade Policies

Gary R. Saxonhouse and T. N. Srinivasan, Editors
Development, Duality, and the International Economic Regime: Essays in Honor of Gustav Ranis

Charles P. Kindleberger *Essays in History: Financial, Economic, Personal*

Keith Acheson and Christopher Maule
Much Ado about Culture: North American Trade Disputes

Alan V. Deardorff and Robert M. Stern *Social Dimensions of U.S. Trade Policies*

Thomas Cottier and Petros C. Mavroidis, Editors
Regulatory Barriers and the Principle of Non-Discrimination in World Trade Law, The World Trade Forum, Volume 2

Bernard Hoekman and Jamel Zarrouk, Editors *Catching Up with the Competition: Trade Opportunities and Challenges for Arab Countries*

Jun Fu *Institutions and Investments: Foreign Direct Investment in China during an Era of Reforms*

Robert M. Stern, Editor *Services in the International Economy*

Keith E. Maskus and John S. Wilson, Editors
Quantifying the Impact of Technical Barriers to Trade: Can It Be Done?

Robert M. Stern, Editor *Issues and Options for U.S.-Japan Trade Policies*

Thomas Cottier and Petros C. Mavroidis, Editors
Intellectual Property: Trade, Competition, and Sustainable Development, The World Trade Forum, Volume 3

Andrew G. Brown
Reluctant Partners: A History of Multilateral Trade Cooperation, 1850–2000

Ka Zeng
Trade Threats, Trade Wars: Bargaining, Retaliation, and American Coercive Diplomacy

Thomas Cottier and Petros C. Mavroidis, Editors
The Role of the Judge in International Trade Regulation: Experience and Lessons for the WTO, The World Trade Forum, Volume 4

Frederick M. Abbott, Christine Breining-Kaufmann, and Thomas Cottier, Editors
International Trade and Human Rights: Foundations and Conceptual Issues, The World Trade Forum, Volume 5

For a complete list of books in the series, please visit
www.press.umich.edu/subjects/econ.html

THE WORLD TRADE FORUM, VOLUME 5

International Trade and Human Rights

Foundations and Conceptual Issues

Frederick M. Abbott, Christine Breining-Kaufmann, and Thomas Cottier,
Editors

Michelle Foster and Thomas M. Fischer,
Associate Editors

THE UNIVERSITY OF MICHIGAN PRESS
Ann Arbor

Published in the United States of America by
The University of Michigan Press
Manufactured in the United States of America
♾ Printed on acid-free paper

2009 2008 2007 2006 4 3 2 1

A CIP catalog record for this book is available from the British Library.

Library of Congress Cataloging-in-Publication Data

International trade and human rights : foundations and conceptual issues /
Frederick M. Abbott, Christine Breining-Kaufmann, and Thomas Cottier, editors.
p. cm. — (World trade forum ; v. 5) (Studies in international economics)
"On August 12-14, 2001 . . . met . . . the fifth World Trade Forum . . . in Berne, Switzerland"—preface.
ISBN-13: 978-0-472-11535-8 (cloth : alk. paper)
ISBN-10: 0-472-11535-9 (cloth : alk. paper)
1. International trade—Congresses. 2. Human rights—Congresses. I. Abbott, Frederick M. II. Breining-Kaufmann, Christine. III. Cottier, Thomas. IV. World Trade Forum (Series) ; v. 5. V. Studies in international economics (Ann Arbor, Mich.)

HF1372.I575 2006
323—dc22 2005052973

The World Trade Forum

The World Trade Forum was founded in 1997 to offer an opportunity for an international in-depth discussion of issues facing the world trading system. The Forum is organized through the cooperation of the Universities of Berne and Neuchâtel (Switzerland). Since the year 2000, it has been held at the newly-founded World Trade Institute in Berne. Forum participants include academics, practitioners, and professionals from government and from international non-governmental organizations. Representing both the legal and economic communities, the participants bring a wide variety of perspectives to the issues of debate.

Each year, one particular topic is chosen as the focus of that year's forum. The participants invited to the conference are requested to prepare a paper on that topic, and then to present the paper for discussion. Question and-answer sessions follow each presentation, and a short analysis by an appointed discussant following the presentation of each group of papers allows for a synthesis of the ideas. At the end of all sessions, a roundtable discussion takes place, in which participants may either make comments on the overall problems of the topic or address questions and suggestions to the other participants in light of the entire series of papers presented.

Following the conference, the authors of the papers revise their submissions for publication in the series of books that accompany the World Trade Forum conferences. An introduction and conclusory analysis by the editors further the synthesis of the topic at hand and aid the reader in determining the overall results of the scholarship.

We are most grateful to the Silva Casa Foundation in Berne for its generous financial support that allows the conferences to take place as well as for its encouragement to pursue the idea of the World Trade Forum, and to the Universities of Berne and Neuchâtel.

The World Trade Forum series was founded in order to help spread the ideas that arise from the careful consideration of the issue presented to interested persons throughout the world. We sincerely hope that this volume achieves this goal.

Contents

Abbreviations and Acronyms

AB	Appellate Body
AEC	African Economic Community
AGOA	African Growth and Opportunity Act
AIDS	Acquired Immunodeficiency Syndrome
AU	African Union
ANCOM	Andean Common Market
CACM	Central American Common Market
CCPR	International Covenant on Civil and Political Rights
CEDAW	Convention on the Elimination of All Forms of Discrimination Against Women
CESC(R)	International Covenant on Economic, Social and Cultural Rights
CFSP	Common Foreign and Security Policy
COMESA	Common Market for Eastern and Southern Africa
DSB	Dispute Settlement Body
DSU	Dispute Settlement Understanding
EAC	East African Community
EEC	European Economic Community
EC	European Community
ECHR	European Convention on Human Rights
ECJ	European Court of Justice
ECOSOC	United Nations Economic and Social Council
ECOWAS	Economic Community of West African States
ECtHR	European Court of Human Rights
EU	European Union
EUT	Treaty on European Union
FAO	Food and Agriculture Organization
FTA	Free Trade Agreement
FTAA	Free Trade Agreement of the Americas
GATS	General Agreement on Trade in Services
GATT	General Agreement on Tariffs and Trade
GDP	Gross Domestic Product
GPA	Government Procurement Agreement
GSP	Generalised System of Preferences
HIV	Human Immunodeficiency Virus
ICESCR	International Covenant on Economic, Social and Cultural Rights
IEEPA	International Emergency Economic Powers Act

ILC	International Law Commission
ILO	International Labour Organization
IMF	International Monetary Fund
LDC	Least-Developed Country
MEA	Multilateral Environmental Agreement
MERCOSUR	Mercado Común del Sur
MFN	Most-Favoured Nation
NAALC	North American Agreement on Labor Cooperation
NAFTA	North American Free Trade Agreement
NEPAD	New Partnership for Africa's Development
NGO	Non-Governmental Organization
OAS	Organization of American States
OAU	Organization of African Unity
OCHCR	Office of the High Commissioner for Human Rights
OECD	Organization for Economic Cooperation and Development
PPMs	Process and Production Methods
USGSP	United States Generalized System of Preferences
USTR	United States Trade Representative
VCLT	Vienna Convention on the Law of Treaties
WHO	World Health Organization
WIPO	World Intellectual Property Organization
WTO	World Trade Organization
WWII	World War II
SADC	Southern Africa Development Community
TBT	Technical Barriers to Trade
TPRM	Trade Policy Review Mechanism
TRIPs	Agreement on Trade-Related Intellectual Property Rights
UDHR	Universal Declaration of Human Right
UN	United Nations
UNCTAD	United Nations Conference on Trade and Development
UNESCO	United Nations Educational, Scientific and Cultural Organization
UNICEF	United Nations Children's Fund
WIPO	World Intellectual Property Organization
WTO	World Trade Organization

Authors and Conference Participants

Authors

FREDERICK M. ABBOTT, Project Co-Director and Edward Ball Eminent Scholar Chair in International Law, Florida State University College of Law, Tallahassee, USA

CHRISTINE BREINING-KAUFMANN, Professor of Law, University of Zurich, Senior Research Fellow, World Trade Institute, Berne, Switzerland

THOMAS COTTIER, Prof. Dr. iur; Director, The World Trade Institute, Berne, Switzerland

CAROLINE DOMMEN, Director, 3D Trade – Human Rights – Equitable Economy, Geneva, Switzerland

PIET EECKHOUT, Professor of European Law and Director, Centre of European Law, King's College, London, UK

FRANK J. GARCIA, Professor of International Economic Law, Boston College Law School, Boston, USA

STEFANIE GRANT, Chief, Research and Right to Development Branch, Office of the High Commissioner for Human Rights (until 2002), Geneva, Switzerland

MICHELLE FOSTER, Senior Lecturer, University of Melbourne Law School, Australia

WALTER KÄLIN, Dr.iur., LL.M (Harvard), Professor of Constitutional and International Law at the Faculty of Law of the University of Berne, Switzerland

ERNST-ULRICH PETERSMANN, Professor of International and European Law, European University Institute and its Robert Schuman Center, Florence, Italy

JOHN H. JACKSON, University Professor of Law, University Law Center, and Director, Institute of International Economic Law at GULC, Georgetown, USA

GABRIELLE MARCEAU, Ph. D., Counsellor for the Legal Affairs Division of the WTO Secretariat, Geneva, Switzerland

SISULE FREDRICK MUSUNGU, Consultant at the South Centre, Geneva, Switzerland

KRISTA NADAKAVUKAREN SCHEFER, Dr. iur., Attorney-at-Law; Lecturer, University of Berne and the World Trade Institute, Berne, Switzerland

ERIC STEIN, Professor Emeritus of Law, University of Michigan, Ann Arbor, USA

ALAN O. SYKES, Frank and Bernice Greenberg Professor of Law and Faculty Director for Curriculum, University of Chicago, USA

JOEL P. TRACHTMAN, Professor of International Law, The Fletcher School of Law and Diplomacy, Tufts University, Medford, USA

SIMON WALKER, Office of the United Nations High Commissioner for Human Rights, Geneva, Switzerland

Other Conference Participants

FELIX ADDOR, Swiss Institute of Intellectual Property
JUERG ABERHARD, Swiss Department of Foreign Affairs
RICHARD BALDWIN, Graduate Institute of International Studies Geneva
EDITH BERNHARDT, World Trade Institute
MARCO BRONCKERS, Stibbe Attorneys-at-Law, Brussels Office
JENS DROLLSHAMMER, Homburger Attorneys-at-law, Zurich
MICHAEL DUTTWILLER, University of Fribourg
ERIK EVTIMOV, World Trade Institute
MARY FOOTER, University of Amsterdam
JOCHEN FROWEIN, Max Plank Institute Heidelberg
MARIANO GARCIA, Graduate Institute of International Studies Geneva
MATTHIAS GERBER, World Trade Institute
CHRISTOPH GERMANN, World Trade Institute
MARTIN GIRSBERGER, Swiss Institute of Intellectual Property
JONELL GOCO, World Trade Institute
CHRISTOPH GRABER, World Trade Institute
VERA GOWLLAND, Graduate Institute of International Studies, Geneva
JAMES HEENAN, European University Institute, Florence
ROB HOWSE, University of Michigan
FRANZISKA HUMBERT, Humboldt-Universität zu Berlin
YUJI IWASAWA, University of Tokyo
JOHN H JACKSON, Georgetown University Law Center
TREVOR TEBOGO KOLA, Embassy of the Republic of South Africa, Berne, Switzerland
DANIEL KRAUS, Swiss Institute of Intellectual Property
PIETER KUIJPER, World Trade Organization
EDWARD KWAKWA, World Intellectual Property Organization
SIMON LACEY, World Trade Institute
VIRGINIA LEARY, University of California Hastings
HOE LIM, World Trade Organization
CHUYANG LIU, World Trade Institute

CARLOS LOPEZ, Graduate Institute of International Studies, Geneva
ARTHUR MATTLI, Swiss Department of Foreign Affairs
PETROS MAVROIDIS, World Trade Institute
WERNER MENG, Universität des Saarlands
SANTANU MUKHERJEE, World Trade Organization
SISULE FREDRICK MUSUNGU, Makerere University
DAMIEN NEVEN, World Trade Institute
JIANQIANG NIE, World Trade Institute
MATTHIAS OESCH, World Trade Institute
SIAN O'NEILL, Kluwer Law International
MARION PANIZZON, Georgetown University Law Centre
FERNANDO PIEROLA, World Trade Institute
BARBARA ROSENBERG, World Trade Organization
KATHLEEN RUBIA, World Trade Institute
DEBRA STEGER, University of Toronto
YOLANDA SCHAERLI, University of Bern
MAHESH SUGATHAN, UNCTAD
VINCENZA TRIVIGNO, Swiss Department of the Economy
THU-LANG TRANWASESCHA, World Trade Organization
ELISABETH TUERK, Center for International Environmental Law
LUZIUS WASESCHA, Ambassador, Swiss State Secretariat for Economic Affairs
JACQUES WERNER, Werner & Assoccies, Geneva
TERESA ZEHNDER, World Trade Institute
GEERT ZONNEKEN, Theodore Goddard, Attorneys-at-law, Brussels Office

Preface

On August 12-14, 2001, more than sixty-five people representing international organizations, as well as representatives from non governmental organizations, government representatives, distinguished academic scholars and students of international human rights and trade law from many different countries met for the fifth World Trade Forum at the World Trade Institute in Berne, Switzerland. The topic which brought them together was 'International Trade and Human Rights – Foundations and Conceptual Issues'.

The conference marked the first public meeting organized by the research project on Human Rights and International Trade. The project was launched by the American Society of International Law under the direction of Professor Frederick M. Abbott, Florida State University College of Law and Professor Thomas Cottier, University of Berne Faculty of Law. It is being conducted in cooperation with the Georgetown University Law Center (Washington D.C.), the Max-Planck-Institute for International Law (Heidelberg) and the World Trade Institute (Berne) and is supported by the MacArthur Foundation. The first conference served the purposes of stocktaking and introducing conceptual issues. The topic encompasses a wide array of issues and themes, ranging from theoretical questions concerning the appropriate relationship between trade and human rights principles, to methods of incorporation of the two schemes in international law.

The papers in this volume make clear that there is an urgent need for further academic engagement with the multifaceted issues raised by the intersection of the two fields. We no longer question whether the link is appropriate and legitimate, but are required instead to grapple with the concomitant questions that arise concerning the appropriate conceptual basis of the link and practical questions inherent in the relationship. The findings underline the need for a conceptual reconciliation of the human rights and trade regimes.

At the same time, the question whether the solution can be found in a general legal framework or rather in a more case-oriented approach, that may differ between different human rights, needs yet to be answered. Therefore, the contributions in this volume will be complemented and further developed by more detailed case studies that are to be discussed at the project meetings in Berne in June 2003 and in Washington D.C. in April 2004.

We thank the Silva Casa Foundation, Berne, who generously supported the conference. We are indebted to the authors, discussants and participants who with their openness and active involvement in the discussions contributed to the success of the conference.

This volume would not have been published without the efforts and the diligent work of the associate editors Michelle Foster and Thomas M. Fischer. Finally, we thank the people at the University of Michigan Press for their support of our project.

The Editors

Part I

Introduction and Conceptual Issues

CHAPTER 1

Introduction

Christine Breining-Kaufmann and Michelle Foster

The World Trade Forum held at the World Trade Institute in Berne, Switzerland on August 12-14, 2001, was the first public meeting organized by the research project on Human Rights and International Trade. The project was launched by the American Society of International Law and is being conducted in cooperation with the Georgetown University Law Center (Washington D.C.), the Max-Planck-Institute for International Law (Heidelberg) and the World Trade Institute (Berne). It is supported by the MacArthur Foundation (USA). The directors of the project are FREDERICK M. ABBOTT and THOMAS COTTIER.

The project aims to study the relationship between institutions and norms regulating international trade, and institutions and norms promoting and protecting human rights. The ultimate objective of the process is to offer recommendations for possible reforms so as to account better for the human rights interests affected by the process of globalization. The initial phase of the project focused on conceptual questions; it will be followed by case studies to be discussed at a conference in Berne in June 2003 and in Washington D.C. in spring 2004.

The first conference, "International Trade and Human Rights – Foundations and Conceptual Issues," held under the fifth World Trade Forum, served the purposes of stocktaking and introducing conceptual issues. It brought together more than sixty-five people representing a wide range of interests and perspectives. Among them were participants representing international organizations, including the Office of the United Nations High Commissioner for Human Rights (the High Commissioner), the World Trade Organization (WTO), the World Intellectual Property Organization (WIPO), as well as representatives from non governmental organizations with an interest in trade and/or human rights, government representatives, distinguished academic scholars and students of international human rights and trade law from many different countries. The participants explored a topic that is becoming increasingly important both in terms of the manifold legal challenges inherent in the intersection of two systems of international law, and in the acute level of public interest in the underlying policy issues. The topic potentially encompasses a wide array of issues and themes, ranging from theoretical questions concerning the appropriate relationship between trade and human rights principles, to methods of incorporation of the two schemes in international law. It is of such potential breadth that, as JOHN JACKSON has observed, one may question whether it is even feasible to attempt to undertake a study which seeks to bring the two discourses (each complex and rich in its own right) together.

Given that the WTO, like its predecessor the General Agreement on Tariffs and Trade (GATT), was conceived as a tool to liberalize trade and thus is based on an instrumentalist concept, the key question is whether and to what extent constitutionalizing the WTO may be necessary or desirable. Several examples have demonstrated that promoting trade liberalization and protecting producers' interests in the context of an increasingly globalized economy may conflict with social policies such as labor standards and human rights interests. It is this conflict that initiated projects like the "Ethical Globalization Initiative" recently launched by the Aspen Institute under the leadership of Mary Robinson.

The papers in this volume make clear that there is an urgent need for further academic engagement with the multifaceted issues raised by the intersection of the two fields. As is evidenced by the contributions, the two fields are institutionally linked in a number of regional and domestic systems, and are becoming increasingly linked at the international level as well. In other words, we have moved beyond the stage of questioning whether the link is appropriate and legitimate, and are required instead to grapple with the concomitant questions that arise concerning the appropriate conceptual basis of the link and practical questions inherent in the relationship.

Legal analysis in this area is still at a relatively early stage and there is a wide range of issues that require further attention, many of which are identified and explored in this volume. A number of fundamental questions arise immediately: What is the purpose of linking trade and human rights? Is there a potential role for human rights in the context of a "bill of rights" for a trade constitution? Is the key goal to uphold human rights principles, harnessing the strength of the international trade regime (including superior enforceability and available sanctions) in pursuance of human rights? Or is it a more modest aim, namely, to ameliorate the potential detrimental consequences of free trade? Or are human rights invoked in order to facilitate the efficient and fair functioning of the free trade regime or to accord its legitimacy? If this is so, is there a risk of the value of human rights being reduced to an economic calculus, of an "economization of human rights? These are important foundational issues, which are often overlooked in the general debate. Inextricably related to these issues is the vital theoretical (and empirical) question concerning whether the two regimes are fundamentally compatible or rather fundamentally inconsistent in terms of aims and policy objectives. In other words, is it possible to achieve coherence between trade and human rights principles?

Once we accept that human rights should be engaged in the trade debate, the question immediately arises as to which human rights should be considered relevant? Should the full range of human rights be invoked? In this respect, it is notable that the contributions reveal an increasing focus on the relevance of economic, social and cultural rights – a set of rights particularly relevant in the trade context but traditionally neglected in favor of civil and political rights in international law. A number of contributions emphasize the importance of a principled legal approach to these questions, based on existing norms and recognized sources of international law. If it is decided that only a subset or "core" set of human rights will be engaged, how does one determine which rights are most relevant? This in turn raises the question as to whether there is a hierarchy of rights in international law.

Another set of issues concerns questions related to the practical intersection of the two regimes. Is it possible to reconcile simultaneous obligations under human rights and international trade law? Should the adjudicating bodies in each regime take into account or attempt to reconcile the obligations inherent in the other regime? This also raises questions concerning institutional competence and cooperation. Should the WTO be involved in developing an autonomous human rights jurisprudence? Or should it rely on existing treaties and norms and on the expertise of the relevant human rights treaty bodies? Should the UN human rights bodies be involved in trade issues? Is there a need for further dialogue between the two sets of institutions, in the words of Mary Robinson, "bilingualism" between the trade and human rights worlds? Can the requisite incorporation be achieved via creative interpretation of existing schemes or is treaty reform necessary? Is it possible to devise a set of broad governing principles to guide interpretation or will the intersection be explored on a case-by-case basis, following a process of balancing various factors in each individual case?

By presenting a selection of the papers discussed at the World Trade Forum 2001, this volume makes a valuable contribution to the debate, as the papers grapple with all of these important issues, in different ways and from different perspectives. The papers can be categorized into three main themes: those that primarily focus on conceptual or theoretical issues by laying the foundations for the debate; those that explore the practical intersection between the international human rights regime and the international free trade regime by analyzing institutional and procedural aspects, and those that focus on relevant developments at the regional level.

Conceptual Issues: Foundations

The papers in this section seek to explore and consider some of the underlying conceptual questions involved in the trade-human rights interface. They highlight the importance of considering the aims and objectives of the trade-human rights link and serve as reminders that any proposal must be based on sound principle.

JOHN JACKSON's paper provides insight into the key theoretical and research questions that require conceptual clarity and further analysis in order to meaningfully explore the trade-human rights link. He highlights the need for consideration to be given to some key policy questions including whether the position that one set of values should always "trump" the other is sustainable or rather whether some compromise or balancing is required. He also suggests that consideration be given to the key underlying objectives of the two sets of regimes: are human rights concerned with human dignity or are they being instrumentalized for promoting other objectives? What are the goals of the free trade system and are they fundamentally compatible or at odds with human rights principles? He outlines some of the salient practical questions including whether the link should be between trade law and a subset of human rights and if so, which rights are to be given priority. He recommends that further analysis be undertaken of the various methods by which a link is established in the different regional and international schemes, and their effectiveness – a challenge taken up in the papers in the second and third category, outlined below. As he notes, a review of the various methods by which the link is made reveals that there is no single template for the linkage, and that creativity is required in thinking beyond "hard" treaty linkages as the only option. JACKSON concludes with a thought provoking set of the salient research questions that should be pursued in the future.

ERNST-ULRICH PETERSMANN addresses some of the fundamental theoretical issues in his chapter examining the relationship between markets, human rights and economic welfare. His paper begins by reviewing the values, principles and objectives underlying the trade and human rights systems respectively, concluding that, in his view, markets and human rights proceed from the same values since the common core of each rests on respect for personal autonomy and individual dignity. He proceeds to note that the effectiveness of markets and of human rights depends on constitutional safeguards, that markets and human rights complement each other, and that specifically, human rights promote the effectiveness of competition, democracy and international governance. In this respect, PETERSMANN outlines six major instrumental functions of human rights: human rights as instruments for reducing the problem of limited knowledge; human rights as incentives for mutually beneficial division of labor; human rights as providing conflict-prevention mechanisms; human rights as guardians against abuse of power; human rights as providing decentralized dispute settlement and enforcement mechanisms; and human rights as sources of democratic legitimacy. Building upon these insights, the final section of the paper develops PETERSMANN's own theory that international law must develop a new "integration paradigm," which would require on the one hand that international human rights law surrender its "anti-market bias" and recognize the importance of economic rights to the freedom and development of the individual, and on the other that emerging international trade law incorporate principles of universal human rights.

ALAN SYKES' paper complements PETERSMANN's in further considering the relationship between economics and human rights and, in particular, issues surrounding their fundamental compatibility. SYKES evaluates some of the key criticisms levied against the international trade system in terms of their economic merit, assessing the extent to which suggestions for protection of human rights values conform to economic principles such as efficiency. From the Chicago-school economic standpoint, increased concern with non trade issues might undermine the essential function of the WTO.

The paper begins with the supposition that trade liberalization raises living standards, which in turn promotes human rights, a well-accepted proposition amongst economists which SYKES proceeds to test empirically, concluding that the data supports the theory that greater openness to trade is correlated with better human rights conditions. He thus deduces that there is no basis for supposing that a more open trading system does systematic damage to human rights, and that any occasional tension can be addressed in a specific and directed manner. Against this background SYKES addresses and evaluates some of the key concerns of critics of the WTO regime including that the WTO system inappropriately impedes the use of trade sanctions as remedies for human rights abuses, that free trade potentially causes damage to the environment and promotes a "race to the bottom" in relation to social regulation, that the global trading regime promotes income inequality, and – with respect to the Agreement on the Trade Related Impact of Intellectual Property Agreement (TRIPS) – that it neglects the needs of the developing world. He concludes that while there are some legitimate concerns, a response that attempts to undermine the free trade regime is not economically sound, and that any tensions in the trade-human rights relationship are best accommodated through tailored interventions that directly address the particular human rights concerns without compromising the wider goals and benefits of the free trade regime.

THOMAS COTTIER's paper aims to provide a framework for better situating the debate on whether institutional links between trade and human rights should be expanded at the international level, by proposing the concept of governance as an appropriate guiding doctrine. He initially makes the distinction between global governance – the idea that a global legal framework must be established which connects international and national law and structures in order to accommodate the challenges presented by globalization; and good governance – a doctrine that has traditionally focused on national law and government and initially emerged in the lending policies of the Bretton Woods institutions. He proceeds to consider the legal basis for principles of good governance and to elaborate on the components of the doctrine, concluding that from the perspective of international law the doctrine of good governance is mainly anchored in human rights principles. With respect to good governance guarantees in current WTO law, his findings suggest that while WTO law has developed a considerable body of law encapsulating doctrines of good governance, it is not based on human rights principles. COTTIER then addresses some of the key conceptual issues in the critiques of good governance and evaluates the case for good governance principles in trade law, before considering the possibility of, and challenges inherent in, invoking human rights principles to buttress and consolidate good governance in the WTO with a view to achieving consistency and enhancing the legitimacy of the trading system.

The Intersection of the International Trade Regime and International Human Rights Law: Institutional and Procedural Aspects

The second broad category of papers comprises those chapters that begin the process of exploring the extent to which international human rights standards can be incorporated or considered in the trade context, in light of the potential inconsistencies and commonalities between the two regimes. The papers consider both general human rights provisions and also specific rights and their application to particular aspects of the trade regime, such as TRIPS.

CAROLINE DOMMEN's paper begins by reflecting on the original purpose and principles of the international human rights regime and international free trading regime (under GATT) respectively, noting their shared aims of establishing multilateral institutional frameworks within which to pursue the objectives of respect for human rights, and cooperation in economic, social and financial policy, in order to promote stability, prosperity and equality. She notes that although both regimes have expanded considerably since their inception, they continue to share consistent and mutually enforceable objectives. Against this background, she proceeds to examine the extent to which economic, social and cultural rights found in a number of important UN covenants, but most notably in the International Covenant on Economic, Social and Cultural Rights (ICESCR), are capable of being applied in the WTO context, in order to respond to concerns about its legitimacy most vocally expressed by developing countries and in international public opinion. In terms of the concerns of developing countries, DOMMEN reviews a number of recent examples in which trade and human rights issues have apparently been in conflict, concerning the production of affordable medication for people suffering from HIV/AIDS, and suggests that reference to state obligations under the ICESCR may have been helpful in the resolution of these disputes. She then submits other ways in which human rights law could be engaged to ensure that the WTO's rules promote the interests of developing countries. In the second part of DOMMEN's analysis, the author notes public perceptions that the WTO favors the economically powerful over the economically disadvantaged, and that it ignores important public interests such as protection of the environment, health and human rights. While acknowledging that there are limits to the ability of the trade regime to address these issues, she suggests that the ICESCR can be a useful and effective tool in complementing the WTO system in order to ensure that trade does not discriminate in favour of the most economically powerful groups within a society.

STEFANIE GRANT's paper approaches the intersection of trade and international human rights issues from an institutional perspective, noting that a number of UN institutions are increasingly considering the extent to which human rights principles can be invoked in the trade context. She observes that the key precipitating factors of this new approach are the recognition, in the past decade, of the importance of economic, social and cultural rights, and the fact that most WTO members are now also parties to the main international human rights covenants, including the ICESCR, raising questions regarding the reconciliation of simultaneous obligations. In this context, she proceeds to review the activities of various components of the UN human rights system – including the Charter Bodies, the treaty bodies and the High Commissioner for Human Rights – in terms of their engagement with the elaboration of the consequences of human rights standards for the trade regime. Following a survey of recent developments, she deduces a number of common elements of the work of the various institutions: concerns regarding issues of procedural fairness at the WTO; concerns that the positive outcomes of the international trade regime benefit the most vulnerable members of society; emphasis on the importance of focusing on the social, cultural, and political dimensions of trade, and not just on economic issues; an increasing emphasis on the need to read trade obligations consistently with human rights obligations; and an emphasis on states' obligations under human rights treaties regarding equality, particularly in the context of the right to health. GRANT concludes by naming some of the remaining challenges in this field, most importantly, the need for further research on the impact of trade liberalization in human rights terms, and the need for increasing dialogue between institutional divisions within the two fields both at an international and national level.

SIMON WALKER of the UN High Commissioner's Office was involved in the drafting of a report on behalf of the High Commissioner on the impact of the TRIPS Agreement on the enjoyment of human rights. The report was produced at the request of the Sub-Commission on the Promotion and Protection of Human Rights, following consultation with the WHO and the WTO. WALKER's paper provides an analysis of this report and complements GRANT's by focusing on one aspect of the UN institutional regime. The report is premised on the recognition that those states negotiating trade rules under the auspices of the WTO are the same states that are parties to the key international human rights conventions (WALKER notes for example that a majority of the WTO members – 113 of 146 as of September 2003 – have ratified the ICESCR) and thus have obligations under both regimes. The tensions between human rights such as the right to health and the right to life on the one hand and protection of intellectual property on the other have become apparent over the last few years. The Declaration on TRIPS and Public Health adopted at the WTO Ministerial Summit in Doha on November 14, 2001, is evidence of the attention that this issue is receiving. The High Commissioner's report first notes that TRIPS acknowledges that intellectual property regimes involve a balancing of the private interests of property holders with aspects of the public interest, and takes the view that this concession to the importance of the public interest is the opening through which human rights standards and principles may enter the TRIPS regime. Notwithstanding this potential, WALKER notes that the TRIPS Agreement does not currently take a human rights consistent approach. However, he proceeds to outline his view that the problems could be remedied in practice by adoption of a human rights consistent interpretation, providing examples of the way in which provisions of the ICESCR can be engaged in the TRIPS context. While optimistic about the potential for consistent interpretation, WALKER also raises the important issue of the difficulties faced by developing countries who wish to uphold human rights obligations but who face political and diplomatic pressure from developed countries to implement "TRIPS plus" policies. This highlights that many of the challenges in this area are not limited to difficulties in the reconciliation of legal regimes, but also require a political commitment to a resolution of the competing interests by states.

Continuing the theme of the intersection between human rights principles and TRIPS, FREDERICK M. ABBOTT's paper provides further analysis and suggestions for possible ways of resolving the many doctrinal and practical issues involved in an attempt to reconcile the two regimes. While the papers in this section thus far have tended to approach the issue of the intersection of international human rights standards with trade issues from a broader, more policy-oriented perspective, ABBOTT's and GABRIELLE MARCEAU's papers provide a more detailed and specific approach which attempts to grapple with some of the most salient practical questions involved in the relationship. One of the key questions is how, in practical terms, human rights norms may be incorporated into the trade regime, particularly in light of the issues of whether there is a hierarchy of international human rights norms, whether some rights are more easily incorporated than others, (especially relevant in relation to economic and social rights which are often framed as obligations of progressive implementation) and which values should be given priority in the case of conflict.

ABBOTT offers a convincing tool for thinking about the answers to some of these questions, in setting out the evolving notion of "core human rights" – a notion developed primarily by the Committee on Economic, Social and Cultural Rights to refer to the minimum core obligations embodied in the Covenant's rights that are non-derogable and immediately enforceable or realizable; in other words not subject to resource constraints. He suggests that further analysis of this concept may yield identification of a category of rights that are of such importance that they must be respected by the multilateral trading system. He then provides specific examples of the way in which this analysis might be undertaken in the context of TRIPS. In terms of resolving potential conflicts between human rights norms and the trading regime, he notes that the Vienna Convention on the Law of Treaties (VCLT) provides some techniques: for example a treaty is void to the extent that it contravenes a peremptory norm. However it is not clear how the notion of core rights (distinct from peremptory norms) would be treated by the VCLT, a topic that deserves further attention. He suggests that in some cases the conflict could be resolved by interpreting the trade provision in a manner that is consistent with the human rights norm. It will be in those cases where consistent interpretation is impossible, that the question of hierarchy of norms, and in particular the developing notion of core rights, may be engaged. Finally, in addition to the technical questions regarding intersection, ABBOTT considers the conceptual issues surrounding the nature of human rights and addresses traditional concerns relating to the alleged vagueness, generality and lack of enforceability of human rights norms, concluding that these traditional concerns do not preclude the incorporation of human rights norms into the trade regime.

MARCEAU's paper presents the most detailed consideration of the practical intersection between trade and international human rights principles, as she focuses on the WTO Dispute Settlement regime and the extent to which it is capable of taking into account and applying international human rights norms. As she identifies at the outset of the paper, if the WTO is seized of a dispute involving a human rights dimension, a range of questions arise, including whether a WTO panel may consider human rights based arguments notwithstanding the lack of reference to human rights standards in the WTO treaty; whether a WTO member can invoke human rights provisions to refuse to comply with a WTO provision; whether human rights provisions have direct application in the WTO system of law; whether human rights considerations can guide interpretation of the WTO treaty and whether WTO members can take action in respect of human rights violations occurring in other member states. In turn, consideration of these questions raises wider issues relating to the nature of the "WTO applicable law" and the extent of WTO jurisdiction.

Turning initially to questions concerning jurisdiction and the applicable law of the WTO, MARCEAU notes a number of features of the WTO regime which suggest that general international law or human rights law does not have direct application in the WTO dispute settlement system: the mandate of the panels and Appellate Body (AB) is defined and limited to WTO matters, panels and the AB are prohibited from adding to or diminishing the rights and obligations of the WTO Agreement, WTO violations can lead only to a specific WTO remedy, and the covered agreements cannot be changed or amended without using the specifically provided procedures. However, this "limited domain" of the WTO does not, in her view, mean that the WTO Agreement exists in a closed system, impervious to principles in general international law, including human rights law. Part II of her paper thus proceeds to consider the ways in which the WTO Agreements are capable of taking into account the general system of international law, in order to ensure that the WTO is not a closed system. Like ABBOTT, MARCEAU refers to the VCLT, although her analysis of the application and significance of the VCLT is more extensive and detailed. In particular, she grapples with the meaning of the little-used but potentially very significant provision in Art. 31(3)(c), which provides that in interpreting treaty obligations, "any relevant rules of international law applicable in the relations between the parties" shall be taken into account. One important aspect of this discussion is the argument that art 31(3)(c) subsumes the principle of "evolutionary interpretation" – a principle of treaty interpretation that has traditionally been invoked particularly in the human rights context, but is increasingly being applied in other contexts as well, including by the WTO AB in the Shrimp-Turtle case. MARCEAU views this provision of the VCLT as providing the basis for some coherence in international law; thus it should be possible to interpret WTO provisions in a manner that allows Member states to respect all their international obligations – including those of human rights. This is particularly so in light of the broad manner in which many of the exceptions in the WTO Agreements are formulated. However, notwithstanding the potential for coherence and consistency, MARCEAU acknowledges that irreconcilable conflict will occasionally arise, albeit rarely. She thus considers the principles that would guide the resolution of such a conflict by the WTO, concluding that since human rights law does not have direct application in the WTO system, it might be possible for compliance with a WTO obligation to involve breach of a human rights provision. One of the most interesting questions on this topic is one also raised by ABBOTT: the significance of the fact that a conflicting human rights norm is one of *jus cogens*. MARCEAU expresses a less concluded view on this question than does ABBOTT, since she regards the question as rather complex and so far unsolved. MARCEAU emphasizes that issues of conflict may ultimately best be resolved by way of state negotiation, in this way raising a similar point as that raised by WALKER: that diplomatic and political elements will be as important as legal factors in respect of many of the issues inherent in the trade/human rights relationship. The final substantive section of MARCEAU's paper considers the extent to which WTO members may act or react to human rights concerns in other states, pointing to examples set out in some of the papers in the next section as evidence of existing practices that raise these issues. While MARCEAU outlines the relevant questions and issues that are raised in this context, she concludes that this is an important area in which further academic work is required. The final section of the paper raises a novel aspect of the trade-human rights nexus, namely the extent to which the procedures adopted by the WTO dispute settlement bodies comply with procedural guarantees in human rights law.

Regional Responses to the Trade/Human Rights Debate

The papers in the third category examine the institutional linkages and jurisprudential developments in the relationship between trade and human rights that have taken place in three important regions: Europe – encompassing both the EU system and the relevance of the European Convention on Human Rights (the ECHR), Africa (in particular within the auspices of the Organization of African Unity) and in the Americas (including the intersection between the Inter-American human rights system and regional schemes of economic integration).

The papers by PIET EECKHOUT, ERIC STEIN, WALTER KÄLIN AND KRISTA NADAKAVUKAREN SCHEFER consider developments in the intersection between trade and human rights as evidenced in the case law of the European Court of Justice (ECJ) (EECKHOUT and STEIN), the jurisprudence relating to the ECHR (KÄLIN) and European foreign policy (SCHEFER).

EECKHOUT provides an interesting and important overview of the way in which the ECJ has considered human rights principles in developing and elaborating on the principles of free trade, with a view to assessing the extent to which the ECJ experience may be instructive and applicable at the WTO level. While acknowledging at the outset that there are some key differences between the regional and international regimes (and thus important limitations on the extent to which experiences at the regional level may be replicated at the international level), he nonetheless convincingly explains the relevance of the experience at the regional level, particularly given that the fundamental rights discourse has been "created" by the ECJ over many years – thus providing a possible judicial precedent for the WTO AB. Following a survey of the ECJ's development of a fundamental rights doctrine, he notes that a number of aspects of the jurisprudence may be of particular relevance for the WTO level. The ECJ has developed a more rights-oriented analysis in respect of cases concerned with free movement of workers and the right of establishment than is the case in respect of trade in goods. This suggests that since trade in services involves the protection of movement of persons across borders, it may necessarily invoke a human rights based analysis, an insight which has relevance for the WTO considering that the national treatment provision in the WTO is analogous to the principle of non-discrimination on grounds of nationality. Another important insight is that human rights based concerns have tended to arise in the EU arena in the context of exceptions to or derogations from the principles of free trade, a phenomenon that is likely to be replicated at the WTO level as well, in the same way as it has been engaged in the context of environment and trade. EECKHOUT also touches on an issue raised by MARCEAU, namely the relevance of human rights for the administration of the trade regime, and he describes the extensive body of case-law that has been developed by the ECJ regarding due process and effective remedies, suggesting that these are issues which will require further consideration in the WTO context in the future.

This last-mentioned point is one of the two key issues considered by STEIN in his short response paper. STEIN focuses particularly on the issue of transparency, and describes the evolution at the EU level from a position where the Community operated in secrecy to the incremental development of codes of conduct and rules of procedure providing for access to documents and the publication of Council proceedings and other important records of its deliberations. He emphasizes the importance of these developments for upholding the democratic nature of the institutions. STEIN's second comment focuses on the controversy that has surrounded the fact that it has been the EU judiciary that has been primarily responsible for developing the fundamental human rights doctrines in the trade context. STEIN suggests that the criticism surrounding the dominance of the judiciary may be instructive when considering the function of the WTO dispute settlement system.

KÄLIN's paper provides a stimulating contrast to EECKHOUT's: he considers the trade related aspects of the ECHR's human rights jurisprudence and in so doing explores a novel aspect of human rights issues, namely, the extent to which the ECHR can be engaged by companies, as opposed to individuals, in the trade arena. He begins by noting that, in contrast to the tradition of natural law according to which individuals are the only bearers of human rights, the ECHR clearly applies to and may be engaged by companies, at least in respect of those rights that are logically applicable to companies (excluding, for example, the right to life). KÄLIN proceeds to analyse the relevance of this application for international trade, noting that since the ECHR applies to everyone within the jurisdiction of a state party, companies from outside Europe could potentially invoke ECHR protection, as has occurred in a number of cases concerning the guarantee of property rights, freedom of expression and procedural rights pursuant to Art 6. In addition, since the ECHR has extraterritorial operation, states parties must respect the ECHR rights of companies abroad whose activities they wish to regulate. The other key aspect of KÄLIN's paper concerns the question whether corporations have any obligations to respect the human rights of third parties, an issue particularly relevant to the international trade context. Although he notes that the ECHR applies directly to state parties only, it is clear that state parties have positive obligations to enforce and uphold the provisions of the ECHR, which can involve the regulation of companies to prevent their contravention of ECHR rights. He notes that this is highly significant in the context of the controversial issue of corporate responsibility for human rights violations. Recent developments, for example in the case involving Unocal's labour policy in Myanmar (Burma), underscore the need for further research in this field as suggested by KÄLIN.

The final paper dealing with the European context is SCHEFER's analysis of the intersection of trade and human rights in European foreign policy. Her paper is based on the premise that the important question in this area is the method by which the protection of human rights can accompany a trade regime. SCHEFER reviews the evolution of foreign policy instruments of the European Community (EC) that aim to secure the protection of human rights outside Europe, noting that the increased concern regarding extraterritorial human rights parallels the EC's growing commitment to human rights within its own territory. She describes developments such as conditionality in partnership and cooperation agreements, preferential trade agreements, policy instruments and the possibility of imposing economic and diplomatic sanctions, concluding that while there are considerable benefits and strengths to these instruments, a number of weaknesses remain. In particular, effective enforcement is often dependent on political will; civil and political rights such as democracy and the rule of law are often emphasized to the exclusion of economic and social rights, and the multiplicity of programs has limited the EC's ability to develop a unified committed policy on human rights.

Turning to the African context, SISULE FREDRICK MUSUNGU's paper reviews the conceptual linkages between regional economic institutions in Africa and human rights, in order to analyze whether there is tension or convergence in respect of the aims of the two regimes. In initially outlining the African human rights regime, he emphasizes the most salient distinctive feature of the African Charter, namely, its treatment of first and generation human rights as inseparable and equal. Interestingly, he explains that most of the instruments establishing the economic groupings in Africa explicitly refer to human rights as an objective or fundamental principle of the economic system. The specific reference to the African Charter in this context suggests that all three generations of human rights are considered fundamental in the formulation of trade rules – a notion that may not be consistent with the development of a core category of rights that must be recognized in the trade context. By contrast to this comprehensive understanding of relevant rights, MUSUNGU explains that the major bilateral trade agreements that involve a link with human rights issues (particular with donor countries) focus on the rule of law and democratic governance: in his view thus approaching the relevance of human rights from the perspective of their importance to the administration of trade.

The final two papers in this section consider developments in the Americas: FRANK GARCIA reviews the integration between the OAS Inter-American human rights system and several regional economic integration systems, while JOEL TRACHTMAN considers the incorporation of human rights principles in US policies and laws relating to trade.

GARCIA identifies two possible broad approaches to the trade-human rights link: the leverage model, which involves conditioning membership in an economic integration system on effective participation in an extrinsic human rights system, and the incorporation model, which involves a more integrated approach that could include, for example, the insertion of a human rights protocol within the economic integration treaty system itself. His paper assesses the extent to which regional developments have adopted the leverage model, focusing on potential links to the OAS human rights system, and in particular to accession to the Inter-American Convention on Human Rights – the core of the human rights protection system in the Americas. GARCIA surveys a number of trading systems, including the North American Free Trade Agreement (NAFTA), the Mercado Común del Sur (MERCOSUR), the Central American Common Market (CACM) and the Andean Common Market (ANCOM), and notes that none of the regimes conditions participation on membership in the OAS, or (more importantly) on accession to the Convention. He notes that failure to link trading regimes to the Convention is primarily explained by the refusal of the US to ratify the Convention – again pointing to the importance of political issues in this debate. Moreover, he observes that to the extent that some linkage has been made, the focus has been on upholding democratic principles which, while important, does not adequately address the wide range of human rights concerns in the region. He concludes by reflecting on potential methods of strengthening the existing tenuous links between trade and human rights, pointing to some positive recent developments such as the Free Trade Agreement of the Americas (FTAA) Quebec Ministerial Declaration as holding future potential.

TRACHTMAN's paper complements GARCIA's in focusing on US unilateralism in the field of trade and human rights. He begins by noting that the US has long been an advocate of the protection of human rights in other countries and to this end has developed a number of domestic schemes that seek to link international trade measures with human rights conditionalities. The purpose of the paper is to consider and analyze the various schemes with a view to assessing the role of unilateralism in international law, and specifically in the area of trade and human rights. TRACHTMAN surveys a number of important measures including the US Generalized System of Preferences, the Massachusetts Burma Statute, the Helms-Burton Act and the Trade Act of 1974, and provides an analysis of their likely compliance with WTO law. His assessment that not all of the measures will be prohibited by WTO law leads him to conclude that there is a lacuna in the law in that international law provides little guidance or regulation in respect of many of these extraterritorial initiatives. In light of this, TRACHTMAN views unilateral actions as dynamic examples of state practice that may contribute to the development of customary international law and play an important role in highlighting and drawing attention to particular human rights situations which may ultimately lead to multilateral institutional action.

Conclusion

As is noted in many of the contributions to this volume, the broad issue of trade and human rights is one that tends to spark a lively debate; often producing heated disagreement and extreme positions. This serves to underscore the importance of further academic engagement with the many controversial and difficult questions – both conceptual and practical – that remain unresolved and unexplored. The contributions in this volume provide an excellent overview of the key issues and controversies in the trade and human rights relationship, identifying possible suggestions and solutions for overcoming some of the obstacles and challenges present in this area and identifying specific questions and issues for further research. It is thus clear that this volume deals with an important and developing area of international law, certain to become increasingly important in future years, as both scholarship and jurisprudence continue to explore the boundaries of the intersection of the two fields.

The findings underline the need for a conceptual reconciliation of the human rights and trade regimes. At the same time, the question whether the solution can be found in a general legal framework or rather in a more case-oriented approach, that may differ between different human rights, needs yet to be answered.

Therefore, the contributions in this volume will be complemented and further developed by more detailed case studies that are to be discussed at the next project meetings in Berne in June 2003 and Washington D.C. in spring 2004. The case studies will focus on the interface between specific human rights and the international trade regime – and particularly on the issues that have been identified during the discussions on the papers presented in this volume. The selected topics are first, the relationship between freedom of expression and competition; second, the right to health, TRIPS and competition law and finally, the right to food and trade in agriculture.

CHAPTER 2

Reflections on the Possible Research Agenda for Exploring the Relationship between Human Rights Norms and International Trade Rules

John H. Jackson

My task in this paper is to ask questions about the difficulties in the dialogue between the legal norms of trade and human rights. The language in the literature regarding human rights on the one hand, and trade on the other presents a *dichotomy of discourses,* like ships passing in the night. Apparently, the roots of this dichotomy relate to the existence of different premises underlying human rights and trade. This article addresses the foundational objectives of both sets of issues and encourages further thinking about the differences and similarities between them. It lays out questions that could assist our understanding of how to reconcile some of the tensions between trade and human rights premises and norms. First, it refers to the parameters that the human rights and trade discussion may adopt. Second, it mentions some aspects of the current practice. Third, with a conceptual purpose in mind, this article asks, "What are the underlying policies on the side of human rights?" and "What are some of the underlying policies on the side of international trade?" The answers to these questions are provided in a kind of sketch, a tip of the iceberg overview based on my observations. Finally, a series of research questions that require further consideration are presented. Clearly, the other papers in this volume drawn from the World Trade Forum in Bern in August 2001, offer many insights relevant to thoughts expressed in this paper.

Before delving into the substance of the human rights and trade interface, there is a point to make about the tone of their respective discourses. The division between trade and human rights is often exacerbated by the approach in the literature. Both sides have perhaps displayed an air of advocacy. Bridging links should not be an advocacy process with a great appeal for human rights on the one hand, or a great appeal for trade rule primacy on the other.[1] Instead, building a dialogue between human rights and trade should come to grips with some of the underlying, deep policy dilemmas. Advancing this far in the discussion requires a framework – a set of parameters.

1. Parameters for the Trade and Human Rights Discussion

The topic of trade and human rights is extraordinarily broad and has many different and complex facets. Its breadth is such that it covers a variety of factors, including a large number of different human rights and a large potential number of different kinds of economic situations. The range of human rights and economic scenarios is so vast as to cast some doubt on whether a study connecting the discourses of trade and human rights can even be undertaken. Indeed such a study cannot be done without constructing/creating some parameters and boundaries around what we are trying to achieve. There are many questions to think about. Should the focus be, for instance, primarily on the WTO and on a *subset* of human rights? That is a research design question requiring time and allocation of resources. It is one of the harder questions yet to be solved.

The next issue relevant to the research design question is whether there *should* be a linkage between human rights matters and international economic policies such as trade. From factual observation the answer is yes – the link is already there. The existing literature on human rights and trade makes the link even more obvious. The speeches and documents from the World Trade Forum, 2001 are clear proof of that. Notwithstanding this acknowledgment to go further and examine the underlying policies of human rights and trade, which in turn will provide key research topics, the natural beginning is to address the current practice connecting the two worlds.

2. Aspects of Current Practice

2.1. Instances Linking Trade and Human Rights

Looking at current practice, it is worthwhile to note the trade-human rights overlap. In this regard, what are the linkages that different institutions have created/established? These linkages are not only present in the European Community and some of its actions in terms of membership, but also in the Lomé Conventions and their successors, as well as a number of other institutions that clearly have a series of linkages. The US has established some linkages in the generalized system of preferences, in the political realm, in some of the attitudes in Congress, in the NAFTA negotiations, and in current negotiations in the western hemisphere. A specific example is the FTAA 2001 Quebec Ministerial Declaration, which is permeated with linkages[2] to human rights and thereby expresses tremendous ambition. (Incidentally, it is amazing that it was signed by a new, conservative US government.) A different question is how well the negotiators really understood what was in it. Furthermore, other linkages can be seen in the AIDS question, government purchasing issues, and the problem of economic sanctions.

2.2. A Broad View of Linkages between Human Rights and Trade

How do all these linkages between human rights and trade relate to each other? They come in many different forms. There is no single template for the concept of linkage. The idea is to avoid being too focused on hard law treaty linkage. Rather, the path can be drawn by thinking broadly of other kinds of linkages, including via soft law, diplomatic pressures, compliance techniques, international law and treaty compliance techniques that downplay retaliation or reciprocal actions. Indeed, the international relations literature has generated a broader view of linkages between human rights and economic policy, encompassing a variety of methods and techniques. After examining the spectrum where the linkages may be found, attention has to be paid to the claims on both sides of this broad divide.

2.3. The Contentions from the Human Rights and Trade Fields

The claim on the one hand, represented in part by some of the papers at the World Trade Forum, 2001, is that human rights must trump everything. For instance, the claim is often made that the human rights objectives must trump trade, relying on the perception that the entire panoply of human rights is a unified field that cannot be distinguished or prioritized. Some imply that the unified field may rise to the level of *jus cogens*. These are issues that require further thought. On the trade side on the other hand, the question is whether the underlying trade goal of increasing wealth, and other goals mentioned below, must be primary, and must prevail. Understanding the goals of human rights and trade in that sense leads to a clash.

In the clash of discourses from both sides, what is most disappointing about the literature is its failure to recognize and take the next step. What must be created in order to maximize the goals in both of these territories? Frankly, this engages a type of balancing test, even though some people dislike this idea. This issue requires hard thinking accompanied by suggestions about "balancing." In this sense, the balancing idea has gone the furthest in the WTO jurisprudence in the area of environment. The Shrimp-Turtle cases are a marvelous example of the tough, nitty gritty struggle (when coming down to difficult, specific instances) of trying to balance the relevant conflicting goals that are present.[3] In addition, the Shrimp-Turtle cases reflect a recognition by the

WTO, institutionally, and the Appellate Body, that there are values other than trade and economic efficiency that have to be considered. These cases reveal that the WTO cannot focus only on trade, and they contain at least some techniques to be applied to the human rights situation.

3. Policy Frameworks

3.1. Grounds for Defending Human Rights: Human Dignity, Free Markets and Democracy

The second major point in this discussion relates to the policy framework. First of all, there are at least two categories of basic assumptions. Interestingly, the literature going back centuries shows a divide. On the one hand, there is the idea that human rights are really an adjunct to human dignity. Accordingly, the human individual, human dignity, and even the human soul, is, by virtue of this humanity, entitled to certain rights.

The second basis however, for the argumentation in respect of at least some human rights, is functional, and truly utilitarian. Some of these are even necessary in order for markets to work. A particular example is free speech. One of the major and traditional market failures that economists often mention is asymmetry of information. That is, the lack of enough information for some market players to make decisions that make sense in the market framework. Free speech is part of that question. For example, John Stuart Mill's writings justify the importance of free speech on utilitarian grounds, accompanied by reference to goals such as the promotion of good government and several other aspects.[4]

Also, it can be argued that human rights have a function in making democracy work. Perhaps this idea postpones or defers the argument that what makes democracy's importance is traceable to the libertarian and human dignity ideas. But it could be said that certain human rights are necessary for a democracy to work, including freedom of speech, the freedom of assembly, and the freedom of movement of persons, at least in a manner that prevents trepidation about being falsely arrested or tortured. So there are a variety of human rights that can be carved out without separating them from, or ignoring, the human rights based on human dignity. This variety of human rights has a strong case as an important set of rights necessary for markets to work. Proving that certain human rights are necessary for markets to operate becomes useful to the arguments in their favor in the political arenas and, particularly, in the business political arenas.

3.2. The Goals of the Free Trade System: Peace, Welfare, Poverty Reduction and Crisis Management

Turning to the area of trade, the search is for the basic goals of the international trade and economic system. At the end of World War II ("WWII"), there were two basic policy assertions made to support the creation of the Bretton Woods system which involved trade, and not just financial institutions (i.e., GATT – and now the WTO – is part of that Bretton Woods institutional system). The first of the two basic policies is keeping the peace. This is what was foremost on the minds of the policy makers at the end of WWII, after having just emerged from the disastrous events that many people thought were at least partly generated by mistakes in economic policy between the two world wars. Of course, there were other causes, too. The conclusion that can be drawn from reading speeches from 1943, 1944, and 1945 is that trade and economic policies are overwhelmingly necessary to maintain peace. Perhaps their weight in the discourse diminished over those years when the world had the luxury of relative peace. The Bretton Woods system can at least be attributed with partly facilitating the avoidance of a World War III, at least in terms of a war of the size of its two predecessors. This element of the Bretton Woods system is very important, although relatively often forgotten. Thus, keeping the peace is an important objective of the world trading system.

Furthermore, the objective of the Bretton Woods system is to enhance global welfare. The idea was to make the pie bigger, instead of fighting over how to divide it up. This is a basic notion, and the philosophy has been attributed to many world political leaders. Though not the single goal of the WTO, enhancing welfare is an essential goal that requires the institution to influence and increase prosperity everywhere in the world.

Over the last few decades, two more goals of the international economic system have emerged. One is the reduction of poverty. The world has a major and persistent problem of poverty or wealth distribution. A key question has been "Who is responsible for addressing poverty and distribution problems in the world?" The answer, until now, has been almost a tunnel vision advocating that the responsibility lies on the *nation state* governments. The question that needs to be raised is "To what degree should the *international system* have a responsibility for wealth redistribution?" This policy question involves further important and controversial issues.

The final policy that underlies the international economic order is the need to manage crises in the context of globalization. It is debated whether "globalization" has progressed, even as compared to the world around 1900 or pre-WWI. There was a lot of free movement of goods, people, and capital during that period. But the last two decades of the 20th century have seen two technological changes that make the current situation remarkably different from that of previous years. One is the reduction in costs and time of transportation, which is significant because transportation was a natural trade barrier for thousands of years. There has been an enormous reduction in transportation time, enabling consumers to obtain perishable goods from abroad by air transport, for instance. There are other indications, such as the diminishing costs of this transport, often ensuring that it is no longer a major trade barrier.

The second technological change is the reduction in costs and time for global communication. This has resulted in reduced transaction costs in terms of trade.

These two elements, the reduction in costs and time for transport and communication, accompanied by a myriad of other factors, mean that the world today faces a situation in which an economic crisis can generate very quickly. The Asian financial crisis narrowly missed becoming a major world economic crisis, but the possibility for such a crisis remains. Crisis management is part of this picture, and one of the questions that arises is the role of the WTO in that kind of crisis management. The role of the WTO in specific circumstances requires consideration in formulating policies.

Thus, two sets of policies have been advanced, namely, human rights policies on the one hand and international trade policies on the other (although there is room to further disaggregate these two categories, which only constitute the tip of the iceberg). This is a starting point in the process of reflecting on human rights and trade. We should begin from those fundamental first principle policies and proceed onward. Notwithstanding views of how simply the WTO could accommodate human rights, the path in introducing them into the WTO system will not be as easy as the environmental situation demonstrated in the Shrimp-Turtle case. There will be line drawing and balancing, together with a search for the meaningful policies and for the appropriate allocation of authority in respect of assessing and implementing those policies.

4. Research Questions

The final part of this article refers to some of the key research questions that need to be further pursued. The research questions herein are divided into two groups. The first group of questions relates to the current practice, and how that demonstrates, one way or the other, the important potential divisions that need to be made. In relation to the legal area the current practice that needs to be examined goes beyond treaty law, and includes soft law and compliance techniques. The assessment of existing practice should focus on whether there are in fact different approaches to different kinds of human rights, such as whether free speech requires one approach, while the prevention of torture requires something different. Next, turning to perhaps the most difficult aspect of the dialogue between trade and human rights, is the task of looking at the future policy implications and issues. In other words, what is the logic of the two subjects, and where does their combination lead?

A fundamental question is "Which human rights?" The list is wide and may include human rights other than free speech, the prohibition of torture, the protection of property, labor rights, health and education rights, and intellectual property. A subsequent question for research design is whether the research of a wide list of rights can be undertaken. Perhaps prioritizing some rights or looking only at some human rights without prioritizing is appropriate.

The second question refers to the linkages where different economic means are and can be used to reinforce human rights. Should these include barriers to imports, tariffs, prohibitions, embargoes, boycotts, etc.? Should the use of taxes be encouraged? If it were possible in some way, should quotas be used? Should labeling and regulatory measures, such as health and purity standards favoring specific interests be permitted? Dealing with critical issues using soft law might prove to be more effective than relying on treaty law. For instance, a recent article in the *Journal of International Economic Law* referred to soft law approaches in the OECD context, which had been more efficient than the WTO approach, particularly in the area of money laundering and corruption.[5] These and other compliance measures require further research.

Third, the likely effectiveness of different approaches requires assessment. It may be that a hard law treaty approach is effective in some ways, for some situations, but not for others. Maybe the current retaliatory framework of the WTO is self-defeating. There are lots of suggestions in that direction, including case studies involving relevant issues. Do economic sanctions really target the right people or at the right institutions, or do they simply hurt the victims themselves in various countries? What works better? Does wealth creation itself provide a greater chance for better human rights? Again these issues need to be further examined.

Fourth, attention must be given to the costs and damages that can occur to competing policy structures where there is a contradiction or tension. The policies can be counter-productive if they single-mindedly confront human rights abusing countries with economic sanctions that slightly enhance human rights in the short run, but undermine the ability of the trade institutions to fulfill their goals, including the creation of wealth, in the longer term. In other words, there is a very strong temptation for protectionist influences to use trade devices to protect workers in the rich countries from competing efforts in poor countries, rather than using trade devices with a strong view to promoting human rights. Advocating protectionist measures under what appear to be human rights justifications is so prevalent in the world today that developing countries adamantly oppose linkages between trade and other areas. They strongly oppose linking human rights, labor rights, and environmental protection principles to WTO measures because they are afraid of the misuse of the measures. Furthermore, they are entitled to be afraid, as some of the jurisprudence relating to the GATT demonstrates. For instance, evidence presented in the WTO's first case on *"United States – Gasoline"* showed that environmental policies were misused in order to prevent competition.[6]

Fifth, "What are the institutional inadequacies?" Institutional inadequacies include issues such as those relating to the structural problems in the WTO. "The WTO 'Constitution' and Proposed Reforms: Seven 'Mantras' Revisited," presents a short inventory of some of the fundamental institutional problems in the WTO such as the consensus rule.[7] Research on institutional problems is important. Perhaps the WTO could better forge linkages between trade and other areas if it weren't for its institutional weaknesses. Other global institutional weaknesses also require attention. In order to study institutional inadequacies, it is necessary to understand the structure of those institutions and to be familiar with institutional processes, for example, it will be necessary to know whether knowledgeable people administer subtle line drawing and balancing tests, or whether administrative processes are just devices to pursue domestic interests. A study of institutional inadequacies would also include inquiries as to whether there is misgovernance or corruption at the national level rendering the nation state unreliable in achieving free trade goals like crisis management or meaningful wealth redistribution. In addition, the question whether there should be importance attributed to democratic institutions as giving the right to participate in regional or international economic institutions, would need to be examined.

Sixth, which trade norms themselves can be said to impinge on human rights? Are there some trade norms that particularly do so? The intellectual property question looms very large at this point, but there are additional trade norms that need to be examined as well.

Seventh, there are the "good governance" questions at the international level. What do international institutions and the WTO need – transparency, participation, *amicus* briefs? Considering the doubts about the institutional viability of the WTO influenced by pessimistic views before the 2001 Doha Ministerial, is the WTO an institution fit to cope with the challenges of today and tomorrow, which include the subject of this study?

Eighth, what are the best ways to implement policies linking trade and human rights? What are the implementation constraints? These are questions involving soft law, hard law, compliance techniques, finger-pointing, and diplomatic pressures of a variety of types.

Finally, the ninth research question relates to the way human rights institutions operate in the real world. In part, it is a question about the old notion of sovereignty, compared to a new notion of sovereignty. Significant issues fall under the question of where to distribute some of the responsibilities and power. Should a decision be made in Geneva or in Brussels, Washington or Sacramento, or even at the local level? These issues are raised in cases like the Massachusetts-Burma case,[8] and in Europe in the current debate on the evolution of the European constitution.[9]

These are the questions for further research. They constitute an extensive list. Unfortunately, the choice among them is not easy. Perhaps there is enough to engage a lifetime of effort and to desegregate and study the issues. However, they are important issues not just for current WTO efforts and negotiations, but also as stepping-stones for the next several decades.

NOTES

1. See some of the other works in this volume.

2. See Third Summit of the Americas, Declaration of Quebec City, April 22, 2001 (site visited on January 31, 2002) <http://www.sice.oas.org/ftaa/quebec/declara_e.asp>.

3. WTO Panel Report, *United States – Import Prohibition of Certain Shrimp and Shrimp Products,* WT/DS58/R adopted May 15, 1998; Appellate Body Report, *United States – Import Prohibition of Certain Shrimp and Shrimp Products,* WT/DS58/AB/R, adopted Oct. 12, 1998; *United States – Import Prohibition of Certain Shrimp and Shrimp Products, Recourse to Article 21.5 of the DSU by Malaysia,* WT/DS58/AB/RW, adopted Oct. 22, 2001.

4. See John Stuart Mill, ON LIBERTY (1859). John Stuart Mill, CONSIDERATIONS ON REPRESENTATIVE GOVERNMENT (1861). John Stuart Mill, UTILITARIANISM (1863).

5. Abbott, Kenneth W. "Rule-Making in the WTO: Lessons From the Case of Bribery and Corruption." *Journal of International Economic Law* 4 (June 2001), 275-296.

6. WTO Panel Report: *United States – Standards for Reformulated and Conventional Gasoline,* WT/DS2/R, adopted Jan. 1, 1996. 103d Cong., 2d Sess. 44 (1994) (testimony of Mary Nichols, Assistant Administrator for Air and Radiation, EPA, June 22, 1994) (site visited on February 2, 2002) <http://web.lexis-nexis.com/congcomp>. The Assistant Administrator for Air and Radiation from EPA stated in her testimony that "the final rule [on reformulated gasoline], however, only allows importers to establish baselines using actual 1990 gasoline test data, or to default to the statutory baseline. The regulations do not let importers use the other baseline-setting methods available to domestic refiners, because they are not expected to be able to accurately predict the quality of gaso-

line imported in 1990." However, she acknowledged that EPA had "learned that PDVSA [Petroleos de Venezuela] probably does have the data necessary to establish accurate individual baselines for their refineries."

7. Jackson, John H. "The WTO 'Constitution' and Proposed Reforms: Seven 'Mantras' Revisited." *Journal of International Economic Law* 4 (March 2001): 67-78.

8. *Stephen P. Crosby v. National Foreign Trade Council,* 120 S.Ct.2288 (2000).

9. See the Council of the European Union, Fundamental Rights, (site visited February 1, 2002) <http://ue.eu.int/df/default.asp?lang=en>; Charter of Fundamental Rights of the European Union, (site visited February 1, 2002) <http://www.europarl.eu.int/charter/pdf/text_en.pdf>; Committee on Legal Affairs and Human Rights, Parliamentary Assembly of the Council of Europe, Report on the Charter of Fundamental Rights of the European Union, Charte 4106/00 (2000), (site visited February 1, 2002) <http://ue.eu.int/df/default.asp?lang=en>. In the debate about Europe's bill of rights the Assembly of the Council of Europe made recommendations with a view to create a consistent coexistence between the system of rights from the European Convention on Human Rights and the Charter of Fundamental Rights of the European Union; see The Daily Telegraph, *Charter of Rights hailed as a turning point for Europe,* September 14, 2000, (site visited on February 1, 2002), <http://news.telegraph.co.uk>. The article illustrates the debate in Britain and other European countries about the Charter of Rights of the European Union.

CHAPTER 3

Human Rights, Markets and Economic Welfare: Constitutional Functions of the Emerging UN Human Rights Constitution

*Ernst-Ulrich Petersmann**

> "Sustainable development is impossible without human rights.... advancement of an interconnected set of human rights is impossible without development"[1]

UN human rights law proceeds from the premise that – as emphasized in the Preamble to the 1966 UN Covenants on civil, political, economic, social and cultural rights – human rights "derive from the inherent dignity of the human person," and "recognition of the inherent dignity and of the equal and inalienable rights of all members of the human family is the foundation of freedom, justice and peace in the world." The Preamble makes clear that human rights precede "the obligation of States under the Charter of the United Nations to promote universal respect for, and observance of, human rights and freedoms," a general obligation universally recognized in UN human rights covenants. Already the Universal Declaration on Human Rights (UDHR) had recognized that "human rights should be protected by the rule of law" (Preamble), yet they exist as inherent birthrights of every human being independent from their legal recognition in UN human rights instruments. The today universal recognition by all states of inalienable human rights has objectively changed the legal status of individuals as legal subjects of international law such that inalienable human rights now exist *erga omnes* and require respect, legal protection and fulfillment of inalienable human rights by all governments. Due to their progressive transformation into international *jus cogens*, the fragmented, treaty-based UN human rights guarantees gradually evolve into a UN human rights constitution limiting the powers also of international organizations.

Human dignity is also recognized as a constitutive principle and fundamental human right in Article 1 of the EU Charter of Fundamental Rights pro-

* Former lecturer of law at the Universities of Hamburg, Heidelberg and the Saarland (Germany), and professor of law at the Universities of St. Gall, Fribourg, Geneva and the Geneva Graduate Institute of International Studies (Switzerland). Former legal advisor in the German Ministry of Economic Affairs, GATT and the WTO. Chairman of the International Trade Law Committee of the International Law Association.

claimed by the European Parliament, the EU Commission and the EU Council in December 2000.[2] Yet, neither UN law nor EU law define their respective concept of human dignity. In national human rights law, only a few national constitutional systems (e.g., in Germany, India, Israel, South Africa) explicitly recognize human dignity as a constitutional value or human right. Political and legal conceptions of human rights differ considerably depending on how human dignity is being defined. For instance, whereas the EC Court protects the "market freedoms" guaranteed in the European Community (EC) Treaty as conferring "fundamental rights" to individuals, human rights lawyers often claim that market freedoms are not directly rooted in human dignity and are fundamentally different from human rights and "fundamental freedoms" protected by human rights law.[3] This contribution begins with a brief clarification of this author's understanding of human dignity and human liberty rights (Introduction) before exploring the relationships among, and complementary functions of, human rights, consumer-driven market competition, individual and democratic self-government and economic welfare (chapters I-VIII).

Introduction and Summary: Human Dignity, Human Rights and Human Liberty Are Indivisible

Regardless of whether human dignity is recognized as the most fundamental human right from which all other rights are following (as e.g., in German and Israeli constitutional law), or whether human dignity is viewed only as a constitutional principle, all six major UN human rights covenants acknowledge in their Preambles the close interrelationship between "the inherent dignity and ... the equal and inalienable rights of all members of the human family." The universal recognition of human dignity as the constitutive principle for human rights suggests that a common understanding cannot be found by interpreting human dignity in the light of theological concepts of "person" (e.g., the creation of man in God's image). The explicit link made in Article 1 of the UDHR between "All human beings are born free and equal in dignity and rights" (first sentence), and "They are endowed with reason and conscience and should act towards one another in a spirit of brotherhood" (second sentence), rather suggests that "reason and conscience" were regarded as the defining elements of humanity and dignity.[4] The appeal to moral conduct "in a spirit of brotherhood" further indicates that "reason and conscience" were referred to not only as anthropological facts, but as sources for moral reasoning enabling mankind to secure universal equal rights as the legal "foundation of freedom, justice and peace in the world" (Preamble UDHR) and of enjoyment by everybody of "an existence worthy of human dignity" (Article 23 UDHR).

This understanding of human dignity as moral and rational autonomy, responsibility and "foundation of freedom, justice and peace" can be further specified following the Kantian view of human dignity as the moral and rational capacity of human beings of exercising one's freedom of choice in a "just" manner respecting the equal autonomy and maximum equal freedom of all others.[5] According to Kant, respect for human dignity and justice requires treating human beings as ends in themselves, respecting their individual choices, and protecting maximum equal freedoms of individuals through ever more precise, national, international and cosmopolitan constitutional rules.[6] As everybody "may seek his happiness in whatever way he sees fit, so long as he does not infringe upon the freedom of others to pursue a similar end which can be reconciled with the freedom of everyone else within a workable general law,"[7] treating a person as an end-in-herself and respecting her freely chosen objectives require legal protection of a human right to maximum equal freedom in the economic area no less than in other areas of human cooperation. For only the individual himself can know, and decide on, his own ends and personal self-development. Hence, human dignity and human liberty are indivisible, as recognized in the 1993 Vienna Declaration adopted by the World Conference on Human Rights: "All human rights are universal, indivisible and interdependent and interrelated."[8]

This contribution proceeds from the Kantian premise that human dignity reveals itself in the moral and rational act of human choice,[9] which merits respect as the source of all value and justifies a *prima facie* right to maximum equal freedom in all areas of personal self-development subject to democratic legislation. In the economic area no less than in other areas, respect for voluntarily agreed and mutually beneficial cooperation among human beings is – as stated in the Preamble to the UDHR – "the foundation of freedom, justice and peace in the world." From this perspective, human survival and personal self-development by means of exercising *economic* freedoms (e.g., freedom of professional and economic liberty as protected in Articles 2, 12 German Basic Law, Articles 15, 16 of the EU Charter of Fundamental Rights) are no less rooted in human dignity than the exercise of personal freedom in non-economic areas.

Recognition of a general constitutional right to liberty, as it can be found in several postwar constitutions so as to better entrench liberty rights against earlier constitutional failures,[10] can be seen as a new phase in the historical evolution of constitutional liberty rights since the Magna Carta (1215) guarantee that "no free man shall be taken or imprisoned but by the law of the land." In longstanding democracies (e.g., England), national constitutional rights to liberty continue to be often construed narrowly as protecting merely freedom from arrest, detention and other bodily restraint.[11] The postwar guarantees of liberty in the UDHR (Article 3) and in the European Convention on Human Rights (Article 5 ECHR) have been drafted and construed in the same Anglo-Saxon perspective. The EC Treaty guarantees of common market freedoms and human rights, however, have been interpreted by the EC Court as protecting much broader personal freedoms (e.g., to move and trade across frontiers) and social rights, including a "fundamental right to human dignity and integrity."[12] The constitutional protection of a general right to liberty, in addition to specific constitutional safeguards of individual freedom, corresponds better to modern theories of justice and to the "indivisibility" of all human rights.[13] It offers additional constitutional and procedural safeguards that are important notably in countries and in international organizations (like the EC) which are not (yet) effectively embedded into longstanding democratic traditions and constitutional constraints. If, proceeding from such a constitutional right to maximum equal freedom subject to democratic legislation, "every person has the right to free development of his personality, to the extent that he does not infringe the rights of others or offend against the constitutional order or public morals" (Article 2:1 of the German Basic Law), then respect for specific legislative guarantees of freedom (e.g., of trade) is legally and judicially protected, as recognized by German courts, also by the general constitutional guarantee of maximum equal freedom subject to democratic legislation.[14] Similarly, the EC Treaty guarantees of common market freedoms and of "freedom to conduct a business in accordance with Union law and national laws" (Article 16 EU Charter of Fundamental Rights) protect individual freedom of personal movement and of trade across frontiers beyond the traditionally narrow scope of "the right to liberty" in Article 5 of the ECHR (now also incorporated into Article 6 of the EU Charter). Respect for maximum personal and legal autonomy of the individual and for rule of law also justifies the moral and legal claim that other, precise and unconditional international guarantees of freedom and non-discrimination (as e.g., the customs union rules in Articles 23-25 of the EC Treaty, Articles III:2, XI:1 of GATT 1994) should, like domestic "market freedoms," be legally respected and protected as parts of the indivisible liberty to which citizens are entitled, subject to democratic legislation, in order to secure their personal self-development in freedom, dignity and peace under the rule of law.

Contrary to the outdated Kantian belief that the state has only a moral responsibility to go beyond equal rules of justice in order to ensure the material well-being of its citizens, UN and EU human rights law recognize that everyone is entitled to the realization of economic and social human rights "indispensable for his dignity and the free development of his personality" (Article 22 UDHR). By recognizing human rights to democratic self-government (e.g.,

Article 21) and "to a social and international order in which the rights set forth in this Declaration can be fully realized" (Article 28 UDHR), UN human instruments also acknowledge the contextual dependence of the realization of human rights on democratic peace and on mutually beneficial international cooperation under the rule of law. Proceeding from these human rights premises, this author has argued for many years that respect for human dignity and legal empowerment of individuals across frontiers also call for recognizing individuals as legal subjects not only of human rights law and of European Union law but also of other precise and unconditional international guarantees of freedom, non-discrimination and rule of law (e.g., in GATT and WTO law), in conformity with the today universal recognition of human beings as legal subjects of modern international law.

Neoclassical economic theory, by contrast, tends to focus one-sidedly on "economic efficiency" in quantitative terms (e.g., increase in GNP and national income) without taking into account the moral and legal human rights objectives of maximizing equal individual liberties and "social justice." The contribution of law to economic welfare has been recognized long since (e.g., by Adam Smith). However, "law and economics," "institutional economics," "public choice" theories and "constitutional economics" have so far failed to analyze systematically the contribution of human rights to economic welfare.[15] Only recently are economists discovering that "human rights make better economic actors," and that economic underdevelopment (e.g., famines, lack of investments, inefficient capital markets) is often due to lack of legal security and of effective protection of human rights. Nobel prize economist Amartya Sen, for example, has suggested to define economic welfare in terms of real substantive freedom and capability of citizens to develop their personality as they would like.[16]

Protection of "economic" and "social human rights" in national laws tends to differ from country to country depending on the particular historical, economic and legal traditions of the countries concerned. In some constitutional democracies, like England and the United States, courts have exercised judicial self-restraint vis-à-vis economic and social legislation by practicing a "double standard" whereby stricter judicial protection is granted to *civil* and *political human rights* than to *economic* and *social human rights*. As US constitutional, economic and competition law is perceived as an adequate legal framework for welfare-increasing competition among citizens, the US Congress has declined to ratify the UN Covenant on Economic, Social and Cultural Human Rights (UNCESCR). The particular focus in EC law, as well as in the national constitutions of some European states, on "economic liberties" and "social rights" confirms the potential importance of individual rights for creating a common market and for promoting social welfare. The EC Treaty guarantees of common market freedoms were rightly characterized by the EC Court as "fundamental freedoms" because they protect transnational citizen rights and mutually beneficial, peaceful cooperation across frontiers in a way European citizens never enjoyed prior to the coming into being of the EC.

The different human rights traditions in Europe and North America are, arguably, both compatible with the universal recognition of the "indivisibility" of civil, political, economic, social and cultural human rights as long as citizens have adequate individual rights and access to the economic resources necessary for their personal development and welfare. By contrast, there is no empirical evidence that protection of civil and political human rights may adversely affect economic and social rights and human welfare; claims by governments in less-developed countries to give priority to economic and social human rights cannot legally justify violations of universally recognized *civil* and *political human rights*, such as rights to free speech and freedom of association.

In UN law, the agreed "indivisibility of civil, political, economic, social and cultural human rights"[17] has not prevented the emergence of separate human rights covenants among which many UN member states selectively "pick and choose." Moreover, the UNCESCR does not protect the economic liberty rights and property rights necessary for promoting economic welfare through mutually beneficial division of labor. Human rights lawyers often neglect freedom of trade, private property rights and non-discriminatory competition as crucial instruments for enabling citizens to acquire the economic resources necessary for the enjoyment of their human rights. By contrast, the European Convention on Human Rights (ECHR) and European Union law have increasingly integrated the various dimensions of human rights into their legal and judicial treaty systems.

This contribution examines interrelationships between human rights, markets and economic welfare. It explains, in chapters I to IV, why markets are a necessary consequence of, and an indispensable means for effective protection of human rights. By assigning liberty rights (e.g., to self-development, freedom of contract, freedom of exchange) and property rights to human and material resources (e.g., intellectual property rights), and by defining individual responsibility and liability rules, human rights create incentives for investments, savings, mutually beneficial cooperation (e.g., through agreed exchanges of property rights), competition and decentralized markets (e.g., labor markets, capital markets, trade in goods). *Economic markets* as well as *political markets* are based on "dialogues about values" and freedom of exchange. Market mechanisms operate as citizen-oriented information- and allocation-mechanisms for a decentralized coordination of producer interests and consumer interests. Market-based and rights-based approaches can promote decentralized incentives and judicial remedies for the realization and enforcement of human rights. The legal recognition of the "indivisibility of human rights" is supported by empirical evidence that economic, political and legal freedoms complement and support each other (e.g., economic liberties contributing to political liberty, democracy forcing governments to prevent unnecessary famines and other human rights violations).

Since protection and enjoyment of most human rights depend on economic resources, and human rights contribute to the economic objective of maximizing consumer welfare through open markets and non-discriminatory competition, chapter V argues in favor of a "new integration paradigm" of international law: On the one side, UN human rights law must overcome its "anti-market bias" and recognize that "economic freedoms" (e.g., to exchange private goods and services) are no less important for the survival and personal development of individuals than civil and political freedoms (e.g., to participate in the democratic supply of "public goods"). For moral, legal and economic reasons (such as scarcity of supply in relation to consumer demand), human rights to liberty should be construed broadly as requiring government compliance with legislative and international guarantees of economic freedoms no less than respect for legal guarantees of civil and political freedoms. On the other side, the emerging global integration law (e.g., of the WTO) must be construed in conformity with the universal human rights obligations of UN and WTO member states. From a human rights perspective, economic policy must aim at enabling every citizen to acquire, own and use the economic resources necessary for the fulfillment of his human rights. Interpreting WTO rules in conformity with human rights does, however, not necessarily imply that e.g., import restrictions are an appropriate policy instrument for dealing with human rights violations in an exporting country.

European integration confirms that linking market integration law with human rights offers an effective strategy for promoting open markets, economic welfare, human rights and democratic peace across frontiers. Economic theory (e.g., on property rights as decentralized incentives for "internalizing external costs") supports the human rights objective of empowering citizens to invoke their individual rights before domestic courts so as to counteract and limit "government failures." Economic theory (e.g., on "countervailing powers") and human rights law also offer arguments for recognizing "market citizens" (e.g., investors, producers, traders, consumers) as legal subjects entitled to judicial protection of their "market rights." The decentralized enforcement of individual market freedoms, property rights, non-discrimination rights and social rights in EC law illustrates the constitutional importance of creating "legal and judicial markets" for the progressive legal clarification and judicial enforcement by self-interested citizens, lawyers and judges of equal liberties and other human rights.

All human rights need to be mutually balanced and implemented by democratic legislation which may legitimately differ from country to country depending on the particular traditions and preferences of their citizens. Protection of human rights aims at protection of individual and democratic *diversity* and at constitutional limitation of abuses of private and public powers which risk destroying freedom and welfare-increasing competition in both *economic markets* as well as *political markets*. Chapters VI to VIII discuss various problems of democratic governance, market regulation and human rights responsibilities of private and public actors at national and international levels.

I. Markets and Human Rights Proceed from the Same Values

Markets emerge wherever personal autonomy and diversity of individual capacities and preferences of investors, producers, traders and consumers are respected. Since the beginnings of written history, marketplaces have been described as cultural centers not only for the exchange of economic goods but also of social services and political ideas (e.g., the agora in classical Athens during the 5th century BC). Limited knowledge, scarcity of resources and the natural tendency of pursuing one's self-interest through social cooperation and division of labor prompt individuals to specialize in the production of scarce goods and services as the most important means for acquiring other goods and services necessary for human survival and for personal self-development. Consumer demand, market prices and competition inform and induce investors, producers and traders to use production factors and allocate resources in a manner enabling mutually profitable exchanges and supply of demand. Empirical evidence confirms that also the modern globalization of markets through international movements of goods, services, persons and investments has enabled trading countries to increase their national economic welfare, to reduce absolute poverty inside countries, and to satisfy and develop diversity of individual supply and demand for economic as well as non-economic goods and services.[18]

Like markets, the idea and legal recognition of "basic individual rights" and "fundamental rights" goes back to the beginnings of written history. Precursors include the rights to asylum granted by Greek city-states; Roman citizenship rights; rights of the nobility and freedom of trade in the Middle Ages (protected e.g., in the Magna Carta 1215); religious freedom guaranteed in the constitutional charter adopted by the Dutch provincial assembly at Dordrecht in 1572; the English *Habeas Corpus Act* of 1679 and *Bill of Rights* of 1689; the French Declaration of the Rights of Man and the Citizen of 1789; and the *Bill of Rights* appended to the US Constitution in 1791. The particular focus of liberty rights (e.g., freedom of religion, freedom of association, freedom to demonstrate, freedom of trade) was often shaped by historical events (such as the schism of the Christian church from the 16th century onwards) and by political struggles against the rulers. Liberation of citizens from discriminatory, welfare-reducing border barriers and transnational protection of freedom, non-discrimination, rule of law, democratic governance, social justice and mutually beneficial cooperation across frontiers are the human rights challenges of the 21st century.

The common core of markets and of human rights rests on respect for personal autonomy and individual diversity. The Kantian moral "categorical imperative" of maximizing equal liberties across frontiers justifies both the idea of inalienable, equal human rights and the economic objective of maximizing consumer welfare through voluntary exchanges and open markets. Human rights and consumer-driven market competition are both designed to protect individual preferences and promote personal self-development based on voluntary social cooperation, decentralized information-, allocation-, coordination- and enforcement mechanisms (such as market prices), and equal basic rights and non-discriminatory competition rules.

II. The Effectiveness of Markets and of Human Rights Depends on Constitutional Safeguards

Markets and competition are not gifts of nature. They depend on property rights (e.g., protecting the freedom to have and use resources exclusively), transaction rights (e.g., to acquire, sell, buy and transfer property titles in scarce resources), freedom of choice and other framework rules for the individual supply of private goods and the collective supply of public goods (such as stable money, legal security, competition rules preventing abuses of market power, social rules promoting social justice). Neither markets nor human rights enforce themselves.

Philosophers, lawyers and economists emphasize long since that liberty, markets and democracy risk destroying themselves unless they are protected by constitutional restraints on abuses of power. In order to overcome this "paradox of liberty" and avoid conflicts between our rational long-term interests and emotional short-term inclinations, individual decisions (e.g., by *Ulysses* when approaching the island of the *sirenes*) as well as collective decisions (e.g., by a democratic majority that wants to hand over the power to a dictator, as in Germany in 1933) need to be restrained by self-imposed rules ("hands-tying") of a higher legal rank.[19] History confirms that, without such constitutional rules, economic markets for the supply of private goods as well as political markets for the collective supply of *public goods* lead to restraints of competition, monopolization and other abuses of market power. Individual and collective liberty thus depend, paradoxically, on legal and constitutional restraints in both private law as well as public law, national and international.[20]

The centuries-old English and American common law tradition of protecting equal freedoms of traders, competitors and consumers against "unreasonable restraint of trade" and "coercion" reflect an early legal recognition of the economic insight that the efficiency of market mechanisms (e.g., for allocating resources in a manner coordinating supply and demand) depends on legal protection of individual freedoms and property rights in both material and intellectual resources. Since World War II, all constitutional democracies in Europe and North America have introduced comprehensive national and international competition rules based on common core principles[21] and on the common historical experience that abuses of private power may be no less dangerous and welfare-reducing than abuses of public power.[22] Whereas modern US competition policy emphasizes the competition policy objective of protecting competition as a welfare-maximizing *process* (rather than protecting *competitors*), EC competition policy continues to admit the legitimacy of protecting also "economic freedom" of competitors in the marketplace even if e.g., vertical restraints neither limit output nor otherwise harm consumers.[23] Yet, notwithstanding the different history and legal framework of competition policies in Europe and North America, there is broad agreement today that

a) the direct objectives of competition policy in Europe and North America should focus on economic efficiency and consumer welfare;
b) the indirect long-term objectives include also dispersion of private and public power and protection of equal opportunities of market participants;
c) other policy objectives (such as protection of small enterprises, social justice) can be pursued more efficiently through other policy instruments (such as tax benefits, production subsidies, labor law, social legislation).

The US Supreme Court has emphasized that "antitrust laws ... are the Magna Carta of free enterprise. They are as important to the preservation of economic freedom and our free enterprise system as the Bill of Rights is to the protection of our fundamental freedoms."[24] The EC's "treaty constitution" recognizes competition law as part of the constitutional task of guaranteeing "an open market economy with free competition" (Articles 4,98,105,157 EC Treaty) based on "a system ensuring that competition in the internal market is not distorted" (Article 3, g). Free movements of goods, services, persons, capital and related payments, non-discriminatory conditions of competition, as well as social rights are constitutionally protected in EC law as "fundamental rights."[25] The single European market could never have been realized without private enforcement of these economic liberties by EC citizens and without their judicial protection by national courts and by the EC Court vis-à-vis governmental and private restrictions and discrimination. EC competition law and the ever more comprehensive EC guarantees of social rights and of regional adjustment assistance are indivisible components of the EC's "economic constitution"[26] and "social market economy" without which political acceptance of the "acquis communautaire" by many less-developed, newly acceding European countries would not have been democratically feasible.

Similar to this emergence of "economic constitutions," the historical evolution of *political markets* for the collective supply of *public goods* (such as democratic self-government) is characterized by the increasingly worldwide adoption of national constitutional restraints based on (1) rule of law; (2) limitation and separation of government powers; (3) democratic self-government; (4) human rights; (5) social justice; and (6) the worldwide historical experience that protection of human rights and "democratic peace" cannot remain effective without international law providing for reciprocal international legal restraints on abuses of foreign policy powers.[27] Similar to economic competition law, the basic objective of constitutional law is to protect freedom of choice, political competition and equal individual rights as legal preconditions for individual and democratic self-government. The definition and mutual balancing of these core principles in national constitutions (e.g., in national catalogues of human rights) and in international "treaty constitutions" (such as the EC Treaty and the ILO Constitution), as well as the protection of human rights through democratic legislation, legitimately differ from country to country, and from organization to organization, depending on the historical experiences and constitutional wisdom of each society. Constitutions recognize a higher legal rank of "inalienable human rights" so as to direct and limit *post-constitutional choices* of government institutions and of citizens within the agreed basic rules.

III. Markets and Human Rights Can Complement Each Other

Consumer-driven markets, human rights and democracy derive values from the individual and his consent. Adam Smith, in his inquiry into the *Nature and Causes of the Wealth of Nations* (1776), concluded that the economic welfare of England was essentially due to its legal guarantees of economic freedom, property rights and legal security for investors, producers, traders and consumers. Modern "law and economics" literature[28] and "institutional economics"[29] have examined in much more detail the interrelationships between legal rules and economic welfare, for instance the contribution of free speech, liability rules, property rights and democracy to the "internalization of external effects" and avoidance of other "market failures" (such as asymmetries in information, discrimination of women, slave work); or the reduction of transaction costs through contract law, litigation rules and law enforcement procedures. The overall conclusion is that equal "individual rights are a cause of prosperity"; and "almost all of the countries that have enjoyed good economic performance across generations are countries that have stable democratic governments."[30]

Economics aims at maximizing *productive efficiency* and *allocative efficiency* as means for reducing the scarcity of resources in relation to consumer demand. The economic recommendations for correcting "market failures" recognize the necessity of government regulation and assume that government institutions have the power, information and motivation for correcting the manifold market imperfections. "Constitutional economics," by contrast, emphasizes the need for limiting and regulating government powers (e.g., monetary, taxing, spending and regulatory powers) and examines the interrelationships between economic welfare and constitutional rules so as to constrain legislative, administrative and other "government failures" by designing a "constitution of liberty" that maximizes economic and social welfare.[31] By assuming that individuals pursue their personal (selfish or altruistic) interests in political markets no less than in economic markets, *public choice theories* explain convincingly why government regulation is often "captured" by "rent-seeking" interests and redistributes income for the benefit of the regulated industries in exchange for political support of the regulators.[32] As majority decisions are replete with opportunities for special interests to exploit the rest of the population, democracy remains sustainable only as *constitutional democracy*. Equal human rights and constitutional guarantees keeping markets and democratic processes open (e.g., by offering "voice," competition and the possibility of "exit") have proven to be indispensable for protecting minorities and individuals against majoritarian despotism and other *government failures*.

As in the case of voluntarily agreed market transactions, the legitimacy of long-term constitutional rules depends upon mutual agreement. Constitutional theories have designed numerous techniques (such as negotiations behind a "veil of uncertainty" over one's future position in society) facilitating agreement on the basic *social contract*. By placing basic personal liberties and other agreed core values beyond the power of majoritarian politics, human rights and open markets facilitate individual consent to the basic constitutional rules and protect individual adjustment to change. If market failures adversely affect human rights, economic theory teaches that governments should correct such market imperfections through "optimal" interventions directly at the source of the problem (e.g., through labor, social and health legislation, prohibitions of cartels and environmental pollution, judicial protection of human rights) without preventing citizens to engage in mutually beneficial trade across frontiers. The human rights to democratic participation in the exercise of government powers, and of individual access to courts, promote a self-enforcing constitution by empowering citizens to protect themselves – through "deliberative democracy," legal, judicial and political remedies – against "government failures" as well as "market failures."

IV. Human Rights Promote the Effectiveness of Competition, Democracy and Worldwide Organizations

The insight that human rights make individuals not only better "democratic citizens" but also "better economic actors,"[33] is of particular importance for international economic integration and rule-making in worldwide organizations where respect for human rights, rule of law and constitutional safeguards (such as parliamentary and judicial control) in the exercise of the limited powers delegated to international organizations are less effectively protected than inside constitutional democracies. In the European Union, the progressive evolution from a sectoral "coal and steel community" toward a customs union, common market, monetary union and political union with a "common foreign and security policy" was democratically acceptable for national parliaments, citizens and national constitutional courts (e.g., in Germany) only because of the simultaneous transformation of the EC Treaty into a "treaty constitution" committed to the protection of human rights, democratic peace, "citizenship of the Union," social justice and judicial review of the rule of law inside the EC.[34] The EC has likewise insisted on the inclusion of *human rights clauses* and *democracy clauses* into its free trade area, customs union and association agreements with more than hundred countries in Europe, Africa, Asia, Latin America and the Pacific.

Human rights organizations and other civil society groups are also requesting the recognition of human rights in WTO law and a consultative status of non-governmental organizations in WTO decision-making procedures.[35] The focus of human-rights on personal autonomy and on democratic diversity corresponds with, and reinforces, the decentralized legal structures of consumer-driven markets and of citizen-driven democracies.

1. Six Major Instrumental Functions of Human Rights Law

Legal doctrine has long since neglected that human rights constitute not only moral and legal rights (e.g., of a defensive, procedural, participatory or redistributive nature), corresponding obligations of governments at national and international levels, and objective principles of justice necessary for protecting "democratic peace" and for limiting abuses of power also by non-state actors (e.g., freedom of association in labor markets). Legal guarantees of civil, political, economic and social human rights also serve information-, incentive-, coordination-, enforcement- and legitimacy-functions for rendering economic and political competition more effective and for solving social problems confronting all societies.[36] For instance:

(1) Human rights as instruments for reducing the problem of limited knowledge: Human rights (e.g., to freedom of information and freedom of the press) entitle individuals to act on the basis of their own personal knowledge and to acquire and take into account the personal knowledge of others. They also protect spontaneous information mechanisms (such as market prices) which enable individuals to take into account knowledge dispersed among billions of human beings even if individuals remain "rationally ignorant" of most of this dispersed knowledge. Such decentralized information and ordering of the actions of diverse persons with limited knowledge reduces the need for centralized government regulation (e.g., laws imposing the majorities' preferences on minorities) which might unnecessarily limit individual freedom and disrupt decentralized ordering (notwithstanding the inevitable need for some centralized ordering e.g., in governmental and non-governmental organizations, companies and families).

(2) Human rights as incentives for mutually beneficial division of labor: Economic transactions are based on the exercise of liberty rights (e.g., to sell and buy) and the transfer of property rights (e.g., in traded goods). Human rights (e.g., property rights, freedom of contract) set incentives for savings, investments and mutually beneficial division of labor among self-interested actors (e.g., by requiring compensation in case of non-fulfillment of contracts or of governmental takings of property rights). They protect individual rights to acquire, buy and sell goods and services necessary for personal self-development but whose supply remains scarce in relation to consumer demand. Equal human rights force people to take into account the interests of others (e.g., by requiring consent to rights transfers) and to settle disputes peacefully based on respect for the rule of law.

(3) Human rights as conflict-prevention mechanisms help to transform the Hobbesian "war of everybody against everybody else" into peaceful cooperation based on equal legal rights. In the economy no less than in the polity, the inevitable conflicts of interests (e.g., between producer interests in high sales prices and consumer interests in low prices) can be reconciled best on the basis of equal liberty rights (e.g., freedom of contract) and other human rights. Human rights enable decentralized solutions also for the "value problem" that human views about "truth" may differ, and value judgments about "the good" and "the beautiful" are not necessarily true.[37] By protecting (e.g., through freedom of religion, freedom of opinion and freedom of the press) diversity of individual values and preventing majorities from imposing their value preferences on minorities, human rights promote peaceful coexistence, tolerance and scientific progress. Effective protection of human rights gives inevitably rise to economic as well as political markets as decentralized means for evaluating scarce resources (e.g., private and public goods and services) in a manner respecting individual freedom and responsibility, promoting dialogues about values, and allocating and distributing resources in accordance with consumer demand.

(4) Human rights as countervailing powers: The history of "human rights revolutions" demonstrates that human rights (e.g., to self-defence *vis-à-vis* illegal abuses of power) offer "checks and balances" enabling citizens to defend their equal rights against abuses of powers and to limit the constitutional task of governments to the "common public interest" defined in terms of equal human rights. By defining core human rights as "inalienable" and requiring respect for the equal human rights of all others, human rights require substantive and procedural justifications of governmental restrictions and promote democratic accountability.

(5) Human rights as decentralized dispute settlement and enforcement mechanisms: Human rights (e.g., of individual access to courts) and corresponding obligations (e.g., for compensation for violations of human rights) set incentives for decentralized enforcement of rules by self-interested, vigilant citizens and for spontaneous, private initiatives to "internalize" harmful "market externalities" (e.g., by invoking property rights and human rights to a clean environment *vis-à-vis* harmful pollution).[38] Human rights require legislative, administrative and judicial protection specifying and balancing human rights, and

thereby promote a living "human rights culture" and continuous adjustment of law and "justice" to changing situations.

(6) Human rights as sources of democratic legitimacy: The human rights to "periodic and genuine elections ... by universal and equal suffrage" (Article 21 UDHR), and to democratic participation in the exercise of government powers (Article 25 UN Covenant on Civil and Political Rights), promote transparent governance based on "the will of the people" (Article 21 UDHR) and on "deliberative democracy"[39] legitimating the exercise of political power at national and international levels. By defining principles of justice which constitutionally limit and guide all government activities, human rights inform and educate people on how they can realize individual and democratic self-government and mutually beneficial cooperation across frontiers while avoiding conflicts with the independent actions of others.

Recognition of the instrumental functions of civil, political, economic, social and cultural human rights for the diverse forms of personal self-development does not contradict the rootedness of human rights in human dignity. As explained in the Introduction, human dignity in the sense of moral and rational autonomy remains the legally recognized source and ultimate objective of all human rights empowering the individual to live one's life in freedom and dignity. The diversity of national and international human rights rules confirms that the legal design and institutional protection of specific human rights may legitimately differ among countries depending on the democratic preferences and resources of their citizens and political communities.

2. Enjoyment and Protection of Human Rights Depend on Economic Resources

As long as unnecessary poverty continues to prevent billions of human beings from enjoying human rights, the empirical evidence on the contribution of human rights to economic welfare is of particular importance for promoting the effectiveness of human rights.[40] Since the economy is no less important for citizens and their human rights than the polity, and most citizens spend most of their time on their economic activities in order to gain the resources necessary for their personal development and enjoyment of human rights, constitutional protection of liberty rights, property rights and other human rights in the economic area is as important as in other areas.[41] Economic markets inducing investors, producers and traders to supply private goods and services demanded by consumers involve democratic "dialogues about values"[42] which are no less important for effective enjoyment of human rights than the "political markets" for the supply of "public goods" by governments.

The economic and human resources needed for the full enjoyment of human rights thus depend on making human rights an integral part of a social and sustainable market economy. Economists increasingly recognize that human rights require defining the goal of economic policy as enabling every citizen to acquire and own the economic resources necessary for exercising his human rights.[43] From a human rights perspective, "market failures" should be defined more broadly as including violations of human rights (e.g., in case of child labor, forced labor and discrimination of women distorting labor markets; discriminatory takings of property rights without adequate compensation distorting capital markets). "Rules of reason" in competition law, and the "public interest clauses" in regional and global integration law (e.g., Article XX GATT), should be construed as justifying government interventions necessary for the protection of human rights and for the correction of market failures (e.g., if private markets do not supply necessary medicines at socially affordable prices). Yet, interpreting "market failures" and "public interest clauses" in conformity with human rights does neither imply that import restrictions are an appropriate policy instrument for dealing with human rights violations in an exporting country, nor that competition authorities should have regulatory powers to protect competitors rather than competition as a process.

The successful integration of human rights into EC law and policies confirms that the economy and "specialized organizations" must not be regarded as autonomous fields unrelated to the human rights of producers, workers, investors, traders and consumers. In order to strengthen the mutual synergies between human rights and integration law also at the worldwide level, UN human rights law must overcome its longstanding neglect of economic liberty rights, property rights and competition safeguards as indispensable means of promoting widespread ownership of economic and human capital (such as health and education) and of preventing small minorities from controlling the economy and polity. WTO members must likewise interpret their declared treaty objectives of "raising standards of living, ensuring full employment and a large and steadily growing volume of real income..., while allowing for the optimal use of the world's resources in accordance with the objective of sustainable development" (Preamble of the WTO Agreement), in conformity with their universal human rights obligations.

V. Globalization of Markets and of Human Rights Requires a New Integration Paradigm

The human rights obligations in the UN Charter and in the UDHR of 1948 were negotiated at the same time as the 1944 Bretton Woods Agreements, the General Agreement on Tariffs and Trade (GATT) of 1947 and the 1948 Havana Charter for an International Trade Organization. All these agreements aimed at protecting liberty, non-discrimination, rule of law, social welfare and other human rights values through a rules-based international order and "specialized agencies" (Article 57 UN Charter) committed to the economic principle of "separation of policy instruments." The postwar UN system envisaged that

- *foreign policies* were to be coordinated in the UN so as to promote "sovereign equality of all its Members" (Article 2:1 UN Charter) and collective security;
- *liberalization of payments* and *monetary stability* were collectively pursued through the rules and assistance of the International Monetary Fund (IMF);
- GATT 1947 and the Havana Charter aimed at mutually beneficial *liberalization of international trade and investments*;
- *development aid and policies* would be coordinated in the World Bank Group;
- and *social laws and policies* would be promoted in the International Labor Organization (ILO) and other specialized agencies (like UNESCO and WHO).

Apart from a few exceptions (such as the explicit references to human rights in the UN Charter, in the statutes of UNESCO and WHO, the Philadelphia Declaration of the ILO), human rights were not effectively integrated into the law of most worldwide organizations so as to de-politicize and facilitate *functional intergovernmental cooperation* (e.g., in the liberalization of trade and payments restrictions) notwithstanding the diverse postwar views on human rights (e.g., in communist countries). In accordance with the "principles of justice" elaborated by modern legal philosophers[44] and reflected in the constitutional law of the leading postwar power,[45] the postwar institutions gave priority to reciprocal international *liberalization* (e.g., in the context of the IMF, GATT, WTO, WIPO and ILO) and to joint *wealth creation.* Economic and social rights and redistribution of wealth were perceived as primarily the responsibility of *national* governments, depending on national resources and value preferences, to be supplemented by "international benevolence."[46] Article 28 of the UDHR recognized: "Everyone is entitled to a social and international order in which the rights and freedoms set forth in the Declaration can be fully realized." Yet, UN human rights law lacks a coherent theory and practice regarding transnational economic and social human rights vis-à-vis not only domestic governments but also foreign governments and international organizations.[47]

Regional integration law, by contrast, has moved toward a different "integration paradigm" linking economic integration to constitutional guarantees of human rights, democracy and undistorted competition. For instance, the "human rights clauses" in the European Union (EU) Treaty, in the association and cooperation agreements between the EU and more than twenty countries in Eastern Europe and the Mediterranean, and in the EU's Cotonou Agreement with 77 African, Caribbean and Pacific states make "respect for human rights, democratic principles and the rule of law ... essential elements" of these agreements.[48] The Quebec Summit Declaration of April 2001 and the "Inter-American Charter of Democracy" of September 2001, adopted by more than 30 member states of the Organization of American States, likewise link the plans for a Free Trade Area of the Americas (FTAA) to the strengthening of human rights and democracy. The proposals, in the WTO Ministerial Declaration of 14 November 2001,[49] for integrating competition, investment, environmental and health protection rules into the global integration law of the WTO, further illustrate the need to examine whether the European and American "integration paradigm" should not also become accepted at the worldwide level in order to promote consensus on a new kind of global integration law based on human rights and solidarity (e.g., regarding the sharing of the social adjustment costs of global integration).

The proposed change from *international functionalism* to *constitutionalism* does not put into question the economic efficiency arguments for "optimizing" and separating policy instruments.[50] However, European integration confirms that the collective supply of public goods (such as global division of labor) may not be politically feasible without comprehensive "package deals" including common responses to "market failures" and redistributive "principles of justice."[51] Less-developed countries, for instance, often perceive market competition as a "license to kill" for multinational corporations from developed countries as long as liberal trade rules are not supplemented by competition and social rules (as in the EC) promoting fair opportunities and equitable distribution of the gains from trade.

In order to remain politically acceptable, global integration law (e.g., in the WTO) must pursue not only "economic efficiency" but also "democratic legitimacy"and "social justice" as defined by human rights. Citizens will continue to challenge the democratic and social legitimacy of integration law if it pursues economic welfare without regard to social human rights, for example the *human right to education* of the 130 million children (aged from 6 to 12) who do not attend primary school; the *human right to basic health care* of the 25 million Africans living with AIDS, or of the about 35,000 children dying each day from curable diseases; and the *human right to food and an adequate standard of living* for the 1.2 billion people living on less than a dollar a day. The new opportunities for the worldwide enjoyment of human rights created by global division of labor (such as additional economic resources, job opportunities, worldwide communication systems, access to new medicines and technologies) must be accompanied by stronger legal protection of social human rights so as to limit abuses of deregulation (e.g., by international cartels, trade in drugs and arms, trafficking in women and children), help vulnerable groups to adjust to change without violation of their human rights, and put pressure on authoritarian governments to protect not only the self-interests of the rulers and of big business but the human rights of all their citizens.

VI. Toward a UN Human Rights Constitution Overcoming the Democracy Deficit of State Centered International Law?

From the peace treaties of Westphalia (1648) up to the UN Charter (1945), the *international law of coexistence* evolved as a system of rights and duties of states focusing on the protection of "sovereign equality" of states (Article 2:1 UN Charter) and on effectiveness of government control over a territory and a population. *Inside democracies*, validity of law depends on respect for human rights and for democratic rule-making procedures. The validity of classical international law rules, however, and the recognition of states as subjects of international law into whose "domestic jurisdiction" other states must not intervene, does not depend on the democratic legitimacy of the governments concerned. Due to its power-oriented character, the lack of legitimacy of classical international law has been criticized long since (e.g., by colonial and other suppressed people) and has rendered a worldwide rule-of-law system impossible.

Since the fall of the Berlin wall (1989), human rights have become universally recognized by all 191 UN member states not only as part of international treaty law (e.g., in the UN Charter and the 1989 UN Convention on the Rights of the Child, ratified by 191 states), but also of international customary law and of the "general principles of law recognized by civilized nations" (Article 38, Statute of the International Court of Justice). The UN's *international law of cooperation* includes also intergovernmental rights and obligations to mutually beneficial cooperation across frontiers and obligations to respect human rights. Yet, UN law secures neither democratic governance nor democratic legislation implementing and protecting human rights, nor judicial protection of human rights.[52] Can the necessary "international governance" for the supply of "public international goods" (such as democratic peace, protection of the "global commons," promotion of human rights and of welfare-increasing division of labor across frontiers) be realized through power-oriented worldwide organizations without democratic governance at the international level and without effective protection of individual liberty rights, property rights and other human rights necessary for a mutually beneficial division of labor among free citizens?

1. Democratic Legitimacy and Accountability of International Organizations Depend on Embedding Them into Domestic Constitutional Systems

International organizations can be perceived as a "fourth branch of government," indispensable for the collective supply of international public goods, whose democratic legitimacy depends on subjecting international rule-making and the domestic implementation of the law and policies of international organizations to parliamentary control, democratic implementing legislation, judicial protection of rule of law and of individual rights, and other domestic constitutional safeguards (such as transparent policy-making in cooperation with representatives of civil society).[53] Regional and worldwide economic integration law, such as the WTO Agreement and the more than hundred free trade area and customs union agreements pursuant to GATT Article XXIV and GATS Article V, derive legitimacy not only from the ratification and implementation of these agreements by national parliaments. No less important is that their substantive legal and judicial guarantees protect individual freedom, non-discrimination, rule of law and welfare-increasing cooperation among producers, investors, traders and consumers far beyond the corresponding legal guarantees in national laws and constitutions.[54]

Economists have long since recognized that international guarantees of market competition, non-discrimination and rule of law, such as those in the 1944 Bretton Woods Agreements and in GATT 1947, can serve "constitutional functions" for enabling citizens to increase their individual and social welfare through mutually beneficial division of labor – guided by the information functions, coordination functions, allocation and distribution functions of market prices and competition across frontiers – without prejudice to the sovereign rights of governments to correct "market failures" and supply "public goods" through national legislation and other government interventions.[55] The liberal trade order before World War I and following World War II illustrated that international market mechanisms – provided they are legally protected and restrained by national and international rules – enable the collective supply of international public goods without a world government.

2. Universal Human Rights Require Democratic Legitimacy and Accountability of International Organizations

The move from "negative integration" (e.g., reciprocal liberalization of discriminatory border restrictions in GATT) toward worldwide harmonization of non-discriminatory internal regulations (e.g., for trade-related services, investments, property rights, competition and environmental rules) raises new concerns about how worldwide rule-making can be legitimized if it is no longer effectively controlled by civil society, national parliaments and "deliberative democracy." Are there alternative means of legitimizing intergovernmental rule-making at the international level even though some of the preconditions of democratic legitimacy – such as a "government of the people, by the people and for the people" (A. Lincoln) – do not exist in worldwide organizations where governments often continue to behave like monarchs treating their citizens as mere objects and negotiating rules behind closed doors without transparent democratic discussion?

Since the 1990s, the universal recognition, in national and numerous UN human rights instruments, of "the inherent dignity and of the equal and inalienable rights of all members of the human family (as) thé foundation of freedom, justice and peace in the world"[56] (Preamble, UDHR 1948) offers a new source of democratic legitimization of international law. As inside constitutional democracies, the legal recognition of an inalienable core of human rights as international *ius cogens* – acknowledged as inalienable "birth rights" of every human being, but not granted by governments – should be interpreted as imposing constitutional restraints on all government powers, including those of international organizations. The fragmented UN human rights treaties, and the human rights bodies set up by them, are increasingly evolving into a "UN human rights constitution," founded no longer only on state-centered treaties but also on universally recognized general principles of law and universal recognition of individuals and peoples as subjects of international law and sources of democratic legitimacy.[57] UN human rights law and the general international law rules on treaty interpretation (as codified in Article 31 of the Vienna Convention on the Law of Treaties) require interpreting international treaties (including the WTO Agreement) in conformity with universally recognized human rights. International courts (like the International Court of Justice and the WTO Appellate Body) should follow the example of the EC Court of Justice and of the European Court of Human Rights by recognizing that UN human rights law binds not only *national governments* but also their collective rule-making in *intergovernmental organizations* and domestic implementation of international rules:

> "Where States establish international organizations, or *mutatis mutandis* international agreements, to pursue cooperation in certain fields of activities, there may be implications for the protection of fundamental rights. It would be incompatible with the purpose and object of the (European Convention on Human Rights) if Contracting States were thereby absolved from their responsibility under the Convention in relation to the field of activity covered by such attribution."[58]

3. Market Integration and Citizen Rights in European and Global Integration: The Role of Courts and Human Rights Organizations

In effecting European integration, citizens, parliaments and courts have forced the EC institutions to recognize that, as stated by the EC Court of Justice, "fundamental human rights (are) enshrined in the general principles of Community law and protected by the Court,"[59] and "respect for human rights is a condition of the lawfulness of Community acts."[60] The European Court of Human Rights has likewise emphasized that the human rights obligations of the more than 40 member states of the European Convention on Human Rights (ECHR) apply also to *collective* rule-making in international organizations.

In most worldwide organizations, however, human rights have not been effectively integrated into multilateral rule-making and policies and are not effectively protected through worldwide adjudication. In contrast to the "Matthews principle" recognized in European law,[61] citizens outside Europe often lack effective judicial remedies to ensure that international obligations undertaken by their governments (e.g. in the WTO) remain consistent with human rights obligations. The UNCESCR offers much less effective legal and institutional safeguards for compliance with economic and social human rights compared with the UN Covenant on Civil and Political Rights (UNCCPR).[62] By not mentioning property rights, and by safeguarding fundamental economic freedoms only in an indirect and inadequate manner (cf. Article 6:2 UNCESCR), the UN covenants do not protect the legal preconditions for creating the economic resources necessary for the enjoyment of human rights. The regular civil society protests against non-transparent rule-making in worldwide organizations, and the often one-sided industry-pressures determining multilateral negotiations (e.g., in the GATT and WTO), are signs of a continuing "clash of civilizations" between a citizen-oriented *human rights culture* and *power-politics* in intergovernmental negotiations and state-centered organizations.

The history of European integration suggests that the emergence of a human rights culture promoting democratic peace and social welfare depends on empowering individuals to defend not only their *civil* and *political* human rights, but also their *economic* and *social rights* through individual and democratic self-government and access to courts. Inside the EC, the judicial protection of "market freedoms," non-discrimination and freedom of competition as fundamental individual rights became an important driving force for the progressive realization of the common market and of "an area of freedom, security and justice" (Article 61 EC Treaty). The EC Court emphasized that economic freedoms "are not absolute but must be viewed in relation to their social function"[63] and with due regard to human rights.[64] The EC jurisprudence on social rights (e.g., "the principle of equal pay for male and female workers for equal work" in Article 141 EC Treaty) contributed to the emergence of a European "social market economy" in which EC member states are required to extend social rights (e.g., to education and vocational training) to nationals of other EC member states.[65]

The UDHR recognizes that "everyone is entitled to a social and international order in which the rights and freedoms set forth in this Declaration can be fully realized" (Article 28). Yet, human rights have not yet been effectively defined and protected vis-à-vis the *collective exercise of government powers in worldwide organizations*. Just as the human rights guarantees and competition safeguards of the EC Treaty have reinforced the legitimacy and effectiveness of European integration and of protection of human rights throughout Europe, human rights law and WTO rules offer mutually beneficial synergies also at the worldwide level for rendering human rights and the social functions and democratic legitimacy of the emerging global integration law more effective. As in European integration, international courts (e.g., the WTO Appellate Body) and human rights organizations (e.g., the UN Committee on Economic, Social and Cultural Rights) should take the lead – with due regard to the "margin of discretion" of democratic legislatures, and to the civil society requests for more effective protection of human rights in worldwide organizations – in interpreting the law of specialized organizations in conformity with universally recognized human rights.

Additional "bottom-up pressures" by civil society representatives, national parliaments and national courts will be necessary for inducing "specialized organizations" and government representatives to respond more actively to their human rights obligations. Just as European integration has benefited from recognizing EC citizens and members of the European Parliament as legal subjects of integration law, UN law and the global integration law of the WTO would acquire additional democratic legitimacy from enabling citizens and parliamentary representatives to participate more actively in the institutional framework of worldwide organizations and in the legal implementation and judicial enforcement of UN human rights law and WTO law.

VII. Social Human Rights and WTO Rules: Need for Deference vis-à-vis Parliamentary Democracy and Specialized Human Rights Bodies

Human rights need to be defined, promoted and mutually balanced through democratic legislation, administrative and judicial protection and international safeguards across frontiers. The "constitutional functions" of the WTO guarantees of freedom, non-discrimination, rule of law and mutually beneficial trade transactions for the corresponding human rights guarantees (e.g., of freedom, non-discrimination and access to courts) are increasingly recognized.[66] The relevance of social human rights for the interpretation and application of WTO rules (e.g., on access to essential medicines), and the model of the "corporatist legal structure" of the International Labor Organization (ILO) for institutional reforms of the WTO, remain, however, controversial. As regards international labor standards, most WTO governments seem to believe that cooperation through technical assistance and capacity building are more effective instruments for the promotion of labor standards than import restrictions which tend to worsen the working conditions in exporting countries and may be neither an effective nor "necessary" remedy (in terms of GATT Article XX) for strengthening labor standards.

The interrelationships between trade rules and the human right to health are increasingly recognized. In the WTO Ministerial Declaration on "The TRIPS Agreement and Public Health" of November 2001, all WTO members "affirm that the Agreement can and should be interpreted and implemented in a manner supportive of WTO Members' right to protect public health and, in particular, to promote access to medicines for all"; WTO members also "reaffirm the right of WTO Members to use, to the full, the provisions in the TRIPS Agreement, which provide flexibility for this purpose."[67] Rather than granting a general waiver from WTO law in favor of the human right to health, WTO members preferred to specify those TRIPS provisions which they understand to grant sufficient flexibility for promoting public health and access to medicines for all.[68] This approach seems consistent with the general principle that human rights are not "absolute" but must be legally implemented through legislative measures taking into account all other human rights.

The universal recognition of human rights calls for construing the numerous public interest clauses in WTO law in conformity with the human rights requirement that individual freedom and non-discrimination may be restricted only to the extent necessary for protecting other human rights. The non-discrimination and "necessity" requirements in the "general exceptions" of WTO law (e.g., in GATT Article XX and GATS Article XIV) reflect these human rights principles. WTO law gives clear priority to the sovereign right to restrict trade if this is necessary for the protection of human rights (e.g., to life, health, food, education, a clean and sustainable environment, and social security). The WTO panel and Appellate Body reports on US import restrictions of shrimps (aimed at protecting endangered species of sea turtles) confirmed that import restrictions may be justifiable under WTO law for protecting human rights values not only inside the importing country but also in other countries and in the High Seas.[69] The dynamic evolution of WTO jurisprudence on trade-related environmental measures suggests that WTO dispute settlement bodies are well aware of the need for interpreting WTO rules with due regard to other international law obligations of WTO Members.

By prohibiting discriminatory and protectionist abuses, the "general exceptions" in WTO law aim at reconciling freedom of trade with the "human rights functions" of safeguard measures restricting liberal trade. In such legal and judicial balancing processes, human rights must guide the interpretation not only of the WTO's "exceptions" and safeguard clauses; the basic WTO guarantees of freedom of trade, non-discrimination, property rights and rule of law likewise protect human rights values (such as individual liberty, non-discrimination, private property and access to courts) that must be taken into account in the legal and judicial balancing processes. Moreover, the right of the importing country to protect the human rights of its citizens needs to be balanced with the corresponding right of the exporting country and also with the economic insight that trade restrictions are only rarely an efficient instrument for correcting "market failures" and supplying "public goods."[70] The recent EC Court judgment interpreting the customs union rules of the EC Treaty in conformity with the human rights guarantees in the European Convention on Human Rights (Articles 10 and 11 on freedom of expression and freedom of assembly) illustrates that judicial protection of human rights may require methodological approaches and judicial balancing methods that differ from those of international trade law.[71]

In past GATT and WTO practice, governments have only rarely referred to human rights e.g., in their invocations of the "general exceptions" (e.g., in GATT Article XX) and other safeguard clauses in GATT and WTO law so as to justify measures "necessary to protect human, animal or plant life or health."[72] There appears to be no evidence, however, that past GATT practice under Article XX has been inconsistent with human rights. GATT dispute settlement jurisprudence, for instance, has never challenged the legality of non-discriminatory and "necessary" safeguard measures under GATT Article XX. Also WTO practice seems to be consistent so far with interpreting the "general exceptions" in WTO law (e.g., Article XIV GATS, Article 8 TRIPS Agreement) in conformity with human rights (such as the rights to health, food, adequate housing and education, or the right to protection of moral and material interests resulting from scientific, literary or artistic production of which one is the author).[73] The numerous "human rights clauses" in international economic agreements concluded by the EC with third countries have likewise been used only rarely for trade restrictions as a remedy for human rights violations.[74] There appears to have been not a single judgment by the EC Court invalidating an EC measure on grounds of human rights.[75]

The increasing human rights jurisprudence by international courts and other human rights bodies may also be of relevance for the judicial interpretation of WTO law. For instance, General Comment No.14 (2000) on the human right to the highest attainable standard of health (Article 12 ICESCR), adopted by the UN Committee on Economic, Social and Cultural Rights in May 2000,[76] defines the right to health as an inclusive right extending not only to timely and appropriate health care but also to the underlying determinants of health, such as availability, accessibility and affordability of health facilities, goods and services. The legal obligations of states to respect, protect and fulfil this human right requires legislative implementation, judicial protection and health policy measures which, "depending on the availability of resources, ... should facilitate access to essential health facilities, goods and services in other countries, wherever possible and provide the necessary aid when required."[77] The General Comment recognizes that trade restrictions e.g., on individual access to essential food, drugs and health services can be inconsistent with the human right to health, and that cooperation might be required also in the WTO for the implementation of the right to health.[78]

The universalization and expanding subject matters of both human rights and intellectual property law have prompted negotiations in various UN bodies and also in the WTO on the clarification of the complex interrelationships between the TRIPS Agreement and human rights. While the need for intellectual property as reward and incentive for research and development (e.g., of new pharmaceuticals) is no longer contested, the proper balancing between the social objectives of the TRIPS Agreement (see Articles 7 and 8), its "regulatory exceptions" (e.g., in Article 6 for "parallel imports," Article 31 for "compulsory licencing," Article 40 concerning abuses of intellectual property rights), and the appropriate scope of intellectual property protection (e.g., for genetic and other living materials, rights of indigenous peoples) raises numerous controversial questions.[79] Yet, the waiver granted from Article 31(f) of the TRIPS Agreement in August 2003 reflects the so far broad agreement that the TRIPS provisions are flexible enough to permit necessary health protection measures so as to ensure access to affordable medicines to treat AIDS and other pandemics.[80]

VIII. Conclusion: Constitutional Functions of the Emerging UN Human Rights Constitution

The ever increasing number of international treaties constituting worldwide organizations, the legal primacy of their respective "constitutional charters" over "secondary law" and – in case of the UN Charter – also over other conflicting treaty rules (cf. Article 103 UN Charter), and the separation and mutual "checks and balances" among the legislative, executive and judicial organs of international organizations – sometimes with compulsory international jurisdiction (e.g., in the WTO and the Law of the Sea Convention) – have promoted the emergence of "international constitutional law" also on the worldwide level.[81] This progressive "constitutionalization" is not limited to international treaty law but – as illustrated by the universal recognition of *ius cogens,*[82] of *erga omnes* obligations[83] and of an "inalienable core" of human rights deriving from human dignity – extends also to general international law. This contribution has argued that – as suggested by the Kantian legal theory on the need for ever more precise national, international and cosmopolitan constitutional guarantees of maximum equal freedom as preconditions for international justice and "democratic peace" – national and international human rights law is evolving into an international "human rights constitution" limiting the powers of all governments and intergovernmental organizations.

The legal preconditions identified by Kant – in his three "definitive articles" for establishing "Perpetual Peace" – are increasingly realized in European integration law: (1) constitutional republics respecting fundamental citizen rights; (2) their international confederation for the collective protection of "democratic peace" and of constitutional order; and (3) cosmopolitan constitutional rules protecting human rights across frontiers. In the second part of his essay on "Perpetual Peace," Kant identified four additional elements[84] that make lasting peace a "realistic utopia" and which have become increasingly effective in European integration: (1) democratic self-government induces rational people to refrain from waging war against other democracies; (2) mutually beneficial trade reinforces the rational self-interest in peaceful cooperation and "peace by satisfaction";[85] (3) public discourse and "deliberative democracy" strengthen "public reason" and constrain selfish power politics; and (4) the antagonistic tendencies in human nature, such as man's "unsocial sociability,"[86] favor dialectic learning processes and progressive entrenchment of constitutional order. With the benefit of 200 years' hindsight, Habermas[87] and others have rightly emphasized that lasting democratic peace requires additional constitutional safeguards within and among states, as they progressively emerge in European integration law, UN law and WTO law.

The UN's standard-setting work and treaty-based reporting, monitoring and technical assistance systems in the field of human rights have contributed to the emergence of a new international and cosmopolitan constitutional law recognizing human dignity, human rights and the self-determination of peoples as new constitutional principles of the traditionally state-centered UN law. Yet, the comparison between UN law and European integration law has revealed a number of weaknesses of UN human rights law. For instance:

a) UN law focuses on rights and obligations of states without adequate clarification of the extent to which UN bodies and other intergovernmental and non-governmental organizations are legally bound to respect, protect and fulfill human rights. Whereas the Council of Europe and the EU are explicitly limited to constitutional democracies, the UN has made no use so far of the legal possibility (e.g., under Article 6 of the UN Charter) of excluding from UN membership states whose governments systematically violate human rights.
b) Even though UN human rights instruments emphasize the indivisibility and interdependence of human rights, the separate UN human rights treaties have led to fragmentation of UN human rights law and human rights bodies. Unlike in EU law, the "constitutional traditions common to the Member States" have not yet become an important source of UN human rights law.
c) Individual complaint procedures exist only in a few UN human rights treaties and remain optional. No UN human rights treaty provides for international judicial remedies.
d) Whereas EU law has dynamically extended the constitutional protection of economic and social rights in view of the need – explicitly emphasized in the Preamble to the EU Charter of Fundamental Rights – "to strengthen the protection of fundamental rights in the light of changes in society," UN human rights law does not empower and protect individuals to enhance their welfare through mutually beneficial division of labor across frontiers.

It is hoped that these and other deficiencies of UN human rights law will be progressively overcome, for instance by means of clarification of the scope of UN human rights and elaboration of additional treaty protocols in UN treaty practice.[88] This contribution has argued that, even if human rights are not explicitly recognized in the constitutive agreements of international organizations, they constitutionally limit all national and intergovernmental powers and call for rights-based development strategies respecting, protecting and fulfilling the inalienable human rights and basic needs of individuals.[89]

BIBLIOGRAPHY

R. Alexy, A Theory of Constitutional Rights, 2002.

P. Alston/M. Bustelo/J. Heenan (eds.), The EU and Human Rights, 1999.

G. Amato, Antitrust and the Bounds of Power, 1997.

K. Arambulo, Strengthening the Supervision of the International Covenant on Economic, Social and Cultural Rights, 1999.

R.E. Barnett, The Structure of Liberty. Justice and the Rule of Law, 2000.

L. Betten/N. Grief, EU Law and Human Rights Law, 1998.

J. Bohman/M. Lutz-Bachmann (eds.), Perpetual Peace. Esssays on Kant's Cosmopolitan Ideal, 1997.

A. Boyle/M. Anderson (eds.), Human Rights Approaches to Environmental Protection, 1998.

W.M. Corden, Trade Policy and Economic Welfare, 1974.

John B. Davis, The Theory of the Individual In Economics, 2003.

Mac Darrow, Between Light and Shadow. The World Bank, the IMF and International Human Rights Law, 2003.

J. Elster, Ulysses Unbound, 2000.

S.J. Evenett/A. Lehmann/B. Steil (eds.), Antitrust Goes Global, 2000.

R.A. Falk, Human Rights Horizons. The Pursuit of Justice in a Globalizing World, 2000.

W. Fikentscher, Wirtschaftsrecht Vol. I, 1983.

W. Fikentscher, Freiheit als Aufgabe, 1997.

D. Gerber, Law and Competition in Twentieth Century Europe. Protecting Prometheus, 1998.

P. Guyer, Kant on Freedom, Law and Happiness, 2000.

F.A. Hayek, Law, Legislation and Liberty, 1982.

T. Hervey/K. Kenner (eds.), Economic and Social Rights under the EU Charter of Fundamental Rights. A Legal Perspective, 2003.

M. Hilf/E.U. Petersmann (eds.), National Constitutions and International Economic Law, 1993.

I. Kant, Political Writings (edited by H. Reiss), 1977.

L. Kaplow/S. Shavell, Economic Analysis of Law, NBER Working Paper No.6960, 1999.

I. Kaul/I. Grunberg/M.A. Stern (eds.), Global Public Goods. International Cooperation in the 21st Century, 1999.

H.H. Koh/R.C. Slye (eds.), Deliberative Democracy and Human Rights, 1999.

R.B. McKenzie, Constitutional Economics, 1984.

D. Kretzmer/E. Klein (eds.), The Concept of Human Dignity in Human Rights Discourse, 2002.

D.R. Lee/R.B. McKenzie, Regulating Government. A Preface to Constitutional Economics, 1987.

M. Mehra (ed.), Human Rights and Economic Globalisation: Directions for the WTO, 1999.

I. Meralli/V. Oosterveld (eds.), Giving Meaning to Economic, Social and Cultural Rights, 2001.

J. Meyer (ed.), Die Grundrechtscharta der EU, 2002.

D.C. North, Institutions, Institutional Change and Economic Performance, 1990.

M. Olson, Power and Prosperity, 2000.

E.U. Petersmann, Constitutional Functions and Constitutional Problems of International Economic Law, 1991.

R. Pipes, Property and Freedom, 1999.

T. Pogge, World Poverty and Human Rights, 2002.

J. Rawls, A Theory of Justice, revised edition 1999.

J. Rawls, The Law of Peoples, 1999.

A.D. Rosen, Kant's Theory of Justice, 1993.

A. Sen, Development as Freedom, 2000.

B.H. Siegan, Economic Liberties and the Constitution, 1980.

P. Sieghart, The International Law of Human Rights, 1984.

United Nations (ed.), The United Nations and Human Rights 1945-1995, UN 1995.

UNDP (ed.), Human Development Report 2000: Human Rights and Human Development, UNDP 2000.

W.K. Viscusi/J.M. Vernon/J.E. Harrington, Economics of Regulation and Antitrust, 2nd ed. 1997.

A.W. Wood, Kant's Ethical Thought, 1999.

World Bank (ed.), World Development Report 2000/2001: Attacking Poverty, World Bank 2000.

NOTES

1. Development and Human Rights. The Role of the World Bank, World Bank 1998, at 2.

2. The text of this Charter is published in the Official Journal of the EC, C 364/1-22 of 18 December 2000. On the controversy over whether Article 1 recognizes a fundamental right to human dignity or merely an objective constitutional principle, see the commentary on Article 1 of the Charter by Borowsky in: J. Meyer (2002).

3. On this controversy see, e.g., E.U. Petersmann, Taking Human Dignity, Poverty and Empowerment of Individuals More Seriously: Rejoinder to Alston, in: European Journal of International Law (EJIL) 2002, 845-851.

4. Cf. K. Dicke, The Founding Function of Human Dignity in the Universal Declaration of Human Rights, in: D. Kretzmer/E. Klein (2002), at 111,117.

5. According to Immanuel Kant, "freedom constitutes man's worth," and "freedom (independence from the constraints of another's will) insofar as it is compatible with the freedom of everyone else in accordance with a universal law, is the sole and original right that belongs to each human being by virtue of his humanity" (cf. I. Kant, The Metaphysics of Morals, at 136; Rosen, at 9,42). According to Kant, equality and all other human rights derive from this universal birthright of freedom. Justice requires, according to Kant, exercising one's freedom in accordance with the moral "categorical imperative" that individuals and a just constitution must allow the "greatest freedom" for each individual along with "the most precise specification and preservation of the limits of this freedom so that it can coexist with the freedom of others." According to Kant, only such national, international and cosmopolitan "constitutional rules of justice" based on ever more precisely defined equal freedoms and democratic self-government offer the prospect of "perpetual peace."

6. On Kant's moral "categorical imperatives" for acting in accordance with universal laws ("Act only in accordance with that maxim through which you can at the same time will that it become a universal law"), for respecting human dignity by treating individuals and humanity as ends in themselves ("So act that you use humanity, whether in your own person or that of another, always at the same time as an end, never merely as a means"), and for respecting individual autonomy ("The idea of the will of every rational being as a will giving universal law") and individual right ("Any action is right if it can coexist with everyone's freedom according to a universal law"), see also A.W. Wood (1999). On Kant's theory of the antagonistic human nature promoting market competition and constitutional "rules of justice," and on the Kantian requirement of transforming the "wild freedom" in the state of nature into lawful freedom through ever more precise national, international and cosmopolitan constitutional rules see also: Petersmann, How to Constitutionalize International Law and Foreign Policy for the Benefit of Civil Society?, in: Michigan Journal of International Law 20 (1999), 1-30.

7. Kant, On the Common Saying: This May be True in Theory, but it does not Apply in Practice, at 74.

8. Paragraph 5 of the Declaration, reproduced in: The UN and Human Rights 1945-1995, at 450.

9. Cf. Rosen at 62. On the distinction, e.g., in German law and in the jurisprudence of the European Court of Human Rights, between human dignity as an absolute core limit to state interference, and secondary rights deriving from the concept of human dignity and subject to limitation, see J.A. Frowein, Human Dignity in International Law, in: D. Kretzmer/E. Klein (2002), at 123.

10. On the constitutional concept of a general right to liberty see: R. Alexy (2002), chapter 7.

11. Cf. Sieghart (1984), section 14.2.5.

12. The quotation is from the EC Court judgment of 9 October 2001, Case C-377/98 Netherlands v. European Parliament and Council (nyr), at para. 70. More generally on economic and social rights in the jurisprudence of the EC Court see: T. Hervey/J. Kenner (2003).

13. See, e.g., J. Rawls (1999), Chapter II, whose conception of "justice as fairness" for defining the basic rights and liberties of free and equal citizens in a constitutional democracy gives priority to maximum equal liberty as "first principle of justice." Rawls' "principle of fair equality of opportunity" and his "difference principle" are recognized only as secondary principles necessary for socially just conditions essential for moral and rational self-development of every person. Kantian legal theory also gives priority to a legal duty of states to ensure conditions of maximum law-governed freedom over moral "duties of benevolence" to provide for the needs of the citizens (cf. A.D. Rosen (1993), at 217; P. Guyer, (2000), at 264 *et seq.*).

14. On constitutional protection of freedom of trade in Germany and other federal states see: E.U. Petersmann (1991), chapter VII.

15. Cf. E.U. Petersmann, Constitutional Economics, Human Rights and the Future of the WTO, in: Aussenwirtschaft 2003, 49-91. For a criticism of economic theories of the individual see: Davis (2003).

16. See A. Sen (2000). On the interdependence between development and human rights see also the World Bank publication referred to in note 1.

17. Cf. also Petersmann, On Indivisibility of Human Rights, in: EJIL 2002, 381-385.

18. See: Globalization, Growth and Poverty: Building an Inclusive World Economy, World Bank 2001.

19. On this paradoxical dependence of liberty on psychological pre-commitments and constitutional restraints see, e.g., J. Elster (2000).

20. See, e.g., R.E. Barnett (2000) and Kant (notes 5 and 6).

21. E.g., prohibition of cartel agreements, of monopolization and other abuses of market power; merger control; transnational cooperation among independent competition authorities.

22. On this common dilemma of market economies and democracy, and on the replacement of the rights-based common law criteria by efficiency-based economic criteria (such as absence of output and price restrictions) in modern US antitrust law, see: G. Amato (1997); D. Gerber (1998).

23. US competition lawyers criticize this European notion of "restriction of economic freedom" on several grounds such as: "(1) its failure to generate precise operable legal rules (i.e., its failure to provide an analytical framework); (2) its distance from and tension with (micro) economics, which does provide an analytical framework; (3) its tendency to favour traders/competitors over consumers and consumer welfare (efficiency); and (4) its capture of totally innocuous contract provisions having non anti-competitive effects in an economic sense" (B. Hawk, System Failure: Vertical Restraints and EC Competition Law, in: Common Market Law Review 1995, 973, at 977-978). For an explanation of the EC position see, e.g.: P. Marsden, The Divide on Verticals, in: S.J. Evenett/A. Lehmann/B. Steil (2000), at 117-136.

24. United States v. Topco Assoc. Inc., 405 U.S. 596, 610 (1972).

25. See, e.g., Case 240/83, *ADBHU*, ECR 1985 531, para. 9: "the principles of free movement of goods and freedom of competition, together with freedom of trade as a fundamental right, are general principles of Community law of which the Court ensures observance." Especially the freedom of movements of workers and other persons, access to employment and the right of establishment have been described by the EC Court as "fundamental freedoms" (Case C-55/94, *Gebhard*, ECR 1995, I 4165, para. 37) or "a fundamental right which the Treaty confers individually on each worker in the Community" (Case 22/86, *Heylens*, ECR 1987, 4097, para. 14). The EC Court rightly avoids "human rights language" for the "market freedoms," the right to property and the freedom to pursue a trade or business in EC law.

26. On the ordo-liberal view of the EC Treaty as an "economic constitution" see, e.g., W. Sauter, The Economic Constitution of the EU, in: The Columbia Journal of European Law 1998, 27-68.

27. For the countless possibilities of defining and balancing these six constitutional core principles in national and international law depending on the particular contexts and preferences see: E.U. Petersmann, Human Rights and International Economic Law in the 21st Century, in: JIEL 4 (2001), 3-39.

28. See, e.g., L. Kaplow/S. Shavell (1999).

29. See, e.g., D.C. North (1990).

30. Olson (2000), at 43, 187. See likewise R. Pipes (1999), who explains prosperity as resulting from "successful struggle for rights of which the right to property is the most fundamental" (p. 291).

31. See, e.g., R.B. McKenzie (1984); J.M. Buchanan, Constitutional Economics, in: The New Palgrave (edited by J. Eatwell, M. Milgate and P. Newman), 1987. On ordo-liberal theories of an "economic constitution" based on a coherent set of "constitutive" and "regulative principles" see also Petersmann (1991), chapter III.

32. On the redistributive nature and "politicization" of government regulations of the economy, and the inseparable unity of the economy and the polity, see, e.g., D.R. Lee/R.B. McKenzie (1987).

33. See: UNDP 2000, p. iii.

34. See: E.U. Petersmann, Human Rights in European and Global Integration Law: Principles for Constitutionalizing the World Economy, in: A. Bogdandy/P. Mavroidis/Y. Mény (eds.), *Liber Amicorum* C.D. Ehlermann (2002), 381-400. Neither in the EC nor in most federal states (including the USA), the constitutional doctrine of limited delegation of powers has prevented ever-expanding and increasingly vague delegations to the higher (federal) level. Judicial protection of human rights and of open markets offers additional constitutional safeguards of individual liberties and deregulation.

35. See, e.g., the report by the International Federation for Human Rights: A.C. Habbard/M. Gulraud, The WTO and Human Rights, November 2001.

36. On the instrumental function of human rights for dealing with the problems of limited knowledge, conflicting interests and abuses of power see, e.g.: R.E. Barnett (2000).

37. On Immanuel Kant's distinction between truth (analyzed in Kant's *Critique of Pure Reason*), value judgments (analyzed in Kant's *Critique of Practical Reason*), and esthetic judgments (analyzed in Kant's *Critique of the Human Ability to Judge*), and on decentralized methods (i.e. markets and democracy) and centralized methods (e.g., dictatorship) to overcome conflicts about value judgments, see, e.g., W. Fikentscher (1997), at 50-51.

38. On the recognition of the importance of human rights for rendering environmental law and environmental protection more effective see: A. Boyle/M. Anderson (1998).

39. See, e.g., H.H. Koh/R.C. Slye (1999).

40. See, e.g., UNDP 2000. On the contribution of liberal trade to economic welfare and to protection of human rights (which, like any legal system, involve economic costs), and, *vice versa*, on the reciprocal contribution of human rights to economic welfare, see the contribution to this book by A. Sykes.

41. On the "double standard" in the jurisprudence of US courts which protect civil and political liberties through higher standards of judicial scrutiny than economic liberties, see, e.g., B.H. Siegan (1980). In European integration, judges review national economic regulations on the basis of much more stringent non-discrimination, necessity, proportionality and human rights standards than in US courts which apply much vaguer "rational basis tests"; cf. the comparative legal study by Petersmann (1991), chapter VIII.

42. Cf. W. Fikentscher (1983), at 10.

43. See, e.g., A. Sen (2000), who argues that freedom (in the sense of "capabilities" of persons to lead the kind of lives they have reason to value) is at once the ultimate goal of economic life and the most efficient means of realizing general welfare. Constitutional economists have long since emphasized that "an economist who is only an economist cannot even be a good economist" (F.A. Hayek, in: McKenzie (1984), at 236).

44. Cf. above note 13 and E.U. Petersmann, Theories of Justice, Human Rights and the Constitution of International Markets, EUI Working Paper 2004.

45. For instance, the Bill of Rights, which had to be appended to the US Constitution in order to secure its ratification, focuses more on "inalienable rights" to life and liberty than on social rights to secure "the general Welfare" (recognized as an objective of the US Constitution in its Preamble).

46. On legal philosophies concerning moral and legal duties of assistance vis-à-vis "burdened societies," the "principle of just savings," a "property-owning democracy" promoting widespread ownership of economic and human capital, and on "distributive justice among peoples" see, e.g.: J. Rawls (1999), chapters 15 and 16. On human rights and "global justice" see: R.A. Falk (2000).

47. On the ethically and legally indefensible, human-made world poverty as a human rights problem see Pogge (2002).

48. The quotation is from Article 9 of the Cotonou Agreemment signed in June 2000 by the EU, the 15 EU member states and 77 ACP countries. On human rights in the external relations law of the EU see, e.g., the contributions by Clapham, Simma, Aschenbrenner and Schulte to: P. Alston/M. Bustelo/J. Heenan (1999).

49. WTO doc. WT/MIN(01)/DEC/W/1 of 14 November 2001.

50. See, e.g., W.M. Corden (1974); W.K. Viscusi/J.M. Vernon/J.E. Harrington (1997).

51. On the need for international organizations and international aid for the provision of "global public goods" see I. Kaul/I. Grunberg/M.A. Stern (1999). The World Bank report on "Globalization, Growth and Poverty: Building an Inclusive World Economy" (2001) emphasizes that open market economies and increased trade offer the best hope for the more than 1 billion people living on less than 1 dollar a day. Over the past two decades of globalization, the successful integration of more than 24 big developing countries into the global industrial economy has increased their income per head (about 5% p.a.) and reduced the number of people in absolute poverty. Countries not participating in the global division of labor have tended to aggravate their poverty problems.

52. See: E.U. Petersmann, Time for a UN "Global Compact" for Integrating Human Rights into the Law of Worldwide Organizations, in: European Journal of International Law 2002, 621-650.

53. This was the "constitutional approach" suggested in Petersmann (1991), chapter IX, prior to the "universalization of human rights" during the 1990s.

54. See, e.g., Hilf/Petersmann (1993).

55. Cf. Petersmann (1991), notably chapter VII.

56. This quotation from the preamble of the UDHR of 1948 is cited in the preambles of most UN human rights conventions, such as the 1989 UN Convention on the Rights of the Child, ratified by 191 states.

57. Cf. Petersmann (note 17), at 383, 385; C. Scott, Toward the Institutional Integration of the Core Human Rights Treaties, in: Merali/Oosterveld (2001), chapter 1.

58. European Court of Human Rights, Third Section Decision as to the Admissibility of Application No.43844/98 by T.I. against the United Kingdom, 7 March 2000, at page 16 (nyr). In *Matthews v. UK*, the European Court of Human Rights found the United Kingdom in violation of the human right to participate in free elections of the legislature even though the law which denied voting rights in Gibraltar implemented a treaty concluded among EC member states on the election of the European Parliament: "there is no difference between European and domestic legislation, and no reason why the United Kingdom should not be required to 'secure' the rights (under the ECHR) in respect of European legislation in the same way as those rights are required to be 'secured' in respect of purely domestic legislation." Cf. European Court of Human Rights, judgment of 18 February 1999 on complaint No. 24833/94, see: Europäische Grundrechtszeitschrift (EUGRZ) 1999, 200.

59. Case 29/69. *Stauder*, ECR 1969. 419, para. 7.

60. Opinion 2/94, ECR 1996 I-1759, para. 34.

61. See the judgment by the European Court of Human Rights mentioned above in note 58.

62. On the absence of governmental and private complaints procedures in the UNCESCR see, e.g., K. Arambulo (1999).

63. Case C-44/94, *The Queen v. Minister of Agriculture*, ECR 1995 I-3115, para. 28.

64. Cf. L. Betten/N. Grief (1998); P. Alston *et alii* (1999).

65. Due to the constitutional limits of EC law, social rights were initially developed in EC law as a function of market integration rather than of the more recent EC Treaty guarantees of "citizenship of the Union" (Article 17) and of "fundamental social rights" (e.g., Article 136). On the need for integrating social rights into market integration law as a means for limiting social market failures (e.g., resulting from an unjust distribution of resources and purchasing power, inadequate opportunities of all market participants to express their "voice" and "exit") see, e.g.: M. Poiares Maduro, Striking the Elusive Balance between Economic Freedom and Social Rights in the EU, in: Alston (1999), at 459.

66. See, e.g., the UN Secretary-General's recent report on "Globalization and its impact on the full enjoyment of human rights," UN documents A/55/342 of 31 August 2000 and A/56/254 of 31 July 2001.

67. See WTO document WT/MIN (01)/DEC/W/2 of 14 November 2001, paragraph 4.

68. In an additional Decision of August 2003, the WTO Council granted a waiver from the obligations under Article 31(f) of the TRIPS Agreement enabling less-developed WTO Members without pharmaceutical manufacturing industries to grant, if necessary, compulsory licenses also for the manufacture abroad and importation of generic medicines from other less-developed countries.

69. See the Appellate Body report of 22 October 2001 on US Import Prohibition of Certain Shrimp and Shrimp Products, DS58/AB/RW, with references to the earlier WTO panel and Appellate Body reports.

70. On the economic theory of "optimal intervention" see Corden (1974). In its Resolution 1999/30 of 26 August 1999 on "Trade Liberalization and its Impact on Human Rights," the Sub-Commission (of the UN Commission on Human Rights) on the Promotion and Protection of Human Rights declared "that sanctions and negative conditionalities which directly or indirectly affect trade are not appropriate ways of promoting the integration of human rights in international economic policy and practice." See also Resolution 1998/12 on "Human rights as the primary objective of trade, investment and financial policy" adopted by the UN Sub-Commission on the Promotion and Protection of Human Rights, and Resolution 1999/30 on "Trade liberalization and its impact on human rights" adopted by the same UN Sub-Commission in 1999.

71. Cf. Schmidberger v. Austria, Case C-112/2000, in: Common Market Law Reports 2003, 1043-1092. Rather than describing the demonstration blocking road traffic on the Austrian motorway as a trade barrier contrary to Article 30 and as being justified either under Article 34 EC Treaty or as

a mandatory requirement permitted by the "rule of reasonable interpretation" of Article 30 EC Treaty, the EC Court avoided these traditional trade law categories and created a new justificatory category for the protection of human rights, referring to the "wide margin of discretion" of the competent authorities regarding a "fair balance" between the common market freedoms and human rights and to the need "to determine whether the restrictions placed upon intra-Community trade are proportionate in the light of the legitimate objective pursued, namely, in the present case, the protection of fundamental rights" (para. 82). Such a "fair balance" is also required in the interpretation of WTO rules. The EC Court's balancing approach rightly implies that invocation of human rights as a justification of trade restrictions must not necessarily "trump" all trade rules designed to limit protectionist abuses (e.g., procedural WTO requirements to carry out and notify a transparent risk-assessment procedure before prohibiting the importation of hormone-fed beef).

72. For an exception, see the submission from Mauritius in WTO document G/AG/NG/W/36/Rev.1 of 9 November 2000, which claims that Article 20 of the Agreement on Agriculture (regarding the taking into account of "non-trade concerns") should be read in conjunction with Article 11 of the UNCESCR recognizing the right of everyone to adequate food.

73. A computer search of references to human rights in WTO panel and Appellate Body reports indicates 10 reports since 1996 where parties, third parties, experts, panelists or the Appellate Body referred to human rights. In the negotiations for the WTO Ministerial Declaration of November 2001 on access to medicines and review of Article 27:3(b) of the TRIPS Agreement, the "Africa Group," for instance, referred explicitly to human rights as criteria for interpreting the TRIPS Agreement. The WTO Secretariat also actively contributed to the discussions leading to the report of the UN High Commissioner for Human Rights on the impact of the TRIPS Agreement on human rights (E/CN.4/Sub.2/2001/13) and to Resolution 2001/21 by the UN Sub-Commission on Human Rights on "Intellectual Property and Human Rights" (E/CN.4/Sub.2/RES/2001/21 of 16 August 2001).

74. The EC's suspension of trade preferences for Yugoslavia in November 1991, for instance, was motivated by the military hostilities in the former Yugoslavia rather than by human rights violations. In the context of the Lomé-Convention, the EC reacted to human rights violations (e.g., in Rwanda) by suspension of financial and technical assistance rather than trade restrictions. The EC's Generalized System of Tariff Preferences (GSP) offers additional preferences to developing countries which respect basic ILO guarantees (such as freedom of association and minimum age for admission to employment); temporary withdrawal of GSP benefits by the EC in response to violations of human rights have been rare (e.g., in the case of Myanmar). There is thus hardly any empirical basis for the criticism (e.g., by P. Prove, Human Rights at the WTO? in: Mehra (1999) at 32) of an alleged "bias of the WTO" because "the primary entry point for human rights concerns would be as justifications for sanctions and trade conditionalities."

75. In his Opinion on the above-mentioned *Schmidberger Case* (note 71), Advocate-General Jacobs stated: "This appears to be the first case in which a Member State has invoked the necessity to protect fundamental rights to justify a restriction of one of the fundamental freedoms of the Treaty" (para. 89). In the few cases where EC acts have been challenged on the ground of violation of human rights, the EC Court did not find an inconsistency with human rights law.

76. See UN document E/C.12/2000/4, CESCR of 4 July 2000 and, on the preparatory work: B.C.A. Toebes, The Right to Health as a Human Right in International Law, 1999.

77. General Comment No.14 (note 76), paragraph 39.

78. See, e.g., paragraphs 41, 43 and 64 of the General Comment No.14 (note 76).

79. See, e.g., G. Dutfield, Intellectual Property Rights, Trade and Biodiversity, 2000.

80. In addition to the WTO Ministerial Declaration of November 2001 and the WTO waiver decision of August 2003, see also the report of the joint WHO/WTO Workshop on Differential Pricing and Financing of Essential Drugs of 8-11 April 2001 (which notes that about 95% of the WHO list of "essential drugs" are not or no longer patented, and differential pricing and international financing of essential drugs are consistent with the TRIPS Agreement).

81. Cf., e.g., C. Walter, Constitutionalizing (Inter)national Governance – Possibilities for and Limits to the Development of an International Constitutional Law, in: 44 German Yearbook of International Law (2001), 171-201; E.U. Petersmann, Constitutionalism, International Law and "We the Peoples of the United Nations," in: H.J. Cremer *et al.*, Tradition und Weltoffenheit des Rechts, Festschrift für Steinberger (2001), 291-320.

82. Cf., e.g., Article 53 of the Vienna Convention on the Law of Treaties.

83. Cf. International Court of Justice Rep. 1970, 3, 32 (Barcelona Traction case).

84. Cf. I. Kant (1795/1977), at 93-130, and T. Mertens, From "Perpetual Peace" to "Law of Peoples": Kant, Habermas and Rawls on International Relations, in: Kantian Review 2002, 60-84.

85. On the distinction between "peace by satisfaction" and "peace by power" see Rawls (1999), at 47.

86. Immanuel Kant (1977), at 44.

87. See, e.g., J. Habermas, Kant's Idea of Perpetual Peace, with the Benefit of Two Hundred Years' Hindsight, in: J. Bohman/M. Lutz-Bachmann (1997), 113-153.

88. For instance, the "General Comments" on human rights treaty provisions adopted by UN bodies – such as the right to adequate food (Article 11 UNCESCR) and the right to the highest attainable standard of health (Article 12 UNCESCR) – clarify, to some extent, the corresponding obligations and duties not only of states but also of intergovernmental organizations.

89. On the practical relevance of a "human rights approach to development" for the practice of international financial and development institutions see: Mac Darrow (2003), at 5 *et seq*.

CHAPTER 4

International Trade and Human Rights: An Economic Perspective

Alan O. Sykes

"The Relationship Between Economics and Rights," my assigned topic for this conference, is a vast subject. Its breadth results in part from the wide array of "human rights" now said to exist, including all manner of economic rights, labor rights, cultural rights, civil and political rights, rights to a clean environment, and perhaps others.[1] The set of economic questions that one might ask about each right is also extensive. For example, is the right in question "efficient" (do those who benefit from it gain enough to be able to compensate those who lose) or is it redistributive? What is the "political economy" of the right – how do we explain which rights are recognized under national and international law and which potential rights are not, and how do we explain the emergence of particular rights over time? What is the function of international human rights treaties, especially when many of them merely bind nations to do what they would do anyway? What is the relationship between human rights and economic development? These are but a subset of the possible lines of economic inquiry, and of course they intersect considerably with the work of political science.

To keep this initial foray into the economics of human rights manageable, I focus on the relationship between the WTO and human rights.[2] The emphasis is on the arguments of World Trade Organization (hereafter WTO) critics who suggest that the growth of the WTO is in one manner or another a threat to human rights. These arguments include the following:[3] (i) Admission to the WTO of nations that violate human rights extinguishes opportunities for the imposition of valuable sanctions to discourage such violations (China is the usual focus of this concern). (ii) Open trade causes production to relocate to areas where environmental standards are lax and results in environmental degradation. Likewise, the competitive pressures that result from open trade cause regulators to lose control over local regulatory matters and precipitate a "race to the bottom" over matters such as social welfare standards, environmental standards, and worker protection legislation. (iii) Open trade exacerbates inequality in the distribution of income.

Although none of these arguments should be dismissed out of hand, I will suggest that none of them provides a terribly persuasive objection to more open trade under the auspices of the WTO. To the contrary, a more open trading system generally tends to promote most of the concerns that come under the rubric of human rights. And to the extent that exceptions arise, conventional economic arguments regarding optimal policy instruments strongly counsel against curtailment of open trade as a solution, and instead argue for tailored measures that directly address the issue in question. I will develop these themes in general terms in Sections I and II, and then deal with the arguments more specifically in Section III.

Section III also briefly addresses a narrower issue that has received considerable attention lately, namely whether the TRIPS Agreement collides with human rights by making essential medicines unaffordable in developing countries. On that issue, the economic response is rather more agnostic, but it is important to underscore the fact that credible patent rights for pharmaceuticals in developing economies may be essential to any progress in the treatment of tropical diseases.

I. Human Rights as a "Normal Good"

Jokes about economists often build on the notion that economists rarely agree with each other. Yet, there is at least one proposition on which virtually all economists agree – trade liberalization raises living standards in the aggregate. As Paul Samuelson once put it, "there is essentially only one argument for free trade or freer trade, but it is an exceedingly powerful one, namely: Free trade promotes a mutually profitable division of labor, greatly enhances the potential real national product of all nations, and makes possible higher standards of living all over the globe."[4] The central agenda of the WTO, of course, is trade liberalization. As WTO membership expands and trade barriers decline over time, therefore, the result will tend to be an increase in the real national product of member nations.[5] This proposition is not merely theoretical; empirical research generally confirms that more open trading systems experience higher rates of economic growth.[6]

In turn, the growth in real income that results from more open trade will promote human rights to the degree that the demand for human rights is "income elastic." There are good reasons to believe that this will be true for many rights. Note that almost all human rights are, in one manner or another, costly. The protection of rights generally requires a legal system that is effective and credible, and such systems do not come without an economic cost. Moreover, many rights require some additional sacrifice of other human wants – minimum wages, rights to unionize, environmental standards, and social security systems, for example, all come at the price of an increase in the cost of goods and services, or an increase in taxation. At some level, therefore, human rights must be "financed" by a reduction in other consumption expenditures that would be made in their absence. Human rights are in this sense akin to ordinary goods and services in that they cost money and, because of the budget constraint that all individuals and societies ultimately face, an increase in "expenditures" on human rights must be accompanied by a decrease in expenditures on other things that people desire.

The expenditures necessary to create and enforce human rights will tend to be less burdensome, other things being equal, in wealthier societies. For in such societies, basic human needs for food, clothing, shelter and the like are more likely to have been met, and more resources will be available for other things. We might therefore expect that wealthier societies will tend to expend more resources (proportionally) on the creation and protection of human rights[7] – that is, we might expect that human rights will tend to be "normal goods" in the language of economics.[8] Anecdotal evidence hints at the correctness of this hypothesis. I suspect that most readers will concur that more developed nations tend to have stronger guarantees of worker rights, higher minimum wages, and greater restrictions on child labor; more developed nations tend to have stronger safety net programs; more developed nations tend to impose greater restrictions on activities that degrade the environment; more developed nations tend to have stronger anti-discrimination norms; more developed nations tend to have stronger protections for the rights of the accused, and so on.

Yet another mechanism may exist to create a favorable linkage between openness to trade and human rights. Openness to trade likely begets a higher rate of interchange of ideas and information between countries. In turn, as people in nations with fewer rights and freedoms become aware of conditions elsewhere, internal pressures for improvement may grow. Isolated societies, by contrast, may be more subject to human rights abuses.

However we need not rely entirely on anecdotes and casual empiricism to believe that rising real incomes and greater openness to trade tend to promote human rights – these tendencies can be seen in empirical data. I assembled per capita gross domestic product (hereafter GDP) data for 195 countries,[9] along with data from third-party sources regarding the quality of human rights country-by-country. I included the so-called "Humana rating" from the 1991 World Human Rights Guide (higher ratings reflect better human rights conditions),[10] the Freedom House ratings on both political rights and civil liberties from its 1999-2000 survey (lower ratings reflect better human rights conditions),[11] and the Index of Economic Freedom Rating for 2000 prepared by the Wall Street Journal (lower ratings reflect better economic freedom conditions).[12] Finally, on the theory that the overall quality of human rights in a nation is likely correlated with the degree to which people want to migrate into the nation (or exit from it), I included data on net migration rates as well (migrants per 1,000 population; a positive rate indicates a net influx of migrants).[13]

Table 1 reports the simple correlation coefficients between per capita GDP and the various indicators of the quality of human rights in each nation (nations with missing values for any human rights index were discarded for that particular correlation). The column labeled "N" denotes the number of observations used for each correlation. All of the results are statistically significant.[14]

Table 1. Simple (Pearson) Correlations With Per Capita GDP

	Corr. Coefficient	N
Humana Rating	0.62	101
Freedom House Political Rights Rating	-0.44	193
Freedom House Civil Liberties Rating	-0.52	193
WSJ Index of Economic Freedom	-0.72	155
Migration Rate	0.38	190

Recalling that better human rights conditions are associated with higher values of the proxy for human rights in rows 1 and 5, and lower values of the proxy in rows 2-4, it can be seen that the results uniformly support the proposition that wealthier nations have better human rights conditions. The relationship holds whether the rights in question are predominantly economic, political or civil. These findings suggest that policies that promote real income growth will also tend to promote human rights across a broad range of concerns.

We have already noted that open trade tends to increase real incomes, but at the risk of belaboring the point it is perhaps instructive to look directly at the relationship between trade policy and human rights indices. The Index of Economic Freedom contains data by country on average tariff rates, which is a reasonably good measure of openness to trade at least in goods markets.[15] Not surprisingly, a strong and statistically significant negative correlation arises between average tariff rates and per capita GDP (that is, more open nations tend to have higher GDP) – the correlation coefficient is -0.48. This relationship is explicable in part by the fact that more open countries tend to have higher growth rates, as noted earlier, and in part by the fact that over the history of the

GATT fewer demands were made for trade concessions from developing countries.[16]

Given the relationship between an open trading system and economic growth, we might expect that average tariff rates would also bear a clear, negative relationship to indicators of human rights (that is, lower average tariff rates tend to occur in nations with better human rights conditions). Table 2 reports the simple correlation between the average tariff rate and the various indicators of human rights employed above.

Table 2. Simple (Pearson) Correlations With Average Tariff Rate

	Corr. Coefficient	N
Humana Rating	-0.60	94
Freedom House Political Rights Rating	0.43	151
Freedom House Civil Liberties Rating	0.44	151
WSJ Index of Economic Freedom	0.54	148
Migration Rate	-0.20	151

Again recall that better human rights conditions are associated with higher values of the proxy for human rights in rows 1 and 5, and lower values of the proxy in rows 2-4. Of course, a lower average tariff rate reflects greater openness to trade. Thus, greater openness to trade is correlated with better human rights conditions according to all of the indicators in Table 2. The results are statistically significant except in relation to the indicator pertaining to the migration rate.

I do not want to make too much of these results. Simple correlations are hardly conclusive proof of a causal relationship between openness to trade and the overall quality of human rights; no doubt some of the causality runs the other way and more sophisticated empirics are needed to discern the true relationship. Moreover, even if openness to trade leads to improved human rights in general, exceptions may arise with respect to particular rights or in respect of specific countries. Nevertheless, there is certainly no basis for supposing either in theory or on the basis of the limited available empirical information that a more open trading system does systematic damage to human rights in any broad sense. To the contrary, everything we know points to a generally favorable relationship between them, and the question then becomes how best to address the occasional tension that may arise.

II. Trade, Human Rights and Policy Instruments

I will begin with some background on the imperfections of markets and of an open trading system. Economists usually discuss such imperfections using the language of "efficiency" and "distribution."

Economic theory does not teach that the unfettered operation of open markets is always desirable. Among the conditions necessary for markets to work well is an absence of "non-pecuniary externalities," defined as effects (favorable or unfavorable) on some individuals that do not pass through the price system resulting from the transactions of other individuals. The paradigm example is pollution – the transaction between a customer and a manufacturer, say, results in productive activity by the manufacturer that causes pollution that harms some third party. In the absence of non-pecuniary externalities, open competitive markets tend to be "Pareto efficient," in the sense that no alternative allocation of resources can make someone better off without harming someone else.[17] However, as a practical matter, externalities such as pollution are commonplace and the possibility arises that corrective government intervention can enhance efficiency.

Moreover, economic theory has essentially nothing to say about distributional equity. Even if an economy is operating "efficiently," the distribution of income may be unacceptably skewed by some criterion. Measures to redistribute income may be judged appropriate even though they often entail some efficiency loss.

It is well known in the international economics literature that open trade may create or exacerbate some problem associated with non-pecuniary externalities or with distributional equity. For example, a lowering of trade barriers may cause a nation to specialize in the production of some good with a production process that is quite "dirty," resulting in a serious local pollution problem. Likewise, the "Stolper-Samuelson" theorem holds that the owners of inputs or "factors of production" used intensively in the production of goods that are displaced by imports when trade becomes more open will tend to suffer reduced real income as a result (conversely, the owners of factors used intensively in exports will tend to enjoy increased real income).[18] If workers in an import-competing industry are at the lower end of the income distribution scale at the outset, for example, more open trade may make them even worse off relative to other workers and the perceived equity of the income distribution may suffer.

Economic theory thus stipulates (the empirical importance of the problem is another matter) that more open trade may cause inefficiency or inequity in some contexts. Not all such effects will infringe "human rights," but some of them may. Commentators increasingly speak of "rights" to environmental quality, for example, and certainly a reduction in the real incomes of less fortunate individuals might be seen as interfering with certain "rights" to an adequate standard of living.

Might such possibilities justify interference with (or opposition to) more open trade? One answer is to be found in the preceding section – more open trade can contribute to overall improvement in human rights even if there are some more narrow tensions. Human rights advocates would be wise not to focus myopically on the negative aspects of open trade to the exclusion of its positive effects.

But there is a further response that builds on another important strand of economic literature. Consider first the case of the harmful non-pecuniary externality that is somehow exacerbated by more open trade, for example, after reciprocal tariff concessions have led some nation to specialize in an industry with high levels of pollution. An economist would say that manufacturers in the polluting industry do not bear the full social costs of their production if they are permitted to impose harms on others without paying for them. If those harmed by pollution have difficulty acting collectively to purchase relief,[19] theory then holds that the "first-best" device for dealing with the pollution externality is to intervene in a manner that raises the cost of the goods produced in the polluting industry to their true social cost, as by imposing a tax on the production of the good in question. After price is increased appropriately, no one will consume the good unless they are willing to bear its full social cost, including the cost of pollution, and the level of production will then be "efficient."

But what about dealing with the pollution problem through trade policy, for example, by retracting the reciprocal tariff concessions that led to the increase in pollution? Theory teaches that this response to the pollution problem is inferior. Even if it reduced pollution towards the appropriate level, it would do so at the cost of raising prices on other goods unconnected to pollution that were covered by the tariff concessions, and this would impose an additional efficiency loss on consumers. Direct intervention in the market that causes the pollution can correct the problem without causing such additional distortions.[20]

A similar line of reasoning applies to the problem of how best to correct any harm to the income distribution caused by more open trade. When the distribution of income is unacceptable, one way to correct it is through progressive income taxes (including negative taxes [subsidies] for the poorest individuals if necessary). Such taxation imposes some cost on the overall level of output because it reduces work incentives. Yet imagine trying to achieve the same degree of redistribution through an alternative policy instrument such as trade policy (perhaps by rescinding the reciprocal trade concessions that led to reduced incomes for workers in import-competing industries). If the degree of income redistribution is the same as under the progressive tax system, then the adverse effect on work incentives should be the same. But efforts to correct income distribution through trade policy impose a further cost by raising consumer prices and impeding efficient specialization of production in accordance with the principles of comparative advantage. Thus, progressive taxes produce fewer efficiency losses and are accordingly the "first-best" way to deal with income distribution problems. Restrictions on trade, like all other legal rules that cause further inefficiencies, are inferior.[21]

The general lesson is one about optimal policy instruments. Whatever the problem that arises, the best intervention will always deal with it at lowest cost. It is exceedingly unlikely that a problem connected to more open trade is best addressed by closing off trade and sacrificing its familiar benefits, rather than through some other policy instrument that directly addresses the problem in question. Even if a more open trading system at times collides with "human rights" in the estimation of some observers, therefore, measures specifically and narrowly tailored to enhance the human rights at issue are more likely to be a cost effective solution than the much cruder device of interfering with open trade and the resulting allocation of productive resources.

III. The WTO and Human Rights: Response to the Critics

In this section I will briefly offer an "economic" response to arguments noted in the introduction: the claim that WTO membership strips the world community of important sanctions against human rights violators; the notion that the growth of trade causes direct harms to the environment or to social conditions generally via a "race to the bottom"; and the suggestion that globalization is harmful because of its effects on income disparities. I also touch on the question whether intellectual property rights in pharmaceuticals are a threat to "human rights" in the developing world.

A. The WTO, Trade Sanctions and Human Rights

Undeniably, the rules of the WTO system interfere with the ability of its members to punish human rights violators by restricting trade with them. WTO members limit their capacity to exclude imports from other WTO members in accordance with "tariff bindings" in the goods area, and various "market access commitments" in the services area. Any trade restrictions in excess of these agreed limits, even in the name of human rights measures, would violate WTO law unless justified by some exception to the WTO rules, or by some superseding mutual agreement between the affected nations. As to the first possibility, although provisions such as Article XX of GATT (now part of the WTO agreements) provide some leeway for trade restrictions in the name of human rights, their scope is unclear and no doubt limited. Regarding the second option, superseding agreements that allow trade sanctions between parties to a human rights dispute will be very rare. Thus, once a nation is admitted to the WTO, the ability of other WTO members to impose trade sanctions (legally) against that nation for human rights violations becomes more restricted.[22]

Notwithstanding these considerations, it is unclear to what extent the admission to the WTO of a nation accused of human rights abuses results in an important loss of external leverage. Recall the debate in the United States over most-favored nation status for China, and the argument of the U.S. administration that open commercial engagement will tend to improve human rights conditions over time. The information presented in Section I, indicating that wealthier and more open nations tend to have better human rights records on average, lends support to this claim. Likewise, policies aimed at isolating human rights violators and excluding them from the prosperity that accompanies open trade may well cause human rights to deteriorate.

Further, it is questionable whether trade sanctions will be effective in promoting changes in human rights policy in the short term. Academic studies regarding the efficacy of sanctions for political purposes accord them mixed reviews, indicating that sanctions often fail for a variety of reasons. The studies suggest, *inter alia*, that sanctions are most likely to be effective when they pertain to matters of modest importance, and when the sanction has the potential to inflict large losses on the target (such as a few percent of GDP).[23] With such factors in mind, consider the problem of promoting human rights in China. Efforts to induce the government of China to alter dramatically its policies toward dissidents are aimed at effecting fundamental changes in the political system that probably cannot be viewed as "modest" under any plausible criterion. Likewise, it is unclear whether trade sanctions against China can succeed at imposing large losses on its economy; unless they are coordinated widely in a multilateral fashion, the nations that impose sanctions may simply see China divert its trade to other nations.

Finally, even if accession to the WTO causes an important loss of leverage over human rights matters in the view of some observers, the discussion in Section II above argues for a narrowly tailored response to the problem. The sensible response is not general opposition to the growth and expansion of the WTO, but an appropriate clarification or amendment of the rules governing exceptions to WTO obligations that would permit human rights sanctions under proper circumstances. I do not mean to advocate such changes, as I think it quite unclear whether the gains from relaxing the rules in this area would be worth the costs in the form of abuses and failed sanctions programs. However, if an important tension really exists here, specific changes in rules and interpretation that better integrate WTO law with international human rights law are the better course.[24]

B. Environmental and "Race to the Bottom" Concerns

Critics of the WTO commonly argue that open trade leads to the degradation of the environment as business relocates to take advantage of lax environmental protection, and further places competitive pressures on environmental, labor, social and perhaps other standards with the result that administrators must sacrifice regulatory goals in these areas in the interest of national competitiveness. Since many of these regulations touch on matters that some commentators view as "human rights," some attention to them is required here.

Economic commentators are largely critical of such claims on both theoretical and empirical grounds.[25] I begin with the theoretical objections.

The first emphasizes the essential lesson of Section I. Open trade increases real incomes on average, and nations with higher real incomes tend to spend more on the environment, on worker safety regulations, on social safety net programs, and so forth. The proposition that an open trading system will tend to reduce the <u>average</u> level of social protection in these areas is thus fundamentally at odds with the evidence that such standards are "normal goods" for the most part – interference with open trade is likely to damage human rights on average, not the reverse.

The second objection challenges the essential premise of the argument that open trade harms the environment (or other matters of social concern) when businesses relocate to take advantage of lower costs. If a business relocates, say, to a jurisdiction that permits more pollution, that phenomenon may well be desirable from an economic standpoint. The harm caused by a particular quantum of pollution is not the same everywhere: geographical differences across jurisdictions may make pollution less harmful in some places (air pollution is much more problematic in the Los Angeles basin, for example); differences in tastes or incomes may also make some societies more tolerant of pollution than others. As a consequence, the social "shadow price" of pollution varies internationally, and it is perfectly appropriate for polluting businesses to locate where the social costs of pollution are lower. The argument is not limited to pollution. As one more (no doubt controversial) example, consider child labor. Where children have few opportunities for schooling and their families live in poverty, the opportunity to work may well leave them better off than otherwise. To the degree that a more open trading system makes possible greater levels of trade in products produced with child labor, affected children may benefit. This is not to deny the sadness of children living in poverty with no access to schooling and poor access to the basics of life, but measures that interfere with their ability to work may leave them worse off yet.

The third theoretical objection relates to the policy instruments analysis of Section II. The fear of a "race to the bottom," slightly rephrased, is a fear that governments will use lax regulatory policies as a means to attract capital to their jurisdiction.[26] But that claim raises its own puzzle – why is capital valuable (at the margin) to the jurisdiction in question? Are the returns to additional capital due to the fact that capital is taxed in a manner that transfers rents from the owners of the new capital to the citizens of the jurisdiction? If not, what is the incentive to attract more capital? If capital is valuable at the margin because of the tax system, why would governments not use the tax system to attract more capital (as through subsidies to new business)? Is that not a more likely way for jurisdictions to attract capital than through suboptimal regulatory policies that sacrifice the environment, the interests of workers, or something else of value?

One response is that the regulatory policy in question is expressly redistributive – government has chosen to tax capital for the purpose of redistributing income, and capital mobility in an open trading system makes it much harder to pursue this policy over the long run.[27] A reduction in taxes can of course mitigate capital flight in this scenario, but it comes at the expense of the redistributive program in question (or creates the need for a different kind of tax to finance it). With the addition of this insight, the more plausible and precise "race to the bottom" claim becomes one about the long-run difficulties of redistributing income from the owners of mobile factors of production in an open economy to the owners of immobile factors.

It is not entirely clear, however, why redistribution needs to proceed in this fashion. If the goal is to aid the poor, for example, taxes on the labor or landholdings of the wealthy may suffice to raise the necessary funds. Hence, the pressure that an open trading system places on established programs of redistribution may be a largely transitory problem that simply requires appropriate adjustments in tax policy.

The fourth line of criticism is closely related. Any inefficient harm to the environment from the growth of trade (putting global commons issues to one side) or any more general "race to the bottom" results from a failure of national political systems to employ proper tools to address social problems. Indeed, the essence of the race to the bottom claim is that domestic regulators will deviate from optimal regulation due to competitive pressures. But if regulators are inclined to deviate from optimal regulation under those circumstances, what reason is there to believe that they would engage in optimal regulation under any circumstances? Put differently, if the concern is that interest group politics distorts regulatory decisions, what reason is there to believe that the distortion will systematically run in the direction of under-regulation in an open trading system? Chicago school economists such as George Stigler and Sam Peltzman have made enormous contributions to the theory of regulation which suggest that much regulation is excessive and unproductive, a result of capture by regulated entities.[28] The same point is made by those on the other side of the political spectrum, and environmental regulation in particular hardly escapes condemnation.[29] Once domestic regulatory policies are seen in their true light – as the highly imperfect product of an interaction among self-interested lobby groups – the fact that they may come under pressure in an open trading system need not be unfortunate. International regulatory competition may well drive out foolish and wasteful regulations rather than undermine valuable ones.[30]

The fifth line of theoretical criticism concerns the question whether there exists any practical, superior alternative to regulatory competition in an open trading system. Economic commentators agree that nations should differ in the degree to which they regulate various areas due to differences in tastes, incomes, geography and other factors. Accordingly, harmonization of regulatory standards is quite undesirable in general.[31] And in relation to the suggestion that international cooperation ought to at least place a "floor" under the level of regulation on many subjects, the response is that there is little reason to trust cooperation to produce an appropriate floor. In the area of labor and environmental standards, for example, the great fear of developing nations is that any international floor on such standards will be driven by protectionist interest groups in the developed countries seeking to raise the costs of their developing country rivals – precisely the fear said by many to have produced the unraveling of the WTO ministerial meeting in Seattle.

The final line of attack on the "race to the bottom" and related claims is not theoretical, but empirical. The bulk of the investigation done in this area pertains to environmental regulations, and seeks to establish one of two things: direct evidence that more open trade has been followed by a lowering of environmental standards, or evidence that businesses relocate to jurisdictions with lax environmental regulations following trade liberalization. In general, empirical evidence of such phenomena is scant: "The literature surveyed is almost unanimous in its conclusion that environmental regulations have not affected interjurisdictional trade or the location decisions of manufacturers. Where studies have found statistically significant effects of such regulations, the effects are always quite small."[32] None of this is meant to deny that some environmental problems may cross jurisdictional boundaries, and that international cooperation can be necessary to address them. But the notion that the growth of world trade has precipitated a noticeable decline in the domestic environmental standards of trading nations is not supported by the available evidence.

No doubt more empirical work remains to be done, and perhaps the picture for policies other than environmental standards will ultimately look rather different. Indeed, as noted above, some commentators do believe that a more open trading system has put serious pressure on certain redistributive policies that in the past have been supported by capital taxes. It is perhaps in this domain that any "race to the bottom" is likely to manifest itself, and to impinge on important "human rights" concerns. But the magnitude of the problem remains unclear, and the ability of governments to substitute alternative methods of redistribution that are not threatened by capital mobility may largely ameliorate it.

C. Income Disparities

Recent decades have brought widening income inequality in many nations.[33] Some commentators link the problem to growing trade, and view it as a basis for resisting the growth of the WTO or other "globalization" initiatives.

To be sure, some of the increased income inequality may be due to more open trade. The Stolper-Samuelson theorem, noted earlier, predicts declining real incomes for factors of production dedicated to the import-competing industries harmed by growth in trade. To the degree that the affected entities are workers already towards the lower end of the income distribution scale (perhaps textile workers in developed countries, as an example), deepening income inequality is surely a possibility.

It hardly follows, however, that resistance to further growth in trade is a sensible response. Much of the increase in income inequality is likely due to other factors. The returns to education have been rising generally,[34] and lower skilled workers are being left behind across the board regardless of their industry. The reason why this is so is something of an economic puzzle, but the general view is that technological progress in modern times favors skilled workers.[35] The empirical evidence on the relationship between trade and wages also tends to find rather little downward pressure on any category of wages from the growth of trade.[36] The primary reasons for widening inequality likely lie elsewhere.

Moreover, as previously noted, open trade promotes the growth of real incomes on average even if some individuals suffer. When the growth of trade harms particular groups of citizens to a degree that is troubling, policies that interfere with trade and reduce overall national income are an unnecessarily costly way of dealing with the problem. Returning to the earlier discussion of optimal policy instruments, transfer programs for the needy would be a superior corrective. Further, if trade-related harms are for some reason deemed worthy of special attention, transfer programs targeted at trade-related harms to groups of workers (such as the Trade Adjustment Assistance Program under U.S. law)[37] can be employed.

This last point raises a broader issue. Income inequality arises for many reasons that have nothing to do with trade, and it is hardly clear that the proper response to income inequality in any way turns on its genesis. Perhaps all that is needed is a sensible network of need-based transfer and safety net programs that, once in place, can address troubling income inequalities whatever their source. Against a backdrop of sensible transfer and safety net measures, open trade can only improve matters by increasing national income and making assistance to the needy more affordable.

D. TRIPS and the Developing World

Although trade liberalization lies at the heart of the WTO agenda and its predecessor the GATT, other matters now come within the WTO system. The most important to date is intellectual property. The WTO Agreement on Trade-Related Aspects of Intellectual Property Rights (TRIPS) requires WTO members to establish effective protection for patents, trademarks, copyrights and other types of intellectual property. It includes detailed rules about the rights that must be protected as well as many of the procedures for protecting them.

One ramification of TRIPS has been an effort in developing countries to create or enhance patent protection for pharmaceuticals. The consequences of this effort for the price and availability of medicines in developing countries has been the subject of considerable attention lately, particularly with respect to the AIDS epidemic in sub-Saharan Africa. Legislation alleged to be inconsistent with TRIPS was the subject of recent litigation in South Africa in a case brought by manufacturers of AIDS medications, a case that eventually was settled.[38] Many commentators have plainly been troubled by the notion that the intellectual property laws required by TRIPS might be used to raise the price or restrict the availability of medications in the context of the desperate circumstances that confront many sub-Saharan nations,[39] and this aspect of the WTO system has been attacked as a particular source of tension with human rights – here, basic rights to medical care.[40]

Economists have something to contribute to this set of issues, but to some degree can merely point out that the wisdom of the various policy options turns on thorny empirical issues. To be sure, economists generally believe that some degree of intellectual property protection is essential to provide innovators with proper incentives to create new ideas and to market them. Yet there is no consensus on the details of an optimal intellectual property system, such as optimal patent length or scope. Accordingly, we cannot be confident that the rules contained in TRIPS enhance economic welfare relative to the set of national rules that would prevail in its absence, or relative to some other hypothetical multilateral agreement.

With respect to pharmaceuticals in particular, no one can say for certain whether existing rules governing pharmaceutical patents afford inadequate protection (suboptimal incentives to innovate) or excessive protection (excessive periods of monopoly pricing relative to what is necessary to encourage innovation). Some studies suggest that the social returns to pharmaceutical innovation are exceedingly high and that more investment in research and development is needed.[41] Commentators skeptical of that view point to the high profitability of the industry, to the billions of dollars that can be made from a successful new drug before generic entry occurs, and to the limited supply of human capital available for productive research. In the end, one can neither prove nor refute the possibility that patent rights in pharmaceuticals create excessive rents for pharmaceutical companies, and that some reduction in patent protection might be socially productive. If so, then the relaxation of pharmaceutical patent protection in developing countries might seem a particularly attractive option given the humanitarian concerns.

In addition, it is unclear the extent to which patent protection in developing countries affects the overall incentives of pharmaceutical companies to conduct research and development. International price discrimination is common in the pharmaceutical industry, with dramatically lower prices being charged for drugs sold to many developing countries. It is possible that revenues from developing country sales for many types of drugs are quite a small portion of current total revenues. The impact of reduced intellectual property protection in developing countries on the returns to pharmaceutical research and development might then be small as well, especially if generic medications sold in developing country markets could be kept out of major developed markets.

Further, even if a reduction in patent protection for pharmaceuticals in developing countries would come at the cost of an important, uneconomical reduction in incentives to innovate, it is possible to imagine devices that would make pharmaceuticals more affordable in developing country markets without affecting incentives to innovate. The most obvious mechanism is direct transfers from the governments of developed nations to help fund pharmaceutical purchases in the developing world – the recent G-8 commitments regarding AIDS drugs are illustrative of this option.[42]

However this discussion requires an important caveat. The AIDS pandemic is not the only infectious disease problem in the developing world – malaria, drug-resistant tuberculosis, and sleeping sickness are among the other notable killers. And unlike AIDS, these diseases are found primarily in developing countries. Little research is being undertaken on these diseases, presumably because pharmaceutical companies do not anticipate returns that would justify the cost. The TRIPS agreement might have some potential to change this situation if pharmaceutical manufacturers perceived that it would create credible patent rights in the developing economies.

Yet, the political pressure has been directed at weakening TRIPs, and of course the Doha ministerial meeting of the WTO produced a Declaration on the TRIPs Agreement and Public Health that opens the door wider to the use of compulsory licensing in response to national medical emergencies, and affirms the right of nations to permit parallel imports (which undercuts international price discrimination by pharmaceutical manufacturers). Although such policies can have the salutary impact of making existing drugs more affordable to those who desperately need them, their prospect may greatly diminish any hope that TRIPs might stimulate new research on tropical diseases.[43]

Conclusion

The opponents of globalization and the WTO point to a wide array of concerns, only some of which can fairly be said to implicate human rights. Economists will find little merit in most of the human rights critiques (like most of the other objections to trade and globalization), and indeed the evidence suggests that the growth of the trading system generally tends to promote rather than undermine human rights. Any tensions are best resolved through tailored interventions that directly address the human rights impairment without sacrificing the wider benefits of freer trade.

NOTES

1. The central instruments under international law are the United Nations Universal Declaration of Human Rights (1948), bifurcated into the International Covenant on Economic, Social and Cultural Rights (1966) and the International Covenant on Civil and Political Rights (1966). Other UN

conventions pertain to such matters as torture and genocide, racial discrimination, and rights of the child. Regional conventions also exist. See generally Louis Henkin, The Age of Rights (New York: Columbia 1990).

2. There is a substantial literature on this general subject, though relatively little of it is expressly economic. For some recent contributions, see Jeffrey Dunoff, Does Globalization Advance Human Rights, 25 Brooklyn L.J. 125 (1999); Frank Garcia, Trading Away the Human Rights Principle, 25 Brooklyn L.J. 51 (1999); Mark Warner, Globalization and Human Rights: An Economic Model, 25 Brooklyn J. Int'l L. 99 (1999); Ernst-Ulrich Petersmann, Human Rights and International Economic Law in the 21st Century: The Need to Clarify Their Interrelationships, 4 J. Int'l Econ. L. 3 (2001).

3. Here I paraphrase the arguments set forth in Human Rights and International Trade: Narrative Project Description, the proposal that forms the basis for this project.

4. Paul A. Samuelson, Economics 692 (9th ed. 1973).

5. Some caveats must be noted. For example, the growth of regional trading arrangements raises the danger of "trade diversion" which could lower real global output if severe enough. Similarly, some WTO rules pertain to matters other than trade liberalization. The rules on intellectual property protection contained in TRIPS, in particular, have an uncertain impact on global output.

6. See Jeffrey Sachs & Andrew Warner, Economic Reform and The Process of Global Integration, 1995 Brookings Papers on Economic Activity 1; Sebastian Edwards, Openness, Productivity and Growth: What Do We Really Know?, 108 Econ. J. 447 (1998).

7. The notion that rights will tend to receive greater protection in wealthier societies is among the themes developed in Richard Posner, The Cost of Rights: Implications for Central and Eastern Europe – and for the United States, 32 Tulsa L.J. 1 (1996).

8. A normal good is defined as a good for which the demand rises as income rises.

9. Data were drawn from CIA World Factbook 2000, available online at www.odci.gov/cia/publications/factbook/index.html.

10. Charles Humana, World Human Rights Guide 3d ed. (Oxford: 1992).

The 40 criteria used in rating each country were distilled from various UN conventions and international treaties. The percentage ratings were determined by awarding a number of points for each question:

3 points if there is an unqualified respect for the freedom or right
2 points if there are occasional breaches of respect for the freedom or right
1 point if there are frequent violations of the freedom or right
0 points if there is a constant pattern of violation of the freedom or right

Questions 7-13 were weighted more heavily because they involve a greater degree of physical suffering. The rating was reached by adding the total points for nonweighted questions to the total for the weighted questions, multiplying by 100, and dividing by 162, the total number of points possible. The average score was 62%.

The forty criteria are:

Freedom to:

1. Travel in own country
2. Travel outside of own country
3. Peacefully associate and assemble
4. Teach ideas and receive information
5. Monitor human rights violations
6. Publish and educate in an ethnic language

Freedom from:

7. Serfdom, slavery, forced or child labor
8. Extrajudicial killings or "disappearances"
9. Torture or coercion by the state
10. Compulsory work permits or conscription of labor
11. Capital punishment by the state
12. Court sentences of corporal punishment
13. Indefinite detention without charge
14. Compulsory membership of state organizations or parties
15. Compulsory religion or state ideology in schools
16. Deliberate state policies to control artistic works
17. Political censorship of press
18. Censorship of mail or telephone tapping

Freedom for or rights to:

19. Peaceful political opposition
20. Multiparty elections by secret and universal ballot
21. Political and legal equality for women
22. Social and economic equality for women
23. Social and economic equality for ethnic minorities
24. Independent newspapers
25. Independent book publishing
26. Independent radio and TV networks
27. All courts to total independence
28. Independent trade unions

Legal rights:

29. From deprivation of nationality
30. To be considered innocent until proven guilty
31. To free legal aid when necessary and counsel of own choice
32. From civilian trials in secret
33. To be brought promptly before a judge or court
34. From police searches of home without a warrant
35. From arbitrary seizure of personal property

Personal rights:

36. To interracial, interreligious or civil marriage
37. Equality of sexes during marriage and for divorce proceedings
38. To practice any religion
39. To use contraceptive pills and devices
40. To noninterference by state in strictly private affairs

11. Freedom in the World: The Annual Survey of Political Rights and Civil Liberties, 1999-2000, Adrian Karatnycky ed. (Freedom House: 2000).

Political rights and civil liberties were each rated by Freedom House on a scale of 1 to 7, with 1 being the most free and 7 being the least free. Countries were assigned a particular number based on responses to the checklists below and the judgments of the survey team at Freedom House. The team assigned initial ratings to countries by awarding from 0 to 4 raw points per checklist item, depending on the comparative rights or liberties present; the only exception is the additional discretionary question B in the political rights checklist, for which 1 to 4 raw points were subtracted, depending on the severity of the situation. After placing countries in initial categories based on the checklist points, the team made adjustments for factors like extreme violence, whose intensity might not be reflected in the checklist questions. The factors considered in each category are:

Political rights: enable people to participate freely in the political process, which is the system by which the polity chooses authoritative policy makers and attempts to make binding decisions affecting the national, regional, or local community. In a free society, this represents the right of all adults to vote and compete for public office, and for elected representatives to have a decisive vote on public policies.

Checklist for political rights:

1. Is the head of state and/or head of government or other chief authority elected through free and fair elections?
2. Are the legislative representatives elected through free and fair elections?
3. Are there fair electoral laws, equal campaigning opportunities, fair polling and honest tabulation of ballots?
4. Are the voters able to endow their elected representatives with real power?
5. Do the people have the right to organize in different political parties or other competitive political groupings of their choice, and is the system open to the rise and fall of these competing parties or groupings?
6. Is there a significant opposition vote, de facto opposition power, and a possibility for the opposition to increase its support or gain power through elections?
7. Are the people free from domination by the military, foreign powers, totalitarian parties, religious hierarchies, economic oligarchies, or any other powerful group?
8. Do cultural, ethnic, religious, and other minority groups have reasonable self-determination, self-government, autonomy, or participation through informal consensus in the decision-making process?

Additional discretionary political rights questions:

A. For traditional monarchies that have no parties or electoral process, does the system provide for consultation with the people, encourage discussion of policy, and allow the right to petition the ruler?

B. Is the government or occupying power deliberately changing the ethnic composition of country or territory so as to destroy a culture or tip the political balance in favor of another group?

Civil liberties: freedoms to develop views, institutions and personal autonomy apart from the state.

Checklist for civil liberties:

1. Are there free and independent media and other forms of cultural expression? (Note: in cases where the media are state-controlled, but offer pluralistic points of view, the Survey gives the system credit.)

2. Are there free religious institutions and is there free private and public religious expression?
3. Is there freedom of assembly, demonstration, and open public discussion?
4. Is there freedom of political or quasi-political organization? (Note: this includes political parties, civic organizations, ad hoc issue groups, etc.)
5. Are there free trade unions and peasant organizations or equivalents, and is there effective collective bargaining? Are there free professional and other private organizations?
6. Is there an independent judiciary?
7. Does the rule of law prevail in civil and criminal matters? Is the population treated equally under the law? Are police under direct civilian control?
9. Is there protection from political terror, unjustified imprisonment, whether by groups that support or oppose the system? Is there freedom from war and insurgencies? (Note: freedom from war and insurgencies enhances the liberties in a free society, but the absence of wars and insurgencies does not in and of itself make a not free society free.)
10. Is there freedom from extreme government indifference and corruption?
11. Is there open and free private discussion?
12. Is there personal autonomy? Does the state control travel, choice of residence, or choice of employment? Is there freedom from indoctrination and excessive dependency on the state?
13. Are property rights secure? Do citizens have the right to establish private businesses? Is private business activity unduly influenced by government officials, the security forces, or organized crime?
14. Are there personal social freedoms, including gender equality, choice of marriage partners and size of family?
15. Is there equality of opportunity, including freedom from exploitation by or dependency on landlords, employers, union leaders, bureaucrats, or other types of obstacles to a share of legitimate economic gains?

12. Gerald O'Driscoll, Jr., Kim R. Holmes & Melanie Kirkpatrick, 2001 Index of Economic Freedom (Heritage Foundation and Wall Street Journal: 2001).

The Index includes a broad array of factors determining economic freedom:

1. Corruption: in the judiciary, customs service and government bureaucracy
2. Non-tariff barriers to trade: such as import bans and quotas, as well as strict labeling and licensing requirements
3. The fiscal burden of government: encompasses income tax rates, corporate tax rates and government expenditures as a percent of output
4. The rule of law: efficiency within the judiciary, and the ability to enforce contracts
5. Regulatory burdens: burdens on business, including health, safety and environmental regulation
6. Restrictions on banks: regarding financial services, such as selling securities and insurance
7. Labor market regulations: established work weeks and mandatory separation pay
8. Black market activities: including smuggling, piracy of IP rights, the underground provision of labor and other services

13. Data were drawn from CIA World Factbook 2000, available online at www.odci.gov/cia/publications/factbook/index.html.

14. In particular, if the various human rights indices are regressed in a simple regression on per capita GDP, the resulting coefficient of per capita GDP is statistically significant at the 95% level.

15. Gerald O'Driscoll, Jr., Kim R. Holmes & Melanie Kirkpatrick, 2001 Index of Economic Freedom (Heritage Foundation and Wall Street Journal: 2001). Nations with economies that are closed to imports were excluded from the sample in preference to assuming some extremely high average tariff rate.

16. See generally John Jackson, The World Trading System 2d ed. 319-25 (MIT: 1997).

17. This proposition is sometimes known as the first theorem of welfare economics. See Hal Varian, Microeconomic Analysis 3d ed. 323-26 (Norton: 1992).

18. See, e.g., Peter Lindert, International Economics 9th ed. 73-77 (Irwin: 1991).

19. This is the mechanism explored by Ronald Coase, The Problem of Social Cost, 3 J. L. & Econ. 1 (1960).

20. See, e.g., Jagdish Bhagwati & T.N. Srinivasan, Lectures on International Trade 185-91 (MIT: 1983).

21. This point is made in quite general terms in Steven Shavell, A Note on Efficiency vs. Distributional Equity in Legal Rulemaking: Should Distributional Equity Matter Given Optimal Income Taxation?, 71 Am. Econ. Rev. (Paps. & Procs.) 414 (1981).

22. Note that many of the targets of trade sanctions imposed in the past for political ends, such as Iraq, Iran and the Soviet Union, were not members of the GATT/WTO system at the time of the sanctions.

23. Perhaps the leading study is Gary Hufbauer, Jeffrey Schott & Kimberley Elliot, International Sanctions Reconsidered 2d ed. 91-115 (Inst. for Int'l Econ.: 1990).

24. This is the general message in Petersmann, supra.

25. The literature is vast. Much of it is collected and referenced in the papers found in Unfair Trade and Harmonization: Prerequisites for Free Trade?, Vols. I & II, Jagdish Bhagwati & Robert Hudec eds. (MIT: 1997) (hereafter Bhagwati & Hudec), and in a symposium issue of the Journal of Economic Law on regulatory competition, published in June 2000.

26. See John Wilson, Capital Mobility and Environmental Standards: Is There a Theoretical Basis for the Race to the Bottom?, in Bhagwati & Hudec vol. 1, supra.

27. This is the essence of the distinction between efficiency-enhancing and redistributive policies in David Charny, Regulatory Competition and the Global Coordination of Labor Standards, 3 J.

Int'l Econ. L. 281 (2000), as well as the point of departure for Dani Rodrik in Has Globalization Gone Too Far? (Inst. for Int'l Econ.: 1997).

28. E.g., Sam Peltzman, An Evaluation of Consumer Protection Legislation: The 1962 Drug Amendments, 81 J. Pol. Econ. 1049 (1973).

29. E.g., Bruce Ackerman & William Hassler, Clean Coal: Dirty Air (Yale: 1981).

30. See generally the symposium in Journal of International Economic Law, June, 2000.

31. Again, see generally sources cited in note 25 supra.

32. Arik Levinson, Environmental Regulations and Industry Location: International and Domestic Evidence, in Bhagwati & Hudec, Vol. I, supra, p. 450.

33. Some of the inequality literature is cited in Dunoff, supra. See also Burtless, C., International trade and the rise in earnings inequality, 33 J. Econ. Lit. 800 (1995).

34. See Gordon Hanson, The Globalization of Production, NBER Reporter, March 22, 2001, p.12; Murnane, R. J., and Levy, F., Why today's high-school-educated males earn less than their fathers did: The problem and an assessment of responses. 63 Harv. Ed. Rev. 1 (1993).

35. Galor, O., and Moav, O., Ability-biased technological transition, wage inequality, and economic growth. 115 Q.J. Econ. 469 (2000).

36. Robert Lawrence and Matthew Slaughter, International trade and American wages in the 1980s: giant sucking sound or small hiccup? 1993 Brookings Papers on Economic Activity 161; Edward Leamer, In search of Stolper-Samuelson effects on US wages, NBER Working Paper, no 5427, January 1998; Kevin Murphy and Finis Welch, F., The role of international trade in wage differentials, in Workers and their wages: Changing patterns in the United States, M. H. Kosters editor, 39-76. (AEI: 1991).

37. See 19 U.S.C. §§2271-2394.

38. South Africa Settles Patent Dispute with Drug Industry, 14 AIDS Litigation Reporter No. 18, p. 6 (June 18, 2001).

39. EU/WTO: Promise to Address Medicine for Poor Countries, European Report, June 27, 2001.

40. The right to the highest attainable level of physical and mental health has long been among the rights recognized in the UN covenants.

41. Kevin Murphy & Robert Topel, forthcoming in Journal of Law and Economics.

42. See Launch of Global AIDS Fund at G-8 Summit Gets Mixed Reviews, Africa News, July 24, 2001.

43. I address these issues at considerable length in another recent paper: TRIPs, Pharmaceuticals, Developing Countries, and the Doha "Solution," 3 Chi. J. Int'l L. 47 (2002). Similar observations may be found in Jean O. Lanjouw, New Global Patent Regime for Diseases: U.S. and International Legal Issues, 16 Harvard Journal of Law and Technology 85 (2002-2003). Lanjouw proposes in essence a two-tier system of patent rights that would provide strong patent protection in developing countries for medicines that address tropical diseases, but would weaken patent protection in developing countries for other medicines.

CHAPTER 5

Governance, Trade and Human Rights

Thomas Cottier[*]

I. Introduction

A. Factual Linkages

The life of the law depends on institutions and structures in manifold and complex ways. Rights and legal obligations, whatever their content, remain without impact in a vacuum. They need to be supported by a large variety of institutions and structures in society, polity, culture, tradition and economics.[1] This is true both for the realization of human rights and for a functioning liberal trading system. Both require, each of them in their own way, supporting institutions and structures that are implied or specifically addressed in legal instruments. Protection and enhancement both of human rights and stable trade relations are highly dependent on appropriate institutional arrangements and frameworks in society at large and the state. Human rights cannot flourish without education, without mutual respect and tolerance, nor without a tradition to respect rights of individuals in society and daily life. They cannot flourish without an accountable government and democracy, without economic prosperity and without the courts as guardians of constitutional rights. An open trading system in addition depends, *inter alia*, on market structures, international communication, cultural interaction and mutual respect, economic efficiency, but also solidarity and safety nets within a society for those who lose in economic integration, regional and global. Both depend on the rule of law, including public and private law. Both, in addition, need to be embedded in international structures in some way or another in a world of mutual interaction and dependence. Both are part of interlocking governance and power into horizontal and vertical separation of powers and checks and balances.

Conversely, many of these supporting institutions also depend on the law. Human rights, as well as the principles and rules of an open trading system,

---

* I am indebted to Jianqiang Nie, Research Fellow WTI, for assistance in completing and annotating this paper. The responsibility entirely remains my own. It builds upon Thomas Cottier, Emerging Doctrines of Good Governance: The Impact of the WTO and China's Accession, in: Frederick M. Abbott (Ed.), China in the World Trading System: Defining the Principles of Engagement, at 119, Kluwer Law International, Boston, 1998.

shape institutions and structures in return and in a process of mutual interaction. Without legal backing, many of them cannot persist and endure in stability. This is certainly true for the state, but also for many institutions in society at large.

The relationship of law, social, cultural and economic institutions therefore is one of mutual dependence and interaction. The same is likely for trade and human rights. This is my basic assumption. We do not have proof of this phenomenon but experience is important. Human rights protection and open markets evolved in parallel, both nationally and internationally.[2] Philosophy, political and historical evidence and economic analysis are likely to establish a close interrelation and perhaps mutual interdependence.

B. Legal Linkages

In a world of factual and real interdependence, the fundamental question before us is whether these different areas should be *institutionally and legally linked* such that they mutually assume responsibility and become legally interdependent. Or, in the alternative, should they be left to factual and political interaction without institutional and legal linkages? The question also arises in relation to trade and human rights.

Answers to this fundamental institutional question are not uniform. They depend on the level of integration. Within nation states, fundamental rights and economic regulation are closely and legally intertwined. Constitutional law addresses the relationship of the two fields. It is unlikely that one prevails over the other completely, and mutual coordination and coexistence is sought. This is also true in European Community case law. Human rights concerns were gradually integrated in a dialogue with national constitutional law.[3] This happened in the case law of the courts, long before efforts to establish a written European Charter of Human Rights was drafted with a view to incorporating it into the treaty system and a future European Constitution. In federal states, sub-federal members are obliged to honor fundamental rights. Persistent violations by a sub-federal entity are likely to result in economic or other sanctions in most federations. It would seem that federal courts and governments generally assume powers to establish such linkages. In the European Union, an institutional linkage between market access and human rights was established as a condition of accession in Article 49 EUT, and membership to the customs union was conditioned on respect of "the principles of liberty, democracy, respect for human rights and fundamental freedoms, and the rule of law" enshrined in Article 6 EUT. Sanctions for human rights violations may result in economic measures by means of withdrawing treaty rights in accordance with procedures set out in Article 7 EUT, as amended. Finally, the European Communities and countries established institutional links between trade and human rights in domestic trade regulations in the context of granting preferential treatment (GSP).[4] They increasingly include such linkages in economic agreements, such as the Cotonou Agreement between the ACP countries and the European Communities.

GATT and the WTO, in a functionalist tradition, do not currently establish comparable explicit linkages between human rights and trade, except in respect of prison labor and UN economic sanctions.[5] The interaction of trade and human rights properly speaking is mainly left, in international law, to *factual* and political relations. Close interactions, however, exist within the rule of law. The question arises whether, on this basis, institutional links between trade regulation, the rule of law and human rights should be institutionally and legally expanded within the multilateral trading system of the WTO.

This question should be discussed in relation to the doctrine of governance. This doctrine encapsulates the relationship between the rule of law, human rights and trade regulation. Today, the term is increasingly used in two ways: *Global Governance* and *Good Governance.* The two do not mean the same thing, but are closely interrelated. The first concept addresses the need to develop a global legal framework, interfacing global and national law and structures, in order to cope with globalization and its ramifications (issues of global policies, multilateral law-making, democratic representation and accountability, dispute settlement and enforcement). On the other hand, the doctrine of Good Governance looks into national governmental structures both in the public and private domain, taking into account the role of civil society (political parties, NGOs, associations media etc). In the trade field, more attention is currently being paid to Global Governance, while the latter prevails in the field of sustainable economic and social development, in particular in the context of aid and concessionary programs.

This paper first explores the concept of Good Governance as it emerged in the lending policies of the Bretton Woods institutions. We discuss the legal basis of Good Governance and its relationship to the rule of law and human rights protection. We explore to what extent Good Governance guarantees exist in WTO law and how they relate to the rule of law and human rights. We explore potential areas for further reinforcing the rule of law and Good Governance on the basis of human rights guarantees, all with a view to achieving overall consistency and to further enhancing the legitimacy of the trading system. Finally, we also consider the concept of Global Governance and seek to place results of the examination of Good Governance in the perspective of this new dimension of governance. The purpose of the paper is to provide a framework for discussing the linkage issue.

II. The Doctrine of Good Governance

A. Evolution

Failures of technocratic social and economic development programs of multilateral and national development agencies led to insights and conclusions that such failures are largely due to the absence of adequate social, political and legal structures upon which to build. After early eras of emphasizing projects of large technical infrastructure, followed by a policy shift to basic needs since 1989, the World Bank and other institutions have increasingly emphasized the need to develop and support adequate structures of governance in the private and public sectors.[6]

These encouraging development activities, in particular within the World Bank, the IMF, OECD and UNDP, gradually acknowledged that sustainable social and economic development strongly depends on the quality of governmental and societal institutions and structures.[7] The doctrine of Good Governance emerged by 1990. It was increasingly integrated into loan strategies, concessionary aid and technical cooperation by multilateral institutions, and in legislation and programs of donor countries.[8] The policy has been implemented by way of shaping conditions with a view to bringing about and accelerating the policy goals of Good Governance.

B. Content and Definitions

"By Governance is meant the exercise of political power to manage a nation's affairs."[9] Good Governance may be defined by way of absence of bad qualities, such as failure to separate public and private affairs, failure to establish a predictable framework of law and government, excessive rules impeding markets, and priorities inconsistent with development needs.[10] According to the OECD, Good Governance encompasses more than just the goals called "Participatory Development," "Democratization" and "Human Rights." It essentially comprises the rule of law, public sector management, controlling corruption and reducing excessive military spending.[11]

More recent work particularly emphasizes the importance of the rule of law and of the protection of property rights as a prerequisite for social and economic development. Markets cannot develop far without effective property rights. And property rights are only effective when three conditions are fulfilled. The first is protection from theft, violence and other forms of predation. The second is protection from arbitrary government actions – ranging from unpredictable, ad hoc regulations and taxes to outright corruption – that disrupts business activity. The third condition is a reasonably fair and predictable judiciary.[12]

The doctrine of Good Governance is not a clearly defined legal concept, let alone a matter of international rights and obligations of States. There are many ways to define governance and Good Governance. However, there seems to be a general consensus regarding key factors . An OECD workshop (including LDCs representatives) names the following as important components of the concept:[13]

- Technical and managerial competence
- Organizational capacity
- Accountability
- Transparency and open information systems
- Participation
- Reliability, predictability and the rule of law

The World Bank's doctrine of Good Governance describes the main tenets of the rule of law as follows:[14]

- The legal system should provide a set of rules known in advance
- The legal system should rely upon rules which are actually implemented
- The legal system should ensure that rules are applied consistently to all (including State) officials
- The legal system must provide an effective, independent mechanism for dispute resolution
- There must be clear rules to govern the amendment of rules, to prevent the arbitrary introduction and rejection of rules, and to remove irrelevant rules

The concept of Good Governance, as defined and applied by the Bank and the IMF and other institutions, remains functional, i.e., it is limited to achieving goals of economic and social development.[15] It cannot formally extend to general political dimensions under the articles of the Bretton Woods institutions. To the extent that the doctrine is applied by national governments in bilateral programs, they are, of course, not bound by this limitation and may adopt a broader definition and content.[16]

C. Legal Foundations

1. A Policy

It is telling that the initiative to emphasize the rule of law and protection of property rights was with World Bank economists facing limitations on achieving sustainable development because of bad governmental structures, and less so with lawyers in the forefront. In search for the causes of failures, economists identified crucial institutional and structural prerequisites for successful economic development. Many of the elements of Good Governance coincide with key attributes of the rule of law. However, it is unclear how the doctrine of the rule of law relates to international law.

It is recalled that, basically, the structures of national government and law enforcement have not been a concern under general international law. It is true that States have always taken a strong interest in structures of governance abroad, for reasons of power, and for reasons of securing trade and commercial interests. Government inference in governance abroad is as old as diplomacy and power politics. Moreover, during the period of colonialism, the relationship between metropolitan powers and colonial governance was withdrawn from international law and made an internal affairs issue for a number of decades in the late 19th and early 20th century.

For obvious reasons, decolonization restored classical doctrines of international law in State practice, despite much human rights rhetoric to the contrary. The doctrines of State sovereignty, non-intervention and self-determination essentially leave these concerns outside the scope of international law. Beyond vague qualifications of a state, such as to be peace-loving or a civilized or effective nation, general international law hardly imposes any particular requirements vis-à-vis governmental structures.[17] Things are different under specific treaties in specific regulatory areas. The WTO is the main example in point and will be discussed shortly. But generally speaking, the state has been the subject, not the object, of international law, and domestic concerns and related rules of international law were essentially limited to the protection of foreign nationals under diplomatic protection.

2. Contract and Conditionality

Specific legal foundations of Good Governance policies of the financial institutions remain weak. *They exclusively rely upon the power to condition loans and concessionary aid.* The legal basis is thus found in the contractual relationship between international organizations or donor countries and recipient governments. As the policy is not shaped in precise legal terms of rights and obligations, the ad hoc contractual basis entails the potential for arbitrary action and conditions. States depending on support by the Bank and the IMF, and on donor States, do not have any means of challenging conditions and their administration. From the point of view of Good Governance, we can hardly consider this to be a good example of the implementation of the rule of law itself. Part of the criticism and resentment expressed and discussed shortly relates to this constellation of issues and may be attributed to insufficiencies in the structures of Global Governance. We return to this after dealing with the WTO.

3. The Rule of Law

Thus, the notions of Good Governance and Global Governance do not form part of the arsenal and instruments of traditional international law. They emerged in political economy and political sciences. Yet, they are closely related to traditional precepts of law. The concepts of property rights, of the rule of law, and the related doctrine of *Rechtsstaat* or *Etats de droit* emerged over centuries and following many battles, and culminated in 19th and 20th century constitutionalism, i.e. government by law, and not by men. Some aspects relate to participatory government and others to transparency in the conduct of business operations.

The mainstream legal communities, unlike economists and political scientists, have so far failed to deal extensively with, and to develop coherent legal theories of, appropriate linkages of international and national structures of governance for social and economic development in the post-colonial era. Attempts were made by the modernist school of Law and Development in the 1970s and 1980s when focused on transplantation of Western legal institutions into developing countries.[18] Studies on the interaction of national and international institutions and structures, however, seem to be only in their beginnings. Thomas Frank discusses them in terms of individual and collective entitlements vis-à-vis states.[19] But we are far from conceptual clarity. The problems we face in discussing the relationship of trade and human rights confirm this point. Underlying state structures, which often lead to, and are the very cause of, violations are not yet addressed by international standards or rules. In the legal mind, the *Westphalian* nation state system is still deeply entrenched.

Lawyers, more than economists and social scientists, essentially still tend to remain within the realm of the nation state and national legal systems, and have done so ever since the end of Roman law universalism. The tradition of positive law and preoccupation with a national legal system prevented the legal profession from developing doctrines of Good Governance that could be universally applied as a set of institutional minimal standards.[20] In my view, it is not a coincidence that the legal profession, and constitutional law in particular, is still behind in developing general legal doctrines of Global and Good Governance from an international angle, transcending the specific setting of a particular country and jurisdiction. The problem of properly locating and sourcing the principle of Good Governance reveals the problem in full scale.

We are thus left with the question to what extent the rule of law with its specific components indicated above finds its foundation in international law. Basic precepts can be partly founded in human rights, in particular those relating to due process of law, discussed below. However, treaty law does not seem to provide for a general and comprehensive concept of the rule of law. The question therefore arises whether it forms part of customary law principles or of the general principles of law of the world's main legal systems. Is it possible to construe the rule of law in customary law, based upon the practice and *opinio juris* of international financial organizations and policies of conditionalities imposed by donor countries? It would seem difficult to do so. What about general principles of law? Again, some of its elements, such as protection of legitimate expectations, or good faith, and equitable principles (estoppel, acquiescence) form part of general principles, but do not cover all of its tenets. Moreover, it is unclear where to draw the line between mandatory, minimal requirements of the rule of law and more advanced forms that would not form part of the core of rules pertaining to international law. Or, is it, in the end, unnecessary to define the rule of law in international law, since its tenets are implemented by way of conditionalities and therefore on the basis of contractual relations? It is submitted that this requires further exploration.

4. Human Rights

Countries accept Good Governance policies as contractual obligations in dealing with donor countries and multilateral agencies. As developing countries depend on loan and aid, conditionality is an effective instrument of implementation outside the realm of general international legal obligations. But this kind of effectiveness renders Good Governance also highly intrusive and potentially vulnerable. The quest for legitimacy made the policy open for justification in terms of human rights. Likewise, the doctrine of Good Governance offered the opportunity to introduce human rights concerns in multilateral and bilateral programs. Accordingly, it was strongly advocated by human rights groups. By and through the doctrine of Good Governance, they succeeded in importing human rights considerations into the IMF and Bank's policies.[21]

Many of the facets of Good Governance described above indeed can be depicted as institutional reflections of human rights principles expressed in national constitutions and the international Bill of Rights. The Universal Declaration of Human Rights,[22] the Covenants on Civil and Political Rights,[23] and to some extent also the Covenant on Economic, Social and Cultural rights[24] depict and reflect goals of Good Governance. The respect of rights inherently entails respect of principles of Good Governance. This is particularly true for the following rights contained in the Universal Declaration: equal protection before the law (Art. 7), effective legal remedies (Art. 8), protection from arbitrary detention (Art. 9), full and fair hearing (Art. 10), the presumption of innocence (Art. 11), protection from arbitrary interference with privacy and family (Art. 12), freedom of movement and residence within the country (Art. 13), right to a family (Art. 16), protection from arbitrary deprivation of property (Art. 17), freedom of thought, conscience and religion (Art. 18), freedom of opinion and expression (Art. 19), freedom of peaceful assembly and association (Art. 20), and right to participate in political life (Art. 21).

While Good Governance doctrines reflect these political and civil rights, it is less clear to what extent in the practice of institutions they also reflect social, economic and cultural rights. To the extent that Good Governance is part of neo-liberal policies, these rights are likely to be taken into account to a much lesser degree. This has been one aspect of the criticism expressed. It is important to note that Good Governance policies seeking legitimacy in a human rights foundation equally need to take into account the policy goals related to second generation rights which affect the large majority of any population, in particular the following provisions found in the Universal Declaration of Human Rights right to social security (Art. 22), right to employment and equal remuneration and right to existence in dignity (Art. 23), right to leisure and holidays (Art. 24), right to an adequate living standard for the person and his family (Art. 25), right to education (Art. 26) and right to participation in cultural life (Art. 27). It is not clear to what extent this is happening, and further research will be necessary on this point.

Conceptually, the international foundations of these standards were laid with the advent of international protection of human rights after World War II. The wide-reaching guarantees of the international Bill of Rights established the foundation of a potentially new international order. It formally turned domestic affairs into potential international obligations and entitlements to intervene. Insistence on non-intervention by newly independent countries and the former Soviet Union rendered such interference weak in practical terms. It is only after the breakdown of the former Soviet Union that human rights are explicitly invoked as justifications for intervention, even explicitly or implicitly in military terms (for example, Kosovo intervention and second Iraq war). The shift of paradigm after World War II began to have real effect only some 50 years later. The Doctrine of Good Governance is one of its emanations.

From the perspective of international law, the doctrine of Good Governance therefore is mainly rooted in human rights. Constitutional theory would further ascribe these structural principles to other institutions of law establishing Good Governance: the rule of law, checks and balances, participatory democracy and transparency. The point is that international law, so far, lacks any category, other than human rights, in general international law by which the structure of states and societies can be defined and assessed. It is not a coincidence that liberal internationalism seeks to expand structural influence on States in terms of individual rights, be it as an emerging right to democracy or a right to development in a most generic sense, or by virtue of third generation rights relating to ecological goals.

III. Good Governance within WTO Law

A. A Rule-Oriented System

Much of what has been said relating to the function Good Governance in the context of financial grants is equally true for trade regulation. Issues of Good Governance are identical and of similar interest from the point of view of trade relations as they are from the point of view of social and economic development in general. Both depend on it, in particular on the rule of law. Good Governance pursued in the realm of financial institutions is also good for the WTO. Human rights and values pursued by the policy are suitable to serve both ends at the same time. Conditionalities imposed by the Bretton Woods institutions are likely to benefit trade relations and assist in implementing specific requirements under WTO law. *Vice versa*, implementation of values and goals of Good Governance in WTO also are likely to benefit social and economic development.

While there has been little discussion in the WTO in terms of Good Governance, and human rights have not been invoked, the law of the World Trade Organization has achieved remarkable regulatory accomplishments in this area. The gradual shift from power-oriented to rule-oriented trade policy brought about increased reliance on the rule of law. Fundamental principles of transparency and domestic legal protection formed part of GATT since the beginning, reflecting both Wilsonian principles of open government after a dark and non-transparent era of international diplomacy leading to World War I, and the economic crisis leading to World War II.

B. The Rule of Law and Transparency

The bulk of WTO law, of course, is dedicated to substantive principles and rules implementing the results of trade negotiations. Many provisions of WTO law, however, relate to legal security, predictability and the avoidance of capricious and arbitrary decisions. They form the basic structures and institutions of the system together with the fundamental principles of non-discrimination (MFN and NT). A number of important principles and rules (non-exhaustive) exist:

- Transparency and publication requirements for national law and precedents (in particular Art. IX GATT, Art. III GATS, Art. 63 TRIPs).
- Judicial protection in matters relating to trade regulation (e.g., Art. VI GATS).
- Concept of reasonable procedures for the acquisition of IPRs (Art. 62 TRIPs); concept of reasonable, objective and impartial administration of service regulation, including informing the applicant (Art. VI GATS).
- Extensive procedural requirements in the administration of countervailing duties (anti-dumping and subsidies) (Agreements on the Implementation of Article VI and XVI of the General Agreement on Tariffs and Trade 1994).
- Notification requirements for draft technical norms and inquiry points (Art. 2.9, Art. 10 TBT Agreement).
- Protection of intellectual property rights, being recognized as private rights (Part II, TRIPs), in particular scientific, literary and artistic production (cf. Art. 27:2 Universal Declaration).
- Extensive rules on enforcement of intellectual property rights (including civil and administrative proceedings, including provisional measures, border controls, standards on timely registration of rights etc. (Art. 42-61 TRIPs).
- Disciplines in order to avoid arbitrary customs valuations (Art. VII, Agreement on Implementation of Article VII of the General Agreement on Tariffs and Trade 1994).
- Extensive procedural requirements in the administration of import licenses (Agreement on Import Licensing Procedures).
- Extensive procedural principles and requirements in the administration of rules of origin (Agreement on Rules of Origin).
- Transparency in Government Procurement: Tender procedures (publication) and legal protection (Plurilateral Agreement on Government Procurement).

It should be noted that these features legally and essentially protect foreign suppliers of goods and services. They stem from the tradition of diplomatic protection. The granting of such rights, however, equally benefits domestic suppliers and thus contributes to Good Governance in general. Governments rarely wish to treat their nationals worse than foreign suppliers. In effect, WTO rules therefore contain prescriptions having a general impact on governmental structures. They contribute to the rule of law. Moreover, we note that the TRIPs agreement establishes property rights. Not only foreign suppliers, but also nationals perhaps in the first place, will benefit from the system implementing these international disciplines. Rules on government procurement are of central importance in terms of combating corruption also for domestic competitors. They contribute to more efficient use of scarce financial resources on home markets.

In sum, we may conclude that WTO law has produced a considerable body of law responding to doctrines of Good Governance. This body of law, however, is focused on the rule of law and limited to trade-related issues. It does not relate to human rights.

IV. Underlying Conceptual Issues

A. The Critique of Good Governance

Before turning to the potential for further expanding elements of Good Governance in the multilateral trading system, it is necessary to address the criticism expressed thus far. The policies of the lending financial institutions, and rights and obligations under WTO law relating to Good Governance, share a common trait of substantially interfering with domestic affairs from the perspective of national sovereignty and the principle of non-intervention. Both areas reveal how much has changed.

The critique of Good Governance as applied by international financial institutions reflects these profound changes. Similar objections are likely to arise against a concept of Good Governance under WTO law, despite different normative constellations and foundations.

A number of objections are raised. First, Good Governance is not as new as it is claimed. It amounts to imposition by the emperor in new clothes.[25] The main arguments can be summarized thus: History shows a long record of interference in structures of other states. The transposition of structural and institutional elements, applied to a different culture and context, explains many failures of the past. It is argued that Good Governance, expounding principles of Western liberal government, does not sufficiently consider cultural diversity. The same concerns can be voiced vis-à-vis WTO Good Governance. They essentially relate to the argument of being prescriptions that are too detailed and too invasive. They are considered too costly for implementation and to cause difficulties in implementation. Good Governance, furthermore, is limited to an economic agenda, essentially focusing on improving market access rights and opportunities. Moreover, while having profound political effects, the doctrine, as applied by financial institutions bound to their functional mandate, cannot take into account the broad range of all human rights concerns involved. Good Governance one-sidedly stresses process and procedural aspects of governance while leaving substance, in particular distribution and equity, aside. There is a one-sided emphasis on political and civil rights at the expense of economic, social and cultural rights. It is argued that the doctrine emerged as a counter strategy against the much more far-reaching (and also interventionist) model of the New International Economic Order.[26] Instead, Good Governance is meant to ensure that development remains within the paradigm of neo-liberal economic policies and seeks to keep to the role of the State at bay. Finally, it is held that the doctrine lacks universality as it is only applied to developing countries, while the structure of government in developed countries, despite all its international negative externalities, remains unimpaired and immune from such implications.[27]

These critical objections are important and protect against the tendency to adopt a naive vision of Good Governance of multilateral institutions, both financial and trade-related. They compel justification of the doctrine in depth, and the consideration of the sensitivities and concerns, in particular in light of the colonial past and legacy. It is submitted, however, that the objections do not convincingly defeat the purpose and basic tenets of Good Governance for a number of reasons.

B. The Case for Good Governance Principles in Trade Law

1. Checks and Balances

The principles of Good Governance, both enshrined in human rights and WTO rules, reflect an important body of human experience in the government of human affairs. They stand for the proposition of government by law, whatever the detailed level of international intervention. The expounded and applied principles emerged, and are still emerging, as answers to government failures and constitutional deficiencies experienced around the world. They reflect human nature and make available institutions and structures of an antidotal nature.

The law of the WTO increasingly affects domestic policies, and a separation of domestic and foreign affairs often is no longer possible (e.g., agriculture, regional policies, IPRs, services).[28] To a lesser extent, the same holds true with structural and procedural requirements. There is a general spill-over effect. Even if Good Governance is, in the field of trade, primarily motivated to support market access and fairness of market condition, these qualities will equally be beneficial for domestic suppliers and consumers in the long run. They contribute to the overall enhancement of Good Governance. It is equally good for people at home. Procedural requirements responding to Good Governance act as an additional check on national governments and the exercise of power. They restrict arbitrariness. They insert what may be called vertical separation of powers and checks and balances, transcending traditional national constitutional law.[29] They are of relevance in dealing with authoritarian regimes. They are equally of importance in democracies where protection of particular minority interests (foreigners and importers) remains important. They assist in stabilizing not only market access rights, but also society and government at large, and contribute to regional and world peace.[30]

2. How Much Prescription?

While the standards in traditional GATT law remained modest and hardly gave rise to complaints, the WTO and in particular the TRIPs Agreement have substantially added increased levels of Good Governance requirements. These levels have caused concerns of excessive intrusiveness. The problem thus is not one of principle. It is one of finding an appropriate prescriptive degree. The question thus arises as to how far minimal standards or harmonization may reach in this field. How far should WTO law go?

While law is a universal concept, it performs significantly different functions in different cultures and societies. Its relationship to other forms and levels of human interaction varies. The role of law increases in individualistic, libertarian societies; it is less prominent/important/prevalent in consensual traditional ones, where customs and tradition exert important stabilizing and regulatory functions. Moreover, approaches to law vary, even within the family of Roman law, let alone with other cultures. All this argues, on the one hand, in favor of traditional reluctance of general international law, in accordance with national sovereignty and self-determination.[31]

On the other hand: *the law follows the merchant.* Trade links build common perceptions and rules. Coordination and harmonization become beneficial and even a necessity. Trading communities and the legal profession do not have difficulties with this and work well globally on the basis of common rules. The *lex mercatoria*, assisting transnational business transactions, has existed for centuries. The same is true for States as a whole. Intervention as such no longer is an argument per se. In a globalizing world of mutual responsibilities, a state cannot claim fully to participate in international relations and the international economy without accepting fundamental rules of the game and predictability. Once it opts for participation in the multilateral system, it accepts that domestic affairs are no longer purely matters of the state alone. People abroad depend on their stability and predictability.

In conclusion, it cannot be a matter of simply adopting and extending a single dominant legal system, and making it global. This is neither compatible with pluralism, nor efficient. Law and culture go hand in hand, and concepts incompatible with a civilization will not work, but will remain without effectiveness. Principles of Good Governance should not be perceived as involving one to one implementation or of involving automatic reproduction of rules predominant in particular industrialized countries and constitutions.[32] Rather, the concept requires appropriate and contextual specification. The level of intrusiveness needs to be assessed in context with Global Governance and its different approaches, ranging from supranational monitoring to inter-governmental networking.

It is submitted that the precise level of detail contained in the Universal Bill of Rights (comprising the Universal Declaration and the two Covenants) poses fundamental problems in this regard. Instead of focusing on core and essential rights suitable to be applied as elements of Good Governance, it translates rights pertaining to developed countries, in particular to the United States and the European Union. While the level of commitment of the United States to international instruments is low, political and civil rights essentially reflect the U.S. Bill of Rights. The same holds true for Europe which, in addition, adheres to the tradition of extensive catalogues of social, cultural and economic rights. As an alternative, we need to search for those elements in law which, over decades and centuries, have proven to be essential companions to human nature and therefore truly common. General and universal principles of law, such as the protection of legitimate expectations, non-retroactivity, proportionality, and due process of law, have been essential components of good and successful government throughout history. We are thus faced with the problem of identifying essential and core standards of Good Governance in the field of economic relations. This is true for conditionality. It is equally true, and even more so, in WTO law, as these standards are binding per se. They cannot be flexibly imposed and withdrawn in a process of trial and error within a lending policy program.

C. Conditionality v. Rule Based Governance in WTO Law

While Good Governance relates to an institutional lending policy, loosely anchored in some, but not all, of the human rights of the Universal Bill of Rights and the rule of law, WTO requirements relating to Good Governance, instead, are detailed, precise and justifiable rules of treaty law. They constitute legal obligations, and are not merely an emanation of an institutional policy. Compliance is assessed by means of suasion (Trade Policy Review Mechanism) or dispute settlement. Implementation may result in suspension of tariff concessions, but it is far from being linked to financial contributions from a donor and lending institution.

Moreover, the rules of the WTO, being treaty rules, apply to all Member States alike. There is no limitation to LDCs in practical terms. It is important to note that many cases arising under the TRIPs Agreement involving issues relating to Good Governance and the rule of law relate to national regulations of industrialized countries, or raise issues within developing countries under the doctrine of consistent interpretation of national or regional law with WTO law.

The traditions of WTO law offer the opportunity of a rule-based doctrine and set of requirements of Good Governance. Unlike conditionality, this implies enhanced transparency, and predictability. It allows for a step by step approach. It corresponds to the rule of law itself. It forms a sound basis within Global Governance.

V. How Far Could WTO Law Go in Support of Good Governance?

In examining the relationship of trade, the rule of law and human rights, the question arises to what extent WTO law should further expand in encompassing additional elements of Good Governance. Formally linking these standards to trade regulation means that implementation of these standards will be made subject to international monitoring, dispute settlement and enforcement by means of withdrawal of market access rights.

A. Enhancing the Rule of Law

A number of suggestions can be made which clearly relate to the rule of law in trade regulation, and further improve domestic institutions and structures essential for an open multilateral trading system.

The following suggestions could be discussed:

- Enhanced rights of Member States to comment on draft legislation of other Members as a tool of dispute prevention (building upon the TBT Agreement).

- More precise rules on publication and transparency regarding national laws and precedents in WTO matters; central publication activities by WTO (online services).
- Commitments to dedicate adequate resources to the judiciary (non-existent today, cf. Art. IX GATT, Art. VI (2)(b) GATS, Art. 41(5) TRIPs).
- Clarification and progress of the impact of WTO law in domestic jurisdictions (issues of consistent interpretation, direct effect and implementation of dispute settlement decisions). This is a major structural issue relating to the role of courts in international trade relations.
- Appropriate extension of civil and administrative enforcement rules of the TRIPs Agreement to other trade-related areas (border controls unrelated to IPRs, tariff quota licensing, subsidies, services, competition).
- General rules on government procurement within GATT and GATS, based upon MFN and non-discrimination.

B. Potential Trade-Related Human Rights Standards

While the proposals above remain within the traditional precepts of WTO law, it is much more difficult to assess to what extent WTO law should encompass proper human rights standards as a means to promote Good Governance in the field of trade – and perhaps beyond. We are faced with the question to what extent human rights concerns should be made part of WTO law. What are the pertinent criteria for doing so? Is it possible to foster goals of Good Governance, in particular rights of individuals relating to dignity and respect, to participation and democracy by means of WTO law? How would the incentives need to be shaped? It is submitted that trade-related rights may be identified and distinguished from the general body of Human Rights guarantees.

Given the structure of the rule-based WTO system, it is submitted that standards should be seriously considered within Good Governance that respond and correspond to market access and equal conditions of competition on markets. There is a potential group of rights or principles that are directly related to the proper and transparent functioning of trade and economic relations. The following may be discussed and explored as potential trade-related human rights under Good Governance beyond the precepts of the rule of law discussed above:

- Protection of moral rights in copyright law as expression of artistic freedom and artistic production closely related to personality and dignity (cf. Art. 9 TRIPs, denying application of Art. 6bis Berne Convention, cf. Article 27:2 Universal Declaration of Human Rights).

- Freedom of information, and access to trade-related information, as an institution and structure to provide transparency of markets and redress asymmetries of information. The problem should be studied taking into account problems of access to information technology. Would this be limited to economically relevant information and necessarily extend to information in general? If not, where to draw the line?
- Freedom of expression, for similar reasons. Moreover, is freedom of expression and freedom of the press (and media in general) a necessary ingredient for stable and predictable markets? How to assess the relationship of trade and political stability and change? Should the freedom expressly relate to economic/political affairs? Where to draw the line?
- Freedom of coalition and assembly, as an important ingredient in bringing about distributional justice among factors of production. Should this be general or limited to trade union rights?
- The right to political participation: To what extent should political institutions be taken into account as essential ingredients in ensuring legitimacy of domestic trade policy and in bringing about equitable distribution through the power of the ballot? To what extent are political rights essential to providing viable safety nets, which provide essential safeguards for an open economy?
- Protection of sexual non-discrimination. To what extent is enhanced protection, in particular of women, an important ingredient in the achievement of the goals of full employment and welfare?
- Protection of real property as an important ingredient for the protection of foreign investment, but also in order to secure ownership of goods and services. Are property rights a condition for decentralized production and markets? The link to competition policies and the prevention of monopoly and oligopoly should be discussed.
- Protection of essential welfare rights (health, food, shelter, primary education). This is likely to be a most controversial point as trade regulation has been based upon comparative advantage and economic efficiency. Yet, is there a long-term shared interest in ensuring fair distribution and the provision of a safety net that, in return, has been an implied condition in industrialized nations to engage in long-term and profound trade liberalization since the end of World War II? How much social welfare is required as a global minimum standard?

The linkage with trade-related human rights poses a number of interesting legal questions. Would this change the legal nature of WTO rules and lead to entitlement of individual operators or not? Would these standards operate as objective standards in order to assess conduct and performance of a Member State, or would they entail new entitlements? How would this affect standing? The matter will depend on institutional and procedural arrangements and cannot be answered in the abstract. The introduction of human rights standards does, as little as rule of law related standards, imply standing by individuals.

Two questions arise as to the legal functions of such elements of Good Governance.

- *Authority*: Should the WTO allow, and under what conditions, Member States to take into account such criteria in shaping their foreign trade relations, in particular in shaping preferential relations? How should such conditions be addressed and framed? The multilateral trading system may have an interest in allowing for human rights policies. It, however, has a similar interest in containing them and preventing abuse for protectionist purposes.
- *Obligations*: Should WTO law, and to what extent, encapsulate such rights and make them subject to positive obligations of Member States, and thus subject to monitoring (Trade Policy Review) and dispute settlement, where such rights are of a justiciable nature?

These points for discussion look almost utopian, certainly today. It is evident that any proposition to enhance even tailor-made (and contained) human rights standards will be opposed and discarded on grounds of massive intrusiveness and denial of self-determination of sovereign States and loss of comparative advantage. Politically, it would also be considered at odds with the traditions of *realpolitik* and would arguably lead to further politicization of trade policy, even if a functional angle to trade policy could be established.

Yet, we need to be aware that the linkage involves issues of long-term legitimacy of the trading system, and the global economic governance at large. A multilateral trading system completely blind to human rights issues will be subject to considerable criticism. As an operational matter, we recall that these linkages within WTO law cannot be unilaterally imposed or practiced by way of conditionality, unlike under the current Bretton Woods Agreements, based upon broad precepts of the Universal Bill of Rights and open textured authority. Instead, these rights and obligations are subject to negotiations in WTO law. A specific catalogue of trade-related human rights could emerge. These rights will be carefully carved out. They are part of the bargaining process. They not only serve as the basis of obligations, but also serve as containment against unilateral action under unilateral human rights policies. They will bind all Parties alike and will not be directed to a certain group of States. They may gradually progress as experience and global integration progresses over a long period of time. The approach is quite different from the Universal Bill of Rights: it is incremental and builds over time in a climate of changing attitudes to Global Governance and the role of multilateral institutions. With such a perspective, it is worthwhile discussing them in light of reflections on Global Governance that take the matter beyond disciplines and limitations of the nation State.

C. Linkage with *Jus Cogens* Rights

A different and more far-reaching approach involves the establishment of a general linkage between trade and human rights. The lack of a specific functional relationship renders trade to becoming an instrument of enforcing human rights per se abroad. At this point, a far-reaching linkage could be established. It would be necessary to demonstrate legitimate goals of enforcing such rights by means of trade sanctions under Good and Global Governance. It is at this stage that the impact of peremptory norms (*jus cogens*) should be studied. Beyond that, and given the massive political implications, it is doubtful whether a proper linkage can be established within the trading system. This would need to be left to political sanctions taken under the Charter of the United Nations peace-keeping efforts.

VI. The Linkage to Global Governance

A. The Responsibility of Global Governance

Good Governance is an important part of Global Governance. It encompasses conditions and requirements that States and their legal systems have to meet in order to participate fully in international relations and benefit from advantages the multilateral economic order may offer. These conditions essentially form part of an overall constitutional system of Global Governance. They essentially provide checks and balances monitored and supported by other governments and multilateral institutions.

Global Governance, however, cannot be limited to prescribing standards of Good Governance to national or regional entities. Global Governance is not limited to prescribing fundamental boundaries. It also needs to provide for entitlements and to support countries in their efforts to bring about stable and prosperous conditions of life. Global Governance is also about the responsibility to render policies of Good Governance possible and successful. It has to create the necessary conditions and assistance to this effect.

These responsibilities belong to the international system and international law at large, and to States and other actors. We need to ask what are optimal framework conditions in international law and the multilateral trading system in support of the rule of law and respect for human rights in Member States. How do we have to shape Global Governance structures in support of Good Governance in different countries? Three issues arise: capacity building, decision-making and participation, and finally, trade policy at large.

B. Capacity Building

The WTO, unlike the financial institutions, only runs, in its present form and size, minimal programs of technical assistance and public investment in transfer of knowledge and technology. Enhancing the rule of law and selective trade-related elements of human rights will primarily require support and assistance in building the necessary and underlying institutions. It necessarily entails major capacity building operations. Enforcement of the rule of law and human rights standards adopted by means of dispute settlement and withdrawal of benefits needs to remain a matter of last resort.

Governments and taxpayers will question why efforts at capacity building abroad need to be substantially increased. The advantages for recipient countries are evident. The advantages for donor countries are less obvious, but are of equal importance in the long run. Governments able to comply with human rights standards are likely able to provide stable political institutions and conditions. They are able to provide basic welfare that allows for open markets in return. They are, in short, able to enhance social and state institutions upon which successful and flourishing trade relations ultimately depend.

It will therefore be necessary to study how funding for capacity building relating to the rule of law and trade-related human rights can be enhanced by the WTO. It could, for example, be part of Global Governance to think about using part of tariff and tax revenues created by international trade for such purposes. Capacity building should develop as a main third leg of the WTO, in addition to the core functions of trade negotiations, monitoring and dispute settlement. It should reach out into the regions and operate from regional offices well acquainted with the problems and needs of the respective countries and economies.

C. Rule of Law and Participation

It follows from what was said above that human rights-related policies must themselves find appropriate legal foundations and be subject to monitoring and judicial review, just as much as rule of law-related obligations in WTO are today. Mere policies of conditionality, based upon broad powers of engagement, paradoxically do not satisfy the conditions that Good Governance seeks to impose upon recipient countries. Instead, human rights policies need to be more firmly and solidly established in law. This is certainly true for the WTO. The Universal Bill of Rights cannot absorb this function. While States are obliged under these instruments, this does not mean that international institutions and others may act without specific authority in international law. It is necessary to define the rules of engagement in a way that ensures that they are predictable. They need to encourage and contain human rights policies both at the same time. It would seem necessary to negotiate additional international instruments that seek to define principles of Good Governance more precisely.

In doing so, it is important to adhere to principles of transparency and accountability in operating principles of Good Governance and other policies in international organizations and diplomacy. Global Governance includes participatory processes and accountability. It is here that participatory claims voiced by civil society need to be taken into account and made part, in a meaningful manner, of the overall process of Global Governance. The linkage of Governance, trade and human rights is inherently related to efforts at bringing about transparent Global Governance. The international system can only ask States and Governments to honor what itself is able and willing to comply with in terms of the rule of law and relevant human rights standards.

In the field of trade, the WTO offers an opportunity to negotiate trade related elements of the rule of law and human rights in a pragmatic process, and in a step by step manner. It is not the tradition of GATT and WTO to enact a Bill of Economic Rights and Obligations. As discussed, it will be a matter of incrementally finding the way forward over a longer period of time, in a process of trial and error, and of gradually building confidence. The same is true for establishing human rights linkages in national or regional autonomous trade instruments or regional agreements. All of this forms part of the constitutional process that defines mutual responsibilities.

Alternatively, and beyond this eclectic approach, is it possible to seek the elaboration of a general instrument of Good Governance in order to provide guidance to multilateral institutions and governments? Discussions beyond incremental changes would assist in triggering a debate on fundamental values of Good Governance and Global Governance. This debate may result in non-binding instruments and recommendations. Part of it may, or may not be implemented, incrementally in specialized organizations, such as the WTO. Part of it may be used as guidelines for conditionalities. Such an instrument could be negotiated between governments. It could be elaborated by civil society or academic institutions and offered/presented for discussion.

D. Trade Policy: Beyond Governance

Finally, optimal framework conditions beneficial to the implementation of Good Governance and human rights need to be studied and, in particular, the implication of trade rules and trade policy needs to be considered in this context. We are, at this stage, facing the large question: what trade rules and trade policies are best suited to assisting and promoting policies of Good Governance? What rules are best served also to promote welfare goals under human rights standards? At this point, the discussion enters substantive matters of trade policy and the broader context of the relationship of human rights and trade. This dimension transcends/goes beyond the scope of governance properly speaking. It requires detailed analysis of the legal and economic impact of different trade policy rules. The problem of interpreting trade rules and the question to what extent human rights should be taken into account in doing so arises in this context of Global Governance. It is submitted that we cannot define policies and obligations of Good Governance without examining the requirements pertaining to Global Governance in relation to international institutions and in international relations. The problem has to be worked at from both ends.

NOTES

1. Thomas W. Wälde and James L. Grunderson, Legislative Reform in Transition Economies: Western Transplants: A Short-cut to Social Market Economy Status, in: Ann Seidman, Robert B. Seidman and Thomas Wälde (eds.) Making Development Work: Legislative Reform for Institutional Transformation and Good Governance, at 79, Kluwer Law International London, 1999. The authors argue that the effectiveness of law is usually intimately linked to the institutional setup of government and economic organizations as well as the shape, force and focus of social and economic forces and their interaction. In the same book, Cheryl W. Gray argues that [a] second necessary (but still insufficient) step toward development of well-functioning legal system in a market economy is establishing a broad set of supporting institutions. Well designed laws may lie dormant without institutional support, id, at 65.

2. Cf. Thomas Cottier, Trade and Human Rights: A Relationship to Discover, in: Journal of International Economic Law, at 111-132, 5 (1) (2002).

3. See, e.g., Grainne de Burca, Fundamental Human Rights and the Reach of EC Law, in: Paul/de Burca, EC Law, Texts, Cases Materials, at 331 Oxford University Press, Oxford 1995; Maya Hertig, L'influence de l'adhésion à l'Union européenne sur la protection des droits fondementaux en Suisse, in: Thomas Cottier & Alwin Kopse (eds.), L'Adhésion de la Suisse à l'Union Européenne: Enjeux et Consequences Schulthess Zurich, at 349, Zurich 1998; P.J.G. Kapteyn & P. Verloren van

Themaat, L.W. Gormeley, Introduction to the Law of the European Communities, 3rd ed., at 282, Kluwer Law International, the Hague, 1998.

4. See the paper by Joel Trachtman in this volume.

5. Art. XX(e), Art. XXI(c) GATT, Art. XIV bis (1)(c) GATS.

6. World Bank, Sub-Saharan Africa- From Crisis to Sustainable Growth, A Long Term Perspective Study (first published in 1989).

7. For instance, International Monetary Fund, Good Governance: The IMF's Role, Washington DC, 1997; The United Nations Development Programme, Human Development Report, New York, 1993; OECD, Participatory Development and Good Governance, Paris, 1995.

8. See World Bank, Sub-Saharan Africa: From Crisis to Sustainable Growth, at 60, Washington DC, 1989; World Bank, Governance and Development, Washington, 1992; World Bank, Governance: The World Bank's Experience, Washington, 1994; World Bank, World Development Report: The State in a Changing World, Oxford 1997; United nations development programme, Governance Policy Paper (last modified in Jan. 1997) http://magnet.undp.org/policy/; IMF, Good Governance: The IMF's Role (last modified on July 2, 1997.) http://www.imf.org/external/pubs/ft/exrp/govern/govindex.htm; International Monetary Fund: Code of Good Practices on Fiscal Transparency – Declaration of Principles, April 16,1998, 37 I.L.M. 942, 942 (1998*);* UNDP: Governance for Sustainable Human Development, UNDP policy document. United Nations Development Programme, 1997; Asian Development Bank, Governance and Infrastructure Development, 1997; African Development Bank, Governance and Development in Africa: Issues and the Role of the African Development Bank and Other Multilateral Organizations, 1993; OECD, Promoting Good Governance workshop, http://www.oecd.org//puma/gvrnance/emef/governance.htm; The European Union also resolved in 1991 to condition its development relationships with poor countries on good governance, Resolution of the Council and of the Member States Meeting in the Council on Human Rights, Democracy and Development in: Bull. EC 11-1991.

9. The World Bank, Governance and Human Rights, at 43, Washington, 1995.

10. Id., at 47.

11. OECD/DAC, Final Report of the Ad Hoc Working Group on Participatory Development and Good Governance (part 1), at 6, OECD Paris 1997, see http://www.oecd.org/dataoecd/44/12/1894642.pdf.

12. See The World Bank, World Development Report, at 41, Oxford, 1997.

13. OECD, Emerging Market Economy Forum Workshop on Public Management in Support of Social and Economic Objectives (http://www.oecd.org//puma/gvrnance/emef/governance.htm).

14. Cf. Ibrahim F.I. Shihata, The World Bank in a Changing World (Selected Essays) Vol. 1 at 85, Martinus Nijhoff Publishers 1991. Shihata defined the rule of law, for the purpose of the World Bank's work on governance issue as: a system which assumes that (a) there is a set of rules which are known in advance; (b) such rules are actually in force; (c) mechanisms exist to ensure the prop-

er application of the rules and to allow for departure from them as needed according to established procedures; (d) conflicts in the application of rules can be resolved through binding decision of an independent judicial or arbitral body; (e) there are known procedures for amending the rules when they no longer serve their purpose.

15. Ibrahim F.I. Shihata, The World Bank in a Changing World (Selected Essays) Vol. 1 at 53, Martinus Nijhoff Publishers 1991.

16. For instance, NEDA (the Netherlands Development Assistance, formerly DGIS) sees good governance as a transparent and responsible application of authority or government in dialogue with the population. Moreover, NEDA distinguishes four basic criteria of good governance: participatory governance; transparent governance; legitimate governance (tasks and responsibilities clearly defined), separation of powers (jurisdiction, government), ruling by the will of population; and effective governance. See Cecilia Kinuthia-Njenga, Good Governance: Common Definitions, at www.unchs.org/english/hdv5n4/intro2.htm.

17. Thomas Cottier, Emerging Doctrines of Good Governance: the Impact of the WTO and China's Accession, in: (F.M. Abbott ed.) China in the World Trading System: Defining the Principles of Engagement, at 120, Kluwer Law International, Boston, 1998.

18. See Francis N. Botchway, Good Governance: The Old, the New, the Principle and the Elements, 13 Fla. J. Int'l. L 159, 175 (2001), referring to Thomas Frank, The New Development: Can American Law and Legal Institutions Help Developing Countries? Wis. L. Rev 767 (1972).

19. Thomas Frank discusses the implications of an emerging international right to democracy, discursive and elective rights of the individual and peoples under the heading of "Fairness in empowerment of Persons and Peoples", Fairness in International Law and Institutions, at 83, Clarendon: Oxford 1995.

20. See Thomas Cottier, supra note 17, at 120.

21. James Thuo Gathii, Good Governance as a Counter Insurgency Agenda to Oppositional and Transformative Social Projects in International Law, in: 5 Buff. Hum. Rts. L. Rev.,107, 174 (1999).

22. Universal Declaration of Human Rights adopted 10 Dec. 1948. G.A. Res. 217A (III) U.N. GAOR, 3rd Sess. U.N.Doc. A/810 (1948).

23. International Covenant on Civil and Political Rights, adopted 16 Dec. 1966, G.A. Res. 2200(XXI), U.N. GOAR 21st Sess., U.N: Doc. A/6316 (1966), 999 U.N.T.S.171.

24. International Covenant on Economic, Social and Cultural Rights, adopted Dec.16, 1966, G.A. Res.220 (XXI), U.N. GAOR, 21st Sess. U.N. Doc. A/6316 (1966) 993 U.N.T.S.3.

25. Antony Anghie, Civilization and Commerce: the Concept of Governance in Historical Perspective, 45 Vill. L. Rev. 887, 911 (2000).

26. See James Thuo Gathii, supra note 21, at 122.

27. Antony Anghie, Universality and the Concept of Governance in International Law, in: E.K. Quashigah and O.C. Okafor (eds.), Legitimate Governance in Africa, at 22, Kluwer Law International, Netherlands, 1999.

28. Thomas Cottier, Emerging Doctrines of Good Governance: the Impact of the WTO and China's Accession, in Frederick M. Abbott (ed.), China in the World Trading System: Defining the Principles of Engagement, at 124, Kluwer Law International, Boston, 1998.

29. id., at 125.

30. id., at 125.

31. id., at 124.

32. id., at 125.

Part II

The Intersection of the International Trade Regime and International Human Rights Law: Institutional and Procedural Aspects

CHAPTER 6

Safeguarding the Legitimacy of the Multilateral Trading System: The Role of Human Rights Law

Caroline Dommen

Introduction

The international human rights regime and the international trade regime were both created soon after the Second World War, with the shared aims of contributing to a better world through institutions for international cooperation. However, the aims of the two regimes appear to have diverged, and a growing number of voices criticize the World Trade Organization (WTO) as it increasingly appears to be seeking to maximize trade rather than to raise living standards in its Member States.

This paper argues that the norms contained in the International Covenant on Economic, Social and Cultural Rights (ICESCR) can go a long way to ensuring that the original objectives of the international trade system are met. Many developing countries and a range of civil society groups, including human rights professionals, have in recent years been increasingly vocal in complaining that the WTO seems to be promoting the private interests of the economically powerful, rather than the public interest. These criticisms are undermining the credibility and perception of legitimacy of the WTO. This paper describes how the ICESCR can be a useful tool to respond to the concerns of developing countries and of civil society, and thus safeguard the WTO's legitimacy as the guarantor of an international trade system designed to promote living standards around the world.

Shared Aims of the International Trade and Human Rights Regimes

The General Agreement on Tariffs and Trade (GATT, the WTO's predecessor) was created at the same time as the United Nations human rights regime, and with much the same aims: to set up a multilateral, institutional framework within which States could cooperate to ensure protection of human rights, and to promote the expansion of trade in order to raise standards of living, ensure full employment and increase incomes around the world. The lack of international institutions was considered to have been an important factor in the degradation of many countries' economic and social situations that caused huge suffering in the 1930s and ultimately led to the outbreak of war. The creation of international institutions for cooperation on economic, social and financial policy was therefore a priority for the builders of the post-Second World War international order.[1]

Now, half a century after their foundations were laid, the UN's human rights regime and the international trade regime have extended in reach, and become ever more sophisticated, complex and important. Since the adoption of the Universal Declaration of Human Rights in 1948, the rules and mechanisms for the promotion and protection of human rights have evolved significantly. Today the UN human rights regime consists of six core treaties and dozens of other instruments and procedures for implementing human rights and holding States and other actors accountable to human rights standards.[2] The underlying aim of the international human rights regime is to shape policy in such a way that it benefits the powerless and takes into account the needs of the often voiceless, most disadvantaged sectors of society. Despite criticisms that the UN human rights system is slow and cumbersome, under-resourced and over-politicised, or inefficient and incomplete, it is undisputed that it has moved towards its objective of helping to protect the rights of the most disadvantaged around the world, and should be supported as it continues to develop ways of fulfilling its goals.

The international trade regime has also greatly expanded since its creation with the adoption of the General Agreement on Tariffs and Trade (GATT) in 1947. At its inception, GATT focussed almost exclusively on trade tariffs. Now the regime consists of wide-reaching rules that govern an increasing range of policy issues, including in areas traditionally solely under domestic policy such as health and safety standards, agriculture, banking, intellectual property and telecommunications. The World Trade Organization (WTO), GATT's successor, came into being in 1995 as the outcome of the Uruguay Round of multilateral trade negotiations, and includes a strong, binding dispute settlement system. GATT's preamble sets out the objectives of international trade relations as being to "rais[e] standards of living, ensur[e] full employment and a large and steadily growing volume of real income." The Agreement Establishing the WTO reiterates these objectives and expands them by acknowledging the particular needs of developing countries, and specifying that trade and economic relations should be conducted in accordance with the objective of sustainable development.[3]

The term "sustainable development" was given common currency by the Brundtland Report, in 1987.[4] Sustainable development is most commonly defined as development that meets the needs of the present without compromising the ability of future generations to meet their own needs. It contains within it two key concepts: the concept of "needs," in particular the essential needs of the world's poor, to which overriding priority should be given, and the idea of limitations imposed by the state of technology and social organization on the environment's ability to meet present and future needs.[5]

By referring to sustainable development, the WTO contains an explicit acknowledgement of the need to give priority to the poor, as well as to improve standards of living. The international human rights regime implicitly aims to benefit the weakest: in this respect the overall objectives of the two regimes point in the same direction. This indicates that there is no inherent incompatibility between WTO objectives and human rights principles, and strongly suggests that it is possible to find a way of developing trade rules to ensure that trade and economic policy are consistent with human rights.

This paper considers the UN's mechanisms for implementing economic, social and cultural rights. It focuses on the International Covenant on Economic, Social and Cultural Rights and explores how and why a human rights approach can be useful in responding to some of the current criticisms and fears regarding the multilateral trading system. In other words, this paper seeks to reply to the question: what can human rights do for the multilateral trading system.[6]

Economic, social and cultural rights – what the International Covenant requires

Within the international human rights legal regime there are a number of instruments that contain requirements for respecting economic, social and cultural rights. These include the Universal Declaration of Human Rights, the Convention on the Rights of the Child and the Convention on the Elimination of All Forms of Discrimination Against Women. However, as the sole instrument that focuses specifically on economic, social and cultural rights (ESCR) worldwide the International Covenant on Economic, Social and Cultural Rights (ICESCR, or Covenant) remains the foundation on which ESCR provisions in other instruments are built.[7] The ICESCR, which is legally binding on 145 States,[8] sets out a number of rights including the right to food, the right to social security, the right to the highest attainable standard of health and the right to education.

The centrepiece of international efforts to promote economic, social and cultural rights is the Committee on Economic, Social and Cultural Rights (Committee), a body of 18 independent experts charged with monitoring implementation of the ICESCR. The Committee's task is mainly discharged through examining the reports that each State party is bound to submit periodically (every 5 years), on progress made and difficulties encountered in implementing the Covenant. The Committee has the legal mandate to cooperate both with the States parties to the Covenant and with the various bodies and specialized agencies of the United Nations concerned with economic, social and cultural rights. Although it is the leading international body with responsibility for economic, social and cultural rights, the Committee's work is complemented by that of other institutions and offices in the UN Human Rights system that study Economic, Social and Cultural Rights and monitor their implementation.[9]

Importantly, the Committee has focussed on clarifying and giving substance to the legal content of the ICESCR's obligations, mainly through "General Comments."[10] This has proved vital given that the imprecise formulation of many of ICESCR's provisions has led to the assertion by some critics that it contains only vague aspirations.

Whilst the ICESCR does not require States to provide food, education, or perfect health to all their citizens directly on ratification, it does impose two important immediate obligations on all States parties. First, they may not discriminate in realization of the Covenant's rights,[11] and second – and most important for our discussions here – the ICESCR requires that each State party "take steps individually and through international assistance and co-operation (...) to the maximum of its available resources" with a view to "achieving progressively" the realization of the rights in the Covenant.[12]

The provision that a State party take steps "to the maximum of its available resources" is noteworthy in that it imposes an obligation on all States parties to take measures towards realization of the rights in the Covenant, regardless of their economic means. Thus the Covenant requires States parties to move as expeditiously and effectively as possible towards full realization of ESCR rights, and implicitly contains the duty on States parties to avoid backward movement (retrogression) from realization of those rights.[13]

Importantly, the requirement that a State party takes steps "to the maximum of its available resources" points to an obligation on each State party, or even on the international community, to assist in the realization of rights in other States parties. The Committee on Economic, Social and Cultural Rights has emphasised that the requirement to take steps "to the maximum of available resources" refers both to the resources available within a State and those available through international co-operation and assistance.[14]

Challenges to the WTO's legitimacy, and a human rights response

It is widely agreed that, in accordance with the preambles of GATT and the WTO, the purpose of the multilateral trade regime is to raise living standards all around the world, rather than to maximize trade *per se*. Yet the two goals of promoting development and maximizing trade have come to be increasingly viewed as synonymous by the WTO and other advocates of trade liberalization.[15] The multilateral framework governing trade is now being subjected to increased criticism by a range of people, including human rights professionals and activists, for being seen to have left its public interest objective behind as it promotes the private interests of those who seek to maximize trade as the overarching goal.

The WTO's image and the perception of its legitimacy is tarnished by criticisms from two main sources: (1) *developing countries*, who feel that it serves the interest of the more powerful economies, and who say that they are still waiting to reap the benefits they were promised in exchange for the concessions they made during the Uruguay Round, and (2) large sectors of the *public* that perceive the WTO as a powerful and uncaring organization that operates behind closed doors to serve the interests of the economically powerful, to the detriment of public interest goals such as protection of the environment, public health and human rights.

Expressions of dissatisfaction from both these sources were most clearly evident in Seattle in late 1999, during the WTO's Third Ministerial Conference. In Seattle, developing countries expressed their displeasure by walking out of the conference room, while a variety of public interest groups expressed their disapproval and anger on the streets. Both developing countries and public groups have continued to express criticism of the WTO's rules and workings in various ways since then.

This paper will set out some ways in which human rights law can be applied to respond to both these sources of dissatisfaction, and contribute to preserving a fair, balanced multilateral trading system.

1. The dissatisfaction of developing countries.

This is perhaps the most serious for the maintenance of a multilateral trading system, as it caused the breakdown of the WTO's Ministerial Conference of 1999, and as the dissatisfaction comes from the WTO's Members themselves, including powerful States such as India, Pakistan and Egypt. Developing countries complain that the international trading system embodied in the WTO contains imbalances in their disfavour. In particular, developing countries have for the past few years been demanding the full implementation of those parts of the WTO Agreement which would be to their benefit.

The Committee on Economic, Social and Cultural Rights has on several occasions reiterated its concern about the extent to which international economic policies and practices affect the ability of States to fulfil their obligations under the ICESCR. Likewise, developing countries have raised their voices within the WTO to lament that WTO rules may limit their latitude to adopt policies that really benefit their countries.

One area that has pitted developing against industrialised countries in the WTO has caught public attention, namely the effect of the WTO's Agreement on Trade-related Aspects of Intellectual Property (TRIPs) on access to medicine. The TRIPs Agreement contains public interest provisions,[16] but in spite of this, many developing countries have come under pressure from private companies or from industrialised countries (most often the US), to implement "TRIPs-plus" obligations. "TRIPs-plus" means accepting obligations that are more stringent than what TRIPs requires, and often involve abandoning the flexibility that TRIPs allows in order to enable countries to ensure that intellectual property legislation promotes social and economic welfare or public health.

Two cases relating to production of affordable medication for people with HIV/AIDS focused the spotlight on this issue in the first half of 2001. In one case, a coalition of pharmaceutical manufacturers (South African Pharmaceutical Manufacturers Association – PMA) brought a legal challenge to the South African courts, contesting a South African law that was to allow the government to import or manufacture cheaper versions of patented AIDS drugs. The other case was brought by the US government to the WTO Dispute Settlement System mechanism. The US claimed that Brazil's Industrial Property Law, under which Brazilian companies would be allowed to produce patented anti-AIDS medicines if the patent-holders did not reduce their prices, violated the TRIPs Agreement. Both these cases were settled, in what was widely seen as a victory for developing countries and a public relations disaster for pharmaceutical companies who were accused of putting profit before the lives of millions of people who are unable to afford life-saving drugs.

The public outcry about pharmaceutical companies' perceived attempts to deprive people with HIV/AIDS of affordable medicines was the catalyst in influencing WTO Members to propose that a Declaration on TRIPs and public health be adopted at their Ministerial Conference, planned for Doha in November 2001.[17] Yet many human rights professionals were surprised that developing countries did not draw more heavily on human rights law in the WTO debate on TRIPs and access to medicines and the proposed declaration on this subject. In April 2001, Brazil did turn to the Commission on Human Rights where it spearheaded adoption of a resolution on access to medication in the context of pandemics such as HIV/AIDS.[18] Apart from this initiative, there were only a few discreet references to human rights in WTO debates on access to medicines, despite the fact that the majority of WTO Members (including most industrialised countries) have legal obligations under the ICESCR to realise the right to the highest attainable standard of health.

A move away from allowing production of generic drugs in cases of diseases that are as serious and widespread as HIV/AIDS is in some countries could well be considered a threat to the right to life. In addition, preventing the availability of affordable drugs constitutes retrogression in the realization of the right to the highest attainable standard of health. And this consideration becomes all the stronger when one recalls that the ICESCR imposes an obligation to devote the maximum of resources available both within a State and through international co-operation to realization of the right to health. Given the requirement of non-retrogression and international cooperation that the ICESCR imposes on its 145 States parties, it is all the more surprising that the WTO debate was framed in terms of public health policy rather than in the stronger terms of legally-binding obligations under international human rights instruments.

Members of the Committee on Economic, Social and Cultural Rights have often pointed out that developing countries could use the Covenant as a "shield" to ward off pressures to adopt economic policies that might interfere with their capacity to realise human rights. As well as using the Covenant as a "shield" in cases of legal challenges such as those involving South Africa and Brazil described above, the ICESCR could also be useful to promote the public interest and the interests of developing countries in other WTO negotiations currently underway.[19] In agriculture for instance, many developing countries are seeking to maintain the right to have "non-trade concerns" recognised, for instance to allow them to restrict imports or maintain subsidies to ensure food security, or to maintain rural employment. In this context, Mauritius has referred to the ICESCR as supporting its view that the WTO's Agreement on Agriculture should allow recognition of non-trade concerns.[20]

Another example of where human rights law would be relevant to ensuring that the WTO's rules promote the interests of developing countries is in the context of ongoing negotiations in the WTO on the scope of the TRIPs Agreement's Article 27.3(b). This Article concerns intellectual property protection of plant varieties and has implications *inter alia* for the right to food and indigenous rights.[21] Here too, human rights law could be used to further the arguments of those who would like the outcome of these negotiations to reflect the public interest, rather than the interests of the private patent-owners (or would-be patent owners) of new plant varieties.[22] There have been few references to human rights in either the WTO's agriculture or TRIPs negotiations. It is however worth noting that one of the few references was by the European Communities, who said that issues such as sustainable development, human development, human rights and sound economic policies may have a bearing on the legitimate exercise of intellectual property rights and should be carefully considered in the review of TRIPs Article 27.3(b).[23]

2. Public perceptions that the WTO favours the rich over the poor, favours private over public interests and rides roughshod over social objectives such as protection of the environment, health and human rights.[24]

For reasons of space, it will not be possible to embark here on a detailed analysis of how human rights norms and procedures can be applied to respond to these concerns. This section of this paper will therefore focus on a point made on the first day of the World Trade Forum, as to whether trade liberalization or the WTO do or can ensure equitable/fairer distribution of wealth.

On the first day of this World Trade Forum, one of the speakers said that stopping or limiting trade would not provide a solution when trade liberalization results in, or exacerbates, unequal distribution of wealth. His comment implied that he understands that we are in an either/or situation: either we promote trade liberalization or we promote respect for human rights. It would follow from his reasoning that respect for human rights is incompatible with trade liberalization. This paper has already referred to human rights law and to the objectives of the WTO to support the view that trade liberalization and trade itself can be carried out in such a way that is compatible with the promotion and protection of human rights. This section will focus on how application of human rights norms can ensure that trade policy does not discriminate in favour of the most economically powerful groups within a country.

As mentioned above, the International Covenant on Economic, Social and Cultural Rights requires that States do not discriminate in the implementation of the rights it sets out. We also saw that the international human rights system has as an objective the protection of the interests of the weak. Yet those who tend to have most influence on trade policy tend to be the economically strong. The most vulnerable or marginalized sectors of society, such as women, subsistence farmers in developing countries, or indigenous peoples often have little understanding or even knowledge of changes in the trade system and the implications of these changes on their lives, and thus their interests are often not considered when trade policy is formulated.

Like the GATT before it, the World Trade Organization has no mandate to intervene in the domestic, distributional questions relating to international trade. Nevertheless, the notion that trade should benefit all – rather than merely favour some powerful sectors of the population over others – was implicit at the time of GATT's creation, as GATT was seen as one part of the international cooperation system, which was also composed of the World Bank, the International Monetary Fund and the UN. GATT's role was to deal with trade, and it was assumed that the UN would deal with the social issues and human rights. Over time, the GATT has turned into the powerful WTO and whilst some seem to have forgotten the public interest objectives set out in their preambles, others overlook that international human rights law (developed to a large extent within the UN) is there to be appealed to in cases when the weak and vulnerable need protection from excesses in the exercise of power by the strong.

In short, in cases where the interests of a particular sector of a country's population are not taken into account by trade policy formulators and the resulting trade policy can be shown either to cause violation of one of the substantive rights of the ICESCR – such as the right to food or the right to health – or to constitute discrimination in the exercise of these rights, those discriminated against can turn to international human rights law. Indeed, human rights law is almost unique in allowing citizens to complain beyond their own State to international human rights bodies when their State's policy has resulted in a violation of their rights.

In this way, application of human rights law is clearly complementary to WTO law by being applied to ensure that a country's trade policy really serves the well-being of a country's inhabitants – or at least, to ensure that one particular group is not systematically discriminated against. Indeed, it is generally acknowledged that trade policy developed in a participatory, inclusive way not only promotes and strengthens democracy but also contributes to the formulation of better policy – policy that is more responsive to the needs of the people.

However, if citizens are to intervene or comment on their country's planned trade policy, they need to know what their country is proposing and preparing to accept in international fora such as the WTO. Access to information and the closed nature of the trade negotiations is an important concern of civil society groups in relation to international trade negotiations such as those that take place in the WTO, and many have been actively campaigning for more transparency in international trade negotiations.[25] These groups would find legal and moral support in Article 21 of the Universal Declaration of Human Rights and Article 25 of the International Covenant on Civil and Political Rights, which provide that citizens have the right and the opportunity to take part in the conduct of public affairs of their country.

Currently many of those working towards ensuring that the benefits of trade are fairly distributed at the domestic level, and respect social priorities such as protection of health, of the environment and human rights are turning to the WTO to make their concerns heard. They should not forget that turning to international human rights mechanisms could be very helpful in clarifying what the relevant legal obligations are, and how they should be implemented.

Concluding thoughts

When discussing the inter-relationship between human rights and trade today, it is essential to recall the assumptions behind the objectives set out in GATT's preamble: that full employment was a sign of a healthy, fully productive economy, that the benefits of a healthy economy could be exported – through importing goods produced in other countries and so contributing to full employment there – and that the purpose of economic growth was to provide what society needed. For better or for worse, the determination of what society needed was, at the time when GATT was negotiated, left to the State.[26]

International cooperation and the determining role of the State were both key elements underlying the post-war economic order. Yet today assumptions about these are very different from those present in the 1940s. Indeed, what will be produced or provided through international economic relations is now determined primarily according to supply and demand – i.e., according to market forces rather than by the State. And developing countries are fighting a constant struggle to ensure that the international trade regime serves their interests rather than just those of the more powerful States or corporations involved in international trade.

These altered assumptions represent a fundamental change – yet we have the same rules or at least the same key principles and wording in the WTO as in GATT. What is the value of this wording today? What are the practical implications of the legal obligation to cooperate internationally? Who should the international trade regime benefit? Can human rights standards help us as we interpret and develop the rules of this trade regime?

Participants in the World Trade Forum might disagree as to the answers to these questions, yet these are issues that must be discussed and considered as they are fundamental to clarifying our views as to whether there is indeed a fundamental underlying difference in objectives between today's international human rights and international trade regimes. Such clarification is necessary to help us chart our way forward on the human rights and trade debate.

NOTES

1. See Caroline Dommen, *Raising Human Rights Concerns in the World Trade Organization – Actors, Processes and Possible Strategies*, 24(1) HUMAN RIGHTS QUARTERLY (February 2002).

2. In addition to the UN human rights system, regional regimes exist in the Americas, in Africa and in Europe. See Hurst Hannum, GUIDE TO INTERNATIONAL HUMAN RIGHTS PRACTICE, 3rd edition, 1999 (Ardsley, New York: Transnational Publishers).

3. See Marrakesh Agreement Establishing the World Trade Organization, Preamble.

4. World Commission on Environment and Development, OUR COMMON FUTURE, Oxford University Press, 1987.

5. Op. cit., p. 43.

6. This question has been posed by Thomas Cottier in the background paper for this World Trade Forum, Trade and Human Rights: Preliminary Thoughts, 13-14 August, 2001.

7. The discussion in this paper focuses on the ICESCR, but it must be stressed that the provisions of other instruments apply, particularly those of the Convention on the Rights of the Child, which is binding on all but two of the States in the world.

8. As at early 2002. The number of States parties to the ICESCR is still just higher than the number of WTO Members (144 in early 2002). The list of States that have ratified the ICESCR is on the web at: www.unhchr.ch/pdf/report.pdf The list of WTO Members can be found on the web at: www.wto.org/english/thewto_e/whatis_e/tif_e/org6_e.htm

9. These include the Commission on Human Rights' Special Rapporteur on the right to adequate housing, the Special Rapporteur on the right to education, and the Special Rapporteur on the Right to Food.

10. General Comments are in a sense the "jurisprudence" of the Committee, prepared and adopted with a view inter alia to providing greater interpretative clarity as to the intent, meaning and content of the Covenant. See for instance, *General Comment No. 14 (2000), The Right to the highest attainable standard of health;* available on the web via: www.ohchr.org/english/bodies/cescr/comments.htm

11. Article 2 (2).

12. Article 2 (1).

13. See *General Comment No. 3 (1990), The Nature of States Parties' Obligations*

14. Id.

15. Dani Rodrik, *Global Governance of Trade as if Development Really Mattered*, background paper prepared by Dani Rodrik for the UNDP Trade and Sustainable Human Development Project, available at: http://ksghome.harvard.edu/~.drodrik.academic.ksg/UNDPtrade.PDF

16. TRIPs Article 7 for instance, specifies that the Agreement should be conducive to social and economic welfare, and Article 8 provides that governments can take public health, nutrition and other public interest concerns into account in formulating their intellectual property laws.

17. On 14 November 2001, at the Doha Ministerial Conference, WTO Members did adopt a Declaration on the TRIPs Agreement and Public Health. See www.wto.org/english/thewto_e/minist_e/min01_e/min01_e.htm

18. E/CN.4/RES/2001/33, 20 April 2001, available on the web via: www.unhchr.ch/html/menu2/2/57chr/resolutions.htm

19. See Caroline Dommen, *The Covenant on Economic, Social and Cultural Rights – A Treasure Chest to Support Developing Countries' Concerns in the WTO?*, in 5 BRIDGES BETWEEN TRADE AND SUSTAINABLE DEVELOPMENT, January-April 2001, available on the web via http://www.ictsd.org/monthly/archive.htm

20. WORLD TRADE ORGANIZATION, *FOURTH SPECIAL SESSION OF THE COMMITTEE ON AGRICULTURE – Statement by Mauritius*, G/AG/NG/W/75, 30 November 2000.

21. See Caroline Dommen, supra note 1.

22. See Caroline Dommen, supra note 19.

23. See WORLD TRADE ORGANIZATION, *REVIEW OF THE PROVISIONS OF ARTICLE 27.3(b) OF THE TRIPS AGREEMENT – Communication from the European Communities and their member States*, IP/C/W/254, 13 June 2001.

24. For more details on these criticisms, see Caroline Dommen, *Economic, Social and Cultural Rights and WTO Work on Intellectual Property – Current Processes and Opportunities (Background paper submitted to the Committee on Economic, Social and Cultural Rights)*, E/C.12/2002/20, 13 December 2000, available on the web via: www.unhchr.ch/tbs/doc.nsf

25. *WTO Discussions Narrow in on Transparency and Civil Society Relations*, 2 BRIDGES BETWEEN TRADE AND SUSTAINABLE DEVELOPMENT, July-August 1998.

26. This was the case in all the different political systems existing at the time the GATT was envisaged, whether in the US and the UK, in socialist Soviet Union or Nazi Germany.

CHAPTER 7

Functional Distinction or Bilingualism? Human Rights and Trade: The UN Human Rights System

Stefanie Grant[*]

A few months ago I was visited by the Geneva trade representative of a major developed country. He had heard that OHCHR was preparing a report on the WTO Agreement on Trade-Related Intellectual Property Rights (the TRIPS Agreement). He wanted to know why, and he expressed sheer incredulity that a trade agreement was any business of a UN human rights institution.

Even five years ago, few would have disagreed with him. But today the UN human rights institutions are increasingly addressing aspects of international trade, and embarking on the difficult task of identifying incompatibilities between international trade rules and international human rights principles. Treaty bodies – most frequently the Committee on Economic, Social and Cultural Rights ("CESCR") – are beginning to frame trade issues in the context of human rights treaty obligations. The Human Rights Commission ("the Commission") and the Sub Commission on the Protection and Promotion of Human Rights ("the Sub Commission") give increasing attention to social and economic issues. The High Commissioner for Human Rights addresses international economic and financial issues as part of her general mandate to "mainstream" human rights.

Why has this taken place? Since the Vienna Conference in 1993, implementation of social and economic rights has moved out of the shadows cast by the cold war, to be recognised as a priority and as an essential element in poverty reduction and conflict prevention. In parallel but separate processes, most states have now ratified the majority of human rights treaties and many have also become WTO members. All WTO members are now parties to one or more of the human rights treaties, with a concomitant legal obligation to respect the rights contained in them.

Human rights discussion on trade related issues takes as its starting point the recognition that for some people living in the developing world the removal of obstacles to trade and capital movements in the last decade has not resulted

* I acknowledge with appreciation the assistance of Simon Walker at all stages in the preparation of this paper.

in accelerated growth and income convergence with more advanced countries. The number of countries classified as LDCs has risen – to 49 – and for the citizens of those countries economic marginalisation has been accompanied by increased poverty and related denials of social and economic rights. It is in this broad context that states have begun to study the impact of the processes of globalisation – including WTO trade treaties – on the enjoyment of human rights.

At the same time there is a recognition that while international law places primary responsibility for implementing human rights on the state, the state's real power to regulate the activities of the private sector, and particularly of large international corporations, is often limited. Given the increasing role of transnational corporations, especially where national provision of basic services such as health, food provision, or education is privatised, the broad human rights obligations of non-state actors need to be clarified. In specific terms, there is concern that the patent provisions of the TRIPS Agreement impact negatively upon the equal access to health care and pharmaceuticals which is required by the right to health provisions of international human rights law.

There is also growing recognition of human rights violations which are carried out through illicit international trade, and facilitated by globalised commerce, travel and communication, such as abusive migration, trafficking, the sale of children, and transboundary dumping of toxic waste.

Human rights and trade issues

For all these reasons, the human rights system – led by the Sub Commission and the Committee on Economic, Social and Cultural Rights (CESCR) – has begun to examine trade, both as a discrete issue, and in its broader context as a core element of globalisation.

In a 1997 report to the Sub Commission, José Bengoa asked whether the human rights system should address economics, or whether these were two radically different spheres. He concluded that human rights, as a code of values juridically accepted at the international level, can legitimately signal the ethically acceptable or unacceptable limits of economic policy measures and economic functioning. The human rights system has the "legal obligation to observe the economic system and to signal the greater or lesser impact it is having in meeting the needs of individual human beings and on their enjoyment of essential civil, economic, social, political and cultural rights."[1]

Earlier, in 1993, another Sub Commission member – Danilo Turk – had expressed concern about the "privatization" of human rights. In a report on social and economic rights, he noted the "rush" to denationalize, leaving economics, politics and social matters to the "whims" of the private sector, including through removal of price controls and subsidies. He expressed concern that price determination by supply and demand and increasing liberalization of foreign trade and payments would inevitably have an impact upon the full realization of economic, social and cultural rights.[2]

The CESCR developed both these lines of approach in its statement to the Seattle WTO meeting,[3] and set the direction for later discussion.

It recognised the advantages of an international trading system as envisioned by the 1994 Marrakech Agreement establishing the WTO, with the objectives of higher standards of living, income growth, full employment and economic growth patterns compatible with sustainable development.

It noted that its own experience in monitoring compliance by states parties to the International Covenant on Economic, Social and Cultural Rights (the ICESCR) had made it "increasingly aware of the extent to which international economic policies and practices affect the ability of states to fulfill their treaty obligations."

It also noted that the "wave of economic and corporate restructurings undertaken to respond to an increasingly competitive global market and the widespread dismantling of social security systems have resulted in unemployment, work insecurity and worsening labor conditions giving rise to violations of core economic and social rights."

It recognised the wealth generating potential of trade liberalisation, but also that liberalisation in trade, investment and finance does not necessarily create and lead to a favourable environment for the realisation of economic, social and cultural rights: "The end which trade liberalisation should serve is the objective of human well being to which the international human rights instruments give expression."

It endorsed a call by the Sub Commission that human rights principles and obligations should be fully integrated in future WTO negotiations, and for a proper study to be undertaken of the "human rights and social impacts of economic liberalisation programs, policies and laws."

It urged the WTO to undertake a review of international trade policies and rules in order to ensure consistency with human rights law, including a review of the impact of WTO policies on the most vulnerable sectors of society.

Subsequent work has built on this initial identification of the interface between trade and human rights.

I will describe the UN human rights system in broad terms, showing its increasing involvement in the issue of trade, and its efforts to establish the link between human rights and the international trade regime, and suggest some of the challenges.

The UN human rights system

The UN human rights system has three elements – the Charter bodies (the Commission on Human Rights ["the Commission"], and the Sub-Commission), the treaty bodies, and the High Commissioner herself. Until recent initiatives in the Commission and Sub-Commission in relation to the TRIPS Agreement, and to access to pharmaceuticals in the context of HIV/AIDS, the Charter-based bodies had considered issues relating to trade only in the context of wider discussions of globalisation.

In 1999 the General Assembly underlined the need to analyse the consequences of globalisation for human rights. The Secretary General then set a framework for discussion, through a report in which he noted that "increased trade and investment has brought significant benefits to many nations and people," with strong evidence to suggest that both are related to higher rates of economic growth and productivity. But the report also noted that trade liberalisation can lead to widening disparities between and within nations, increase people's vulnerability to external economic variations and shocks and as a result put at risk the realisation of fundamental human rights. The report then identified issues and questions on which the views of states were to be sought.[4]

The Commission and the General Assembly also have before them the reports of Commission-appointed special rapporteurs, an increasing number of them are starting to focus on issues which have a direct or indirect bearing on international trade, and on matters which may be affected by trade rules such as the right to food. The activities of private companies are considered by some country special rapporteurs – for example in the case of Sudan where attention has been drawn to the activities of oil companies in conflict zones – and several thematic experts have mandates to report on illicit trade such as the sale of children, the dumping and movement of toxic waste, and trafficking.[5]

In 1999, the Commission acknowledged that globalisation is not merely an economic process but has social, political, environmental, cultural and legal dimensions that have an impact on human rights, and that these impacts may differ from country to country. It requested the Sub-Commission to undertake a study.[6] In 2001, the Commission's resolution on globalization requested the OHCHR to prepare a report on the human rights impact of globalization, in co-operation with the UN Conference on Trade and Development,[7] which is the first – and welcome – initiative to recognise the need to bring together the institutional perspectives of trade and human rights.

The Sub-Commission is now devoting significant attention to issues relating to trade, globalisation and human rights.[8] In 2000, it began to focus on specific trade issues. Its resolution on "intellectual property rights and human rights" noted that the implementation of the TRIPs Agreement could affect enjoyment of such human rights as the right to enjoy the benefits of scientific progress, the right to health, the right to food, and the right to self-determination. It also noted that actual or potential conflicts exist between the implementation of the WTO's TRIPS Agreement and the realization of economic, social and cultural rights in relation to technology transfer to developing countries, the consequences of protecting plant varieties on the right to food, the patenting of genetically modified organisms, bio-piracy and the reduction of indigenous and other communities' control over their genetic and natural resources and their cultural values.[9] The Sub-Commission requested a report from the High Commissioner, and this will be addressed by Simon Walker this afternoon.[10]

This year's discussion focussed also on the GATS (General Agreement on Trade in Services) Agreement. Members took as their starting point the state's obligation under international human rights law to ensure universal access to basic services such as health and education, requested a report from the High Commissioner, and encouraged analysis by agencies on the human rights implications of the liberalisation of trade in services under the framework of the GATS.[11]

In a related resolution on intellectual property and human rights, the Sub Commission asked the High Commissioner to seek observer status within the WTO, to review the patent as a legal instrument from a human rights perspective, and to analyse the impact of the TRIPS Agreement on the rights of indigenous peoples.[12]

The Sub-Commission is also examining the working methods and activities of corporations (an initiative which is distinct from the Global Compact).[13] In 2000 Sub-Commission member David Weissbrodt formulated "Draft Universal Human Rights Guidelines for Companies."[14] The draft guidelines reflect substantive international law, and there are hopes that they will be the basis for a legally binding instrument.

The treaty bodies oversee the six principal human rights treaties.[15] Each treaty has a supervisory committee of independent experts whose primary function is to review reports from states on treaty implementation. The committees also provide authoritative and expert interpretations of specific treaty provisions, through their general comments.[16] Their work is respected by governments, and increasingly influential. In August 2001, a nine member US delegation, led by the Assistant Attorney General, reported on US law and practice to the Committee on the Elimination of Racial Discrimination. Two weeks later, a twenty member official Japanese delegation, and forty NGO representatives, came to Geneva to present Japan's report on its measures to implement the International Covenant on Social, Economic and Cultural Rights.

This is a young system. The Convention on the Rights of the Child (the CRC) came into force only in 1990. There is still little case law regarding civil and political rights and has yet no social and economic rights jurisprudence because neither the CESCR nor the CRC can consider individual cases, although the recent adoption of an optional protocol allowing individual complaints in relation to the Convention on the Elimination of All Forms of Discrimination Against Women (the CEDAW) may yield some relevant jurisprudence in the future, given the fact that CEDAW contains both civil and political and economic and social rights. The CRC has been ratified by all UN member states except the US and Somalia, and thus constitutes a unique common legal standard, which combines economic, social and cultural rights with civil and political rights in one treaty.

The CESCR's general comments on food, housing, education and health[17] bind its 145 states parties,[18] and have assumed something of the status of rules of the road, for example in analysis of the impact of trade rules on the supply of basic services. Of particular importance is their identification of the four constituent elements of accessibility which must be met in provision of a basic service: non discrimination, physical accessibility, economic accessibility, and information accessibility. The Committee is now drafting a General Comment to clarify the protection given to intellectual property in Article 15(1)c[19] of the Covenant. A consultation in 2000 with experts from WTO, WIPO and UNESCO, academic experts and NGOs identified a wide range of issues and questions requiring discussion and resolution, including: what balance should be struck between human rights and intellectual property rights, how can intellectual property rights be made more "egalitarian," how can indigenous – collective – knowledge be protected given that intellectual property rights are individual rights, how can traditional knowledge be recorded in data bases usable by patent examiners and so protected, and how to prevent a negative impact on the right to food by, e.g., reducing farmers' access to seeds where patents are taken out on parts of plant varieties.[20]

Common elements

Reviewing these discussions and developments, some common elements can be identified.

Fairness. General Assembly and Commission resolutions typically make the general assertion that while globalization, including trade liberalization, holds out opportunities; it also presents challenges which are not being met by current international standards.[21] More specifically, there is concern that procedures within the WTO should conform to principles of procedural fairness. In the words of the Sub Commission special rapporteurs on globalisation, if the dispute resolution system "is to serve the purpose of meting out justice within the existing international trade regime, it will have to win the confidence of a wide spectrum of members as a professional, impartial and accessible system."[22]

Vulnerability. There is concern to ensure that the benefits of the evolving international trading regime will be shared equitably by all, in particular by the most vulnerable sectors of different societies.[23]

Focus. Many of the charter body resolutions on globalization and trade liberalization underline that globalization, including trade liberalization, has focussed too much on its economic dimensions to the neglect of social, cultural and political dimensions, without recognising the human being as the central subject of development.[24]

Legal coherence. Although all WTO members are parties to some human rights treaties, trade rules and human rights principles have developed in isolation from each other, and concerns are increasingly expressed that states should now review their obligations under both types of treaties and, where their actions/policies are inconsistent with their treaty obligations, bring them into conformity. The Sub Commission special rapporteurs have proposed a "restatement" of human rights law, in the form of minimum guidelines for institutions that are designing the policies and principles of globalisation. They argue that the application of human rights standards "should be the commencement point from which multilateral lending institutions embark on the formulation of their policies, rather than a point of reference when things have gone wrong."

Equality and nondiscrimination. The ICESCR's General Comment interpreting article 12 on the right to health spells out the state's duty "to adopt legislation or to take other measures ensuring equal access to health care and health related services provided by third parties," and to ensure that "privatisation of the health sector does not constitute a threat to the availability, accessibility, acceptability and quality of health facilities, goods and services."[25] Earlier this year, the Commission reflected this in a resolution calling on states to pursue policies "in accordance with applicable international law ..." which would promote "(t)he accessibility to all without discrimination, including the most vulnerable sectors of the population, of ... pharmaceuticals or medical technologies."[26]

Obstacles and challenges

Many aspects of the functioning of the international trade system – both positive and negative – are not very well understood, particularly by human rights experts. This ignorance has encouraged anxiety over its negative effects, and held back analysis based on a solid grasp of the relationship between trade rules and human rights principles. There has been too little research on the impacts of trade liberalization from a human rights perspective. Some work is now underway in some specialised agencies. UNICEF is examining the impact of liberalised trade on children through country studies, using the CRC as its point of reference. The Food and Agriculture Organisation is reviewing the impact of liberalised trade and agricultural imports on small farmers.

There is an urgent need to move from discussion which is based on anecdotal evidence to research based assessements. Research in this field should give priority to three questions:

How can we empirically measure the impacts – positive and negative – of entry to the international trade regime,[27] and specifically of WTO trade rules, on human rights, and what conclusions can properly be drawn? The absence of an individual complaints mechanism for social and economic rights under the international human rights treaties means that no case law has developed within the UN system which can be used to flag issues and "diagnose" problem areas. But states themselves, and NGOs, can use the treaty body country review process to identify specific areas or instances in which international trade rules have required national legislative or policy changes which have then impacted negatively upon human rights.

In what ways does this country and case specific material show a conflict between international trade rules and international human rights law? Are states being encouraged to liberalize beyond the requirements of the WTO? Is there evidence to show that liberalised service provision – for example in education – has negatively affected universal or equal access to primary education?

Where the private sector expands, and the state reduces its provision of, for example, basic health care in favor of health services provided by private companies, what steps should the state take to fulfil its obligation to protect and respect human rights, and what are the consequent duties of private actors?

Calls for coherence between the principles of trade and human rights are not only about reconciling two distinct bodies of international law. They also require reconciliation of institutional divisions at a national level – which sometimes amount to a virtual "lobotomy" – between government officials who work in trade ministries, and those working in the human rights fields often in distinct ministries, such as foreign affairs or justice. At the national level it is often the case that the officials who prepare reports to the human rights treaty bodies have little contact with other colleagues who are responsible for implementing international trade treaty obligations.

Even in Geneva, specialists in the two areas often work in isolation from each other, and this is particularly the case in larger missions. Shortly before meeting the trade representative of whom I spoke at the start, I heard a diplomat from a small African country discussing the interface between human rights and WTO issues with great fluency. When I asked how she had been able to develop expertise in both areas, she explained that hers was a very small diplomatic mission, and she was therefore responsible for both trade and human rights.

This "functional distinction" still afflicts most national governments. But it is now beginning to change in Geneva, with regular contact taking place between OHCHR, WTO, UNCTAD and other international agencies. The CESCR's day of general discussion on intellectual property perhaps offers a model.

This is very much a work in progress. Speaking in Prague at the Annual Meeting of the World Bank and the IMF in 2000, the High Commissioner called for a new "bilingualism" between the language of international human rights and the language of international trade. This meeting is an important stage in that learning process.

NOTES

1. Economic and Social Council, *The relationship between the enjoyment of human rights, in particular economic, social and cultural rights, and income distribution*, Final report prepared by Mr. José Bengoa, Special Rapporteur to the Sub-Commission on Prevention of Discrimination and Protection of Minorities, 30 June 1997, (E/CN.4/Sub.2/1997/9).

2. Economic and Social Council, *The realization of economic, social and cultural rights*, Final report presented by Mr. Danillo Türk, Special Rapporteur to the Sub-Commission on the Prevention of Discrimination and Protection of Minorities, 3 July 1992, (E/CN.4/Sub.2/1992/16).

3. Committee on Economic, Social and Cultural Rights, *Statement of the United Nations Committee on Economic, Social and Cultural Rights to the Third Ministerial Conference of the World Trade Organization*, 26 November 1999, (E/C.12/1999/9).

4. For example: From the perspective of the promotion and protection of human rights, how can economic growth be channelled equitably? "To what extent does article XX (of the General Agreement on Tariffs and Trade) indicate a point of convergence between trade rules and international human rights law?" "One question that has been raised from a human rights perspective is: how can international rules be adapted to protect and promote the cultural rights of indigenous peoples

and other groups?" See General Assembly, *Globalisation and its impact on the full enjoyment of all human rights*, Preliminary report of the Secretary-General, 31 August 2000, (A/55/342), paras. 17 and 19.

5. Economic and Social Council, *Situation of Human Rights in the Sudan*, Report of the Special Rapporteur to the Commission on Human Rights, 19 April 2000, (E/CN.4/2000/36), paras. 19, 21.

6. Economic and Social Council, *Globalization and its impact on the full enjoyment of all human rights*, Resolution, Commission on Human Rights, 28 April 1999, (E/CN.4/1999/59), para. 4.

7. Economic and Social Council, *Globalization and its impact on the full enjoyment of all human rights*, Resolution, Commission on Human Rights, 20 April 2001, (E/CN.4/2001/32), para. 9.9.

8. As early as 1992, Special Rapporteur Danilo Türk submitted a report to the Sub-Commission on the Realization of Economic, Social and Cultural Rights, which set the direction for later discussion in the Commission on trade issues. The report discussed a number of issues that are relevant to the globalisation and human rights debate today, structural economic issues that obstruct the realization of economic, social and cultural rights, popular participation, the role of the State, the question of income distribution, and the part played by the international financial institutions. E/CN.4/Sub.2/1992/16, op. cit.

9. Economic and Social Council, *Intellectual Property Rights and Human Rights*, Resolution, Sub-Commission on the Promotion and Protection of Human Rights, 17 August 2000, (E/CN.4/Sub.2/RES/2000/7), Preamble.

10. See Economic and Social Council, *The impact of the Agreement on Trade-Related Aspects of Intellectual Property Rights on the enjoyment of human rights*, Report of the High Commissioner, 27 June 2001, (E/CN.4/Sub.2/2001/13).

11. Economic and Social Council, *Liberalization of trade in services and human rights*, Resolution of the Sub-Commission on the Promotion and Protection of Human Rights, 15 August 2001, (E/CN.4/Sub.2/RES/2001/4), para. 2.

12. Resolution 2001/21 requests the High Commissioner (i) to seek observer status with the WTO for the ongoing review of the TRIPS Agreement; (ii) to consider the need for an examination and, if necessary, to conduct such an investigation into whether the patent, as a legal instrument, is compatible with the promotion and protection of human rights and corresponding State obligations; (iii) to undertake an analysis of the TRIPS Agreement on the rights of indigenous peoples. (E/CN.4/Sub.2/RES/2001/21).

13. In 1994, 1995 and 1997, it requested reports on the relationship between the enjoyment of human rights and the working methods and activities of transnational corporations. In 1998 the Sub-Commission decided to set up a Working Group on transnational corporations *inter alia* to identify and examine the effects of the working methods and activities of transnational corporations on the enjoyment of human rights, as well as to analyse existing standards regulating the activities of transnational corporations as they relate to human rights. In 1998, it issued a "Working document on the impact of the activities of transnational corporations on the realization of economic, social and cultural rights."

14. Principles relating to human rights conduct by companies, working paper prepared by David Weissbrodt, E/CN.4/Sub.2/2000/WG.1. Weissbrodt identified the context in these terms: "... the emergence of the increasingly integrated global economy; the prominence of international trade and investment; the growth of information and communications technology facilitating rapid transmission of information; increasing privatisation; concerns about the impact of globalisation and trade on human rights; ...shareholder and stakeholder demands for greater openness and public accountability... and increased reliance on voluntary compliance with international standards applicable to companies."

15. International Covenant on Civil and Political Rights, International Covenant on Social, Economic and Cultural Rights, Convention against Torture, Convention on the Elimination of Racial Discrimination, Convention on the Elimination of Discrimination against Women, Convention on the Rights of the Child.

16. See, e.g., General Comments by the Committee on Social, Economic and Cultural Rights on the nature of states parties obligations, the right to adequate housing, the duty to give effect to the Covenant (on social, economic and cultural rights) in the domestic legal order. (HRI/GEN/1/Rev.4, 7 February 2000).

17. See above, and E/C.12/2000/4,CESCR.

18. Now 150 States Parties.

19. "The right of everyone to benefit from the protection of the moral and material interests resulting from any scientific, literary or artistic production of which he is the author" (A.15(1)c ICESCR.).

20. See, e.g., A. Chapman, *Approaching intellectual property as a human right: obligations related to article 15(1)(c)*, Paper presented on the Day of General Discussion, 28 November 2000, (E/C.12/2000/12).

21. Article 28 of the *Universal Declaration on Human Rights* is seen as a point of departure: ("E)veryone is entitled to a social and international order in which the rights and freedoms set forth in this Declaration can be fully realized."

22. "We wish to underscore... that it is only through such a system that all parties can seek a balanced application of the trade regime which takes into consideration not only the logic of the market, but also available safeguards regarding human rights and environmental standards. ...(T)here will have to be serious stocktaking of its performance ...Priority must be given to ensuring the independence, impartiality and representative nature of panels and of the [Appeal Body], accessibility by developing coutries, stronger remedies and internal and external transparency of the dispute settlement procedures." Economic and Social Council, *Globalization and its impact on the full enjoyment of human rights*, Report of the Special Rapporteurs of the Sub-Commission on the Promotion and Protection of Human Rights, 2 July 2001, (E/CN.4/Sub.2/2001/10), para. 48.

23. E/C.12/1999/9, op. cit.

24. As required by the *Declaration on the Right to Development*, article 1.

25. CESCR, *The right to the highest attainable standard of health*, General Comment No. 14, 4 July 2001, (E/C.12/2000/4), para. 35.

26. Economic and Social Council, *Access to medication in the context of pandemics such as HIV/AIDS*, Resolution of the Commission on Human Rights, 20 April 2001, (E/CN.4/RES/2001/33), para. 2(b).

27. See, e.g., fears that China's membership in the WTO will negatively affect social provision (e.g., education, food, housing). "Competition from foreign agriculture is expected to hasten the huge migration of people from the countryside into the cities. The influx will strain urban social services and worsen unemployment..." *International Herald Tribune*, September 2001.

CHAPTER 8

TRIPS and Human Rights: Preliminary Reflections

Frederick M. Abbott[*]

The first order of business at the trial of the case brought by the pharmaceutical industry against the government of South Africa was the petition by the Treatment Action Campaign (TAC) for admission as amicus curiae. Much of TAC's written submission to the court consisted of statements by individuals who were suffering from AIDS, or whose family members had died from the condition. The advocate for the patent holders, who opposed the petition, argued that the government adequately represented the interests of the people of South Africa, that the patent holders and the government between them would make the appropriate legal arguments, and that admission of TAC would be redundant and inappropriately time consuming. The High Court in Pretoria was filled with supporters of TAC and other AIDS activist groups, many of those supporters HIV-positive, and some rather ill. Judge Bernard Ngoepe looked around the courtroom, and told the advocate for the patent holders that TAC, representing the interests of thousands of South Africans suffering from AIDS, brought a "special dimension" to the case and would be admitted to the proceedings.[1]

I. Introduction

We are considering the relationship between human rights and trade-related aspects of intellectual property rights (TRIPS). Intellectual property rights (IPRs) have always reflected a balancing of general public interests and private stakeholder interests, and in this sense IPRs take into account social welfare concerns as well as those of individual inventors and artists. While the balance struck in the TRIPS Agreement is flawed,[2] it is capable of flexible interpretation and amendment. Human rights represent the values for establishing a glo-

---

* This paper was initially written and presented in August 2001, and it generally reflects the situation as of that date. It has been updated to include reference to the Doha Declaration on the TRIPS Agreement and Public Health, adopted 14 November 2001. A separate paper addressing the right to health, competition principles and TRIPS has been prepared for the second meeting of this Project in June 2003, and that paper more generally incorporates developments subsequent to August 2001.

bal constitutional balance between the interests of the public and the private holders of IPRs.

We are collectively at a somewhat early stage of analyzing, from a legal standpoint, the relationship between human rights and the TRIPS Agreement. The observations in this paper reflect the preliminary nature of this inquiry.

From a legal perspective, the sources of human rights relating to TRIPS are customary international law, the Universal Declaration of Human Rights, and various other human rights instruments including the International Covenant on Civil and Political Rights (ICCPR) and the International Covenant on Economic, Social and Cultural Rights (ICESCR). The Report prepared by the Office of the High Commissioner for Human Rights, entitled "The impact of the Agreement on Trade-Related Aspects of Intellectual Property Rights on human rights," insightfully surveys the relevant human rights instruments and their potential application to TRIPS issues.[3]

The idea or concept of human rights as it applies to the field of IPRs involves something beyond the specific norms we may identify in human rights instruments or customary law. Human rights involve the shared perceptions of individuals regarding basic questions of right and wrong, fairness and equity. When an overwhelming part of the world's public perceives a situation as unjust, and expresses its concern, that shared perception itself becomes a part of our human rights dialogue, and informs public policy makers in their actions. Human rights take on character, and become appropriately multidimensional in the context of specific cases, and reflect the spirit of the times.

Lawyers may incline to be dismissive of public perception because the legal profession is by nature analytical, and the lawyer prides him or herself on objectivity and precision. Yet laws do not operate in clinical isolation from events, and events (particularly those of great moment) are rarely analytical and precise. One does not stop a war on a legal technicality.[4] In the combating of social wrongs, it is the shared perception of the public, and the willingness of the public to take on the responsibility for setting things back in their proper order, that matters.

Meetings in the TRIPS Council on access to medicines that ultimately resulted in the Doha Declaration on the TRIPS Agreement and Public Health flowed largely from efforts by developing WTO Members to deal with public health problems affecting their people. The TRIPS Council did not begin taking access to medicines issues seriously because the OECD governments became more enlightened about the consequences of TRIPS and patents. Rather, this took place because the worldwide public did not accept that the rights of pharmaceutical industry patent holders should take precedence over the rights to life and health of millions of individuals. The human rights dimension will play a substantial role in the response of the WTO and other multilateral organizations to public health issues. It is precisely because fundamental human rights are at stake, and that these rights are paramount in public consciousness, that the legal situation will adapt.

II. Human rights and TRIPS

a. Core and relative human rights

Human rights are held by individuals and groups, and are both affirmative and negative in nature.[5] There is considerable discussion in human rights literature,[6] considered also in refining the work program of this Project,[7] as to whether certain human rights may be defined as "core" rights. The identification of core rights might assist lawyers and policy-makers to avoid or resolve conflicts with other bodies of rules, such as trade rules, and to better appreciate which areas should be most protected against intrusion.[8]

Distinguishing between "core" and relative human rights is not straightforward. It is not a matter of placing *jus cogens* human rights on one side of the ledger, and other human rights on the other. The UN Committee on Economic, Social and Cultural Rights has, for example, indicated that rights subject to progressive realization under the Covenant necessarily entail a "core" obligation that is not the subject of progressive realization, stating for example:

> "12. … it should also be recalled that the Committee's General Comment No. 3, adopted in 1990, confirms that States parties have a 'core obligation to ensure the satisfaction of, at the very least, minimum essential levels of each of the rights' enunciated in the Covenant. As the Committee observes, without such a core obligation, the Covenant 'would be largely deprived of its *raison d'être.*' More recently, the Committee has begun to identify the core obligations arising from the 'minimum essential levels in relation to the rights to health, food and education.' The Committee wishes to emphasize that any intellectual property regime that makes it more difficult for a State party to comply with its core obligations in relation to health, food, education, especially, or any other right set out in the Covenant, is inconsistent with the legally binding obligations of the State party."[9]

The identification of core rights may be important in applying human rights in the interpretation and application of the TRIPS Agreement. If a human right is considered "core," inviolable and non-relative, then such right may not be subject to "balancing" as against non-core or relative interests. If the concept of core rights has currency, the "right to life" would certainly be among them. Government authority is precluded from taking life, at least without due process of law.[10] As a core right, the right to life is a negative right, protecting the individual against intrusion on his or her person. (An important question is at what stage a government's dereliction in addressing risk to life may be construed as an abrogation of its obligation not to take life. This question arises in relation to public health, when governments fail to act against a clear and present danger to their citizens.) A relative right or interest cannot be invoked by a government as the justification for taking human life. Moreover, protection of core rights is not subject to "progressive realization." Governments may not invoke the absence of adequate resources as a justification for taking life, torture, arbitrary arrest and detention, or discrimination.

Non-core rights are relative in differing degrees. Non-core human rights may be the subject of progressive realization. Important examples are the right to education and the right to health. It is recognized that the provision of adequate education and health care each require the expenditure of resources, and that governments are constrained by resource-limitations.[11] It would be unrealistic, and may undermine the degree to which the obligations are given credence in the international community, to say that all people everywhere shall immediately have proper access to adequate education and health care, if many governments are not in a position to provide that access. However, the fact that a human right is subject to progressive realization does not imply that a government is not under a binding obligation – it is. But the government also has a certain flexibility to balance the various interests of society so as to address all of its important human rights responsibilities. Human rights that are relative and/or subject to progressive realization must be balanced within the framework of the TRIPS Agreement, which unarguably has a potential (and realized) impact upon them.

The notion that human rights may be set along a continuum from "*jus cogens*" to "core" to "non-core/relative" creates a complex picture when approaching potential or realized conflicts in implementation of rule systems. This picture is considered later in the paper.

b. Human rights instruments prescribe that individuals have rights in respect of their creations, and to protection of their personhood

The Universal Declaration of Human Rights and the International Covenant on Economic, Social and Cultural Rights each recognize a right of individuals to the fruits of their scientific and expressive creations.[12] Furthermore, rights dealing with protection of personal integrity may be relevant in areas such as protection of personal names against abusive practices, as well as to moral rights.[13]

c. Rights in creations balanced within human rights instruments[14]

The rights to the fruits of creative efforts are not absolute. While the Universal Declaration prescribes the protection of "the material interests" resulting from creation, the nature of those material interests was at the time of the Declaration, and today, determined by national legislation. At the time the Declaration was adopted, for example, the term of patents varied widely among countries (as did the scope of subject matter coverage). Thus "the material interests" were and are by definition relative.

Article 15, ICESCR, speaks of the right of creators to "benefit" from the material interests resulting from their creations. It does not prescribe a specific level of benefit.

That the rights of individuals to benefit from their scientific and literary creations are relative non-core rights does not diminish their importance. There are few "non-relative" human rights. While genocide and slavery are not justifiable in any context, even the right to life is subject to the relative interests of society in countries that apply the death penalty in criminal proceedings.

d. Rights in creations potentially distinguished as between individual and enterprise rights[15]

Human rights are attributed to individuals and, in some settings, to groups. In the context of benefits from creative efforts, individuals not infrequently assign all or part of their economic interests to legal persons (i.e., business enterprises). This differentiates rights in creative works from "core" rights, such as the right to life and to be free from torture, because the latter are inalienable. Whether enterprises are the beneficiaries of human rights is a difficult question. As vehicles for personal enterprise, they may enjoy a certain element of subsidiary or derivative protection. Yet the very term "human rights" would appear to signal that the subjects of human rights are individuals whose personal rights, to the extent they become tied up in business, may enjoy derivative protection.

III. The TRIPS Agreement as a new form of international instrument

a. Characteristics of the TRIPS Agreement[16]

The TRIPS Agreement was the first GATT-WTO agreement prescribing a positive normative system for implementation in national law. It reflected a more substantial preemption of domestic regulatory discretion than had previously been accepted within the GATT 1947 legal system. The establishment of domestic enforcement standards enhanced the reduction of discretion from customary levels.

During its negotiation, the economic and social impact of the TRIPS Agreement was largely unquantified. While the effects of tariff reductions and quota elimination were and are subject to reasonably sound *ex ante* economic analysis, economists lacked the data and analytical tools with which to predict effects of TRIPS implementation.[17] Even today, the most sophisticated analysts of the TRIPS Agreement acknowledge that substantial gaps remain.

The TRIPS Agreement was designed to solve a producer-perceived problem of inadequate returns on research and development (R&D) investment. Trade negotiators had modest input from constituencies other than producers that would be affected by the Agreement. Trade negotiators did not in general coordinate adequately with other parts of government affected by the outcome of negotiations, e.g., public health officials.[18]

b. Public interest balancing

Since the advent of IPRs, legislatures and courts have been called upon to weigh the interests of "property" holders and those affected by the grant of exclusive rights. Perspectives on the proper balance change over time. In his classic 1950s work on the economics of the patent system, Fritz Machlup assumed that important medicines would not be freely exploited under patent monopoly.[19] By contrast, industry and markets today assume that "blockbuster" cancer medicines will return enormous monopoly rents.

The TRIPS Agreement reflects part of the continuum in balancing interests in stimulating creation, on one side, and common public interest in dissemination of information and knowledge, on the other.[20] This balance is principally reflected in national and regional laws that incorporate industrial policy and public interest considerations, but also is historically reflected in multilateral instruments largely administered by the World Intellectual Property Organization (WIPO).

The balance of public and private interests in intellectual property rights is typically informed by constitutional rules or principles. The TRIPS Agreement attempts to transpose a constitutional balance between private stakeholders and public interest to the multilateral level. There is a strong argument that transposing constitutionally-balanced rights into a multilateral organization with limited internal capacity for constitutional balancing is an inherently problematic undertaking.[21]

Various TRIPS internal mechanisms reflect the public interest side of balancing.[22] Relevant provisions include, *inter alia*:

- The Preamble regarding objective of non-distortion in trade, recognition of public policy objectives of national laws, maximum flexibility for least developed countries
- Article 1:1 right of states to implement as appropriate to national legal system and practice
- Article 2:1 incorporation of other multilateral instruments, e.g., Article 5 of Paris Convention
- Article 6 preclusion of dispute settlement regarding exhaustion
- Article 7 references to contributions to dissemination of technology, advantages to users, and contribution to social welfare
- Article 8:1 references to public health and nutrition, vital areas of socio-economic and technological development
- Article 8:2 prevention of anticompetitive practices
- Article 9 incorporation of Berne Convention standards that define copyright to protect literary and artistic works (i.e., creative expression), and incorporate rights of fair use, etc.
- Article 13 exceptions to copyright
- Article 15:2 recognition of grounds for denying trademark registration
- Article 16 incorporation of general tests for trademark infringement, including requirement of likelihood of confusion
- Article 17 exceptions to trademark rights
- Article 26:2 exceptions to design rights
- Article 27:1 flexibility in application of conditions of patentability and permitting of differentiation (as contrasted with discrimination) in field of technology and whether imported or locally produced
- Article 27:2 permitting of exclusions for public ordre, morality, protection of human, animal, plant life and health, and environment
- Article 27:3(a) permitting of exclusions for diagnostic, therapeutic and surgical methods

- Article 27:3(b) permitting of exclusion for plants, animals and essentially biological processes, other than non-biological and microbiological processes; and flexibility in protection of plant varieties
- Article 30 exceptions to patent rights
- Article 31 authorization of grant of compulsory licenses
- Article 39 implicit recognition of non-protected status of information in public domain
- Article 39:3 limitation of data protection to that "against unfair commercial use"
- Article 40 authorization of legislation and enforcement of competition principles to IPRs
- Article 41:5 recognition of limitations on enforcement resources
- Article 42 elaboration of defendant's rights in civil proceedings
- Article 65 general application of transitional arrangements
- Article 66:1 extended transition period for least developed countries, and indication of intention to allow extensions "duly motivated"
- Article 66:2 obligation on developed countries to provide incentives for technology transfer to least developed countries
- Article 67 encouragement of technical assistance
- Article 71 security exception, limited but including recognition of obligation to maintain international peace and security

c. The rule-exception hierarchy

Generally speaking, the TRIPS Agreement frames protection of private rights in the form of positive obligation, and addresses public interest issues by way of negative or exceptional rights. An alternative would be to formulate protected public interests as positive rights or obligations of states, and to establish IPRs as reflecting exceptional exclusivity in information based on specific policy objectives. For example,

> "WTO Members are obligated to establish conditions under which adequate and effective health care is provided to individuals within their territories. In order to achieve that objective, Members may grant patent rights to promote investment in innovative technologies, provided that patent rights do not act as an obstacle to achieving the objective of adequate and effective health care."

d. The Doha Declaration on the TRIPS Agreement and Public Health

The initial draft of this paper was presented in August 2001 in the period of the run-up to the Fourth WTO Ministerial Conference in Doha, with an audience including a number of persons active in those negotiations, and engendered an intensive discussion. It was evident that the perceived interests of pharmaceutical patent holders, on one side, and advocates of greater limitations on patent rights in the interests of enhanced access to medicines, on the other, were in sharp contrast.

The negotiating history and a more complete analysis of the Doha Declaration appear elsewhere.[23] It is important to emphasize here that the Doha Declaration is manifestly a human rights instrument, as well as a trade instrument. At paragraph 4, it states:

> "We agree that the TRIPS Agreement does not and should not prevent Members from taking measures to protect public health. Accordingly, while reiterating our commitment to the TRIPS Agreement, we affirm that the Agreement can and should be interpreted and implemented in a manner supportive of WTO Members' right to protect public health and, in particular, to promote access to medicines for all."

The Members of the WTO have agreed by consensus that the TRIPS Agreement "does not and should not" prevent them from taking measures to protect public health. The Agreement "can and should be interpreted and implemented in a manner supportive of WTO Members' *right to protect public health*, and in particular, to promote access to medicines for all."

The Declaration acknowledges the "right to protect public health." In any implementing action under the TRIPS Agreement, and in any dispute settlement proceeding, this "right to protect public health" must be acknowledged and given effect. That right may indeed come into conflict with the right of patent holders under Article 28, TRIPS Agreement, to prevent third parties from making, selling or importing medicines. Those rights will need to be balanced against one another, taking into account that the objective of the right to health is to "promote access to medicines for all."

IV. TRIPS and human rights

a. Access to medicines

The TRIPS Agreement has a present and prospective impact on a wide range of human rights. The area in which concern has so far been most intense involves the impact of pharmaceutical patents on the rights to life and health. Patents by nature and function increase prices of pharmaceutical products above ordinary competitive-market prices, thereby reducing affordability and access. Although access to medicines is influenced by various factors in addition to price, e.g., regulatory controls and health care infrastructure, this does not eliminate the basic impact of price effects.[24]

Patents are used to stimulate investment in the development of new medicines, and a balance must be struck between negative price-related access effects and positive future R&D effects. Accomplishing this balance complicates the human rights agenda.

The TRIPS Agreement also regulates trademarks, copyrights and rights in data submitted for regulatory purposes. These TRIPS interests have significant effects on access to medicines. In addition to their source identification and goodwill functions, trademarks have been invoked in efforts to prevent generic producers from using capsule colors commonly known among doctors and patients. Copyright has been invoked in efforts to prevent the duplication of information in doctor and patient leaflets. Certain rights in data submitted for regulatory purposes have been used to block the registration of generic medicines. However the legal merits of these uses of IPRs under TRIPS Agreement rules are viewed from the perspective of private right holders; a different view might emerge when viewed through the lens of the right to health.

b. Rights of speech/expression and political association affected by copyright

Copyright by definition provides the right to prevent reproduction and distribution of expressive works, and thereby acts as a restriction on freedom of speech. There is as yet very modest attention given to the question at the multilateral level of the extent to which governments may limit the scope of copyright in the interest of promoting freedom of expression. Although the TRIPS Agreement, including by incorporation the Berne Convention, acknowledges that governments may provide exceptions to the rights of copyright holders, there is only indirect acknowledgement that human rights interests in freedom of speech may be implicated by its rules. As the right to political association is dependent on the freedom of expression, so too is that right implicated by the TRIPS Agreement.

c. Rights of personality/identity affected by trademark and geographical indication

Trademarks and service marks perform important identification functions that intersect with the rights of personality and identity. The support that trademarks and service marks provide to identity may not be adequately recognized from a human rights standpoint. As instruments of market control, trademarks and service marks may also inhibit individual access to essential products. Geographical indications – associating products with places on the basis of characteristics or reputation – may have important implications for developing country agriculture, both positive and negative. They may also affect the right of communities to control their identity, which may have cultural or human rights implications.

d. Rights of peoples in resources and traditions affected by patents and other IPRs

The rights of communities in relation to their resources are directly affected by TRIPS Agreement rules on patent and plant variety protection. Matters such as disclosure of the geographic origin and source of biological materials are relevant to the protection of biodiversity and to the achievement of sustainable development. This of course implicates the relationship between the TRIPS Agreement and the Convention on Biological Diversity, among other instruments related to sustainable development.

The rights of communities in designs and folklore are affected by TRIPS Agreement rules on copyright and design protection. Traditional commercial criteria for copyright and design protection may undervalue the rights of communities in their collective creations.

V. Human Rights as the Vehicle for Constitutional Balance

a. Rule-making

1. The multilateral level

To what extent were governments negotiating the TRIPS Agreement obligated to take into account human rights norms, and to what extent must present and future negotiations take into account human rights norms?

From a legal standpoint, the Vienna Convention on the Law of Treaties (VCLT), Article 53, prohibits (or renders void) treaties that conflict with peremptory norms (*jus cogens*). So, if the TRIPS Agreement or an amendment to it authorized slave trading among WTO Members, for example, it would be void *ab initio*.

The most appropriate rule-modifying body for eliminating a conflict between the TRIPS Agreement and a peremptory norm would be the Ministerial Conference of the WTO, which would recommend an amendment to TRIPS Agreement rules to be submitted for acceptance by the Members.

If the TRIPS Agreement, or an amendment to it, is in conflict with a rule of a human rights treaty and the parties to both agreements are the same, the VCLT rules on the application of successive treaties on the same subject matter would apply.[25] If the parties are not the same, then a judicial or dispute settlement body would need to resolve the conflict by application of customary rules of treaty interpretation (as reflected in the VCLT). There is no evident prohibition on the conclusion of successive treaties with conflicting rules, provided that parties to the treaties are prepared to provide a remedy for their inconsistent conduct.

Introduction of the notion of "core" human rights, as distinguished from *jus cogens*, adds a complication to the analysis. Assuming that states may not adopt a treaty that violates a peremptory norm, but they may adopt a treaty conflicting with the norms of another treaty, does the analysis hold if the affected rules embody "core" rights? Does international law provide for a more nuanced relative hierarchy of norms? We might at least venture that the judge, in considering the merits of a case, will consider the relative intensity of norms in framing his or her perspective and decision. The question of a more formal basis for establishing a hierarchy demands greater attention.

International law does not prohibit states from agreeing to modify a rule of customary international law by treaty.[26] Thus, WTO negotiators might choose to modify or disregard, as among themselves, a customary rule of human rights law by treaty. One of the functions of treaty-making is to allow for the modification of custom. However, the introduction of the concept of "core" human rights again complicates this analysis. While states may modify or supercede a rule of custom by treaty, may they modify or supercede a "core" human right as well?

At the normative level, the question arises whether the WTO is an appropriate forum for negotiation of rules that affect human rights.[27] Two points seem appropriate in reply: first, there are structural imbalances at the WTO that make it a poor choice of institution wherein to negotiate rules with effects on social welfare. Negotiations at the WTO are conducted by trade delegations that largely represent producer group interests.[28] This inevitably leads to solutions that are weighted in favor of the most economically powerful producers.[29] In short, the WTO is not an optimal forum for the negotiation of TRIPS rules which have human rights consequences. This may suggest reform of the WTO decision-making processes.

Second: governments do not so far appear inclined to reform the WTO decision-making processes. This suggests that it may be necessary to continue negotiating rules attuned to human rights in alternative forums where such interests may be better accommodated. Even here the options are limited because of two phenomena: (1) most or all international institutions reflect to some degree or other the same problem of imbalanced governance as the WTO, and (2) the international institutions with more balanced decision-making structures tend to lack the effective power of the WTO, and therefore to present less forceful possibilities for improvement.

2. The national and regional level

Human rights norms, such as the right to life and health, are often reflected in national constitutions. It may be substantially more realistic for governments to develop and apply rules supportive of human rights interests at the national (or regional) level than by attempting to accomplish the adoption at the WTO of consensus-based rules taking into account human rights interests. In this context, the human rights rules developed at the "softer" multilateral institutions, such as the UN Human Rights Commission and the WHO might be relied upon by national institutions as support for the local implementation of human rights policies.

Concrete implementation of TRIPS Agreement rules occurs at the national level, and it is here that better attention might be paid to rule-making.

The main defense against TRIPS implementation contrary to human rights interests is the national constitution, which should require that the government protect the human rights interests of its citizens. The extent to which the constitution may be used in WTO dispute settlement proceedings as support for progressive interpretation is as yet untested,[30] but it is an avenue that would appear to have significant promise. The United States Trade Representative, for example, might have substantial difficulty making an argument that WTO rules should take precedence over national constitutional rules since (a) the U.S. Supreme Court has held that a treaty may not deprive a citizen of a constitutional right[31] and (b) Congress would surely object to the position that the U.S. Constitution can be overridden by WTO/TRIPS rules.

b. Conflict resolution

1. Multilateral level

There is potential complementary or competing jurisdiction between the International Court of Justice and the WTO DSB/Appellate Body (AB) in application of the TRIPS Agreement, WIPO-administered treaties and human rights instruments.[32] A state subject to a WTO DSU complaint could file a claim for breach of human rights obligations at the ICJ. In the context of a UN Charter-based complaint, the ICJ has the potential strong enforcement mechanism of referral to the UN Security Council.[33] The UN Charter by its terms takes precedence over other treaties to which its members are party,[34] but this same rule does not apply to human rights instruments outside the Charter. There is no clear hierarchy between decisions of the ICJ in so far as they relate to instruments other than the Charter, and decisions of other judicial bodies, such as the WTO Appellate Body.

Implementation of the TRIPS Agreement potentially conflicts with human rights, both core and relative. There was a juridical tradition within the GATT 1947 that it operated as a "self-contained" regime. This tradition was firmly broken down by cross-references to WIPO Conventions in the TRIPS Agreement, and by the Appellate Body in the *Shrimp-Turtles* decision.[35] Yet judicial bodies, including the WTO DSB/AB, are regulated by governing instruments that may restrict their application of external sources of law. The AB is instructed by the DSU to render decisions regarding interpretation of the covered agreements,[36] applying customary rules of interpretation of public international law.

If a peremptory human rights norm is engaged then, as prescribed by Article 53 of the Vienna Convention on the Law of Treaties (VCLT),[37] the AB would be required to void any conflicting rule (or the entire offending agreement). Thus, if the right to life is a peremptory norm, and if the mandatory patenting of pharmaceuticals directly conflicted with the right to life (hypothetically), the AB would be required to void the applicable rule of the TRIPS Agreement.

In many contexts, however, the relevant human rights norm will not be peremptory, and the AB might be presented with the question how a TRIPS Agreement rule that conflicts with a treaty-based relative human right should be interpreted. It would seem apparent that the AB should attempt to apply rules so that the operation of one treaty is consistent with the operation of the other. This will give the AB both the right and the obligation to adopt an interpretation of the TRIPS Agreement supportive of the right to health.

The more difficult problem arises when a rule of the TRIPS Agreement is inconsistent with a non-peremptory human rights rule; that is, if the AB is unable to develop a "consistent interpretation." The AB might be able to apply the VCLT rule regarding successive treaties on the same subject matter, particularly if the parties to both treaties are the same. If not, and absent any further elaboration, since the AB's authority is to decide on the interpretation of the covered agreements, including TRIPS, it would be difficult from a juridical standpoint to conclude that a human rights treaty-based norm should be given priority within the framework of the WTO. One of the Members in the dispute may be in breach of a human rights obligation, but this is not something within the AB's competence to remedy.

Might the concept of the "core" human rights obligation, that is not a peremptory norm, shift the balance in decision-making by the AB? As noted earlier, the potential impact of "core" human rights demands further attention. The effect of core rights conceptually might depend on the forum at which identification of the core norm is made. For example, because the Ministerial Conference in the Doha Declaration indicated that WTO Members have the "right to protect public health" so as to promote access to medicines for "all," the Ministerial Conference may have identified a core right in the context of the TRIPS Agreement. Does the identification or particularization of a right to protect health by the Ministerial Conference change that value into one that should, at a minimum, be treated on the same plane as the TRIPS Agreement from the standpoint of the hierarchy of norms considered by the AB? Might such identification signal an intention that the right to protect health has a stronger relative weight than other rules in the context of TRIPS Agreement interpretation?

What if the identification of the "core" right were made by the Committee on Economic, Social and Cultural Rights that issues definitive interpretations, by way of Comments, of the ICESCR? What if the identification were made by the UN General Assembly?

As a preliminary matter, the AB seems more likely to give full effect to decisions by the Ministerial Conference for a number of reasons, including the latter's authority to render authoritative interpretations of the WTO Agreements and, under the VCLT, Article 31 to reflect agreements by the parties as to the interpretation of the covered agreements. Yet as to external bodies, their authority may depend on context, though that is something which will require further elaboration.

The lack of a direct inroad by human rights treaties (or customary rules) into the WTO legal system is something that may be considered a gap in the system. In many cases, however, application of the concept of consistent interpretation should provide the AB with authority to apply human rights rules.

A hypothetical case

As illustration, negotiations are underway at the TRIPS Council for a solution to the problem presented by Article 31(f), TRIPS Agreement that facially precludes exports under compulsory license of a predominant part of production. Suppose that prior to conclusion of negotiations, a developed country – perhaps the Netherlands – grants a compulsory license within its territory solely for the manufacture and export of essential medicines that are urgently needed at low cost by developing country WTO Members.

In analysis of the legal issue, would the AB be required to stay within the strict terms of the TRIPS Agreement, or would it be able to consult the UN Declaration on Human Rights, or the International Covenant on Economic and Social Rights? Could the AB look at the legislation adopted in the Netherlands and say that while, in a strict sense, it may appear inconsistent with Article 31, TRIPS Agreement, the WTO must take into account that its Members also affirmed the UN Declaration on Human Rights, and that the Dutch are acting consistently within their TRIPS obligations (e.g., using Article 30) to supply developing countries with needed medicines?

So far, the DSB (or AB?) in the *Shrimp-Turtles* case has acknowledged the relevance of international instruments, outside the WTO texts, for purposes of aiding interpretation. But how far does this flexibility extend? Could the Netherlands argue that its WTO legal obligations are conditioned on its respect for its international human rights obligations? Could, for example, the Netherlands invoke article 103 of the UN Charter and argue that the Declaration, elaborating on obligations under the Charter, in fact takes precedence over WTO rules?

What if the AB rules against the Netherlands, and that country brings a claim at the ICJ arguing that suspension of its concessions under the WTO Agreement (in reaction to its exercise of rights under human rights instruments) constituted an international delict that should result in an award to it of damages? How would the ICJ treat a decision of the AB/DSB?

2. National and regional level

Regional and national courts may apply human rights instruments and the TRIPS Agreement either directly or by consistent interpretation. As illustration, in the South Africa pharmaceuticals case, South African courts were asked by *amicus curiae* to balance competing claims under international human rights instruments to which South Africa is party, and the TRIPS Agreement. In a subsequent case in South Africa, the Constitutional Court used constitutional rules reflecting human rights as a benchmark for evaluating the reasonableness of conduct by the government in relation to the supply of essential medicines.[38]

As noted above, it may be very difficult for a complaining Member to persuade the AB that another Member's application of a constitutionally protected right is subject to successful challenge at the WTO, particularly when that protected right derives from principles of international human rights law.

c. Addressing critiques of human rights rules

A traditional critique of using human rights norms to inform economic law is that the former are "too vague" or "unrealistic." Administrators and judicial bodies are said to face difficulties in applying human rights standards because of their generality. It is argued that this compares unfavorably with the specificity of trade rules and the level of application and enforcement. Carried to its logical conclusion, the argument suggests that it would be inappropriate for "hard" trade disputes to be resolved by reference to "soft" human rights law.

1. Vagueness

Human rights may, of course, be understood and expressed in different ways. In a limited sense, human rights may be understood as a certain set of core or fundamental rights that protect individuals against the intrusion of government authority, such as the right to life and the right to be free from arbitrary arrest and detention. In a broader sense, human rights may be understood to embody social entitlements such as the right to a free education.

As a starting point, it might be observed that "human rights" are no more vague than "trade rights," absent more specific denomination. Trade rights may variously embody rights of national treatment, most favored nation treatment, administrative transparency, absence of quota restrictions, and so forth. Until these rights are specifically agreed upon by governments in the context of trade negotiations, they are not part of the system of trading rules that are applied by the WTO Dispute Settlement Body. The WTO agreements are the product of a long evolution in which rules have been refined from broad to specific.[39]

Human rights norms are continually being refined in a variety of contexts. National/regional courts and administrative tribunals provide interpretations of these norms both in the context of the interpretation of national/regional rules,[40] and in the less frequent application of multilateral human rights instruments.[41] Various bodies of international organizations also work to provide formal and informal guidance regarding the content of human rights norms.[42]

The International Court of Justice and the international criminal courts are rendering decisions that interpret the content of human rights.

If the complete body of international human rights instruments is considered as a whole, it may be that indeterminacies and inconsistencies exist. Yet the same would certainly be true if the complete body of international trade agreements is considered as a whole.

2. Enforcement

While governments disregard trade rules with considerable regularity, it may be that compliance with trade rules is on the whole more consistent than compliance with human rights instruments. Without substantial empirical study, it is difficult to determine whether this is the case. Assuming that compliance with trade rules is more consistent than compliance with human rights rules, a few tentative hypotheses for this phenomenon might be offered.

Governments that fail to fulfill promises regarding human and social rights may do so because of lack of resources with which to meet their progressive commitments. It may not be that governments fail to take these commitments seriously, but that no amount of good intention will provide resources where none are available.

The implementation of trade rules, by way of contrast, usually does not require the expenditure of substantial resources. Although domestic industries may be adversely affected, it is relatively inexpensive to lower a tariff or reduce a quota, while on the other hand it may be enormously expensive to provide education and health care.

Governments face identifiable costs in failing to comply with trade rules. Trade privileges are likely to be withdrawn from a non-complying government, and the withdrawal of export privileges will generate a reaction from a domestic industry constituency. There is a political cost to non-compliance.

A government that routinely disregards the human rights of its citizens may be doing so because of internal security concerns, and may not be susceptible to domestic political pressure short of violent action. The international community generally reacts to human rights violations with concrete action in exceptional circumstances, which often involve more than local human rights issues.

Do most governments adhere to international human rights standards most of the time? Is attention predominantly drawn to the cases in which such rights are not observed? It may be that compliance with human rights norms is generally under-identified.

Accurately answering the question whether governments treat trade concerns more seriously than human rights concerns would be a complex undertaking. We might posit that governments are less likely to be penalized by the international community for human rights violations than for trade rule violations. If so, the reasons for this are not simple.

3. Possible solutions to the problems of vagueness and non-enforcement

The alleged problem of "vagueness" in human rights law might be addressed by multilateral and/or national legislative identification of "core" human rights against which IPRs can be balanced. Of course, judicial bodies are responsible for identifying and applying human rights *jus cogens* norms.[43]

Regarding the question of enforcement, judges may make use of the technique of looking to state practice in the application of human rights instruments.

4. Are intellectual property rights unique?

Rights in tangible (and non-IPRs-based intangible property) frequently conflict with human rights to life and health, but tangible property rights are not often interfered with on grounds, for example, that more equitable distribution would protect right to life. Is there a special characteristic of intellectual property that makes it more susceptible to regulatory interference than physical property? Perhaps it is that IPRs protect knowledge and information that might otherwise be capable of wide application in the public interest, whereas physical property tends to have localized utility. This would account for a different set of balancing rules.

The human rights to life and health are implicated each time an individual with a serious illness is unable to afford a therapeutic patented pharmaceutical. In some countries, social welfare policies provide for universal access to medicines; in others, access depends on financial capability. To what extent are human rights rules implicated in the micro-case of the individual unable to afford a medicine in a comparatively wealthy state? Are human rights to life and health relative in the sense of the scale of the effects on groups? These questions require further exploration.

VI. Alternative approaches to addressing crisis situations

a. Invocation of fundamentally changed circumstances or force majeure

Assuming that WTO Members were confronting substantial difficulties in addressing public health or other vital interests as a consequence of TRIPS rules, there are legal mechanisms other than the application of human rights instruments to aid in addressing those difficulties. One such rule is that of fundamental changed circumstances or *rebus sic stantibus*. This is embedded in the VCLT, Article 62(3), providing that unforeseen and fundamentally changed circumstances provide a party to a treaty with a right to suspend its operation.

A difference between application of the doctrine of changed circumstances and human rights instruments is that the former is episodic, while the latter may result in more enduring interpretative changes.

VII. Trading system concerns

Some trade specialists express concern that attention to human rights will interfere with the efficient operation of the global economy. Proposals to protect human rights are sometimes referred to as "disguised protectionism." While human rights doctrines may be capable of misuse, it would seem to over-simplify matters to suggest that market mechanisms will appropriately account for human rights absent regulatory intervention. Markets by their nature account for individuals as factors of production and as consumers.[44]

IPRs holders express concern that failure to provide high levels of protection will impede their research mission and in the long run undermine global public welfare. This also is an over-simplified response to achieving an appropriate balance between life and health, and interests in innovation. Balancing in TRIPS requires that interests be evaluated in their context.

Throughout the history of the international IPRs regulatory system, rights granted to creators have been subject to balancing against other social interests. This balancing has typically taken place at the national or regional level in the framework of a constitution. The TRIPS Agreement largely removed IPRs regulation from the traditional constitutional framework, giving broad rights to producers and exceptional rights to the public. The most evident means for resurrecting and maintaining a balance is for WTO Members to apply their constitutions to the application of TRIPS Agreement rules. The national and regional constitution will in most cases advance individual and group human rights. Moreover, this route does not require forcing a consensus on rebalancing the TRIPS Agreement at the WTO, an avenue that has proven rather difficult.

Yet in some cases the national constitution and its application will also require protection at the multilateral level, and it is here that the AB will need to step in to identify and apply relevant human rights principles that will maintain a reasonable semblance of balance. The academic community, including those involved in this research project, should help to lay the groundwork. There may yet remain the need to change the WTO rules to give greater force to human rights principles. That is a further step in which this research project may aid, but which will also depend on political interest and will.

NOTES

1. Trial notes of F.M. Abbott.

2. The TRIPS Agreement, according to many expert commentators, represents a flawed bargain in the sense that great economic pressure was brought to bear on developing countries to establish private stakeholder interests without adequate evaluation of public interest consequences from a developmental perspective. See Contributions on TRIPS in THE POLITICAL ECONOMY OF INTERNATIONAL TRADE LAW: ESSAYS IN HONOR OF ROBERT HUDEC (eds. Daniel Kennedy and James Southwick), Cambridge University Press 2002.

3. See Report of the High Commissioner, *The impact of the Agreement on Trade-Related Aspects of Intellectual Property Rights on human rights*, Commission On Human Rights, Sub-Commission on the Promotion and Protection of Human Rights, Fifty-second session, Item 4 of the provisional agenda, E/CN.4/Sub.2/2001/13, 27 June 2001.

4. As of yet, the proclivity to genocide has yet to be halted because of a treaty.

5. The right to freedom from torture, for example, is a "negative right" in that it stands as a bar to government and governmentally supported conduct. The right to education, for example, is largely a "positive right" in that it imposes an obligation upon governments to take positive steps.

6. See, e.g., Theodor Meron, *Note and Comment: On the Inadequate Reach of Humanitarian and Human Rights Law and the Need for a New Instrument,* 77 A.J.I.L. 589 (1983), and Dinah Shelton, *Hierarchy of Norms and Human Rights: Of Trumps and Winners,* 85 SASK. L. REV. 299, 309 (2002).

7. Meeting of Project Advisory Board, [March 2001], at Georgetown University Law Center.

8. It has been suggested that the rights to life, to freedom from slavery and torture, to freedom from arbitrary arrest and detention, and to non-discrimination, might begin to form the basis of a core. Core rights are immediately effective and inviolable. Rights of political association and expression, to housing and education, and to basic health care, might be considered more relative, and in some contexts to be subject to "progressive realization." Yet, as noted by the CESCR, relative rights may also include a minimum core.

9. Id.

10. There is, of course, ongoing controversy over use of the death penalty in criminal proceedings.

11. See, e.g., Committee on Economic, Social and Cultural Rights, Twenty-Seventh Session, Geneva, 12-30 November 2001, Substantive Issues Arising in the Implementation of the International Covenant on Economic, Social and Cultural Rights, Economic and Social Council, E/C.12/2001/1514, December 2001.

12. Article 27(2), Universal Declaration of Human Rights (1948):

"Everyone has the right to protection of the moral and material interests resulting from any scientific, literary or artistic production of which he is the author."

Article 15, International Covenant on Economic, Social and Cultural Rights (1966):

"1. The States parties to the present Covenant recognize the right of everyone: ...

c. To benefit from the protection of the moral and material interests resulting from any scientific, literary or artistic production of which he is the author.

2. The steps to be taken by the States Parties to the present Covenant to achieve the full realization of this right shall include those necessary for the conservation, the development and the diffusion of science and culture. ..."

13. For example, Article 12 of the Universal Declaration provides:

"No one shall be subjected to arbitrary interference with his privacy, family, home or correspondence, nor to attacks upon his honour and reputation. Everyone has the right to the protection of the law against such interference or attacks."

A similar set of rights is found in the International Covenant on Civil and Political Rights:

"Article 17:

1. No one shall be subjected to arbitrary or unlawful interference with his privacy, family, home or correspondence, nor to unlawful attacks on his honour and reputation.
2. Everyone has the right to the protection of the law against such interference or attacks."

14. See analysis in Report of High Commissioner, supra, regarding article 15 of International Covenant on Economic, Social and Cultural Rights (ICESCR).

15. Id.

16. UNCTAD/ICTSD, RESOURCE BOOK ON TRIPS AND DEVELOPMENT (Cambridge, 2005) and UNCTAD, COURSE ON DISPUTE SETTLEMENT, WTO, Module 3.14, TRIPS.

17. Accord KEITH E. MASKUS, INTELLECTUAL PROPERTY RIGHTS IN THE GLOBAL ECONOMY, at xv (IIE 2000)

18. Absence of coordination and cooperation among policy fields remains a systemic and persistent problem in governments at all levels of economic development.

19. Machlup asked: "The great inventor of the polio vaccine, Dr. Salk, generously contributed his idea to society without applying for a patent. If he had taken a patent on his process and sold it to a company which exploited it restrictively enough to make high profits, would the American public have stood for it?"

He also said: "It is more than probable that the socially most important inventions, say, of drugs or vaccines for the cure or prevention of cancer, would not be allowed to be exploited with the same monopolistic restrictions that are freely tolerated in the exploitation of patents on hair curlers, bottle caps, or television screens."

Fritz Machlup, An Economic Review of the Patent System, Subcomm. On Patents, Trademarks and Copyrights, of the Committee on the Judiciary, 85th Congress, 2d Sess.

20. Id., and Frederick M. Abbott, *The Enduring Enigma of TRIPS: A Challenge for the World Economic System*, 1 J. INT'L ECON. LAW 497 (1998).

21. See Thomas Cottier, *Limits to International Trade: The Constitutional Challenge,* 94 ASIL Proc. 220 (2000), and Eric Stein, *International Integration and Democracy: No Love at First Sight,* 95 A.J.I.L.489 (2001).

22. See UNCTAD-ICTSD Resource Book, supra note [16].

23. Frederick M. Abbott, *The Doha Declaration on the TRIPS Agreement and Public Health: Lighting a Dark Corner at the WTO,* 5 J. INT'L ECON. L. 469 (2002).

24. See, Frederick M. Abbott, Study Paper 2a, WTO TRIPS Agreement and Its Implications for Access to Medicines in Developing Countries, for British Commission on Intellectual Property Rights (Feb. 2002).

25. VCLT, Article 59:

"Termination or suspension of the operation of a treaty implied by conclusion of a later treaty

1. A treaty shall be considered as terminated if all the parties to it conclude a later treaty relating to the same subject-matter and:

(a) it appears from the later treaty or is otherwise established that the parties intended that the matter should be governed by that treaty; or

(b) the provisions of the later treaty are so far incompatible with those of the earlier one that the two treaties are not capable of being applied at the same time.

2. The earlier treaty shall be considered as only suspended in operation if it appears from the later treaty or is otherwise established that such was the intention of the parties."

26. See exchange between Michael Glennon, Jochin Frowein and Frederick Abbott in transcript of PARLIAMENTARY PARTICIPATION IN THE MAKING AND OPERATION OF TREATIES, (S.A Riesefeld and F.M. Abbott eds. 1994), at 403-415.

27. Consider a thought experiment:

Scenario 1: Trade Ministers are flying into Doha where one item on the agenda is a draft Declaration on TRIPS and Public Health. Of the 140 Ministers flying to the meeting, only one is HIV-positive, and he lives in an OECD country where antiretroviral drugs are made available under his health insurance plan.

Scenario 2: Trade Ministers are flying into Doha where one item on the agenda is a draft Declaration on TRIPS and Public Health. Of the 140 Ministers flying to the meeting, 139 are HIV-positive, and each of them has been ordered to refrain from taking any antiretroviral medicine until those drugs have been made affordable to the typical resident of a Sub-Saharan African country.

Would the debate on TRIPS and access to medicines, and the resulting Ministerial Declaration, be any different depending on the Scenario? The intention of the thought experiment is to suggest that attitudes toward the relevance of human rights to the proper balancing of public and private interests in TRIPS may be conditioned by the perspective of the observer.

28. Is the WTO Ministerial Conference, or are trade negotiating rounds, suited to addressing human rights interests, particularly in light of the reciprocity-based character of the negotiations? Consider, for example, whether it is appropriate for Country A to exchange a concession on the terms of patent protection for pharmaceuticals with a concession by Country B to allow market access for textile products. Does the fact that higher pharmaceutical prices and limited access will result in a deterioration of public health conditions in Country A factor into these negotiations?

terms of patent protection for pharmaceuticals with a concession by Country B to allow market access for textile products. Does the fact that higher pharmaceutical prices and limited access will result in a deterioration of public health conditions in Country A factor into these negotiations? How does the fact that improved market access for textiles may offset the price increase for pharmaceuticals affect this equation?

29. See Eric Stein, International Integration and Democracy: No Love at First Sight, 95 A.J.I.L.489 (2001).

30. In the India-Mailbox case the U.S. used the Indian constitution as an affirmative weapon in arguing that India's alleged administrative instructions would not have effect in Indian law. [cite]

31. Reid v. Covert, 354 U.S. 1 (1957.

32. See ERNST-ULRICH PETERSMANN, THE GATT/WTO DISPUTE SETTLEMENT SYSTEM (1997), at Introduction.

33. Though the fact of veto rights at the Council makes its use as an enforcement body potentially problematic.

34. Article 103, UN Charter.

35. United States – Import Prohibition of Certain Shrimp and Shrimp Products, AB-1998-4, WT/DS58/AB/R, 12 Oct. 1998.

36. Art. 1:1, DSU "The rules and procedures of this Understanding shall also apply to consultations and the settlement of disputes between Members concerning their rights and obligations under the provisions of the Agreement Establishing the World Trade Organization (referred to in this Understanding as the 'WTO Agreement') and of this Understanding taken in isolation or in combination with any other covered agreement."

Art. 3:2, DSU "The dispute settlement system of the WTO is a central element in providing security and predictability to the multilateral trading system. The Members recognize that it serves to preserve the rights and obligations of Members under the covered agreements, and to clarify the existing provisions of those agreements in accordance with customary rules of interpretation of public international law...."

37. VCLT, Article 53:

"Treaties conflicting with a peremptory norm of general international law (jus cogens)
A treaty is void if, at the time of its conclusion, it conflicts with a peremptory norm of general international law. For the purposes of the present Convention, a peremptory norm of general international law is a norm accepted and recognized by the international community of States as a whole as a norm from which no derogation is permitted and which can be modified only by a subsequent norm of general international law having the same character."

38. See Minister of Health v. Treatment Action Campaign, Constitutional Court of South Africa, Case CCT 8/02, decided 5 July 2002, discussed in paper for second Berne meeting, Frederick M. Abbott, *Integrating the Human Right to Health and Competition Principles in the Context of TRIPS.*

39. This process has been widely noted. See, e.g., F.M. Abbott, *The Intersection of Law and Trade in the WTO System: Economics and the Transition to a Hard Law System*, in UNDERSTANDING TECHNICAL BARRIERS TO AGRICULTURAL TRADE 33 (DAVID ORDEN AND DONNA ROBERTS EDS., 1997).

40. Human rights instruments may affect interpretation of national/regional rules either through direct application, or through application of principle of consistent interpretation.

41. Note experience of European Court of Human Rights in applying ECHR to expression and IPRs disputes.

42. See, e.g., Committee on Economic, Social and Cultural Rights, *The right to the highest attainable standard of health*: 11/08/2000.E/C. 12/2000/4, CESCR General Comment 14 (General Comments), article 12 of the International Covenant on Economic, Social and Cultural Rights.

43. As a potential claim, consider the following:

"The rights of individuals to life and health are fundamental human rights that are superior to the rights of individuals and enterprises in intellectual property."

This broad claim embodies a number of more specific features:

- That the right to life is a fundamental human right.
- That the right to health is a fundamental human right.
- To the extent that ownership of intellectual property is a human right, that right is inferior to the rights to life and health.
- Enterprises are distinguished from individuals.

Assuming that each element of this claim is valid from a legal standpoint, what specific relevance would it have for interpreting the WTO TRIPS Agreement?

44. The tobacco industry recently carried pure market economics to a logical but absurd conclusion, advising the Czech Republic that killing people through cigarette smoking is a cost-effective means to deal with budgetary constraints otherwise imposed by an aging population.

CHAPTER 9

A Human Rights Approach to the WTO's TRIPS Agreement

*Simon Walker**

Introduction

I am particularly pleased to have been asked to talk about the human rights angle in relation to our discussions on trade. I am pleased for the simple reason that although it seems to be fashionable to critique trade in human rights terms, the human rights angle is very often lost. As a result, our critique risks losing focus and thus losing its added value. In 2000, the High Commissioner called for bilinguism between the human rights and trade worlds. I think we have come a long way in bridging this gap – and today, I think we have a constructive dialogue between the Office of the High Commissioner and the WTO. However, I realize there are other gaps we have to bridge – between law and economics, and even between international organizations and the academy. In particular, we must be careful when reducing human rights to an economic calculus. Human rights are about minimum legal standards to protect human dignity of individuals – in particular vulnerable individuals and groups of individuals – but not corporations.

The report

Having said that, I will turn to a summary of the High Commissioner's report on the impact of the Trade-Related Aspects of Intellectual Property Rights (the TRIPS Agreement) on the enjoyment of human rights (document E/CN.4/Sub.2/2001/13).

The report was requested by the Sub-Commission on the Promotion and Protection of Human Rights in August 2000. The Office started work on it early in 2001 with a long process of internal discussion which led ultimately to review and approval of the methodology by the High Commissioner. As part of the drafting process, the High Commissioner requested that the report be based on consultations with the WHO, WTO, UNAIDS and WIPO. All of those or-

---

* The following comments are made in the author's personal capacity and do not necessarily reflect the position of the High Commissioner for Human Rights or her Office.

ganizations were approached, and consultations were subsequently held with the WHO and the WTO. Consultations were held prior to drafting, as well as post drafting, and were particularly helpful in establishing a constructive dialogue between our organizations. The report was submitted to the Sub-Commission and was discussed last week.

In brief, the report provides a framework for a human rights analysis of the WTO's TRIPS Agreement and then focusses specifically on one human right, namely the right to health.

The *point of departure* for the report is that the states negotiating trade rules within the WTO are the same states sitting in the Commission on Human Rights. 111 Member States of the 141 Members of the WTO have ratified the *International Covenant on Economic, Social and Cultural Rights* (ICESCR). All but one have ratified the *Convention on the Rights of the Child* (CRC). Most of the rights in the Universal Declaration are arguably part of customary international law and many states have included it in their constitutions. Given these concurrent obligations on states, the question therefore is: How can these states implement trade rules in ways that also promote and protect human rights?

The report begins by examining the *balance* within the TRIPS Agreement in light of states' obligations under Article 15 of the ICESCR. Article 15 sets out the human right of authors to their moral and material interests in new creations and inventions. On the other hand, the article sets out the right of everyone to enjoy the benefits of scientific advancement. The question becomes one of balance – how to weigh private interests of authors with the public interest in the innovation and wide dissemination of technology.

This notion of balancing public and private interests is not new to IP systems – in fact it lies at their very base. A patent is granted for a limited time to an inventor as an incentive to invent. However, in order to obtain the patent, the inventor has to disclose the best method of peforming the invention. On expiration of the patent, the innovation enters the public domain and so benefits the public. This avoids the possibility of an innovator keeping secret the best method for performing an invention.

Similarly, *the TRIPS Agreement acknowledges the need for balance.* The objectives of the Agreement under Article 7 state that:

> The protection and enforcement of intellectual property rights should contribute to the promotion of technological innovation and to the transfer and dissemination of technology, to the mutual advantage of producers and users of technological knowledge and in a manner conducive to social and economic welfare, and to a balance of rights and obligations.

The principles of the agreement allow states to:

> Adopt measures necessary to protect public health and nutrition, and to promote the public interest in sectors of vital importance to their socio-economic and technological development.

Other articles allow states to take measures in the public interest such as to exclude from patentability inventions on public morality grounds, including to protect human, animal or plant life or health or to avoid serious prejudice to the environment (Article 27(2)).

The Agreement accepts that rights holders also have responsibilities and so allows states to take measures to provide for compulsory licenses (Article 31) as well as to protect against anti-competitive practices (Articles 8 and 40). The agreement obliges developed countries to take measures to promote technology transfer to least developed countries.

The High Commissioner sees these references to public interest issues and responsibilities of rights holders as flexibilities or openings in the Agreement towards a human rights approach to intellectual property protection. Reference to issues such as public health, food security, and the promotion of technological development can be interpreted to allow the fulfillment of the right to health, the right to food and the right to development. Balancing rights with responsibilities responds to the need for balance identified in Article 15, referred to above. Special and differential treatment for least developed countries might promote to some extent human rights notions of affirmative action.

Does the TRIPS Agreement take a human rights consistent approach?

The short answer is no. And I indicate four reasons why this is so.

First and foremost, public health, food security and development concerns are included in the TRIPS Agreement as exceptions. *But human rights are not exceptions.* A human rights approach to the TRIPS Agreement would put the promotion and protection of human rights at the heart of the objectives, not as exceptions to commercial objectives.

Second, while the TRIPS Agreement does include public interest objectives and does indicate some of the *responsibilities* of IPR holders, it does not set out clearly what these responsibilities are. The Agreement goes into considerable detail in setting out the content and modes of enforcement of intellectual property rights but only refers to the responsibilities of IPR holders – such as compulsory licensing or anti-competion laws – as options. Thus the Agreement could be said to be weighted in favour of rights holders.

Third, the TRIPS Agreement includes forms of IP protection relevant to industrialized countries, but not necessarily useful for *knowledge rich but eco-*

nomically poor people. Of course, the TRIPS Agreement allows states voluntarily to develop and implement national legislation such as petty patent protection. But again, while industrial property protection comes within the realms of *obligation*, other forms of intellectual property protection that might be more beneficial for individual innovators come within the realm of *option.*

Finally, there is the issue of *whether a one-system-fits-all approach to intellectual property protection is appropriate for states enjoying very different levels of technological development.* While of course this is an issue for the negotiating parties, I would just note one human rights issue, namely: Have the negotiators of the TRIPS Agreement bargained away their obligations under the *Declaration on the Right to Development*, namely under Article 2(3) which states:

> States have the right and the duty to formulate appropriate national development policies that aim at the constant improvement of the well-being of the entire population and of all individuals, on the basis of their active, free and meaningful participation in development and in the fair distribution of the benefits resulting therefrom.

I would just flag one other issue that was not developed in the report which I believe is important – and this is the question of cost. The legislative and administrative costs involved in implementing the TRIPS Agreement are significant, in particular for least developed countries. Will the introduction and implementation of IP legislation and the establishment of patent and trademark offices drain resources from least developed countries which might better be spent on setting up hospitals or getting child workers back to school? Where is the public benefit here? Further, if, as some commentators have suggested, least developed countries are only meant to set up patent offices that rubber stamp decisions to grant patents already issued by the USPTO, the EPO or the Japanese Patent Office, how does this sit with the human rights concern that patents should be granted only after an appropriate weighing up of the value to the public of granting private rights to technology holders?

So, is the bottle half empty or half full?

While I would argue that the TRIPS Agreement in its present form does not coincide with a human rights approach to intellectual property protection – is this the end of the story? Or could these imbalances be remedied in practice through human rights consistent implementation? Is the bottle half full or half empty? I am an optimist – and I would say that they can. The remainder of the High

Commissioner's report focusses on the right to health as a first step in ensuring human rights consistent implementation of the TRIPS Agreement.

I will not go into great detail on the discussion of the right to health and health aspects of intellectual property systems, although I would refer to the General Comment on the right to health by the Committee on Economic, Social and Cultural Rights (E/C.12/2000/4). I will go straight to the example included in the report as a means of illustrating one way in which the flexibilities of the TRIPS Agreement can be implemented so as to protect the right to health. The case in question is the HIV/AIDS programme in Brazil.

The Brazilian Government, since 1998, has implemented an HIV programme aimed, in part, at providing affordable essential HIV treatments to a growing number of Brazilians living with HIV. Due to an impressive display of political will, the Brazilian Government has provided treatments through local drug production, bringing costs down from an estimated US$530 million to US$ 319 million. Local production of drugs has led to reductions in costs of, on average, 70%. The programme has reduced AIDS deaths by 50% and reduced hospitalizations due to opportunistic diseases by 80%.

Most of the drugs in the HIV programme are off-patent. However two of them are subject to Brazilian patents held by overseas pharmaceutical companies. The purchase through importation of these drugs is currently taking up 36% of the programme's budget. Consequently, the Government has entered into negotiations with the suppliers to lower the prices.

In case the pharmaceutical companies do not agree to lower prices, a local research institute has commenced proceedings for the grant of compulsory licenses over the production of the drugs and has also started research to develop the drugs locally. In the meantime, the Government has managed to get sufficient price reductions on one of the two drugs and is still negotiating on price reductions for the second drug. The possibility of the award of a compulsory license over the drugs has been an effective negotiating tool for the Brazilian Government in obtaining price reductions.

Compulsory licensing is possible under Articles 68 and 71 of the Brazilian Intellectual Property Law. Compulsory licenses can be awarded on a number of bases including on the grounds of national emergency or public interest. These terms are defined in the Presidential Decree on Compulsory Licensing of 1999 which states that:

> There are considered to be within the public interest those facts, among others, related to the public health, nutrition, protection of the environment, as well as those of primordial importance to the technological or social and economic development of this country.

Similarly, the TRIPS Agreement, under Article 31, allows states to take measures to provide for compulsory licenses, including in the case of a national emergency or other circumstances of extreme urgency or in cases of public non-commercial use. The right to health, as elaborated in the General Comment of the Committee on Economic, Social and Cultural Rights, includes a right to affordable, essential drugs, as set out in the WHO's essential drug list. Given that the use of compulsory licensing provisions – consistent with WTO rules – is assisting the Brazilian Government to provide affordable HIV treatments (which are included on the WHO list), the Brazilian case can be seen as an example of best practice where the flexibilities of the TRIPS Agreement are being used in ways to promote the right to health – and specifically the right to access affordable essential drugs.

There are *certain limitations* on the universal relevance/applicability of this example, and I will highlight just two. First, while Brazil is in a position to implement the TRIPS Agreement in ways that take advantage of the flexibilities within the Agreement, many least developed countries are not. The issue here, of course is probably a development question, and would still exist with or without a TRIPS Agreement. The second issue is what is known as TRIPS plus. In spite of the existence of human rights compatible flexibilities in the TRIPS Agreement, certain developed countries apply trade and diplomatic pressure on key developing countries to implement standards higher than those required by the TRIPS Agreement. Apart from the fact that one of the objectives of the TRIPS Agreement was to avoid such resort to unilateral action, the question arises how easily such higher IP standards sit with states' obligations to protect human rights.

One of the *key recommendations* of the High Commissioner in her report therefore is as follows:

> The High Commissioner joins WHO in recommending that developing countries be cautious about enacting TRIPS plus legislation that is more stringent than present requirements under the TRIPS Agreement without first understanding the impact of such legislation on the protection of human rights.

Points for discussion

I would just like to raise an issue that in fact became the key issue in drafting the report – although it is not particularly clear from the text – namely, are intellectual property rights human rights?

The original resolution which led to the submission of the High Commissioner's report also requested a report by the Secretary-General. Rather than prepare a second analytical report, the Office decided to send out a request for information to states, international organizations and NGOs. The response was overwhelming and, as a result, we decided to submit the original report plus an addendum of late responses, which was as large as the original.

When sending information requests to NGOs, normal practice dictates that we send a request only to ECOSOC affiliated organizations. However, given the exceptional nature of the subject matter, we also sent a request to IP institutes and organizations. Thus, the responses covered a wide terrain and some were quite colourful. Indeed some of the responses – including from one of the organizers of this forum – made claims along the lines of, "of course, intellectual property rights are human rights." Only last week, the European Commission sent a letter to the Deputy High Commissioner including such gems as, "In addition, many have rightly argued that the WTO and the TRIPS Agreements are also, in a way, human rights' agreements ..." At an OHCHR briefing to international organizations this May, a representative of the WTO discussed the access to drugs issue as a conflict between two human rights – namely the right to health and patent rights (as human rights). I am not sure what the practical implications of such a linkage would be, but putting corporate-held patents over pharmaceuticals on the level of a moral right that suggests a right of universal coverage could have undesirable effects. Imagine, for example, a pharmaceutical company claiming that its fundamental and inalienable rights would be infringed by the grant of a compulsory license.

And this is where I would like to emphasize the relevance of "the human rights angle" to our discussion. Unless we clearly base our discussion in the fundamentals of human rights, the debate will increasingly be skewed by such misinterpretations.

In any case, this prompted me to do some research to see what exactly the drafters of the Universal Declaration really meant when they included authors' rights as human rights. And the results were interesting. I will summarize them in two points:

First, to my surprise, the drafters were referring to copyright and patents. This should be qualified by the fact that drafters from common law systems (the US, the UK, Australia, New Zealand and Canada) denied the linkage between intellectual property rights and human rights. Further, at least some of the drafters from civil law countries were much more concerned with the protection of moral rights of authors – rights not to have works denigrated – rather than material rights of authors – rights over commercial use and so on. Nonetheless, the drafters clearly came to a consensus that copyright and patents were included within the protected subject matter.

Second, and here is where we come to the fundamentals of human rights, *the drafters were clearly referring to the protection of individual authors.* Although in fact little attention was given to the issue, they had in mind Marie Curie and inventors working away in attics without central heating, working for the benefit of humanity. There is no evidence to suggest that they even considered intellectual property rights as corporate-held rights, or rights that would become so central to international trade. At a time when intellectual property rights are overwhelmingly held and exercised by corporations, it is essential that the distinction is maintained between the rights in the TRIPS Agreement, and human rights in intellectual property.

A more appropriate way to view the TRIPS Agreement and the rights contained in the Agreement is as a mechanism for operationalizing human rights in intellectual property. In other words, so long as the implementation of the TRIPS Agreement (and the exercise of intellectual property rights therein) achieves the right balance – i.e., it promotes the rights of individual authors as well as the rights of everyone to benefit from scientific progress – the TRIPS Agreement could be a vehicle for implementing human rights obligations. However, I think there needs to be considerably more empirical research before such conclusions can be drawn.

The way forward

I will finish with just a few comments on last week's Sub-Commission debate on the TRIPS Agreement. The discussion came under item 4 of the Sub-Commission's agenda "economic, social and cultural rights." The agenda item was wide, and covered a range of other topics, including rights to drinking water, the report of the Special Rapporteurs on globalization, the role of the International Financial Institutions and so on.

The discussion was lively and certainly more sophisticated than in previous years, suggesting a hopeful trend that the international human rights programme is beginning to become more conversant in trade and financial matters. However, there remain several misconceptions on all sides.

The WTO, IMF and World Bank all made contributions to the discussion and most of the Sub-Commission experts who spoke welcomed this contribution. Some of the experts, the WTO and some NGOs spoke on TRIPS. The WTO focussed on the TRIPS Agreement as being part of the solution to public health issues and not the problem, and underlined the flexibility in the Agreement that could allow it to be used to promote public health. They also noted that the WTO Secretariat was assisting states in understanding the opportunities offered by the flexibilities in the Agreement.

The *experts* of the Sub-Commission raised the following issues concerning the TRIPS Agreement:

- The fact that saying something was an intellectual property right does not automatically make it a human right
- The need for the Sub-Commission to focus further on the TRIPS Agreement due to the important role it plays in the world economy
- The need for the Sub-Commission to acquire a technical understanding of the TRIPS Agreement as a means of pursuing a constructive dialogue with the WTO and other organizations and actors
- The need to focus on Article 15 of the ICESCR in discussions on the TRIPS Agreement
- The apparent shift in favour of intellectual property rights holders due to the TRIPS Agreement
- The need to examine new forms of intellectual property protection beyond patents that would be more appropriate to meeting the needs of the international community
- The fact that only larger developing countries are in a position to take advantage of the flexibilities in the TRIPS Agreement
- Encouragement for further dialogue with the WTO

The Sub-Commission adopted a new resolution on "intellectual property and human rights" (E/CN.4/Sub.2/RES/2001/21). The Sub-Commission made the following requests:

- That the High Commissioner seek observer status on the TRIPS Council
- That the High Commissioner submit a report to next year's Sub-Commission on the issue of the impact of the TRIPS Agreement on the rights of indigenous peoples
- That the Commission on Human Rights agree at its next session in Spring 2002 to convene a seminar on the issue of the TRIPS Agreement and human rights.

Finally, as a postscript, the High Commissioner has maintained her focus on intellectual property and the right to health. In October 2001, the High Commissioner, speaking at a meeting on globalization in Ghent, Belgium noted that international trade rules must avoid double standards where emergency measures such as compulsory licensing of antibiotics for the anthrax problem in developed countries are acceptable while compulsory licensing of drugs to treat pandemics is contested.

CHAPTER 10

The WTO Dispute Settlement and Human Rights

*Gabrielle Marceau**

Introduction

WTO dispute settlement and human rights[1] is only a small part of the wider issue of ethics in trade. Human rights aspects of trade actions also cover an important spectrum of moral, ethical, political, social and legal issues. Allegations of conflicts between trade considerations and trade rules, and the respects of human rights, are made regularly. For some, WTO obligations would somehow encourage, lead to, authorize, or permit human rights violations and the WTO treaty should be condemned.[2] Others have argued that violators of human rights are necessarily violators of WTO.[3] Others want to use human rights considerations to justify deviations from WTO market access rules[4] or to condition preferences and advantages.[5] Some recall that WTO Members are bound by the human rights consequences of their trade actions. States' inconsistent positions in human rights and trade fora are often alleged. Many would suggest that conflicts between systems of laws (trade and human rights) and thus systems of values must ultimately be addressed as matters of policy through political arenas, and that dispute settlement, by itself, is unlikely to resolve the issues.[6]

In trying to break down and expound relevant aspects of this debate, I have been asked to examine a very small angle of this multidimensional issue of trade and human rights: WTO dispute settlement and human rights. It is actually quite possible that the WTO dispute settlement system can be seized of a dispute carrying human rights arguments either in support of the complaint or the defense. In this context human rights and WTO dispute settlement may be called to answer the following types of questions: Can a WTO panel accept human rights allegations when there are no references to human rights in the WTO treaty? Can a WTO Member invoke human rights provision to refuse to

---

* The views expressed in this paper are strictly personal and do not bind the WTO Secretariat or the WTO Members. In the preparation of this paper I have greatly benefited from many discussions and exchanges with Hélène Ruiz-Fabri, Brigitte Stern and Joel Trachtman. I am also grateful to Tenu Avafia, Lorand Bartels, Milton Churche, Mireille Cossy, Pieter Jan Kuijper, Simon Lacey, Morris Lipson, Lisa Pearlman, Mara Valenti, Sandiago Vilalpando, Simon Walker and Jochem Wiers for their comments on earlier drafts.

comply with a WTO provision? Does human rights law have direct application in the WTO system of law and before WTO courts? Can a Member invoke human rights consideration in its interpretation of WTO rights and obligations? Can WTO Members legislate in using human rights consideration taking place exclusively on another state, without violating international law on jurisdiction? All these questions are but some aspects of the issue of the relationship between WTO law (and WTO dispute settlement) and human rights.

The concept of "dispute settlement" is also broad: it may cover the procedural aspects of a dispute settlement mechanism. An important systemic issue of dispute settlement is concerned with the concept of the "applicable law", i.e., the system of legal norms binding on WTO Members, as WTO Members, and providing for effective remedies. In this paper I suggest that WTO law is a specific sub-system of international law with specific rights and obligations, specific claims system, specific violations, specific enforcement mechanisms and specific remedies in case of their violation. Dispute settlement is also concerned with the distinct but parallel question of the limited jurisdiction and incapacity of WTO adjudicating bodies to apply and enforce[7] norms other than those of the WTO, including human rights law. The methods and tools used by WTO adjudicating bodies in the interpretation of the "WTO applicable law" are important as well. In this paper I try to develop these three aspects in relation to human rights law, with a discussion of the procedural aspects at the end.

Part I of this paper suggests therefore that the issue whether WTO Members can invoke human rights law to refuse to comply with WTO obligations (including allegations of "conflicts" between WTO and other norms of international law) can only be adequately answered when keeping in mind the nature of the "WTO applicable law" – a specific system of law – as well as the limited competence and jurisdiction of WTO adjudicating bodies. Part II discusses the interpretation of the WTO applicable law in taking into account, when relevant, human rights law. It is suggested that a good faith interpretation of the relevant WTO and human rights provisions should lead to a reading of WTO law coherent with human rights law. The recent Doha Declaration on TRIPS and Public Health is a good example of such coherent reading of WTO provisions taking into account potentially relevant human rights law.

Yet even if their occurrence would be very rare, pure conflicts between WTO law and human rights, including *jus cogens*, are conceptually possible and Part III examines the issue. It concludes that WTO law generally does not receive the direct application of non-WTO norms, such as those of human rights. WTO adjudicating bodies do not appear to have the competence to reach any conclusion that a non-WTO norm has been violated or any conclusion that effectively add, diminish or amend WTO law. Arguably *jus cogens* would have direct effect in WTO applicable law; its violation by a WTO provision would terminate the WTO treaty in its entirety or at least the violating provision. Some may argue that WTO panels and the Appellate Body do not have the capacity to determine the nullity of a WTO treaty provision (or a national measure applying a WTO provision) for violation of *jus cogens*. Others would suggest that the customary prohibition against any violation of *jus cogens* is such as to invalidate *ab initio* any violating provision, a legal reality that binds all States and all institutions. In this sense this customary prohibition would be part of the WTO applicable law. In most, if not all, cases the strong presumption against a violation of *jus cogens* will lead to an interpretation of WTO law which avoids such violation. In any case, WTO Members in violation of non-WTO norms, such as human rights law, remain subject to rules on State responsibility. There is no perfect coherence between the human rights and the WTO systems of laws and jurisdictions.

In Part IV, I slightly touch upon what is probably the most important and complex issue in the trade and human rights debate: that of the WTO jurisdiction. Issues related to and encapsulated in the debate of the WTO jurisdiction, include (1) the state of WTO law on PPMs, (2) whether and how foreign policy considerations are to be used in regulatory and preferential distinctions, (3) generally whether and how WTO provisions can allow WTO Members to act upon extrajurisdictional matters and (4) conflicts and overlaps of jurisdictions. The analysis of the reach of the WTO jurisdiction is difficult and calls for further reflection. To what extent can WTO Members' trade regulatory and preferential distinctions take into account, be based on, react to, or force policy and regulatory changes to, human rights situations taking place entirely and exclusively in another Member's territory?

Lastly, Part V focuses on procedural aspects of WTO and human rights dispute settlement processes. There are very few areas of procedural and judicial overlaps between human rights dispute settlement procedures and those of the WTO. Human rights treaties are mainly concerned with obligations of States *vis-à-vis* individuals while the WTO is essentially a government to government forum. However, it is useful to examine whether the WTO dispute settlement mechanism can learn and benefit from procedural tools developed in human rights proceedings and whether human rights jurisdictions could benefit from Members' experience with WTO dispute settlement procedures.

I. The "WTO applicable law" and the "limited jurisdiction" of WTO adjudicating bodies[8]

The nature and process of WTO dispute settlement mechanism and the reach of Article 23 of the DSU, will often "attract jurisdiction" over any dispute involving any trade restrictions. Therefore, the issue of the "applicable law" between WTO Members and the distinct but related issue of the incapacity of panels and the Appellate Body to make recommendations enforcing autonomous norms of international law, such as those on human rights, must be examined.

A. The DSU will attract jurisdiction in favour of WTO adjudicating bodies

The WTO dispute settlement mechanism can be triggered easily and quickly, and panels and the Appellate Body will often be expected to make rapid rulings, arguably at the exclusion of other jurisdictions for any WTO-related grief.

1. Presumed legal and economic interests sufficient to initiate any of the WTO dispute mechanisms

Unlike requirements for standing in many international tribunals, the criteria for initiating DSU proceedings are easily met. In *US – Wool Shirts and Blouses,* the Appellate Body noted: "If any Member should consider that its benefits are nullified or impaired as the results of circumstances set out in Article XXIII, then dispute settlement is available."[9] Similarly, in *EC – Bananas III*, the Appellate Body referred to "potential export interest":

> ... a Member has broad discretion in deciding whether to bring a case against another Member under the DSU. The language of Article XXIII:1 of the GATT 1994 and of Article 3.7 of the DSU suggests, furthermore, that a *Member is expected to be largely self-regulating in deciding whether any such action would be "fruitful."*... The United States is a producer of bananas, and a *potential export interest* by the United States cannot be excluded.... We also agree with the Panel's statement that: ... with the increased interdependence of the global economy, ... Members have a greater stake in enforcing WTO rules than in the past since any deviation from the negotiated balance of rights and obligations is more likely than ever to *affect them, directly or indirectly.* (Emphasis added.)[10]

Although in practice a Member must have some authentic interest to invest in the initiation of WTO dispute settlement proceedings, the *Korea –*

Dairy Panel rejected the notion that evidence of any economic or legal interest must be provided before WTO proceedings can be triggered.[11] Therefore an allegation that another Member has violated a WTO provision is often sufficient to formally trigger the regular WTO dispute settlement process through a simple request for consultations in writing and copied to the DSB.

2. Quasi-automaticity, reversed consensus and the rapidity of the WTO dispute settlement mechanisms

The WTO dispute settlement mechanism functions according to a principle of reversed consensus (also called negative consensus). According to this new principle, many steps and procedural stages happen automatically, within predetermined time-limits, unless by consensus, WTO Members agree otherwise.[12] When requested a panel must be established, reports of the panel and Appellate Body must be adopted by the DSB and retaliatory sanctions must be authorized. The entire dispute process should be completed within 9 to 12 months. So far, panels and the Appellate Body have respected quite well the deadlines envisaged in the DSU.[13] After the adjudication process (if immediate implementation is not possible) a "reasonable period of implementation" is given to the losing party and varies between 8 and 12 months. At the expiry of that period of implementation parties if they disagree on the WTO consistency of the implementing measure must return before the panel and the Appellate Body before sanctions can be authorized by the DSB. A quick arbitration process is also available if parties do not agree on the level of retaliatory sanctions. In other words, the mechanism is expedient and it is very difficult for any party to a dispute to "block" it. The WTO dispute settlement system proceeds very rapidly compared with any other international adjudication process. WTO Members find these aspects quite convenient and the mechanism is well used.

Allegations that WTO trade is affected would generally suffice to initiate formally the dispute process. Arguments based on human rights considerations – in support of the complaint or the defense – would not in any way change the automatic procedures of the DSU. Human rights arguments will therefore be made once the panel process is well engaged and will be examined with the claims and the defense.

3. The reach of Article 23 of the DSU: Prescriptive and exclusive jurisdiction

Article 23 of the DSU entitled "The Strengthening of the Multilateral System" provides that:

> 23.1 When Members seek the redress of a violation of obligations or other nullification or impairment of benefits under the covered agreements or an impediment to the attainment of any objective of the covered agreements, they shall have recourse to, and abide by, the rules and procedures of this Understanding.
>
> 23.2(a) ... Members shall: (a) *not make a determination to the effect that a violation has occurred*, that benefits have been nullified or impaired or that the attainment of any objective of the *covered agreements* has been impeded, *except through recourse to dispute settlement in accordance with the rules and procedures of this Understanding*, and shall make any such determination consistent with the findings contained in the panel or Appellate Body report adopted by the DSB or an arbitration award rendered under this Understanding." (Emphasis added.)

Article 23 of the DSU is maybe one of the fundamental provision of the DSU. Not only does it prohibit unilateral measures,[14] and arguably some state "behaviour" that would potentially "threaten the multilateral trade system,"[15] but it provides that the WTO has exclusive jurisdiction for matters relating to WTO grieves.[16] Article 23 of the DSU does not, however, resolve the complicated issue of overlaps and conflicts of jurisdictions touched upon in Part IV:D below.

As a means of ruling out any such unilateral measures and subject them to the WTO membership surveillance, Article 23 of the DSU was drafted so that WTO Members have in advance provided WTO adjudicating bodies with exclusive jurisdiction to address violations of WTO provisions. It is possible to "opt out" of the DSU standard procedure by resorting to arbitration under Article 25 of the DSU, if both parties agree. The arbitration process provided for in Article 25 of the DSB remains under the surveillance of the DSU, notably for its implementation (Articles 21 and 22 of the DSU). [17] In this paper I will refer to the general dispute mechanism of panels and the Appellate Body and not the various possibilities offered by Article 25 of the DSU rarely used.[18]

Therefore once a WTO Member has made a formal allegation that a WTO provision has been violated, the final determination rests exclusively with the DSB which will proceed rapidly to adjudicate the dispute. Arguments dealing with human rights considerations may very well be raised during this fast WTO process. Now what can panels and the Appellate Body do?

B. The WTO panels and the Appellate Body have a delegated and limited jurisdiction

WTO panels and the Appellate Body are creation of the DSU, extending the provisions of Articles XXII and XXIII of GATT 1947. Article 3.1 of the DSU provides that "Members affirm their adherence to the principles of management of disputes heretofore applied under Articles XXII and XXIII of GATT 1947, and the rules and procedures as further elaborated and modified herein." All WTO multilateral trade agreements, except GATS, contain a cross-reference to the provisions of Articles XXII and XXIII of GATT and the DSU.[19] GATS refers only to the DSU as it has its own Article XXII and XXIII on dispute settlement.

Under Article XXIII of GATT 1947, CONTRACTING PARTIES were given the authority to assess whether a benefit accruing to a contracting party had been nullified or impaired (or the attainment of the objectives of the GATT was being impeded) as a result of a violation of the GATT.[20] Early on a smaller group of experts were mandated by the CONTRACTING PARTIES to provide them with recommendations whether a GATT provision had been violated. Such panel's recommendations had to be adopted by the CONTRACTING PARTIES to be binding.[21]

Pursuant to GATT Articles XXII and XXIII and the DSU, WTO Members[22] have delegated to panels and the Appellate Body the power to adjudicate their disputes and make recommendations to the DSB. The parameters of this competence of the WTO adjudicating bodies are determined in the DSU. The DSU defines the jurisdiction (mandate) of panels (and the Appellate Body) with reference to (1) allegations of WTO violations by the complaining party(ies); (2) the specific type of remedies/conclusions that panels and the Appellate Body they may recommend; and (3) the prohibition imposed on them to add or diminish WTO law.

1. The mandate of panels: To determine whether provisions of the WTO "covered agreements" have been violated: Articles 1, 4, 7 and 11 of the DSU

Pursuant to Article 1.1, the DSU will apply to disputes brought under the "covered agreements." "Covered Agreements" are listed in Annex 1 of the DSU to include all the multilateral trade agreements, except the TPRM (and the plurilateral agreements if so notified to the DSB). the covered agreements are thus the WTO agreements. Article 4 refers to consultations being initiated on allegations of violations of any of the covered agreements. Article 7.1 provides that the mandate of the panel is "*[t]o examine, in the light of the relevant pro-*

visions in (name of the covered agreement(s) cited by the parties to the dispute), the matter referred to the DSB by (name of party) in document ... and to make such findings as will assist the DSB in making the recommendations or in giving the rulings provided for in *that/those agreement(s).*" (Emphasis added.) Article 7.2 adds that "Panels shall address the relevant provisions *in any covered agreement or agreements* cited by the parties to the dispute... ." (Emphasis added.) Article 11 of the DSU also suggests a limited jurisdiction for panels. It requires a panel to "make an objective assessment of the matter before it, including an objective assessment of the facts of the case and the *applicability of and conformity with the relevant covered agreements*, and make such other findings as will assist the DSB in making the recommendations or in giving the *rulings provided for in the covered agreements.*"[23] (Emphasis added.)

In sum the mandate of panels and the Appellate Body is defined and limited to WTO matters: to apply and enforce the WTO covered agreements.[24] Claims of human rights violation could not be pursed before WTO courts. Human rights provisions that cannot be read into the covered agreements could not be enforced by WTO adjudicating bodies.

2. Panels and the Appellate Body are prohibited from adding or diminishing rights and obligations of the WTO Agreement[25]

Articles 3.2 and 19.1 of the DSU are unambiguous: "... Recommendations and rulings of the DSB cannot add to or diminish the rights and obligations provided in the covered agreements" or (Article 19.1) "...in their findings and recommendations, panels and the Appellate Body cannot add to or diminish the rights and obligations provided in the covered agreements." At best WTO adjudicating bodies could make "suggestions,"[26] yet such suggestions refer to the way the Member may implement and correct the situation condemned by the recommendation that a "WTO provision has been violated." This limitation confirms that to WTO panels cannot enforce or give effect to non-WTO rules, since in doing so they would necessarily add or diminish WTO law. It also confirms that the mandate of panel is to interpret and apply, give (direct) effect to WTO law. WTO adjudicating bodies could not enforce or give effect to human rights provisions that are not in the covered agreements.

3. WTO violation can only lead to specific WTO remedy

As further discussed in Section C:3 below the DSU provides for a standard panel or Appellate Body recommendation: "to bring the measure found inconsistent in conformity with the provisions of the covered agreements." Panels are invited to make suggestions for the manner in which the measure should be brought into conformity but such suggestions are not binding and cannot be enforced.

A single jurisdiction may be authorized or required to use different "applicable law" in different circumstances. The "jurisdiction" (or competence) of panels and the Appellate Body and the relevant "applicable law" between two WTO Members are two legally distinct concepts.[27] The issue of the "applicable law" is relevant because it identifies the set of rights and obligations that binds WTO States and can be enforced before WTO courts. The applicable law is the law that can be given (direct) "effect" between WTO Members, as WTO Members, and before WTO adjudicating bodies. Inherent to the concept of applicable law is that of the applicable remedies. The WTO applicable law is the system of law (rights and obligations) that binds WTO Members and that the WTO adjudicating bodies use and apply to provide effective remedies in case of their violation.

C. The WTO applicable law, a specific sub-system of international law

In the WTO, the applicable law and the jurisdiction/competence of panels are both defined with reference to the WTO law: the covered agreements. The provisions on the limited jurisdiction of panels mirror those on the applicable law between WTO Members. It is suggested that the WTO sub-system of law contains specific rights and obligations and provides in details for the consequences of their violation. Articles 1, 3, 4, 7, 11 and 19 of the DSU identify the source of the subject-matter of adjudication and the specific remedies: the covered agreements. To the extent that specific rights and obligations and specific remedies have been identified in the WTO treaty, WTO Members are presumed to have set up a system that contains a specific applicable law. If this is so, WTO law is a specific sub-system of international law that does not receive directly the other sources of international law (yet, unless contrarily indicated, its provisions are presumed to be compatible and coherent with those of general international law).[28] What is WTO law then? The line between the normal evolution and expansion of the WTO law (through the development of secondary legislation for instance and the formal amendment of WTO) including its liberal interpretation on the one hand, and an illegal addition or diminishing of WTO law on the other hand, is sometimes difficult to draw.

1. Specific obligations – specific claims

Obligations of WTO Members are those contained in the covered agreements identified in Annex 1 and 2, together with relevant secondary legislation. Article II of the Marrakech Agreement Establishing the WTO provides that WTO

Members are bound by that agreement as well as the provisions of Annexes 1, 2 and 3; Article XVI:5 provides that reservation to WTO obligations are possible only pursuant to provisions of the multilateral trade agreements, and none of them contains any such reservation process. The WTO obligations and rights are those of the covered agreements. Claims can relate only to violations of any of the covered agreements.[29]

2. Specific system of enforcement

As discussed above Article 23 of the DSU has been interpreted as prohibiting any form of non-authorized unilateral action. Grieve relating to WTO rights and obligations can only be brought before WTO courts and according to the DSU procedures.

3. Specific remedies

Article 19.1 of the DSU provides:

> "Where a panel or the Appellate Body concludes that a measure is inconsistent with a covered agreement, it shall recommend that the Member concerned bring the measure into conformity with that agreement. In addition to its recommendations, the panel or Appellate Body may suggest ways in which the Member concerned could implement the recommendations."

This provision can be read as excluding remedies under general international law on State Responsibility. In *US – Import Measures*, the Appellate Body seems to have concluded that once the challenged measure has been removed, no further remedial action is possible; the standard remedy "bring your measure into conformity" would not include the possibility, for instance, of obtaining financial compensation for lost trade opportunities:[30]

> 81. We note, though, that there is an obvious inconsistency between the finding of the Panel that "the 3 March Measure is no longer in existence" and the subsequent recommendation of the Panel that the DSB request that the United States bring its 3 March Measure into conformity with its WTO obligations. The Panel erred in recommending that the DSB request the United States to bring into conformity with its WTO obligations a measure which the Panel has found no longer exists.[31]

The DSU regulates numerous aspects of Members' remedial actions, their implementation and their surveillance by the DSB.

(1) Regulation of the period of implementation, when immediate implementation is not possible, i.e., the "reasonable period" (Article 21.1 of the DSU), including the possibility of arbitration on that reasonable period in case of disagreement between the parties (Article 21.3 of the DSU).

(2) The requirement that following the first six months of the reasonable period and until full satisfaction.

- the non-implemented DSB recommendations remain on the DSB agenda;
- 10 days before each DSB meeting the Member at fault must provide a written "status report" of its progress in the implementation of the recommendations and rulings (21.6 of the DSU).
- at each of those meetings the Member at fault must thus provide to the DSB an explanation on the status of its implementation, together with a public explanation as to how it intends to implement and remedy the illegal situation.

(3) Obligation of the faulty Member to reply to any other WTO Member entitled to raise any matter relating to the issue of implementation of DSB recommendations and thus request information and ask questions to the concerned Member(s). If the matter is one brought by a developing country, the DSB is obliged to consider whether further action might take place (Article 21.7 of the DSU).

(4) If the dispute was initiated by a developing country, the DSB is obliged to consider (alternative and) appropriate action. In doing so it shall take into account not only the trade coverage of the measures but also their impact on the economy of the developing country (Article 21.8 of the DSU).

(5) Article 21.5 of the DSU regulates the determination of the WTO compatibility of the remedial action (the implementing measure) by a WTO adjudicative body and excludes any other forum or means to do so.

(6) The regulated possibility of temporary, voluntary and WTO compatible trade-compensation pursuant to Articles 3.7 and 22.1 of the DSU.

(7) The regulated (albeit quasi-automatic) authorization mechanism to Members to use retaliatory sanctions (Article 22.2-22.6 of the DSU).

(8) The obligation to rely on WTO arbitration in case of disagreement between the parties, for the determination of the level of sanctions (Article 22.6-22.7 of the DSU).

(9) The exclusive jurisdiction of WTO arbitrators to determine a level of sanction "equivalent" to the level of nullification (a criteria distinct from the "appropriate" benchmark under general international law).

The DSU specifically defines the WTO applicable remedies, i.e., the only remedies available for violations of the WTO. This limitation on available remedies is another evidence that the applicable law between WTO Members is limited to WTO law, i.e., the covered agreements. This seems to have been the conclusion reached by the panel in *US – Certain EC Products*:

> 6.133 (…) In short the regime of counter-measures, reprisals or retaliatory measures has been strictly regulated under the WTO Agreement. It is now only in the institutional framework of the WTO/DSB that the United States could obtain a WTO compatible determination that the European Communities violated the WTO Agreement, and it is only in the institutional framework of the WTO/DSB that the United States could obtain the authorization to exercise remedial action. [footnote 170: Therefore, in the WTO context, the provision of Article 60 of the Vienna Convention on the Laws of Treaties (1969) on this matter does not apply since the adoption of the more specific provisions of Article 23 of the DSU.]

4. The Covered Agreements cannot be changed or amended without using the WTO-specific procedures

Panels and the Appellate Body cannot make a finding that a non-WTO provision, such as a human right treaty, has superseded a relevant WTO provision as in doing so they would in effect be amending the WTO treaty, contrary to general international law and WTO rules on amendment. It is indeed difficult to conceive situations where a panel would set aside a WTO provision in favour of another treaty or customary provision claimed to have superseded the relevant WTO provision, without amending the WTO, at least between the two disputing States and potentially with regarding to other WTO Members not party to the superseding treaty.

Under general international law,[32] and as provided for, a superseding treaty provision can be considered as "amending" another treaty provision only if it does not affect the rights or the performance of other states under the superseded treaty. Could it be argued that two WTO Members can modify (a concept distinct from amending) their bilateral rights and obligations without affecting the rights of other WTO Members? For instance, two WTO Members could require that human rights be respected as a condition for trade *between them only*. Arguably, the other WTO Members – not subject to such human rights requirements – could not claim that their market access rights would be reduced by the existence of this bilateral requirement and may therefore not initiate any WTO dispute process. Can two WTO Members modify their WTO rights and obligations between the two of them only? Can two WTO Members "add to or diminish" their respective WTO rights and obligations if they do not affect the trade opportunities of third WTO Members? If the WTO obligations are always the same for all Members – and it can be argued that they are – such bilateral modification of WTO rights and obligations may simply not be possible without affecting the rights of other third WTO Members. In light of the GATT/WTO basic rule on the most-favoured national principle (MFN), one may conceive many situations where the specific rights or obligations provided for in a bilateral treaty may effectively reduce the rights or obligations of other WTO Members not party to this bilateral treaty. It is worth noting the concluding remarks of the Appellate Body in the recent *US – Section 211 Appropriation Act* where it stated that when a Member's TRIPS related measure affects some Members, the obligations of national treatment and most-favoured nation principles oblige the provision of similar advantage to all Members.[33]

5. The "implied powers" resulting from the obligation to adjudicate WTO disputes with objectivity

Schoenbaum has suggested that the provisions of Article 11 of the DSU which calls on panels to "make such other findings as will assist the DSB in making the recommendations or in giving the rulings" is "an implied powers clause which should be interpreted broadly so that the panels and Appellate Body can decide all aspects of a dispute."[34] As argued in this paper, many non-WTO issues will often need to be addressed and interpretation of international and national legal instruments need to be performed in order for panels to apply and enforce WTO law. But these considerations will be performed only to the extent necessary to interpret and apply WTO law, not do decide "all aspects of a dispute."[35]

Article 11 of the DSU can however been read as providing panels with the necessary power and the obligation to ensure that the application of the covered agreements and its administration of the dispute process for their enforcement are done objectively. This objectivity calls for a good faith interpretation of the substantive and procedural provisions of WTO law, in light of general international law that binds WTO Members. This would notably include the right and obligation of panels to adopt specific rules of procedure on due process etc. Part V examines this power in the context of the procedural aspects of the WTO dispute settlement procedures.

D. Conclusion: The limited "domain" of WTO[36]

Joel Trachtman early on insisted on the limited "domain" of the WTO dispute settlement mechanism, noting in particular the fact that panels and the Appellate Body are prohibited from adding and diminishing rights and obligations of Members under the WTO Agreement. His analysis concentrate on the limited capacity of WTO adjudicating bodies to enforce any non-WTO law that would add or diminish to the covered agreements. I would like to suggest that the WTO applicable law participate into the limited domain of the WTO law in identifying specific rights and obligations and specific remedies. This limited jurisdictional domain of WTO law and WTO adjudicating bodies does not, however, reduce the obligations of WTO Members to comply at all times with their other international law obligations. This limited domain of WTO only exacerbates the lack of coordination between the WTO system of law and other systems of international law.

In *Korea – Government Procurement*, the Panel reached the conclusion that "[c]ustomary international law applies generally to the economic relations between WTO Members. Such international law applies to the extent that the WTO treaty agreements do not 'contract out' from it."[37] I would like to suggest that the meaning of this statement is simple and obvious: WTO Members remain bound by all their obligations under general international law at all times. While they are Members of the WTO, States must continue to respect all their other international obligations, including their human rights obligations. The state of international law will therefore influence the scope and the reach of WTO rights and obligations which must be interpreted in light of this general obligation imposed on States to comply with all their obligations in good faith, including those on human rights, with a view to avoiding conflicts with other parts of international law. At the same time, the WTO applicable law may not receive non-WTO norms directly and non-WTO law does not have direct effect into the WTO system. In addition, WTO adjudicating bodies are capable of enforcing the state of international law between the two WTO disputing parties if it implies an addition or diminution of the covered agreements.

Joost Pauwelyn rightly has argued that a distinction must be established between the "applicable law" and the "jurisdiction" of panel: for him "the jurisdiction of WTO panels is limited. The applicable law before them is not."[38] For Pauwelyn, Members are presumed to have accepted the binding effect and the direct application of general international law into the WTO law. For him, if the relevant conflict rules demonstrate that a non-WTO rule must prevail, "then the WTO rule cannot be applied (and the defendant wins)." For Pauwelyn this would not result in "requiring the WTO panel to judicially enforce the other rule of international law" and "the panel would not be 'diminishing' the rights of the complainants," as the complainant would have agreed to these conflict rules in the first place.[39]

For Pauwelyn, when panels are giving full effect to a non-WTO rule that will supersede WTO rules, a panel is not "enforcing" the non-WTO rule because the WTO Members are presumed to have accepted the application of conflict rules of general international law, as part of the covered agreements. For me, on the contrary, allowing a non-WTO provision on human rights (or others) to supersede and set aside a WTO provision and therefore in giving a legal effect to this non-WTO provision, can only be viewed as adding or diminishing the WTO covered agreements (or amending it).

Lorand Bartels has argued that the DSU does not place any a priori restrictions on the sources of international law applicable in a WTO dispute. For him, Articles 3.2 and 19.1 of the DSU act as conflict rules which ensure that covered agreements prevail over any other norms to the extent of any inconsistency.[40] Although the ultimate result of Bartels' suggestion is the one recommended in this paper, there is no justification or benefit in considering Articles 3.2 and 19.2 of the DSU as conflict rules. Nothing in the wording of Articles 3.2 and 19.1 seem to indicate any intention of the drafter to envisage conflict situation (which they have done on other occasion with Article XVI:4 of the Marrakesh Agreement and the General interpretative Note to Annex 1A). For Bartels therefore in situation of silence of the WTO treaty, rules of general international law would find direct application – since there could not be any "conflict." It is suggested the application (or direct effect) of non-WTO law provisions into WTO law system will always lead to an addition or diminishing of the covered agreements.[41]

This WTO applicable law (specific obligations and specific consequences of their violation) seems to exclude the direct application of rules of general international law, including those on state responsibility. General international law continue to bind WTO Members and remain relevant and benchmark in the interpretation of WTO law. In the recent *US – Cotton Safeguard*, the Appellate Body after analyzing the safeguard provisions of the WTO Agreement on Textiles and Clothing stated:

"Our view is supported further by the rules of general international law on state responsibility, which require that countermeasures in response to breaches by states of their international obligations be commensurate with the injury suffered."[42]

This would confirm the view that WTO law is to be analyzed and interpreted consistently with general international law (and in taking into account all relevant rules of international law) which can be used to identify the parameters of WTO rights and obligations. General international law or human rights law cannot find direct application between WTO Members and before WTO adjudicating bodies. The lack of coordination and coherence between the two systems of law (WTO law and general international law) and the overlap of jurisdictions, are issues discussed in Part IV:D below. States parties to the potentially superseding treaty maintain their rights outside the WTO jurisdiction pursuant to rules on state responsibility.

II. The interpretation of the WTO applicable law using general international law, including human rights, when relevant

The limited domain of the WTO does not mean that the WTO Agreement exists in a closed system hermetic to general international law and to human rights law.[43] To the contrary, the obligation for States to implement all their obligations in good faith,[44] the wording of many WTO provisions and principles of interpretation *require* panels and the Appellate Body to use or to take into account the various other treaties, customs and general principles of law, including those relating to human rights, when interpreting, and assessing compliance with, WTO provisions.

A. Interpretations that will avoid conflicts with Member's relevant human rights obligations

In its first dispute, the Appellate Body made it clear that the WTO Agreement could not be read in "clinical isolation from public international law."[45] Article 3.2 of the DSU requires the WTO agreements to be interpreted in light of customary rules of interpretation which leads, among other references, to the Vienna Convention on the Interpretation of Treaties (Vienna Convention). Article 3.1 of the Vienna Convention offers tools to perform this exercise, the first of which is the ordinary meaning of the terms of the treaty, in light of the object and purpose of that treaty. Article 31.2 describes what can be considered as "context." Article 31(3)(b) refers to any subsequent practice in the application of the treaty which establishes the agreement of the parties regarding its interpretation. Article 31.3 mandates that related actions of the parties as well as other relevant rules of international law, may be taken into account together with the context.

1. Article 31.3(c) of the Vienna Convention

Article 31.3(c) of the Vienna Convention is particularly relevant when interpreting treaty obligations, such as those of the WTO Agreement, which interact with various treaties. Article 31.3(c) provides that "There shall be taken into account, together with the context: ... (c) any relevant rules of international law applicable in the relations between the parties." 1. Article 31.3(c) of the Vienna Convention.

Rules of international law

The term "rules of international law" seems to refer to all public international law sources, including those relating to human rights when relevant. Thus, all sources of international law, including international customs and general principles of international law (Article 38.1(b) of the ICJ Statute),[46] or general principles of (domestic) law accepted by nations (Article 38.1(c) of ICJ Statute), would have to "be taken into account." Some treaties would also have to be taken into account (Article 38.1(a) of the ICJ Statute).

Applicable to the relations between the parties

The requirement that any such rule be "applicable to the relations between the parties," implies that the international law rule must apply, thus be binding on the parties. But which parties? One narrow interpretation would read "parties" as meaning all WTO Members. In other words, for a non-WTO treaty to be used to interpret WTO obligations, it and the WTO Agreement would require identical membership. This approach seems to have provided the basis for the *Tuna II* panel's decision to exclude any consideration of CITES because it was a multilateral agreement signed only by some of the parties to the GATT.[47] While this approach provides a conceptually clear rule, it suffers from a number of problems. It would greatly reduce the number of outside treaties and legal principles that could be used to interpret WTO obligations under Article 31.3(c). Few international agreements, if any, will have identical membership, although some may have a wider membership. But to request that such non-WTO treaty have at least the WTO membership would also create illogical situations. As WTO Membership grows, fewer international agreements will match its membership. This would lead to the paradoxical result that the WTO would, at least in theory, become more isolated from other international systems of laws as its membership grows. In addition there may be principles and provisions in an international treaty (with smaller membership) which have become a customary rule of international law binding on all countries, even if non-signatory to that treaty. Moreover, from a legal perspective, the "identical membership" approach (at the WTO membership) does not seem to be consistent with that adopted by the Appellate Body in *Shrimp*, which examined CITES and a number of other MEAs, many of which did not have the same membership as the WTO.[48]

Another more sophisticated criterion, yet stringent, would be to allow the use of rules in treaty open to wide *membership*. For instance, Article 3 of Annex 1 of the SPS Agreement, Articles 4 and 5 of the TBT Agreement and Article VI:5 of the GATS refer to standards developed in relevant international (or even regional) organizations as being those organizations whose membership is *open to* all Members of the WTO.[49]

Joost Pauwelyn[50] has suggested that only international law rules that have been accepted or tolerated by all WTO Members can be taken into account when interpreting WTO provisions. On the other hand, Pauwelyn would provide bilateral treaties with direct effect (being enforced by panels to the extent that they may supersede WTO provision and allow a Member to avoid a violation of a WTO provision). It is difficult to understand why such treaty-having-now-become-binding-on-WTO-Members-and-thus-part-of-the-WTO-applicable-law (and part of the legal context of other WTO provisions) could not be "taken into account" in the interpretation of other provisions of the WTO Agreement. Arguably, using Pauwelyn's criteria, the silence of Members would authorize the use of non-WTO norms that would be binding only a small group of States.

A broader interpretation of the terms "applicable in the relations between the parties" would allow the use of treaties between a smaller or different group – more than one WTO Member, but less than the whole WTO membership – to interpret WTO obligations. This interpretation is supported by the different usage of "parties" throughout Article 31 and in Article 31.3(c). Article 31.2(a) refers to "any agreement relating to the treaty which was made between *all the parties*," and Article 31.2(b) refers to an instrument by "*one or more* parties" and accepted by "the *other* parties." Therefore, it could be argued that the use, without these qualifications, of "the parties" in 31.3(b) and (c) allows consideration of treaties signed by a subset of the WTO membership that is less than all the parties, but more than one of the parties.[51] With human rights issues, the membership of such other human rights treaties will often be at least as broad as that of the WTO.

In other words, 31.(c) would potentially reach a series of binding norms; parties to the disputes must be parties to these rules of international law. What finally determines which of all those international law rules are to be used is rather the relevance of this rule of international law in light of the nature of the WTO provisions that is interpreted.

Relevant rules of international law

The third element – and a crucial one – of Article 31.3(c) is the reference to "relevant" rule of international law. It is suggested that the reach of the provision will be determined with reference to the type and nature of the WTO obligation at issue. Since many of the WTO obligations are multilateral in their nature, international law rules to be used for their interpretation, should also be multilateral in their nature. But some obligations are either negotiated bilaterally or have application between a small group of WTO Members.

For example, the Appellate Body has used for the interpretation of the WTO, and made otherwise reference to, treaties with different membership than that of the WTO. In *EC – Bananas III*, the WTO provision under examination was the Lomé waiver, adopted pursuant to Article IX of the Agreement Establishing the WTO. The Appellate Body used the Lomé Convention in its interpretation of the WTO waiver. This was logical since the waiver, albeit multilaterally approved, was concerned with special rights and obligations of a group of WTO Members. The said Lomé Convention was "relevant." In *EC – Computer Equipment*,[52] the Appellate Body blamed the panel for not referring to the HS Classification treaty when interpreting the WTO Schedule of the United States, while the membership of the HS treaty is different from that of the WTO. In *US – Shrimp*[53] the Appellate Body examined the term "exhaustible natural resources" in light of both the Convention on Biological Diversity and the Convention on the Conservation of Migratory Species of Wild Animals – albeit here it can be argued that the definition therein was generally accepted by all WTO Members. In *EC – Poultry*[54] the Appellate Body said that the bilateral agreement between Brazil and the European Communities could also be relevant (under 32 of the Vienna Convention) when interpreting Brazil's Schedule. In the interpretation of Article XXIV on regional trade agreements, Article 31.3(c) could possibly point to agreements between a smaller group of WTO members than full membership.

Article 31.3(c) is a tool, an indicator of the norms/rules of international law that must be taken into account in the interpretation of treaties, such as that of the WTO. It indicates three variables to be assessed in the determination of whether a specific norm is to be used. The identification of such "rules" for the interpretation of a specific WTO provision is a legal issue that is appealable before the Appellate Body. The evidentiary appreciation of the compliance with such rules is generally under the exclusive jurisdiction of panels unless of the three situations condemned by the Appellate Body in *EC – Hormones* ("disregard" and "distortion" and "misrepresentation" of the evidence) exist.[55]

In sum the assessment of which rule of international law applicable to the relations between the parties is relevant in the interpretation of a WTO provision is to be assessed on a case-by-case basis in light of the nature of the WTO provisions at issue, keeping in mind that there may be different degrees of relevance. In fact, Article 31.3(c) of the Vienna Convention can be viewed as an obligation on panels to be "aware of" – and take them into account – what is otherwise international law between the WTO disputing parties. In all cases, the reliance of relevant provisions of general international law and their necessary examination by a panel would always be performed "only to the extent necessary to interpret [the WTO provision]."[56]

2. Evolutive interpretation

Article 31.3(c) also subsumes the principle of "evolutionary interpretation,"[57] a principle that is of particular importance when dealing with concepts such as those of "human rights" or the invocation of GATT Article XX(a) "public morals" or Article XX(e) "prison labor," which have constantly evolved since the creation of the United Nations. In *US – Shrimp*, when interpreting the term "exhaustible natural resources" in Article XX(g), the Appellate Body referred to a number of non-WTO sources of international law after having noted that that concept had evolved. The Appellate Body stated:

> The words of Article XX(g), "exhaustible natural resources," were actually crafted more than 50 years ago. They must be read by a treaty interpreter in the light of contemporary concerns of the community of nations about the protection and conservation of the environment. While Article XX was not modified in the Uruguay Round, the preamble attached to the *WTO Agreement* shows that the signatories to that Agreement were, in 1994, fully aware of the importance and legitimacy of environmental protection as a goal of national and international policy. The preamble of the *WTO Agreement* – which informs not only the GATT 1994, but also the other covered agreements – explicitly acknowledges "the objective of *sustainable development*..."[58]

From the perspective embodied in the preamble of the WTO Agreement, we note that the generic term "natural resources" in Article XX(g) is not "static" in its content or reference but is rather "by definition, evolutionary."[59]

Sinclair stated, in respect of Article 31.3(c), that:

> "there is some evidence that the evolution and development of international law may exercise a decisive influence on the meaning to be given to expressions incorporated in a treaty, particularly if these expressions themselves denote relative or evolving notions such as 'public policy' or 'the protection of morals.'"[60]

The International Court of Justice (ICJ) has made use of an "evolutionary" approach in certain cases, including most recently in the *Case Concerning the Gabcíkovo-Nagymaros Project (Hungary/Slovakia)* where it stated: "...[The] Treaty is not static, and is open to adapt to emerging norms of international law."[61] The ICJ did the same in the *Case of the Aegean Sea Continental Shelf (Greece vs Turkey)* when it wrote: "It follows that in interpreting and applying reservation (b) with respect to the present dispute the Court has to take into account the evolution which has occurred in the rules of international law concerning a coastal State's rights of exploration and exploitation over the continental shelf."[62] In the NAFTA context, an Arbitration Group recently concluded that the use of the term "GATT" in the cross-reference from the provisions of the FTA and NAFTA had to be interpreted to mean GATT as it evolved into the WTO Agreement.[63] The European Court of Justice has also made use of such principle: "Finally, every provision of community law must be placed in its context and interpreted in the light of the provisions of Community law as a whole, regard being had to the objectives thereof and *to its state of evolution at the date on which the provision in question is to be applied.*" (Emphasis added.)

The European Court of Human Rights has also made use of the evolutive interpretation, since it considers the Convention "as a living instrument which must be interpreted in the light of present-day conditions." To come at the interpretation "imposed" by the changes that have occurred since the Convention was drafted, the European Court usually compares the legislations of the contracting Countries in order to find out which evolution they have been passed through. The Court also takes into consideration the relevant international instruments on the subject-matter at dispute.[64]

In the context of import restrictions imposed for human rights considerations, a WTO Member may want to justify its actions by invoking the exception of "public morals" in Articles GATT XX(a) and GATS XIV(a), or "prison labour" in GATT Article XX(e) or concepts such as "security" or "emergency in international relations" exceptions pursuant to GATT Article XXI and GATS Article XIV *bis*. There is no jurisprudence interpreting so far such concepts and it is far from clear whether the violation of human rights could be covered by the terms "protection of public morals." Having said this, the evolution of the GATT exceptions bring about interesting questions.

For instance, faced with the absence of reference to "prison labour" in the list of GATS exceptions of Article XIV, it may be possible for a panel to conclude that the term "public moral" of GATS Article XIV(a) has evolved (from the GATT days) to include "prison labour." At the same time it would be difficult to conclude that the reach of GATT Article XX(a) "public morals" is narrower than that of GATS Article XIV(a) referring to similar "public morals and public order" concept. Has the term "public morals " in GATT XX evolve to cover what the term "public morals and public order" of GATS XIV(a) now reach? How can a single measure be exempted under GATS for a policy reason condemned under GATT? Questions arise if the "security" exceptions (in Articles GATT XXI or GATS XIV *bis*) were invoked to justify trade restrictions based on human rights. Can the interpretation of Article GATT XXI(b)(iii) "emergency in international relations," remain impermeable to the evolution of the concept of "threat to peace and security" in general international law authorizing the use of force and other Chapter VII measures by the Security Council and individual States when faced with crisis and massive violations of human rights taking place entirely in another States?

In sum it is argued that Article 31.3(c) of the Vienna Convention aims at promoting some "coherence" in international law, so that the treaty being interpreted and other relevant international law rules are read in a way that is mutually supportive and avoids conflict. The WTO Agreement, as with any other treaty, should be interpreted taking into account other relevant and applicable rules of international law, including human rights. In this context, it should generally be possible to interpret WTO provisions in a way that allow States to respect all their international law obligations, including those of human rights law.

B. Examples of human rights provisions alleged to be relevant in the interpretation of WTO provisions

Human Rights provisions relevant and applicable to the parties to a dispute would indeed have to be taken into account when interpreting WTO provisions that deal with a subject-matter also address by specific or general human rights law. Robert Howse and Katau Mutua have argued that the WTO treaty, including the reference to sustainable development in the preamble, provisions of the TRIPS Agreement, and Article XX should be interpreted in light of the treaty (even subsequent) commitments by the relevant parties.[65]

The sources of human right law are important.[66] An important difficulty in dealing with human rights treaties is the fact that they are often drafted in rather general terms and frequently there is no consensus on their implications. Jose Alavarez identifies well this problem in a commentary on Howse and Mutua's paper.[67] What is the "right to health"? What is the "right to food" and what does it entail in terms of rights and obligations of states? Why and how are they relevant to WTO obligations? As mentioned in the previous section of this article, the "relevance" of the non-WTO rule is determinant in the identification of the non-WTO rules that can be used in the interpretation of WTO applicable law.

It has been suggested[68] (before the Doha WTO Ministerial Conference) that the "human right to health" was determinant when interpreting the TRIPS Agreement, including developing countries' right to make full use of the compulsory licensing provisions of Article 31 of the TRIPS Agreement, or to make use of parallel importations. In the opinion of proponents of this human rights argument,[69] the TRIPS Agreement, in particular in light of the preamble, Articles 1, 7 and 8 which call for a "balanced" reading of the agreement, should be interpreted in light of Articles 55 and 56 of the United Nations Charter, Articles 25 and 27 of the Universal Declaration on Human Rights, Articles 12 and 2 of the International Covenant on Social Economic and Cultural Rights as further discussed in General Comment No. 14 and 3 of the Human rights' Committee, all referring to the right to health. Robert Howse further argued that even the WHO Policy Statement relating to the issue before the WTO panel, should have been taken into account when interpreting the balancing requirements under Articles 7 and 8 of the TRIPS Agreement.

Caroline Dommen has argued human rights could be invoked by Brazil to defend (part) of its health programme challenged under the TRIPS Agreement by the United States.[70] For her, Brazil could rely on Article 2 of the International Covenant on Economic, Social and Cultural Rights ("Economic Covenant") obliging States to take steps individually and through international assistance to the maximum of its resources with a view to achieving progressively the full realization of the rights set up in the Covenant, including an adequate standard of living, housing, work, education, food, health etc.

Some have suggested that the "human right to food" may be invoked by developing countries when interpreting provisions of the Agreement on Agriculture. Mauritius has invoked the right to food in the context of the issues of food security and non-trade concerns for developing countries. Mauritius has argued[71] that pursuant to Article 20 and the Preamble of the Agreement on Agriculture,[72] non-trade concerns should be taken into account in the continuation of reform process and this includes the developing countries' right to food. In support of its allegation, Mauritius stated that during the last 50 years, a number of international legal instruments relating to nutritional concerns and the right to food have been developed. For Mauritius, the fundamental right of everyone to be free from hunger is recognised and guaranteed access to adequate food is the responsibility of the State. For Mauritius, when interpreting the obligation (including those of negotiation) under the Agreement on Agriculture, the problems of both food-importing and food-exporting countries should be taken into account "*to ensure an equitable distribution of world food supplies in relation to need.*[73]

At the Bern conference in August 2001 Simon Walker submitted the Report of the High Commissioner on Human Rights on "The Impact of the TRIPS Agreement on Human Rights" which advocates a "human rights approach to the TRIPS Agreement."[74] Referring to Articles 7 and 8 of the TRIPS Agreement which call for an interpretation and application of the TRIPS Agreement conducive to social and economic welfare and a balance of rights and obligations," the Report makes at least 10 recommendations where the TRIPS Agreement would be interpreted and enforced in line with human rights. This report contains multiple examples of possible interpretations of the WTO taking into account human rights law. Arguably the Doha Declaration on TRIPS addressed some of those issues and as such would constitute an expression of this possibility to reconcile WTO provisions and relevant human rights law. Mauritius then referred to a series of international instruments that offer further parameters on the content of such right to food: (1) the Universal Declaration of Human Rights which in Article 25-1 states that everyone has the right to a standard of living adequate for the health and well-being of himself and his family, includes a right to food; (2) the International Covenant on Economic, Social and Cultural Rights (ICESCR), adopted by the UN in 1996, namely Article 11.1 of the Covenant which recognizes the right of everyone to an adequate standard of living for himself and his family, including adequate food; (3) the 1996 World Food Summit which emphasised that access to sufficient and adequate food is a right applying to everyone. (Objective 7.4 of the Plan of Action adopted by consensus at the Summit underlines that "governments, in partnership with all actors of civil society, will, as appropriate... make every effort to implement the provisions of Article 11 of the ...Covenant....") For Mauritius, the government commitments relating to the right to food are basically result-oriented, and the international conventions do not prescribe any specific policy instrument. WTO instruments should therefore be used accordingly.[75]

The above list of examples does not diminish the difficulty of identifying which "rule of international human rights law" would be relevant when interpreting the specific WTO provisions or when assessing compliance with a WTO provision. What is this human right to food? Article 11 of the Economic Covenant, as detailed in the General Comment No 12, Article 24(2)(c) of the Convention on the Rights of the Child, Article 12(2) of the Convention on the Elimination of All Forms of Discrimination Against Women, Article 25 of the Universal Declaration on Human rights, the first Commitment of the 1996 Rome World Food Summit Political Declaration and Plan of Action, Article 10(b) of the Declaration on Social progress and development, Articles 1 and

2(3) of the Declaration on the Right to development and Articles 1 and 2 of the Universal Declaration on the Eradication of Hunger and Malnutrition offer specific parameters of such concept.

What is the right to health? Human rights activists refer generally to a series of treaties and international declarations that offer definitions and criteria for such right to health. Specific references and criteria exist in Article 5(e)(iv) of the Convention on the Elimination of All Forms of Racial Discrimination, Article 12(1) of the Convention on the Elimination of All Forms of Discrimination Against Women, and Articles 23, 24 and 27 of the Convention on the Rights of the Child. Regional human rights treaties which declare that human beings have a right to health would include Article XX of the Helsinki Final Act, Article 1 of the Declaration on the Rights of Disabled Persons, Article 27 of the Declaration on the Use of Scientific and Technological progress in the Interests of Peace and for the benefit of Mankind, the Declaration of Alma-Ata on primary health Care, the Preamble and Article 1 of the Declaration on the Right to Development as well as the Cairo Declaration on Population & Development, the 1995 Copenhagen Declaration on Social development and the 1995 Beijing Declaration and programme of Action on the Rights of Women. The Declaration on the Right and Responsibility of Individuals, Groups and Organs of Society to Promote and Protect Universally Recognized Human Rights and Fundamental Freedoms and the United Nations Millennium Declaration could also serve as useful instruments – whether in and of themselves binding or not – when interpreting WTO provisions dealing with health matters.

Although this preliminary identification of international instruments dealing with the rights to food or the right to health is necessary, it is not sufficient to consider them relevant to the interpretation of a specific WTO provisions. To our benefit the Committee on Economic, Social and Cultural Rights has adopted a series of interpretations of many provisions of the Covenant on Economic and Social rights;[76] the legal value (and the general acceptance by States) of such Committee Reports is not clear. To the least these Comments can be viewed as statements by Human Rights experts of the Human Right Committee that can be used as expert doctrine for the interpretation of human rights law.

C. The normative and flexible nature of certain provisions of WTO and human rights law

Many WTO provisions are drafted in flexible terms so as to provide WTO panels "flexibility" in the assessment of WTO compliance. For instance, Articles

GATT XX and GATS XXI exceptions are more of the nature of "standards," as opposed to specific "rules" – to borrow the analytical framework and distinction introduced by Joel Trachtman.[77] Their application will call for further "completion" – by panels – of the specific parameters of such WTO prescriptions, in light of the specific circumstances of each dispute.[78] Trachtman also suggested that under GATT Article XX type of provisions, panels are requested to "complete the WTO contract" or "fill in gaps"[79] left intentionally by the WTO legislators to the WTO adjudicators.

Although I agree with Joel Trachtman's analytical framework, I have difficulties with the use of terms such as "gap" or "to be completed" as they carry the idea that something was missing from the text of the WTO. Nothing was missing. As suggested by Trachtman, some provisions of the GATT, such as Article XX, were intentionally drafted in general terms to allow for the flexibility that is necessary for a single norm to be used in numerous and distinct factual circumstances. Article XX refers to policy considerations and impose behaviour obligations which can be best drafted only in general terms and which will require panels to balance various factual and legal elements on a case-by-case basis.

For example, GATT Article XX authorizes measures necessary for the protection of public morals or health etc.... Determination of compliance under GATT Article XX is thus a mixed question of facts and law. As mentioned in the previous discussion on the "evolutive interpretation," references to concepts of "public order" or "public morals" or "prison labour" or "health" may call for the examination of relevant human rights instruments to define the parameters of such concepts. In determining whether a measure is "necessary to protect public morals,"[80] pursuant to Articles GATT XX(a) or GATS XIV(a) while following the criteria established by the recent jurisprudence on this matter,[81] a panel could be entitled to examine the participation of concerned Members in such human rights treaties when relevant: (1) as evidence of the "importance of the values and common interests" protected by the measure; (2) as evidence of the efficacy of the chosen measure; (3) as evidence of the good faith and consistent behaviour of the concerned Member. Moreover, in *US – Shrimp*[82] the Appellate Body made clear that the examination of the United States' participation in similar other regional or bilateral treaties was a factual matter relevant in the assessment of its good faith efforts; the same could be done with relevant human rights treaties. Other factual elements could include declarations in national and international forums, decisions of human rights jurisdictions, other relevant general declarations by States on the importance and primacy of human rights, relevant resolutions of the ILO or the General Assembly, all of which would constitute public knowledge or factual information which the panel can obtain pursuant to Article 13 of the DSU.

It is certainly correct that WTO Members, as states, are bound by all their international law obligations. States are also presumed to negotiate all their treaties in good faith, thus, in keeping in mind all their other international law rights and obligations. States should thus be able to comply with all their international law obligations simultaneously, including those of human rights law and WTO law. A good faith interpretation of both the relevant human rights law – as the panel will be called to interpret such human rights provisions to determine its content and whether it is relevant to the interpretation of the WTO provision – and WTO law should generally avoid any conflict and allow for a coherent reading of both sets of law.[83]

III. The irreconcilable conflicts between WTO provisions and those of human rights law

Conceptually, irreconcilable conflicts remain possible. In *Argentina – Textiles*, the Appellate Body stated that "Argentina did not show an irreconcilable conflict between the provisions of its MOU with the IMF and the provisions of Article VIII of GATT 1994."[84] This implied that such a possibility of a pure irreconcilable conflict between the WTO and other treaties may exist.

A. Definition of a conflict

The issue of the definition of what is a "conflict" is relevant to the discussion on the WTO relationship with other treaties. Ultimately, only when there is a conflict between two treaty provisions must one of them be set aside (either as suspended or abrogated, Article 30.4, 41 and 60 of the Vienna Convention). In all other situations, all States' obligations are cumulative and must be complied with simultaneously.

The fact that a single (or many Members) may be in compliance with the WTO Agreement and in violation of human rights treaty does not imply that there is a conflict between provisions of the WTO Agreement and those of any specific human rights treaty. Conflict is a rather specific and narrow concept:

> ... [T]echnically speaking, there is a conflict when two (or more) treaty instruments contain obligations which cannot be complied with simultaneously. ... Not every such divergence constitutes a conflict, however. ... Incompatibility of contents is an essential condition of conflict.[85]

> … a conflict of law-making treaties arises only where simultaneous compliance with the obligations of different instruments is impossible. ... There is no conflict if the obligations of one instrument are stricter than, but not incompatible with, those of another, or if it is possible to comply with the obligations of one instrument by refraining from exercising a privilege or discretion accorded by another. (…) The presumption against conflict is especially reinforced in cases where separate agreements are concluded between the same parties, since it can be presumed that they are meant to be consistent with themselves, failing any evidence to the contrary.[86]

Thus, for a conflict to exist between a WTO provision and a provision of a human rights treaty, evidence must be put forward that the WTO mandates or prohibits an action that a human rights treaty conversely prohibits or imposes. The arising of such situations would be rare. In fact, one would have to be able to demonstrate that compliance with the WTO necessitates violation of a human right treaty.

In the WTO context, this narrow definition of a conflict was confirmed in *Guatemala – Cement,*[87] when the Appellate Body, while discussing the possibility of conflicts between the special and additional rules of the DSU for anti-dumping disputes, and the general provisions of the DSU stated: "A special or additional provision should only be found to *prevail* over a provision of the DSU in a situation where adherence to the one provision will lead to a violation of the other provision, that is, in the case of a *conflict* between them." Recently, in *US – Hot Rolled Steel*, the Appellate Body confirmed a narrow definition of "conflict."[88]

There is no principle of effective interpretation between treaties. Governments change as do their political ideologies, and with the passing of time a single State may end up signing two different treaties or treaties with contradictory obligations or provisions. But a conflict is a conflict, although the occurrence of conflicts between different treaties may be higher than conflicts within a single treaty where all provisions were negotiated together and at the same time. Since the main objective of rules of interpretation is to identify the intention of the parties, it is suggested that "conflicts" should be interpreted narrowly, in order to avoid situations where a third party will take upon itself to set aside a previously negotiated treaty provision in favour of the exclusive application of a superseding provision.

Therefore if relevant human rights provisions are alleged, a WTO panel should first decide whether the human rights law is relevant and if so, it shall attempt to reconcile the interpretation of both laws. In case this is not possible, the panel would then be faced with a pure conflict. The panel should recognize that human rights law does not have direct effect between the parties and that it is prohibited from reaching any conclusion that would add or diminish the covered agreements.[89]

Finally it may be useful to note that as with MEAs,[90] two categories of potential conflict may occur: a) conflict with a provision in a human rights treaty stating a substantive human right (e.g., prohibiting forced labour); b) conflict with a provision in a human rights treaty setting out certain measures that the parties to the treaty (or an institutional body) could/should take to protect a substantive human right (e.g., trade bans on goods produced with forced labour). Any conflict with the WTO is more likely to concern category (b) rather than (a) – i.e., conflict with the means by which states are seeking to protect/achieve certain human rights, rather than a conflict with those human rights. The legal distinction may be minimal, but from a political point of view a type (a) conflict with the WTO would be more explosive and embarrassing than a type (b) conflict.[91]

Another distinction can be drawn between "direct conflicts" between two treaties and the conflict in the application of a treaty, i.e., when a specific implementation of a treaty provision by a specific State leads to conflicts of obligations for that State or inconsistencies between rights and obligations in different treaties.

B. Conflicts with human rights provisions other than those of a *jus cogens* nature

In theory, a WTO provision could be superseded by another treaty or customary provision including human rights law. Through the operation of Articles 30 and 59 of the Vienna Convention, a human rights provision which is adopted after the WTO treaty (*lex posterior*) or which is more specific (*lex specialis*) will supersede a (conflicting) WTO provision. Articles 30 and 59 of the Vienna Convention, nonetheless, refer to "successive treaties relating to the *same* subject-matter."[92] Accordingly, one view may be that they would not be applicable to settle "conflicts" between a WTO provision and a provision regarding human rights contained within another treaty, since they would not be dealing with the same subject-matter. Another view could be that the "subject-matter" refers to that of the specific provisions of the two treaties that are overlapping.

As far as human rights norms having a customary character is concerned, the general maxim according to which "*lex posterior generalis non derogat priori specialis*"[93] may very well often apply. This principle states that "a later law, general in character, does not repeal an earlier law which is special in character."[94] This principle seems to have been recognized by the International Court of Justice in the Gabcikovo-Nagymaros Project[95] and by the WTO Appellate Body in *EC – Hormones* case.[96] In both these cases, the courts were of the view that it was not necessary to determine the "status" of the precautionary principle since, even if they had found that it has attained the status of customary law, it would not have superseded the obligations arising for the parties under the treaty provision in dispute, interpreted according to its ordinary meaning. As a consequence, it is difficult to see how a customary rule on human rights, which by definition will be general, even arisen after the WTO, could supersede a treaty provision, unless there is the consent of the contracting parties or the *lex posterior generalis* has a peremptory character.

In Part I of this paper, I have suggested that the WTO applicable law is limited to the covered agreements including institutional actions pursuant to the covered agreements. Therefore human rights provisions that are not included into the WTO covered agreements cannot have direct effect or find application in that WTO legal system. Moreover, to the extent that the superseding provision adds to, diminishes, or amends the rights and obligations created by the covered agreement, WTO adjudicating bodies would not be able to enforce the non-WTO provision or give it direct effect in the WTO applicable law.

Under general international law, and as suggested in Part I(2)(iii) above, it is difficult to imagine a practical situation in which a human rights provision would supersede a WTO provision without at the same time amending a provision of the covered agreement, at least with regard to WTO Members not parties to any such superseding treaty.[97] Can two WTO Members modify their WTO rights and obligations as between themselves only? Can the DSB (in adopting recommendations of Panels and the Appellate Body) "add or diminish" WTO rights and obligations of two disputing Members even if trade opportunities of other WTO Members are not directly affected? Articles 3.2 and 19 of the DSU seem to answer categorically no.

C. Conflicts with obligations *jus cogens* (or peremptory norms of international law)[98]

Allegations of a conflict between a WTO provision and a peremptory norm of international law may be more complex; violations of norms of *jus cogens* are strictly prohibited and arguably *jus cogens* automatically annul or modifies any inconsistent provisions. Is this prohibition limited to those States parties to the Vienna Convention? Has *jus cogens* reached a customary status pervasive to all systems of laws? And what is *jus cogens*? When and how can it be invoked, what are the consequences if a WTO provision appears inconsistent with *jus cogens*? Can a WTO panel or the Appellate Body identify a norm as having reached a *jus cogens* status? Can WTO courts determine the consequences of its violation by a WTO provision or a member's specific application of WTO norm? Can WTO courts violate *jus cogens*?

The Fédération Internationale des Ligues des droits de l'Homme (FIDH)[99] suggested that Articles 56[100] and 55[101] of the UN Charter must be interpreted in light of the Covenants and the Human Rights Universal Declaration, which covers all human rights (not only *jus cogens*) and therefore the obligation of States to take actions and measures for the protection of human rights includes all human rights. Thus, since Article 56 is part of the UN Charter, and Article 103 of the UN Charter states that in case of conflict the UN Charter supersedes any other treaty, the provisions of Article 56, interpreted to include all human rights, will supersede any other treaty obligation, including those of the WTO Agreement. This reading is quite expansive. Generally, only a few human rights are recognized as having acquired the status of "peremptory norms of international law" (*jus cogens)*, providing them with normative hierarchical superiority over WTO provisions in cases of conflict.[102]

The customary nature of such peremptory norms is recognized by Article 26 of the Rules on State Responsibility of the International Law Commission (ILC):[103] "Compliance with peremptory norms: Nothing in this chapter precludes the wrongfulness of any act of a State which is not in conformity with an obligation arising under a peremptory norm of general international law." All states may invoke the state responsibility of any other state in violation of *erga omnes* obligations, including those peremptory norms (*jus cogens*).

In its 5th commentary the ILC stated:

> The criteria for identifying peremptory norms of general international law are stringent. Article 53[104] of the Vienna Convention requires not merely that the norm in question should meet all the criteria for recognition as a norm of general international law, binding as such, but further that it should be recognized as having a peremptory character by the international community of states as a whole. So far, relatively few peremptory norms have been recognized as such. But various tribunals, nationals and international, have affirmed the idea of peremptory norms in contexts not limited to the validity of treaties. Those peremptory norms that are clearly accepted and recognized include the prohibitions of aggression, genocide, slavery, racial discrimination, crimes against humanity and torture, and the right to self-determination.

Where there is an apparent conflict between primary obligations, one which arises for a State directly under a peremptory norm of general international law, it is evident that such an obligation must prevail. The processes of interpretation and application should resolve such question without any need to resort to the secondary rules of States responsibility. In theory one might envisage a conflict arising on a subsequent occasion between a treaty obligation, apparently lawful on its face and innocent in its purpose, and a peremptory norm. If such a case were to arise, it would be too much to invalidate the treaty as a whole merely because its application in the given case was not foreseen. But in practice such situations seem not to have occurred. Even if they were to arise, peremptory norms of general international law generate *strong interpretative principles* which will resolve all or most conflicts. (Emphasis added.) Many WTO provisions are drafted in terms of general prohibitions, giving Members flexibility in the implementation of their WTO obligations. Because of the nature of WTO obligations and the subject-matters they cover, it is difficult to envisage a direct or primary "conflict" between any WTO provision and one of the above listed peremptory norms. Moreover, the drastic consequence of a conflict with *jus cogens* are such as to call for a strong presumption of conformity with *jus cogens*, (especially in light of Article 44.5 of the Vienna Convention which precludes separability of treaty provisions in situation of Article 53.) The ILC itself seems to recognize that interpretative principles will resolve all or most apparent and direct conflicts with *jus cogens*:

One may argue that it is possible that a WTO provision "apparently lawful on its face and innocent in its purpose" is implemented by a Member in such a way as to violate the *jus cogens vis-à-vis* another Member. Can a WTO panel or the Appellate Body reach a conclusion that a national measure implementing a WTO right or obligation is in violation of *jus cogens*? Arguably a panel or the Appellate Body can only determine whether a violation of a WTO provision, not of *jus cogens*, has occurred. Moreover, recommendations and remedies of the WTO dispute settlement system are strictly regulated in Article 19 of the DSU. The only recommendation by panels and the Appellate Body is "to bring the WTO inconsistent measure into conformity with the covered agreements." What should a panel or the Appellate Body do in such circumstances? Should it simply report to the DSB that it is faced with a situation of potential clash or violation of *jus cogens* and refrain from further ruling?[105]

Hélène Ruiz-Fabri has emphasized[106] the important link between the procedures and the substantive norm in matters relating to *jus cogens*, at least as far as the Vienna Convention is concerned. The pre-notification requirement (Article 65 of the Vienna Convention), the reference to consultations and conciliation (Article 65.3 of the Vienna Convention and 33 of the UN Charter) and the ICJ dispute settlement (Article 66(a)) were negotiated to ensure that allegations of *jus cogens* are not abused and as a necessary protection of conventional obligations: *pacta sunt servanda.*[107] Although Article 66 "supplements" other dispute settlement mechanisms, she has argued that there does not appear to exist at the moment any universal jurisdiction – other than the ICJ – that has the structural and institutional capacity to make declarations regarding *jus cogens.* She doubts that the Appellate Body has the capacity to "apply" the Vienna Convention as such since it is mandated to apply the covered agreements. If she accepts the existence of some "ordre public de droit international," including norms of *jus cogens*, she deplores the lack of any effective procedural and institutional mechanism to operationalize such norms:

> C'est au minimum l'idée que certaines normes auraient une supériorité substantielle, qu'elles ne sauraient être écartées par des volontés particulières et que leur transgression serait considérée comme d'une gravité particulière. Mais les institutions juridiques qu'on a imaginées pour traduire cette supériorité, en sorte d'y relier les caractéristiques qui sont celles des règles d'ordre public, sont inabouties ou assez largement ineffectives. Les raisons ont été bien identifiées: elles sont d'ordre structurel et résident principalement dans le défaut des éléments organiques qui garantiraient et donneraient vie à ces institutions.[108]

Can a panel or the Appellate Body be of the view that the pervasive nature of *jus cogens* has already terminated the conflicting separable WTO provision[109] and that the panel is only stating the state of WTO law, as affected by *jus cogens*? The panel would not be adding or diminishing WTO law since the covered agreements would have been changed automatically by *jus cogens* even before the panel was requested. In other words, the panel or the Appellate Body would act in conformity with the DSU by applying the WTO provisions as changed by *jus cogens*: Article 3,5 DSU, in fact, mandates them to reach solutions "*consistent* with the (covered) agreements." Or is it rather that the relevant WTO provision has "disappeared" and the panel would then be faced with a form of WTO *non-liquet.*[110] All these questions call for further reflection and research.

In practice the situation may pose itself differently. First, the relevant norm of *jus cogens* could always be used in the interpretation of the challenged WTO provisions or the national measures and this should generally suffice to avoid conflicts with *jus cogens*. And this may be the real impact of such concepts – it affects the general thinking of people, governments and judges.[111] Second, faced with such allegations, a panel or the Appellate Body may simply state something like "even in admitting that we have the capacity to apply and enforce the Vienna Convention, in particular the provisions of Articles 64 and 65.4, we don't need to examine this question as we are of the view that the provision at issue does not have the meaning suggested by the parties and rather means that ..."

Another angle must be examined. The WTO has its own international legal personality. As such, the WTO is bound by international law insofar as its functional international personality permits it to be so bound. Treaties signed by the WTO institution are subject to the provisions of the 1989 Vienna Convention on the Law of Treaties Between States and International Organizations or Between International organizations, which provisions, including those on *jus cogens*, are similar to those of the 1969 Vienna Convention for treaties between States. Could one say that a panel's conclusion that would tolerate, lead or encourage a Member to violate its human rights obligations, would bring about the international responsibility of the WTO? Then, how would the "victim" Member be entitled to invoke this liability and where? Should we rather conclude that in such a case the WTO would not be the legal person taking the measure that would violate human rights law. The WTO Member taking the measure would itself be in violation of *jus cogens*.

D. The remaining state responsibility of Members violating a human right law

The issue of WTO Members' state responsibility for violation of human rights law is not a matter of WTO dispute settlement. Yet it is important to keep in mind the fact that WTO Members remain responsible for the consequence of human rights violations. In situations where a human right provision would supersede a WTO provision but as such could not be received by the WTO legal system and could not be enforced by WTO panels, the State invoking the human right provision would remain entitles to invoke the application of the rules on state responsibility. Article 30.5 provides that:

> Paragraph 4 [*lex posterior*] is without prejudice to article 41, or to any question of the termination or suspension of the operation of a treaty under article 60 or to any question of responsibility which may arise for a State from the conclusion or application of a treaty, the provisions of which are incompatible with its obligations towards another State under another treaty.

The ILC (2001) Rules on State Responsibility addresses the consequences of the violation of international obligations, including those relating to human rights (whether peremptory norms or others).[112] The cumulative application of Articles 42[113] and 48 lead to the conclusion that violations of some human rights provisions entitle the states directly injured or specifically affected, as well as and a wider group of such States (recognition of *erga omnes* obligations)[114] to claim state responsibility.[115] The states directly injured or specifically affected could use countermeasures – other than in the form of unilateral trade restrictions contrary to GATT/WTO provisions. The other states could also invoke the state responsibility of that state violating a peremptory norm (*erga omnes*), and take the remedial actions listed in Article 48.2:[116] (i) Cessation of the internationally wrongful act, (ii) and assurances and guarantees of non-repetition in accordance with Article 30; and (iii) Performance of the obligation of reparation in accordance with preceding articles, in the interest of the injured State or of the beneficiaries of the obligation breached.

In other words, the violation of human rights (or even *jus cogens*), albeit not enforceable before WTO adjudicating bodies, does not free the violating state from any remedial obligations. The benefits obtained in one forum (say the WTO) may be nullified by the application of the rules on state responsibility.[117]

E. Preliminary conclusion

This article suggests that (1) there is an obligation to interpret the WTO provisions in light of other relevant rules of international law, including relevant human right law dealing with the same subject matter; (2) This first obligation together with the general principle of good faith by which States are presumed to have negotiated their treaties – WTO and human rights – in good faith and to comply with all their international law obligations simultaneously, lead to a presumption against conflicts between the WTO and human rights treaties; (3) Situations of conflicts between the provisions of the WTO and those of human rights are difficult to conceive; (4) But if conflicts were to be identified, it is suggested that the WTO is a specific sub-system of international law in which non-WTO law (including human rights law) cannot find direct application; (5) in all cases, WTO adjudicating bodies cannot enforce human rights obligations and rights of WTO Members if in doing so they would be adding or diminishing provisions of the covered agreements; (6) WTO Members, victim of a human rights violations maintain their right under rules of states responsibility against the violating state; (7) As to *jus cogens*, it is not clear whether WTO adjudicating bodies have the legal capacity to make any declaration relating, in particular, to the nullity *ab initio* of the said conflicting WTO provision or WTO treaty;[118] (8) In situations of conflicts with human rights law (including *jus cogens*) in the "application" of or implementation of WTO law by a WTO Member, the WTO adjudicating body should be encouraged to report to the DSB, emphasising the limitation of the DSU process on the matter.

IV. The overall "jurisdiction" issue inherent to human rights considerations in trade-related measures

Human rights policy interacts with international trade law at many points leading to specific actions which could eventually be taken to the WTO dispute settlement system. From a WTO dispute settlement perspective, each type of measure involving human rights aspects will necessitate a legal assessment of the specific WTO provisions at issue. One difficult issue is whether a WTO Member can invoke and rely on human rights considerations occurring entirely in another state.

For instance, in this conference Joel Trachtman has identified US legislations that could be seen as having human rights aspects, the effects of these measures on international trade, as well as their WTO compatibility. He refers to domestic regulations where the regulatory distinctions are concerned with human rights (which would call for an Article III analysis and the related PPM issues); border restrictions based on human rights considerations (which would require assessment under the WTO exceptions provisions, Articles XX and XXI of GATT and XIV and XIV *bis* of GATS, in light of the existing jurisprudence); government procurement criteria based on human rights considerations (which would have to be assessed with reference to obligations contained in the Government Procurement Agreement); the Enabling Clause's criteria and gradation mechanisms as well as conditions attached to GSP preferences when relating to human rights considerations (which would call for an assessment of Members' right *vis-à-vis* "preferences," the issue of like product, exceptions etc...). Frank Garcia has discussed the reference to human rights considerations in regional trade agreements and their compatibility with GATT Article XXIV (and V of GATS) in light of the relevant jurisprudence could further be examined.[119] Krista Schefer has identifed situations where human rights are used in foreign trade policy instruments that may include trade components. From a WTO dispute settlement perspective, the WTO compatibility of such bilateral or multilateral agreements could also be challenged.

To this list of measures involving human rights considerations, one may add the possibility of labelling requirements with human rights references – involving the application of the TBT, GATT or even parallel GATS provisions;

other regulatory distinctions applicable for trade in "services" – involving the examination of Article XVI GATS market access and Article XVII national treatment conditions, scheduling criteria and related like services and MNF issues as well as GATS domestic regulation criteria and GATS Article VI:4 issue; human rights considerations in investment regulations (which would raise TRIMS/SCM/GATT III, I/GATS issues); rules of origin (and the related agreement) as well as human rights considerations in the analysis of the agriculture commitments (including the green box and the requested development box).

It is not the purpose of this paper to make an exhaustive list of trade measures that could include human rights considerations or even to attempt to assess their compatibility in the context of WTO dispute settlement. Rather, the purpose of the present section is simply to suggest that when human rights considerations are used in trade-related measures,[120] it highlights three very difficult (and overlapping) issues in WTO law which are in need of further examination. First, is the status of process and production methods (PPM), second, the status of other non-product-related regulatory or preferences distinctions based on policy considerations. These two issues are part of an overall debate over the reach of the "WTO jurisdiction," i.e., the rights of WTO Members to act or react extraterritorially under WTO law and under general public international law.

Human rights considerations are in some cases examined from a PPM perspective (such as child labour used for the production of goods and services). Human rights considerations in trade measures may also be expressed in terms of a (general or specific) policy of an exporting country which has no direct link to the specific product or services imported. Most often the invoked human rights actions or behaviour take place abroad, i.e., outside of the territory/jurisdiction of the country imposing the human-rights based measure.[121] I would like to suggest a few points about these general issues with a view to encouraging further discussions of this matter in the more specific context of human rights.

A. The issue of PPMs

The first set of issues relate to the status of PPMs in WTO law. Authors have written on the issue of PPMs in the context of the trade and environment debate and I apologize for not referring to this rich literature.[122] To sum up the situation, it may be said that the GATT case law does not seem to accept any of PPMs considerations as the basis for regulatory distinctions under Article III. For example, in *US – Measures Affecting Alcoholic and Malt Beverages*[123] a Minnesota tax credit for micro-breweries was invalidated, even though it was available to foreign as well as domestic brewers, because the beer, though produced by a different method, was deemed like, and discriminatory tax treatment was therefore an Art. III violation. The most significant GATT PPM jurisprudence, the *Tuna/Dolphin* cases,[124] did not even address Art. III, which was interpreted to apply only to measures that affect "products as such"[125] but rather analyzed a US import ban on tuna from countries whose dolphin protection standards did not meet those set out in US law (a process-based measure) under GATT Art. XI, and found a violation. The measure was considered not to be protected by Article XX. In *Tuna I*, the extraterritorial location of the dolphins seemed to have been fatal and the panel did not offer much discussion as to whether Article XX could protect PPM. However, in *Tuna II* although the panel recognized that XX(g) actions are not explicitly limited to responses to events or actions within domestic jurisdiction,[126] it did not discussed the issue of PPM under Article XX as such.

Under the WTO Agreement, the *US – Shrimp* dispute presented similar facts and was analyzed at the Panel level in a similar manner, but the Art. XI violation found by the Panel was not challenged by the US and therefore the Appellate Body did not get to consider whether PPMs should be analyzed under Art. III.[127] The WTO jurisprudence seems to suggest that "likeness" refers to likeness in physical properties, and therefore differences in processing histories (including human rights considerations) cannot generally cause unlikeness. Contrary to others' views, it is suggested that the Appellate Body has not opened up the likeness test in *EC – Asbestos*, in finding that the Border Tax Working Party Criteria – physical characteristics, end-use, consumers' habits and tastes and tariff classification – "are neither a treaty-mandated nor a closed list of criteria will be used to determine the legal characterization of products."[128] The Appellate Body found that the determination of likeness requires consideration of any evidence which indicates whether the products are in a competitive relationship in the marketplace, as the purpose of Art. III is to prohibit protectionism:[129] "If there is – or could be – *no* competitive relationship between products, a Member cannot intervene, through internal taxation or regulation, to protect domestic production."[130] In determining whether this competitive relationship exists in practice, the Appellate Body[131] seems to have focused a good deal on the physical characteristics of the products namely their carcinogenicity or toxicity. Although it stated that each and all of four criteria must each time be examined,[132] despite the possibility of conflicting evidence from those criteria,[133] it arguably gave a heavier weight to physical characteristics or at least differences in physical characteristics when it wrote:

> 118. We consider this to be especially so in cases where the evidence relating to properties establishes that the products at issue are physically quite different. In such cases, in order to overcome this indication that products are *not* "like," a higher burden is placed on complaining Members to establish that, despite the pronounced physical differences, there is a competitive relationship between the products such that *all* of the evidence, taken together, demonstrates that the products are "like" under Article III:4 of the GATT 1994. In this case, where it is clear that the fibres have very different properties, in particular, because chrysotile is a known carcinogen, a very heavy burden is placed on Canada to show, under the second and third criteria, that the chrysotile asbestos and PCG fibres are in such a competitive relationship.
>
> [...]
>
> 136. It follows that the evidence relating to properties indicates that, physically, chrysotile asbestos and PCG fibres are very different. As we said earlier, in such cases, in order to overcome this indication that products are *not* "like," a high burden is imposed on a complaining Member to establish that, despite the pronounced physical differences, there is a competitive relationship between the products such that, *all* of the evidence, taken together, demonstrates that the products are "like" under Article III:4 of the GATT 1994.[134]

Ultimately, *EC – Asbestos* focuses on physical characteristics and determines that evidence relating to health risks (carcinogenicity, or toxicity) associated with the product can be examined under the existing Border Tax categories of physical properties and consumer tastes and habits.[135] The difficulty is to appreciate the links between the determination of the competitive relationship and the focus on the physical characteristics of the products, or even the sum of the four identified criteria. The facts were very specific to this case and the Appellate Body has indeed also used broad language in talking about the obligation of panels to evaluate "all the relevant evidence."[136]

Thus, the question whether non-physical process-based distinctions, such as those based on human rights violations in production methods, could be considered as resulting in "unlikeness" for the purposes of Art. III national treatment obligation between imported and domestic like products (as well as for the purpose of the MFN obligation of GATT Article I) has not been answered by the jurisprudence. Yet it will be necessary to examine this issue in depth, because human rights considerations, by definition, will never affect the physical characteristics of imported products.

B. Policy considerations not directly related to specific imports

Another question is whether any policy considerations have a place in WTO law. In general international law, some are of the view that while States do not have jurisdiction to prescribe with respect to standards related to domestic policy preferences such as working conditions or remuneration of workers. Furthermore, even where a fundamental norm has been violated, a State may not act to coerce third party nations into adopting its policy of punishment towards the offending State. According to Brigitte Stern, even a good intent/desirable policy goal cannot be used to justify illegal extraterritorial action.[137] Treaties may, however, provide otherwise. Does Article III (Art. XX?) authorize the consideration of human rights policy of the exporting countries unrelated to specific imports? Can such policy considerations be used as criteria for providing trade preferences, including those in regional trade agreements?

From early GATT jurisprudence, a panel in *Belgian Family Allowances*[138] considered a levy on imports purchased by Belgian governmental entities which originated from countries deemed to have a system of family allowances less generous than that put in place by Belgium. The Panel found the social policy consideration irrelevant in assessing the consistency of the levy with the requirement that like products be treated equally.

Under the WTO, the Appellate Body decision in *US – Shrimp* made clear that certain policies can be taken into consideration under certain subparagraphs of Art. XX.[139] The question is, evidently, which ones. Article XX contains a closed list of such policies, which, by nature deserve to be interpreted in an evolutive manner. While the Appellate Body found that conservation policy justifications are permissible under Art. XX(g), the country-based nature of the regulation at issue, its lack of flexibility and discriminatory application in the manner in which the challenged measure was implemented and applied, led the Appellate Body to find that the real policy consideration of the United States was not to protect and conserve sea turtles, but rather to influence other WTO Members to adopt the same comprehensive regulatory regime.

The application of the "necessity" requirements under Article XX(b) and the obligation to implement treaty provisions in good faith operate to ensure that its allowance of policy considerations is not abused.[140] Importantly, for the Appellate Body, the policy consideration which has so far justified a unilateral action reflects a "shared policy value."[141] A finding of shared policy value serves to fulfill these good faith and necessity requirements. The problem, however, as many have recognized, is how to identify and weigh which policy considerations are international values, so as to be permissible Art. XX justifications.[142] And yet it is not even clear whether only internationally shared value would be covered by Article XX policy, as the Appellate Body has already authorized Members to set standards at the level they consider appropriate, even above international standard.[143] It may be suggested that statements made in other treaties and forums (even political ones) can be used to trace evidence of such shared policy values and that the protection of (some) human rights may be among those. Since human rights considerations are usually based on policy considerations, this matter will necessitate further research. Labelling requirement (even voluntary) trade preferences and other foreign policy instruments with trade components are directly concerned.

C. The general issue of "jurisdiction" in the WTO[144]

A final set of questions involve the issue of jurisdiction which in fact include and overlap with the two above-mentioned debates.[145] Under general international rules on State responsibility, it is usually argued that States are generally prohibited from using countermeasures to influence another State's policies within its own territory.[146] Yet history has shown that States often seek to impose their sanctions on those outside their jurisdiction by means of trade action. How, then, does the WTO Agreement deal with the issue of extraterritoriality?

Some of the sub-paragraphs of GATT Art. XX and GATS Art. XIV are explicitly concerned with actions taken abroad. One clear example is Article XX(e), relating to the products of prison labour. As the *Tuna II* panel recognized with respect to XX(g), the safe harbours of the other subparagraphs are not explicitly limited to responses to events or actions within domestic jurisdiction.[147] Furthermore, Articles GATT XXI and GATS XIV *bis* address security exceptions, which will often result from action taken outside domestic jurisdiction.

In *Tuna I*, a GATT Panel considered that Art. XX(b) and (g) did not permit trade action for the purpose of enforcing domestic laws in another country, reasoning that such permission would allow each country to "unilaterally determine the conservation policies from which the other Contracting Parties could not deviate without jeopardizing their rights under the General Agreements."[148] In this view, GATT law did not allow States to justify illegal trade actions on the basis of behaviour which occurred beyond their territorial boundaries. In *Tuna II*, the Panel engaged in a more nuanced discussion of jurisdiction. It first recognized that Art. XX(g) did not explicitly spell out a limitation on the location of the exhaustible natural resource to be protected, and found that the exception could be used in order to conserve exhaustible natural resources located outside its territory.[149] Yet, in this case, it found that the measure was taken to force other countries to change their policies, and therefore could not be primarily aimed at conservation of a natural resource or rendering effective domestic production or consumption restrictions, and therefore did not come under the XX(g) exception. Neither *Tuna I or Tuna II* were ever adopted by the CONTRACTING PARTIES, and this jurisprudence continued to evolved under the WTO law – as did the rules on jurisdiction in general international law.

In *US – Shrimp*, the Appellate Body found that on the facts presented, while neither party had claims of any rights of exclusive ownership over sea turtles, the fact that they were an exhaustible natural resource and some populations of these species were highly migratory, passing in and out of the waters subject to the rights of US jurisdiction, created a sufficient "nexus" between the migratory and endangered marine populations involved and the United States for the purpose of Art. XX(g).[150] Although factually questionable, this seemed to suggest that the interest in the regulated product need not be a territorial one.[151] Reference to "shared value" may be seen as an attempt to formulate a coherent jurisdictional test to assess when a country has a sufficient interest in a policy such that Article XX will excuse unilateral action against a producer which violates that policy.

The question which follows from this analysis is whether this "nexus" is the analytical matrix which will be used under other sub-paragraphs of XX which will be more directly implicated where trade action is taken in respect to human rights violations? In *US – Gasoline*, the Appellate Body said that given the different textual constructions of the various subparagraphs, it would be unreasonable to suppose that the Members intended to require "the same kind or degree of connection or relationship between the measure under appraisal and the state interest of policy sought to be promoted or realized."[152] This suggests that the "nexus" required will vary based on the particular policies and the legal provision at issue.[153]

Under general public international law on extraterritoriality, the "nexus" iterated *in US – Shrimp* can be conceptualized as an "effects" test, but its definition is far from clear. While it is generally accepted that actions abroad which have an impact or produce effects in a State provide that State with jurisdiction over the matter, the nature of the effects test is not settled.[154] Looking specifically at the area of human rights, if a State violates a fundamental norm, either conception of the general international law permits any country to punish the violator.[155] Stern would argue, however, that the European view of the effects test does not permit a country to go after third party countries in order to coerce them into joining in the punishment of the violator. Furthermore, it may not permit a country to punish a primary violator of what is simply a human rights policy in the country seeking to assert jurisdiction.

Bernhard Jansen has suggested that there may be situations where it is justified to take trade measures to pursue non-economic objectives, even in the absence of any evident attachment to the territorial jurisdiction of the importing state. In the environmental context, he argues that where an endangered species is confined to a territory of a single state which takes action to threaten its survival and is not prepared to negotiate with international community, public international law (WTO law?) may evolve in such a way as to accept universal jurisdiction in certain circumstances. This proposal can be viewed as a way of saying that where the policy implicated is a clearly shared value, and the violator a clear outlaw, the need for a formal traditional jurisdiction over the regulated product itself can be very attenuated.[156]

The softened requirement for a "nexus" can also be viewed in parallel to the growing consideration for a "universal jurisdiction" over violations of certain universal values, which would include some human rights. Universal jurisdiction has already been recognized for some international crimes. Brigitte Stern describes this universal jurisdiction of States in the following way:

> En dehors des compétences qui sont reconnues aux états par le droit international [territoriale, personelles et matérielle] le droit international leur attribue également, dans certaines hypothèses limitées, ce qu'on appelle une compétence universelle, c'est-à-dire la possibilité pour chaque état de protéger, par le biais de la répression de certains actes, les intérêts fondamentaux de l'humanité.
>
> La définition des actes mettant en danger l'humanité a varié au cours du temps et est certes encore destinées à évoluer. (...)
>
> ... on peut dire que sont considérés comme intérêts communs essentiels, deux types d'intérêts: d'une part ceux qui sont communs en ce sens que tout etats peut être indistinctement touché et donc lésés dans ses intérêts propres si certains actes sont commis, et d'autre part ceux qui sont communs parce que'il touchent à l'essence de l'humanité et sont donc possédés en partage par tous les Etats.[157]

A similar concept of universal jurisdiction would apply to *erga omnes* obligations as now codified by the ILC Rules on State Responsibility.[158]

Developments in the context of Chapter VII of the UN Charter may offer a way for WTO law in this area. Traditionally, violations of human rights within a State's domestic market was protected from retaliatory action by other states (especially countermeasure or the use of force) by Article 2.4 of the Charter, which insists that "All Members shall refrain in their international relations from the threat or use of force against the territorial integrity or political independence of any state, or in any other manner inconsistent with the Purposes of the United Nations." In the recent years, however, massive violation of individuals' rights and human rights has been used as the legal basis for action under UN Chapter VII action, which requires a determination of a "threat to peace, breach of the peace, or act of aggression" in order to justify measures not involving armed force or those involving force so as "to maintain or restore international peace and security." For example, actions taken with respect to Liberia, Iraqi, Somalia, Bosnia and Rwanda have all had as their legal basis internal matters and their impact on human beings. For instance, Antonio Cassesse has suggested that a new rule of international law may be in the process of crystallization whereby certain large scale human rights violations create a threat to peace and trigger authorization of self-defense or unilateral action, where Security Council authorization proves impossible to obtain.[159] If such unilateral force can be used again massive violation of human rights, it suggests that less intrusive unilateral economic actions would be even more permissible in such circumstances.

Returning to the WTO Agreement, the GATT Art. XXI security exception may be argued to be wider and more flexibile than the concept of "threat to peace and security" under Ch. VII of the UN Charter. If this latter concept is moving ahead to include human rights violation within a state as a trigger, the concept of security under the WTO Agreement should surely do the same. Furthermore, while a threat to peace for the purposes of Chapter VII would require massive human rights violation, a lesser degree of violation may satisfy the requirements of GATT Art. XXI or GATS Art. XIV, as well as GATT Article XX(a) or GATS XIV(a).

D. Overlaps/conflicts of jurisdictions

Related to the above legal issues is that of overlapping judicial jurisdictions. It is possible that a single dispute or related aspects of the same dispute be adjudicated before different tribunals, such as the Human Rights Committee and a WTO Panel or the Appellate Body. This may lead to situations where jurisdictions may reach different and even opposite conclusions. It may also lead to a waste of resources, unnecessary procedures and inconsistent development of international law.

At present, in international law, no rules (other than specific treaty provisions) limit States in their decision to choose between two jurisdictions; principles of international commercial law such as *forum non coveniens, res judicata*, litispendance, abuse of process and procedural rights etc., cannot find application in the overlap of jurisdictions between public international law tribunals.... States' choices seem based on economic, political and legal opportunities. In addition, the wording of Article 23 of the DSU makes it clear that a WTO adjudicating body always has the authority and even the obligation to examine claims of violations of WTO obligations.

The availability of multiple jurisdiction does not reduce the responsibility of a WTO State found to have violated another treaty including a possible exclusive jurisdiction provision of that other treaty.[160] Hence the need to encourage coordination between WTO and other jurisdictions (including those addressing human rights), although at present nothing limits the jurisdiction of WTO Panels and the Appellate Body once that jurisdiction exists.[161]

Those issues relating to the WTO jurisdiction are most complex and certainly not limited to the application of the WTO exceptions provisions. Whether regulatory distinctions or preferences can relate to human rights taking place in another State's territory will be relevant for their WTO assessment under GATT, TBT, TRIMS, GATS and TRIPS and is most relevant in the context of the Enabling Clause and other types of preferences. Further research and discussions are needed if one wants to offer a comprehensive understanding of the relationship between human rights law and WTO law.

V. The procedural aspects of human rights and WTO dispute settlement mechanisms

Finally another aspect of WTO dispute settlement may be concerned with the procedural aspect of the process; this is the object of this last section.

Human rights treaties (and law) deal with rights of individuals. Human rights are often categorised as civil and political (in principle applicable without government intervention being needed) and social, cultural and economic rights (where often the conditions to enjoy such rights are to be provided by positive government action). Also, one may distinguish between rights of substantive nature (such as the right to life) and of procedural nature (such as the right to a fair trial).

The classic function of civil and political human rights is to protect human beings against arbitrary behaviour by government bodies, thus constraining such bodies in the exercise of powers conferred on them or assumed by them. The provisions on the right to a fair trial refer mostly to criminal proceedings, but sometimes also to judicial proceedings in general. A considerable number of human rights have received international status through such UN instruments as the Universal Declaration of Human Rights, the International Covenant on Civil and Political Rights (CCPR), and the International Covenant on Economic, Social and Cultural Rights (CESC).[162] The European Convention on Human Rights (ECHR) provides for an individual petition procedure in Article 34, including NGO petitions. Individual petitions are only admissible if local remedies have been exhausted. The European Union is committed to respect fundamental rights as guaranteed by the ECHR, and its Member States may take action in case of a serious and persistent breach by a Member State of such rights.[163] The European Court of Justice interprets the European Union and European Community Treaties in accordance with the ECHR.[164]

In the WTO context, as in any public international law sphere, individuals have their interests represented by their governments. The object of most WTO provisions is to regulate actions by States and provide other States with the right to complain, although the jurisprudence has recognized that (as with other sectors of public international law) individuals may, at least indirectly, be affected by WTO violations.

A. Examples of procedural prescriptions in human rights treaties

Many human rights treaties provide for a right to an effective remedy (including compensation); a right to a fair trial; a right to be represented; a right to *habeas corpus* remedy (specific to criminal procedures); a right to an appeal; a right to due process and a right to administrative justice.

1. The right to an effective remedy

Article 8 of the Universal Declaration of Human Rights (UDHR) provides that "Everyone has the right to an effective remedy by the competent national tribunals for acts violating the fundamental rights granted him by the constitution or by law." This has been echoed furthermore, in the Declaration on the Right and Responsibility of Individual Groups and Organs of Society to promote and protect Universally recognised Human Rights and Fundamental Freedoms and according to Article 13 of the European Convention on Human Rights.

2. The right to a fair trial

Article 8 of the Universal Declaration of Human Rights (UDHR) provides that "Everyone has the right to an effective remedy by the competent national tribunals for acts violating the fundamental rights granted him by the constitution or by law." This has been echoed furthermore, in the Declaration on the Right and Responsibility of Individual Groups and Organs of Society to promote and protect Universally recognised Human Rights and Fundamental Freedoms[165] and according to Article 13 of the European Convention on Human Rights.

For instance, Article 9 of the UDHR states that "No one shall be subjected to arbitrary arrest, detention or exile" while Article 10 adds that "Everyone is entitled in full equality to a fair and public hearing by an independent and impartial tribunal, in the determination of his rights and obligations and of any criminal charge against him." According to Article 11, "Everyone charged with a penal offence has the right to be presumed innocent until proved guilty according to law in a public trial at which he has had all the guarantees necessary for his defence. [...]"

Article 6 European Convention on Human rights (ECHR) and Article 14 International Covenant on Civil and Political rights (CCPR), both refer to a "fair and public hearing by an independent and impartial tribunal." The ECHR adds "within a reasonable time," while the CCPR adds "competent" to "tribunal." Both address the rights of individuals ("everyone" and "all persons").

The Human Rights Committee, when considering individual petitions under the Optional Protocol, holds closed meetings (Article 5.3 Optional Protocol). Hearings of the ECHR, on the contrary, are in principle public (Article 40 ECHR).

3. The right to be represented

Article 14.3(d) CCPR and Article 6.3(c) ECHR, guarantee persons charged with a criminal offence the right to defend themselves in person or through legal assistance and, if necessary, to be given such assistance free "when the interests of justice so require." Article 14.3(d) CCPR which explicitly provides the right for a criminal suspect to be tried in his presence, and defend himself in person (the latter is also mentioned in Article 6.3[c] ECHR).

4. The right to an appeal

Article 14.5 CCPR guaranteeing everyone convicted of a crime the right to his conviction and sentence being reviewed by a higher tribunal.

5. The right to due process

The right to due process is embodied in Article 9(2) of the Declaration on Rights and Responsibility.[166] This is enforced by the Basic Principles on the Independence of the Judiciary[167] and can be found most importantly in Article 14(3) of the CCPR.[168]

6. The right to administrative justice

The right to administrative justice is inter-linked with the right to due process as expounded above and pertains to provide an expedient, fair and timely judicial process. Although made reference to in several sections of the CCPR, it is not directly referred to. It is arguably indirectly contained in Article 14(3) of the ICCPR. Furthermore, Article 4 of the Convention on the Rights of the Child makes direct reference to the right of the child to administrative justice.[169] Two important components of the right to administrative justice are the right to be heard (referred to as the *audi alteram partem* principle) and the absence of bias in a hearing (otherwise referred to as the *nemo judex in propria causa* doctrine).

B. Are the procedural prescriptions of the DSU in compliance with the prescriptions of human rights treaties?

As mentioned, individuals are supposed to have their interests represented in the WTO dispute settlement process by their governments. Although WTO disputes are about rights and obligations of Members, they may indirectly affect individuals, mostly in an economic sense.[170] Depending on their domestic rules, individuals may trigger their government to start WTO dispute settlement proceedings (e.g. TBR in EC, Section 301 in US).

1. To the extent the WTO dispute settlement process affects individuals (directly)

(a) Amicus curiae briefs

WTO adjudicating bodies are ahead of other international States-to-States tribunals in accepting *amicus curiae* briefs from non-State actors.[171] The Appellate Body has decided that panels may take into consideration information submitted to them by individuals or non-governmental organizations, even if such information has not been sought and not been included in parties' submissions.[172] The Appellate Body has also decided that the same goes for itself: "We are of the opinion that we have the legal authority under the DSU to accept and consider *amicus curiae* briefs in an appeal in which we find it pertinent and useful to do so."[173]

(b) Right to participate in the dispute settlement process with a Member

In general, a Member State party to a dispute is free to determine the composition of its delegation in panel and Appellate Body proceedings. This includes the decision to enlist the services of private counsel as well as any other individual. The issue (the participation of private counsel) first arose in *EC – Bananas III,* where the Appellate Body stated: "We can find nothing in the Marrakesh Agreement Establishing the World Trade Organization (the 'WTO Agreement'), the DSU or the Working Procedures, nor in customary international law or the prevailing practice of international tribunals, which prevents a WTO Member from determining the composition of its delegation in Appellate Body proceedings... We rule that it is for a WTO Member to decide who should represent it as members of its delegation in an oral hearing of the Appellate Body."[174]

This ruling, which applied to Appellate Body proceedings, was extended to panel proceedings in *Indonesia – Automobiles*.[175] WTO Members are now regularly represented by private counsel at all stages of the Panel and Appellate Body proceedings.

(c) National legislation using the representation aspects of the US Section 301; should they be multilateralized?

Some States (such as the United States and the European Communities) have national legislation which provide for the right of individuals or groups with collective goals to force their own government into initiating dispute settlement mechanisms under specific circumstances. The EC new Trade Barriers Regulations of 1994 and the US Section 301 of the 1974 Trade Act are examples of such mechanisms.[176] Article 1904.5 of NAFTA provides that upon request from an individual, the NAFTA parties will initiate the dispute settlement mechanism envisaged in NAFTA chapter 19. Since rights of individuals may be directly affected by trade measures,[177] it may be beneficial to envisage their multilateralisation.

(d) Right of individual to request information (SCM/TBT/SPS agreements, and enquiry points under GATS) that can be enforced by government before WTO jurisdictions

Various WTO agreements oblige Members to publish domestically any regulation affecting trade; Article X of the GATT reflects this basic obligation reiterated in other more specific agreements. Interested parties are also entitled under the TBT and SPS Agreements to request from any Member, information on regulation that may affect the former's trading rights. States are also obliged to take into account the position of interested parties in their investigations and determinations of trade remedies. In addition, pursuant to the GATS, Members have the obligation to establish "enquiry points" where information affecting the service suppliers and service traders must be available.[178]

2. As a comparison of the dispute settlement mechanisms for human rights violations (only applicable by analogy as "general rules of procedure" or "principles of law")

(a) Right to a fair trial/due process/objective assessment

Article 11 of the DSU has been interpreted to require panels and the Appellate Body to respect due process, fairness, to make an objective assessment of the facts, and to limit itself to the WTO applicable law.

The Appellate Body has, on various occasions referred to "due process," *inter alia* in observing that detailed standard working procedures for panels would help to ensure due process and fairness in panel proceedings.[179] Other references to due process concerned an appellant requesting the Appellate Body to reverse a panel's finding on procedural matters,[180] the duty of parties engaged in a dispute to be forthcoming as to claims and facts involved,[181] and the adequate opportunity for parties to respond to evidence submitted.[182] The objective assessment of Article 11 of the DSU includes an obligation to "act in good faith, respecting fundamental fairness" [in an investigation process].[183]

(b) Independence of panelists and the Appellate Body members

Citizens of a disputing Member are prohibited from acting as panelists. The same nationality requirement does not apply to members of the Appellate Body. Panelists, members of the Appellate Body, arbitrators, experts and WTO staff assisting and to some extent members of the Textile Monitoring Body (TMB) are subject to a detailed set of Rules of Conduct that were adopted by the DSB in December 1996.[184] These Rules of Conduct are the most sophisticated rules applicable to participants in international dispute settlement and are the result of more than two years of negotiations initiated by the Preparatory Committee for the WTO.

The covered persons are subject to general obligations: to be independent and impartial, to avoid direct or indirect conflicts of interest and to maintain confidentiality (Section II); these obligations are already contained in the DSU. To ensure that these obligations are respected, each covered person is expected to: (1) adhere strictly to the provisions of the DSU; (2) disclose the existence or development of any interest, relationship or matter that that person could reasonably be expected to know and that is likely to affect, or give rise to justifiable doubts as to, his or her independence or impartiality; (3) take due care in the performance of his or her duties to fulfil these expectations, including through avoidance of any direct or indirect conflicts of interest in respect of the subject matter of the proceedings; (4) consider only issues raised, and necessary to fulfil his or her responsibilities within the dispute settlement proceeding and not delegate this responsibility to any other person. The Rules of Conduct which contain four different challenge mechanisms have been used on a few occasions.[185]

(c) Audi alteram partem

While the panel's Working Procedures are silent on this point, the panel process always envisages the exchange of (generally at least two sets of) submissions and right to rebuttals. The same applies to questions which are answerable by either party; parties are usually invited to provide answers to any questions asked by any other party or third-parties involved in the dispute.

The Appellate Body's Working Procedures provide for the possibility of finding against a Member that fails to appear:

> [29] Where a participant fails to file a submission within the required time periods or fails to appear at the oral hearing, the division shall, after hearing the views of the participants, issue such order, including dismissal of the appeal, as it deems appropriate.

(d) Right to legal representation

As discussed above, in the *EC – Bananas III* (AB) and *Indonesia – Automobiles* dispute, the issue of the participation of private counsels was settled and it is now a general practice that Members are assisted by private lawyers and other consultants before WTO adjudicating bodies.

On 17 July 2001, the Advisory Centre on WTO Law was officially established as an independent intergovernmental organization. At present the Agreement has thirty-two Signatories: nine developed countries, twenty-two developing countries and one economy in transition. All Least Developed Countries are beneficiaries of the Centre by definition. Legal advice is provided to them at a beneficiary rate, though not free. Membership of the Centre remains open to all WTO Members and those in the process of accession to WTO through an accession procedure.[186]

(e) Right of appeal

All panel rulings, including those under Article 21.5 reviewing implementation measures can be appealed. There is however, no appeal for arbitration decisions under Articles 25, 21.3(c) and 22.6 of the DSU. At the moment there is no interlocutory appeals. It should be noted that most international tribunals do not provide for a right to appeal and that in human rights convention appeals exist mainly in the case of criminal cases.

(f) Burden of proof

In WTO dispute, the burden of proof is always on the country challenging the sovereignty of States to adopt the measure of its choice. States are presumed to act in good faith and to comply with all their international obligations.[187] Explicit defenses (like under XX GATT) impose an autonomous burden of proof.

(g) Rules on evidence

Article 11 DSU and the Working Procedures in Appendix 3 do not establish time limits for the submission of evidence to a panel. The latter do, however, distinguish between two stages in panel proceedings. During the first stage, the complainant sets out its claims and supporting evidence, and during the second, rebuttals are made by the parties of the arguments and evidence submitted by other parties. Panels have the discretion to accept additional evidence even late in the proceedings.[188] However, panels must be careful to observe due process, which entails providing the parties adequate opportunity to respond to evidence submitted.[189]

If a party refuses to provide information sought by the panel, the panel has the authority to draw adverse inferences from such refusal.[190] Of course, the panel may not ignore or disregard other relevant facts, as it must make an "objective assessment" under Article 11 DSU.[191]

Articles 11.2, 13 and Appendix 4 of the DSU provide panels with a great deal of power to seek and obtain evidence and information generally from any source. According to the Appellate Body, the comprehensive nature of the authority of a panel to "seek" information should be underscored.[192]

(h) The right to an effective remedy[193]

The DSU mechanism is arguably easily invoked: it can be triggered by a simple allegation, without any *prima facie* need to prove any specific economic or legal interest while the actual effect of any violation is also presumed. The effectiveness of the system can also be assessed with reference to the type of remedies therein envisaged. As discussed above the standard remedy under WTO law is for the losing party to bring its measure into conformity with the relevant and applicable WTO provision. This is to be done within an agreed or arbitrated reasonable period of implementation which varies from 8 to 12 months. There is generally no financial compensation of any sort for loss of trade opportunities (and this may be considered a weakness for some Members).

Since remedies are explicitly addressed in details such as the possibility of declaratory judgment (as it was done by the Appellate Body in *US – Certain EC Products*[194]); preliminary rulings;[195] cessation pursuant to Articles 3.7 and

19.1, 21.1, 22.1 of the DSU; excuse pursuant to Article 22.6 of the DSU; WTO compatible, temporary and voluntary trade-compensation pursuant to 3.7 and 22.1 of the DSU; and regulated sanctions, it can be argued that remedies under general international law are not available to WTO Members before WTO adjudicating bodies, including cross-retaliation pursuant to Article 22 of the DSU.

Pakistan has indeed suggested that new forms of remedies should be negotiated to include namely the possibility of financial and or retroactive compensation.[196] Interlocutory injunction may also be envisaged for serious breach of WTO obligations, urgent matters and perishable goods.

(i) Developing countries' status

The DSU contains various provisions allowing further flexibility and procedural benefits in favor of developing countries. Examples of provisions attempting to favor developing countries can be found in Articles 3.12, 4.10, 27.2, 8.10, 21.2, 21.7, 21.8, 25 and 27 of the DSU. An important and related issue is who really benefits from such provisions within the said countries, which is, again, more of a distribution issue, outside of the influence of the WTO.

So far the jurisprudence has been sensitive and careful to safeguard the rights of developing countries. For example, in *EC – Bananas III*, the Appellate Body rejected the GATT practice of refusing private counsel before panels and stated that: "... we can find nothing in the ['*WTO Agreement*'], the *DSU* or the *Working Procedures*, nor in customary international law or the prevailing practice of international tribunals, which prevents a WTO Member from determining the composition of its delegation in Appellate Body proceedings" and this allowed small delegations to bring along private counsels.[197] In *US – Shrimp (21.5)*[198] the Appellate Body put a great deal of emphasize on the need to ensure that when imposing unilateral measures pursuant to Article XX of GATT, the importing countries maintains enough flexibility in its application of the said measure so as to ensure that developing countries exporting shrimps can use alternatives methods of complying with the goal and policy pursued by the importing country.

3. Preliminary findings

The process and procedures followed by WTO adjudicative bodies can certainly be improved and chances are that in the context of the Doha Development Round many suggestions would ensure the consideration of such improvements. If many people from the civil society challenged the confidentiality of such process and the need for rules allowing for the consideration of *amicus cu-*

riae briefs by panels and the Appellate Body, one may reach the conclusion that generally the procedural mechanism of the WTO dispute settlement system does not appear to reveal any failure to respect the basic human rights procedural prescriptions.

Some thoughts in conclusion

There is no doubt that WTO Members are bound by their human rights obligations. In light of the international law presumption of good faith, States are presumed to negotiate treaties in good faith, i.e., taking into account all their such international obligations. Therefore WTO Members must comply with their human rights obligations and with their WTO obligations at the same time without letting a conflict arise between the two sets of legislations. Hence, it is only reasonable to expect that WTO adjudicating bodies would interpret WTO provisions taking into account all relevant international obligations of WTO disputing States. In this paper I suggest that, because of the inherent flexibility of many of the WTO obligations, including the wording of many WTO provisions, it will be possible for WTO Members to respect both their human rights obligations and their WTO obligations at the same time. The WTO applicable law appears to be a fairly complete sub-system of international law which must however be interpreted as having been drafted and as evolving coherently with the rest of international law. In any case, in a situation of irreconcilable conflict between a WTO provision and human rights law, panels and the Appellate Body cannot reach a conclusion that a non-WTO provision has superseded a WTO provision, as in doing so they would be adding or diminishing or amending the WTO treaty, contrary to clear prescriptions of the DSU.

Situations of conflicts between the system of human rights law and that of WTO law may in fact be best considered as a matter for negotiation by States, rather than for dispute settlement. But all this depends on the willingness of WTO Members to provide treaties dealing with human rights and subject matters other than trade, with a dispute settlement mechanism as powerful as the one put in place by the WTO Agreement. In fact, the issue is not a legal one and not one of dispute settlement as such. It is a political one.

The procedural aspects of the dispute settlement mechanism of the WTO would appear to respect the main rules found in human rights treaties. If anything, a possible solution to existing human rights violations include the need to strengthen the investigative powers and dispute settlement mechanisms in human rights treaties to enhance their effective implementation. The use of human rights experts, evidence gathered by human rights bodies and the involvement, when relevant, of human rights material in the panel process may also ensure further coherence between the WTO Agreement and human rights treaties. Institutional agreements reinforcing the dispute settlement mechanism of other human rights treaties would reduce the attractiveness of the WTO dispute settlement mechanism.

NOTES

1. On WTO and Human Rights see generally: P. Ala'I, "A human rights critique of the WTO: some preliminary observations," *Geo. Wash. J. Int'l. Rev.*, 33 (2000/2002), p. 537-533; A.E. Appleton, "The World Trade Organisation: implications for human rights and democracy," *Thesaurus Acroasium*, 29 (2000), p. 415-462; J. Bhagwati, "Trade linkage and human rights," *The Uruguay Round and beyond: essays in honour of Arthur Dunkel*, Berlin: Springer, 1998, p. 241-250; S.H. Cleveland, "Human rights sanctions and the World Trade Organisation," *Environment, Human Rights and international trade / ed. by F. Francioni*, Oxford: Hart Publishing, 2001, p. 199-261; M. Cohn, "The World Trade Organization: elevating property interests above human rights," *Ga. J. Int'l & Comp. L.*, 29 (2001), p. 247-440; T. Flory, N. Ligneul, "Commerce international, droits de l'homme, mondialisation: les droits de l'homme et l'Organisation mondial du commerce," *Commerce mondiale et protection des droits de l'homme: les droits de l'homme à l'épreuve de la globalisation des échanges économiques*, Bruxelles: Bruylant, 2001, p. 179-191; H. Lim, "Trade and human rights: what's at issue?" *J.W.T.*, 35 (2001), p. 275-300; E.-U. Petersmann, "From 'negative' to 'positive' integration in the WTO: time for 'mainstreaming human rights' into WTO law," *C.M.L.R.*, 37 (2000), p. 1363-1382; A.H. Qureshi, "International trade and human rights from the perspective of the WTO," *International economic law with a human face / ed. F. Weiss, E. Denters and P. de Waart*, The Hague: Kluwer, 1998, p. 159-173; P. Stirling, "The use of trade sanctions as an enforcement mechanism for basic human rights: a proposal for addition to the World Trade Organization," *Am. U.J. Int'l L. & Pol'y*, 11 (1996), p. 1-46. A fundamental dispute settlement issue of the debate on trade and human rights is that of the jurisdiction matters under WTO provisions, as reflected already in the PPMs and policy considerations debates that have taken place in the trade and environment area. Can WTO Members' regulatory distinctions or preferences make reference to (some – and which ones) human rights situations or policies occurring in another? If so, why, when and how and under which multilateral surveillance mechanism, if any?

2. In addition to a series to Activists' allegations one may refer to the first report of the Expert Group of the Sub-Commission on Human Rights, 15 June 2000 which became known as the Nightmare Report (having qualified the WTO as the nightmare of human rights and developing countries) – E/CN.4/Sub.2/2000/13.

3. Robert Howse and Makau Mutua have written: "It is absurd to expect a country that systematically violates basic human rights to faithfully execute and implement the processes that WTO agreements require." I would tend to agree with Jose Alvarez commenting on Howse Mutua's paper that "Many human rights violators routinely comply with international economic agreements and many prominent defenders of human rights, including the United States, have trouble adhering to and complying with some international agreements" in: Trade and The Environment: Implications for Global Governance: How Not to Link: Institutional Conundrums of an Expanded trade Regime, 7 *Wid.L.Symp.J.1.* (Spring 2001).

4. One may think of the invocation of GATT Articles XX or XXI or GATS Articles XIV or XIV*bis*.

5. One may think of labelling requirements referring to human rights considerations and the possibility of human rights considerations in GSP preferences.

6. See for instance Jose Alvarez, "Comments on Howse and Makau's paper" in: Trade and the Environment: Implications for Global Governance: How Not to Link: Institutional Conundrums of an Expanded Trade Regime, 7 *Wid.L.Symp.J.*, 1 (2001).

7. "Enforce" will be defined as providing for effective remedies.

8. On this issue see generally: Gabrielle Marceau, "A Call for Coherence in International Law," *Journal of World Trade*, (1999) Vol. 5, No. 33; Gabrielle Marceau, "Conflicts of Norms and Conflicts of Jurisdictions," *Journal of World Trade*, (2001) Vol. 35, No. 6, p. 1081; Joel Trachtman, "The Domain of WTO Dispute Resolution," (1999) *Harvard International Law Journal*, Vol. 40, No. 2, p. 333; Joost Pauwelyn, "The Role of Public International Law in the WTO: How Far Can We Go?" *American Journal of International Law*, (2001) Vol. 95, No. 3, p. 595; Lorand Bartel, "Applicable Law in WTO Dispute Settlement Proceedings," *Journal of World Trade*, (2001) Vol. 3 No. 35, p. 499; Thomas J. Schoenbaum, "WTO Dispute Settlement: Praise and Suggestions for Reform," *International and Comparative Law Quarterly*, (2000) Vol. 47, p. 647; David Palmeter and Petros Mavroidis, "The WTO Legal System: Sources of Law," *A.J.I.L.*, Vol. 92, No. 3, p. 398.

9. Appellate Body report on *United States – Measures Affecting Imports of Woven Shirts and Blouses from India*, WT/DS33/AB/R, (*US – Wool Shirts and Blouses*) adopted on 23 May 1997, p. 13.

10. Appellate Body report on *European Communities – Regime for the Importation, Sale and Distribution of Bananas*, WT/DS27/AB/R, (*EC – Bananas III*) adopted on 25 September 1997, paras. 135 and 136.

11. It did, however, note: "Even assuming that there is some requirement for economic interest, we consider that the European Communities, as an exporter of milk products to Korea, had sufficient interest to initiate and proceed with these dispute settlement proceedings." Panel Report on *Korea – Definitive Safeguard Measure on Imports of Certain Dairy Products*, WT/DS98/R, (*Korea – Dairy*), adopted on 12 January 2000, para. 7.14.

12. For instance Article 6.1 of the DSU envisages that after the period of consultations (Article 4.7 of the DSU), the complaining party can request the establishment of a panel which "shall be established at the latest the second time the matter appears on the agenda of the Dispute Settlement Body, unless by consensus the WTO Members decide not to do so" (Article 6.1 of the DSU). In practicable terms, a complaining Member will never agree to participate in a consensus decision not to establish a panel that it has just requested (unless it gets somehow satisfaction). The same is true for the adoption of panel and Appellate Body reports and for the imposition of sanctions: when requested such actions must take place unless by consensus WTO Members decide not to do so. Some say that the process is more or less into the hands of the complaining party who must agree to suspend it; otherwise it will proceed along pre-established stages. To ensure the effectiveness of

the process, each time the action of the Dispute Settlement Body (DSB) is formally required, any Member can call a meeting of the DSB on a 10 to 15 days notice period. Members are also given rights to appeal panel findings, to call for different forms of arbitration during the DSU process as well as other procedural rights.

13. William Davey, "Has the WTO Dispute Settlement Exceeded its authority?", JIEL (2001) Vol. 4, No. 1, p. 79.

14. Unilateral measure is defined here are measures other than those explicitly authorized by the WTO. See para. 111 of the Appellate Body report on *US – Import Measures on Certain Products from the European Communities*, WT/DS165/AB/R, (*US – Certain EC Procucts*) adopted on 10 January 2001: "Article 23.1 of the DSU imposes a general obligation of Members to redress a violation of obligations or other nullification or impairment of benefits under the covered agreements only by recourse to the rules and procedures of the DSU, and not through unilateral action. Subparagraphs (a), (b) and (c) of Article 23.2 articulate specific and clearly-defined forms of prohibited unilateral action contrary to Article 23.1 of the DSU. There is a close relationship between the obligations set out in paragraphs 1 and 2 of Article 23. They *all* concern the obligation of Members of the WTO not to have recourse to unilateral action."

15. In the *US – Section 301* Report, this seems to have been one of the conclusions reached by the Panel – in that case, the threat of unilateral determinations by a powerful State, the United States. The Panel was of the view that the "indirect effect" of the admittedly non-mandatory US Section 301, the risk of unilateral determination (both having "chilling effect" on Members and the marketplace), as well as the overall systemic damage of any spill-over effect of such discretionary legislation, were such – in particular in light of the economic power of the United States – as to lead to a conclusion that the United States, in maintaining such Section 301, appeared *prima facie* to be in violation of Article 23 of the DSU.

"An important reason why Article 23 of the DSU must be interpreted with a view to prohibiting any form of unilateral action is because such unilateral actions threaten the stability and predictability of the multilateral trade system. Unilateral actions are, therefore, contrary to the essence of the multilateral trade system of the WTO."

Panel Report on *US – Section 301-310 of the Trade Act of 1974*, WT/DS152/R, (*US – Section 301*), adopted on 27 January 2000, at para. 6.14, see also paras. 7.71 to 7.94.

16. See the Panel report in *US – Certain EC Products* at para. 6.133.

17. For Ohlhoff and Schloemann the system contained in Articles 4 to 22 of the DSU only applies where the parties to the dispute cannot agree on the resolution of the dispute by "expeditious arbitration within the WTO," which according to Article 25 can "as an alternative means of dispute settlement … facilitate the solution of certain disputes that concern issues clearly defined by both parties." See "Rational allocation of disputes and 'constitutionalisation': Forum choice as an issue of competence" in: *Dispute Resolution in the WTO*, James Cameron & Karen Campbell (Ed.), at p. 318.

18. Note that in recent proceedings under Article 22.2 and 22.6, the United States and the European Communities have used Article 25 arbitration to arbitrate the level of sanctions resulting for the refusal of the United States to bring its measure into conformity of the TRIPS Agreement in *US – Copyright Section 110(5)*, WT/DS 160/ABR25/1.

19. See Article 4.11 of the DSU and its footnote that lists them all.

20. Article XXIII also envisages the possibility of disputes on the basis of non-violation and situation complaints. Non-violation claims would imply allegations that a Members' action, although not in violation of the WTO, has been such as to nullify the trade benefits of another complaining Member. On the issue of non-violation see the Appellate Body discussion in *EC-Measures Affecting Asbestos and Products Containing Asbestos*, (*EC – Asbestos*), WT/DS135/AB/R, adopted on 5 April 2001, paras. 182-190.

21. For a detailed description of the evolution of the dispute settlement mechanism of the WTO, see MTN.GNG/NG13/W/4/Rev.1.

22. See Article 2(b) of GATT 1994 which provides that contracting parties should be read WTO Members; Article XXI of GATT is now replaced by the institutions identified in the WTO Agreement including the DSB, in the case of DSU related matters.

23. The limited jurisdiction of WTO adjudicating bodies has, arguably, been confirmed by the Appellate Body in *EC – Poultry*, where it had to assess the legal value of a bilateral agreement (the Oilseed Agreement) between Brazil and the EC. The Appellate Body stated: "In our view, it is not necessary to have recourse to either Article 59.1 or Article 30.3 of the *Vienna Convention*... As such, it [the Schedule of the EC] forms part of the multilateral obligations under the *WTO Agreement*. The Oilseeds Agreement, in contrast, is a bilateral agreement negotiated by the European Communities and Brazil under Article XXVIII of the GATT 1947, as part of the resolution of the dispute in *EEC – Oilseeds*. As such, the Oilseeds Agreement is not a 'covered agreement' within the meaning of Articles 1 and 2 of the DSU. Nor is the Oilseeds Agreement part of the multilateral obligations accepted by Brazil and the European Communities pursuant to the *WTO Agreement*, which came into effect on 1 January 1995. The Oilseeds Agreement is not cited in any Annex to the *WTO Agreement*. Although the provisions of certain legal instruments that entered into force under the GATT 1947 were made part of the GATT 1994 pursuant to the language in Annex 1A incorporating the GATT 1994 into the *WTO Agreement*, the Oilseeds Agreement is not one of those legal instruments." Appellate Body Report *on European Communities – Measures Affecting the Importation of Certain Poultry Products*, WT/DS69/AB/R, (*EC –Poultry*) adopted on 23 July 1998, at para. 79 (Emphasis added.)

24. In the absence of extraordinary mandate pursuant to Article 7.3 of the DSU or the arbitration process of Article 25.

25. Joel Trachtman in his article "The Domain of the WTO Dispute Settlement System," Op. cit. used as sub-title this prohibition to add or diminish WTO provision, hence referring to the determinant implications of that provision.

26. Article 19.1 *in fine* reads as follows: "In additions to its recommendations, the panel or the Appellate Body may suggest ways in which the Member concerned could implement the recommendations."

27. The conceptual distinction between the jurisdiction of an adjudicating body and the relevant "applicable law" was well identified by Joost Pauwelyn, in: "The Role of Public International Law in WTO" Op. cit. at p. 554 and Lorand Bartels, in: "The Applicable Law" Op. cit., at p. 502.

28. Article 23 of the DSU provides exclusive jurisdiction to WTO adjudicating bodies to provide remedies for any WTO grieve. It would be a denial of justice to conclude that provisions of the covered agreements could be superseded by non-WTO rules which, *de facto* and *de jure*, could not be enforced or apply by WTO panels and the Appellate Body since they are strictly prohibited from adding or diminishing existing covered agreement.

29. Articles 3 and 6 and 7 of the DSU.

30. But in the absence of effective remedy, setting aside the peculiar political and legal contexts of this dispute, is rather peculiar, this Appellate Body's conclusion confirms that it considers itself capable of issuing declaratory rulings.

31. See the Appellate Body report in *US – Certain EC Products*, at para. 81.

32. Article 41.1(b)(i) of the Vienna Convention.

33. Appellate Body Report on *US – Section 211 Omnibus Appropriation Act of 1998*, WT/DS176/AB/R, *(US – Section 211 Appropriations Act)*, adopted on 1 February 2002, para. 363: "However, where a WTO Member chooses not to recognize intellectual property rights in its own territory relating to a confiscation of rights in another territory, a measure resulting from and implementing that choice must, *if it affects other WTO Members*, comply with the *TRIPS Agreement*, by which all WTO Members are voluntarily bound. In such a measure, that WTO Member must accord 'no less favourable treatment' to the nationals of *all other WTO Members* than it accords to its own nationals, and must grant to the nationals of all other WTO Members 'any advantage, favour, privilege or immunity' granted to any other WTO Member. In such a measure, a WTO Member may not discriminate in a way that does not respect the obligations of national treatment and most-favoured-nation treatment that are fundamental to the *TRIPS Agreement*."

34. Thomas J. Schoenbaum, "WTO Dispute Settlement: Praise and Suggestions for Reform," *I.C.L.Q.*, (2000) Vol. 47, p. 647, at p. 653.

35. See the Appellate Body Statement in para. 162 of the *EC – Bananas III* Report: "Thus, we have no alternative but to examine the provisions of the Lomé Convention ourselves *in so far as it is necessary to interpret the Lomé waiver.*" (Emphasis added.) See a more extensive discussion of this issue of what can be interpreted – domestic law and international law instruments in Gabrielle Marceau and Jennifer Morrissey "Clarifications of the DSU brought by WTO Jurisprudence" in: *Trade and Agriculture*, (ed. Joe Macmahon) (2001) Cameron May, at p. 143.

36. I have borrowed the expression from Joel Trachtman "The Domain of WTO Dispute Resolution," Op. cit., p. 333.

37. Panel Report on *Korea – Measures Affecting Government Procurement*, WT/DS163/R, (*Korea – Procurement*) adopted on 19 June 2000, para. 7.96.

38. Joost Pauwelyn, "How Far Can We Go?" at p. 566.

39. Idem.

40. Lorand Bartels, "Applicable Law," p. 506.

41. In an exchange of email Milton Churche has suggested that the issue of what constitutes adding to or diminishing the covered agreements may not be straightforward. One could run an argument that panels and the Appellate Body are only applying customary rules of treaty interpretation in establishing that certain provisions of the WTO have been superseded by a non-WTO treaty. If so, then the panel and the WTO Members have to respect this interpretation. This is as much a part of Article 3.2 of the DSU as the requirement about not adding to or diminishing the rights and obligations in the covered agreements. Indeed, if this line of reasoning held, could one not argue that DSB recommendations based on an interpretation of WTO provisions consistent with customary rules of treaty interpretation cannot be seen as adding to or diminishing these rights and obligations (as the WTO provisions – and therefore these rights and obligations – cannot be read [and do not exist] in isolation from these rules)?

42. "Our view is *supported further* by the rules of general international law on state responsibility, which require that countermeasures in response to breaches by states of their international obligations be commensurate with the injury suffered. In the same vein, we note that Article 22.4 of the DSU stipulates that the suspension of concessions shall be equivalent to the level of nullification or impairment. This provision of the DSU has been interpreted consistently as not justifying punitive damages. These two examples illustrate the consequences of breaches by states of their international obligations, whereas a safeguard action is merely a remedy to WTO-consistent "fair trade" activity. It would be absurd if the breach of an international obligation were sanctioned by proportionate countermeasures, while, in the absence of such breach, a WTO Member would be subject to a disproportionate and, hence, "punitive," attribution of serious damage not wholly caused by its exports. In our view, such an exorbitant derogation from the principle of proportionality in respect of the attribution of serious damage could be justified *only if the drafters of the ATC had expressly provided for it, which is not the case.*" (Footnotes omitted, emphasis added.)

Appellate Body Report in *United States – Transitional Safeguard Measure on Combed Cotton Yarn from Pakistan*, WT/DS192/AB/R, (*US – Cotton Safeguard*) adopted on 5 November 2001, at para. 120. The same is true for the use of the principle of "due diligence" in paras. 67, 76, 77 and 79 and with its use of "good faith" in para. 81 of the same report.

43. I regret the very negative connotation given by some to the term "self-contained regime," while, on the contrary, such systems if they exist – far away from being insensitive and unreceptive to general international law – are evidence of a high level of legal sophistication sufficient for not having to rely on more general provisions of general international law and state responsibility. A legal sub-systems that is "clos" (French term for self-contained) is a specific system of law that provides for specific obligations and the specific consequences of their violation. There is nothing pejorative there. Self-contained regime cannot mean that a system of law would "suffice" itself. Rather it refers to specific *rights and obligations* that provides for effective *remedies* in case of their *violation*. In WTO, these three variables are specifically identified. Yet WTO must "breathe" the rest of international law and its interpretation will reflect it. Thus it is not unreasonable to suggest that the WTO is a specific system, as described in Article 53 of the Rules on state Responsibility. Another suggestion could be that if most provisions of the WTO are sufficiently specific to exclude the application of the general Rules on State Responsibility, the obligation of objectivity contained in Article 11 of the DSU would call for the direct application of provisions on State Responsibility to "complete" the operationalization of WTO law, as long as it would not be viewed as an addition or diminution of WTO law.

44. Article 26 of the Vienna Convention on the Law of Treaties (Vienna Convention): "Every treaty in force is binding upon the parties to it *and must be performed by them in good faith.*" (Emphasis added.)

45. Appellate Body report on *United States – Standards for Reformulated and Conventional Gasoline,* WT/DS2/AB/R, ("*US – Gasoline*"), adopted on 20 May 1996, p. 18.

46. Panels and the Appellate Body have made use of general principles of international law to support their interpretation based on the ordinary meaning of the terms of the WTO Agreement. For instance, in *Canada – Terms of Protection,* in discussing the non-retroactivity of some provisions of the TRIPS Agreement, the Appellate Body stated that: "This conclusion is *supported* by the general principle of international law ... which established a presumption against the retroactive effect of treaties." (Appellate Body report on *Canada – Patent Term of Protection,* WT/DS170/AB/R, adopted on 12 October 2000, para. 71) In *US – Shrimp* it stated that: "The chapeau of Article XX is, in fact, but one *expression* of the principle of good faith" and it reiterated that "good faith" was a pervasive statement in its Review Report on the US implementation measure (Appellate Body report on *US – Import prohibition of Certain Shrimp and Shrimp Products,* WT/DS58/AB/R, (*US – Shrimp*), adopted on 6 November 1998, para. 158, and in the Review Report WT/DS 58/AB/R/RW at paras. 123 and ff). In *United States – Tax Treatment for "Foreign Sales Corporations,"* WT/DS108/AB/R, (*US – FSC*), adopted on 20 March 2000), para. 106, the Appellate Body stated that Article 3.10 of the DSU was an expression of the good faith general principle of law (para. 106). In *US – Hot-Rolled Steel,* the Appellate Body stated: "We see this provision as another detailed expression of the principle of good faith, which is, at once, a general principle of law and principle of general international law, that informs the provisions of the AD Agreement, as well as other covered Agreements" (Appellate Body Report on *United States – Antidumping Measures on Certain Hot-Rolled Steel Products from Japan,* WT/DS184/AB/R, (*US – Hot Rolled Steel*), adopted on 23 August 2001, at para. 101). In *US – Cotton Safeguard,* the Appellate Body referred to the principle of due diligence when interpreting the investigating obligations of Members under Article 6 of the Agreement on Textiles; it also made parallels with the principle of proportionality, the rules on state responsibility and referred to the "pervasive general principle of good faith that underlies all treaties" (para. 81).

47. GATT Panel Report on *Tuna II,* at para. 5.19.

48. We note that the Appellate Body did not specify which Article 31 provision it relied on when using these international environmental agreements to interpret the Article XX(g) term "exhaustible natural resources." However, these agreements could be characterised as "relevant rules on international law applicable in the relations between the parties" under Article 31.3(c).

49. The TBT Decision on Principles for the Development of International Standards, Guides and Recommendations with Relation to Articles 2, 5 and Annex 3 (Annex 4 to G/TBT/9) refers to "transparency," openness, impartiality and consensus, effectiveness and relevance, coherence and the development dimension as criteria to be used for the determination whether such standards contained in a non-WTO treaty could be relevant for the purpose of assessing the compatibility of any measure with the TBT Agreement.

50. Joost Pauwelyn, "The Role of Public International Law in the WTO," Op. cit., at p. 576.

51. An argument by Palmeter and Mavroidis also lends weight to this approach. They argue that "the parties" refers to the parties to a dispute. This position reinforces the view that Article 31.3(c) may be used where treaties have different membership. However, their approach while illustrating their interpretation, can only be considered a partial one, as the Vienna Convention is not used exclusively in the case of disputes. A better approach is that "parties" may refer more generally to a subset of all the parties to the treaty under interpretation. Palmeter and Mavroidis, "The WTO legal system: Sources of Law," *A.J.I.L.*, Vol. 92, No. 3, p. 398.

52. The Appellate Body report on *European Communities – Customs Classification of Certain Computer Equipment*, WT/DS62, 67, 68/AB/R, (*EC – Computer Equipment*) adopted on 22 June 1998. See also on this issue, Gabrielle Marceau, "A Call for Coherence in International Law" Op. cit., at p. 123-127. Lorand Bartels, pointed to the fact that the Appellate Body (at para. 93) criticised the panel for taking into account the practice of only one party *to the dispute*, thus apparently violating Article 31(3)(b), and it also later (at para. 85) referred expressly to Article 31(3) before stating (at para. 89) that "a proper interpretation of Schedule LXXX should have included an examination of the Harmonized System and its Explanatory Notes." This amounts to an acceptance of the submission of the European Communities, which expressly stated (at para. 13) that, by virtue of Article 31(3)(c), the treaties constituting the Harmonized System and its Explanatory Notes (which were not concluded by all WTO Members) should "be relevant in interpreting the obligations of the European Communities under Schedule LXXX vis-à-vis WTO Members which are also Members of the World Customs Organization (the 'WCO')." Lorand Bartels, "Article XX of GATT and the Problem of Extraterritorial Jurisdiction: The Case of Trade Measures for the Protection of Human Rights," *Journal of World Trade*, Vol. 36, No. 2. p. 353. See also on this issue, Gabrielle Marceau, "A Call for Coherence in International Law" Op. cit.

53. The Appellate Body report on *US – Shrimp* at footnote 111. It noted, in relation to the former, that both Thailand and the United States had signed but not ratified the convention. And it noted, in relation to the latter, that India and Pakistan had ratified, but that Malaysia, Thailand and the United States are not parties to the convention. The Appellate Body did not explicitly refer to Article 31.3(c).

54. Appellate Body report on *EC – Poultry*, at para. 82.

55. See Appellate Body Report in *European Communities – Measures Concerning Meat and Meat Products*, WT/DS26, 48/AB/R, (*EC – Hormones*), adopted 13/2/98, at para. 133.

56. Appellate Body finding in para. 162 of the *EC – Bananas III* . Note also that domestic legislation may also need to be interpreted. In *India – Patent,* the Appellate Body said in certain circumstances, it was permissible to refer to national law: "*There was simply no way for the Panel to make this determination without engaging in an examination of Indian law*. But, ... in this case, the Panel was not interpreting Indian law 'as such'; rather, the Panel was examining Indian law solely for the purpose of determining whether India had met its obligations under the TRIPS Agreement." (Emphasis added.) Appellate Body Report on *India – Patent Protection for Pharmaceutical and Agricultural Chemical Products*, WT/DS79/1, (*India – Patent*), report adopted 2 September 1998, paras. 67-8. In *US – 1916 Act*, the panel stated that even if the text of the law in question were clear on its face, it was necessary to examine the domestic application of that law, its historical context and legislative history and subsequent declarations of US authorities in order to asses its compatibility with WTO law, Panel Report on *United States – Antidumping Act 1916*, WT/DS136, (*US –*

1916 Act), adopted on 26 September 2002, at para. 6.48. See also panel report in *United States – Section 337 of the Tariff Act of 1930*, adopted 7 November 1989, BISD 36S/345. In all those reports the domestic law was interpreted to determine compliance with WTO law.

57. For an examination of the use of the "evolutive interpretation" principle in other fora, see Gabrielle Marceau "Conflicts of Norms and Conflicts of Jurisdictions," Op. cit. at p. 1088-1089 and Gabrielle Marceau, "A Call for Coherence in International Law," Op. cit., at page 120-123.

58. Appellate Body report on *US – Shrimp* at para. 129.

59. Appellate Body report on *US – Shrimp* at para. 130. It is also worth recalling this passage from *Japan – Taxes on Alcoholic Beverages*, WT/DS8, 9, 11/AB/R, (*Japan – Alcoholic Beverages*), adopted on 1 November 1996, at page 34: "WTO rules are not so rigid or so inflexible as not to leave room for reasoned judgements in confronting the endless and ever-changing ebb and flow of real facts in real cases in the real world. They will serve the multilateral trading system best if they are interpreted with that in mind." See also the conclusion of the ECJ in *CILFIT* (Rec. 1982, p. 3415, at 3430): "Finally, every provision of community law must be placed in its context and interpreted in the light of the provisions of Community law as a whole, regard being had to the objectives thereof and *to its state of evolution at the date on which the provision in question is to be applied.*" (Emphasis added.)

60. I. Sinclair, *The Vienna Convention on the Law of Treaties*, 2nd ed., (1984, Manchester, MUP) p. 139. See also Mustafa Kamil Yasseen, *L'Interpretation des traités d'après la Convention de Vienne sur le droit des traités, Recueil de Cours*, 1976 – III, tome 151, p. 64, and Taslim Olawale-Elias, *The Doctrine of Inter-temporal Law*, A.J.I.L., Vol. 74, (April) 1980, p. 292.

61. In the *Case Concerning the Gabcíkovo-Nagymaros Project (Hungary/Slovakia)*, (1997) ICJ. See also *Namibia (Legal Consequences) Advisory Opinion* (1971) I.C.J. Rep. 31.

62. *Case of the Aegean Sea Continental Shelf (Greece vs Turkey* ICJ (1978), p. 4, at paras. 78–80. See also *Namibia (Legal Consequences) Advisory Opinion* (1971) I.C.J. Rep., 31.

63. Arbitral Panel Established Pursuant to Article 2008 of the North-American Free-Trade Agreement, Final report: *In the Matter of Tariffs Applied by Canada to Certain U.-Origin Agricultural Products* (2 Dec. 1996).

64. The most significant cases in which the European Court of Human Rights applied an evolutive interpretation are: *Tyrer*, Serie A, Vol. 26, adopted on 28 April 1978, at para. 31; *Marckx*, Serie A, Vol. 31, adopted on 13 June 1979, para. 41. See also the judgment in *CILFIT* (ECJ (1982), p. 3415, at 3430) where the evolutive interpretation was used by the ECJ. Also, J. Boulouis, *Les méthodes d'interprétation de la CJCE, Répertoire de droit communautaire*, Dalloz; R. Kovar, *La contribution de la Cour de justice à l'édification de l'ordre juridique communautaire, Rec. des cours de l'académie de droit europ.*, Vol. IV, T. 1, 1993; H. Gaudin, *Les principes d'interprétation de la Cour de justice des Communautés européennes et la subsidiarité, Rev. des Affaires européennes*, 1998, n° 1, p. 10.

65. Robert Howse and Katau Mutua, "Challenges for the World Trade Organisation," Rights and Democracy, 2000.

66. See the paper of Yuji Isawasa in this publication on sources of human rights law.

67. Jose Alavarez, Comments on Howse and Makau's paper, p. 3.

68. For instance see the unpublished paper of Richard Elliott, "International Human Rights Law, Access to Medicines, and the Interpretation of the WTO Agreement on Trade-Related Aspects of Intellectual Property Rights," November 2001; Papers from the Legal Assistance Center, Windhoek, Namibia (2001); Peter N. Prove, "Human Rights Within the WTO," The Lutheran World Federation.

69. See for instance Robert Howse, "The Canadian Generic Medicines Panel, A Dangerous Precedent in Dangerous Times," *Journal of World Intellectual Property*, Vol. 3, No. 4, p. 493 (2000).

70. See WT/DS 199. See Caroline Dommen, "Covenant on Economic, Social and Cultural Rights: A Treasure Chest of Support for Developing Countries' Concerns in the WTO," BRIDGES January-April 2001, at p. 21.

71. See Document G/AG/NG/W/36/Rev.1.

72. The Preamble of the Agreement on Agriculture recalls that the long-term objective "is to establish a fair and market-oriented agricultural trading system" and notes that "commitments under the reform programme should be made in an equitable way among all Members, having regard to non-trade concerns, including food security and the need to protect the environment; having regard to the agreement that special and differential treatment for developing countries is an integral element of the negotiations ..."

73. Article 11.2.b of the International Covenant on Economic, Social and Cultural Rights.

74. E/CN.4/Sub.2/2001/13.

75. It should be noted that Mauritius invoked such human right law provisions, not in dispute settlement context, but in support of its interpretation of Article 20, dealing with the obligation of Members to undertake negotiations but in claiming that in doing so Members' negotiations and the WTO policy reform ought to be undertaken in a way that is consistent with other multilateral commitments.

76. The Committee on Economic Social and cultural Rights in its general comment defines or narrows the otherwise potentially ambiguous application of the right to food and what obligations are imposed on state parties as a result of this right. According to the Committee, "The right to adequate food, like any other human right, imposes three types or levels of obligations on States parties: the obligations to respect, to protect and to fulfil. In turn, the obligation to fulfil incorporates both an obligation to facilitate and an obligation to provide. The obligation to respect existing access to adequate food requires States parties not to take any measures that result in preventing such access. The obligation to protect requires measures by the State to ensure that enterprises or individuals do not deprive individuals of their access to adequate food. The obligation to fulfil (facilitate) means the State must pro-actively engage in activities intended to strengthen people's access to and utilisation of resources and means to ensure their livelihood, including food security. Finally, whenever an individual or group is unable, for reasons beyond their control, to enjoy the right

to adequate food by the means at their disposal, States have the obligation to fulfil (provide) that right directly... ." For comments on the right to food see E/C.12/1999/5; on the right to health see E/C.12/2000/4.

77. Joel Trachtman, "Trade and ... Problems" *European Journal of International Law* (1998) Vol. 9, No. 1, p. 32, at 45.

78. It is interesting to note that this distinction bears some resemblance with the old distinction between "traité-loi" and "traité contrat" where the first is drafted in general terms like the legislation in civil law countries with general normative provisions and the former was evidence of more precise syllagmatic commitments. This distinction, which is intellectually satisfying however proves not to be very useful in practice as it has not lead to different regimes of treaties. In practice most would argue that many treaties have both types of provisions.

79. Joel Trachtman, "The Domain of WTO Dispute Settlement System," Op. cit., at p. 346 and Joel Trachtman, "Trade and ... Problems," Op. cit.

80. On the interpretation and application of the "Public Morals" exception of GATT Article XX(a) see Marie-Joëlle Redor, "L'ordre public: Ordre public ou ordres publics; Ordre public et droits fondamentaux." *Actes du colloque de Caen*, 12 et 12 mai 2000, Bruylant (2001); Christoph T. Feddersen "Focussing on Substantive Law in International Economic relations:" The "Public Morals" of GATT's Article XX(a) and "Conventional" Rules of Interpretation," *Minn.J.Global Trade*, Vol.7, at p. 75 and Steve Chartnovitz, "The Moral Exception in Trade Policy," *Virginia Journal of International Law*, Spring 1998. Reprinted in part in "Forty Years of Scholarship," *Virginia Journal of International Law*, Spring 2000.

81. The recent jurisprudence – See the Appellate Body Reports in *Korea – Imports Measures on Fresh, Chilled and Frozen Beef*, WT/DS161, 169/AB/R, (*Korea – Various Measures on Beef*), adopted on 10 January 2001, paras. 161-164, reiterated in *EC – Asbestos*, paras. 171-172 – has established that the determination whether a measure which is not "indispensable," may nevertheless be "necessary" involves a process of weighing and balancing a series of factors which include (1) the importance of the common interests or values protected by the measure, (2) the efficacy of such measure in pursuing the policies aimed at, and (3) the accompanying impact of the law or regulation on imports or exports. The more vital or important the policies it is aimed at, the easier it would be to accept as "necessary" a measure designed for that purpose. Criteria have also been developed to ensure that while a Member has a *prima facie* right to maintain the types of measures necessary to enforce chosen policies, that Member should be able to demonstrate its good faith in that its measures are not applied in a discriminatory manner or as disguised restriction on trade.

82. "128. (...)First, we used the Inter-American Convention to show that 'consensual and multilateral procedures are available and feasible for the establishment of programmes for the conservation of sea turtles.' In other words, we saw the Inter-American Convention as evidence that an alternative course of action based on cooperation and consensus was reasonably open to the United States. Second, we used the Inter-American Convention to show the existence of 'unjustifiable discrimination.' The Inter-American Convention was the result of serious, good faith efforts to negotiate a regional agreement on the protection and conservation of turtles, including efforts made by the United States... 130. (...)The Panel compared the efforts of the United States to negotiate the Inter-American Convention with one group of exporting WTO Members with the efforts made by

the United States to negotiate a similar agreement with another group of exporting WTO Members. The Panel rightly used the Inter-American Convention as a *factual reference* in this exercise of comparison. It was all the more relevant to do so given that the Inter-American Convention was the only international agreement that the Panel could have used in such a comparison." in *US – Shrimp (21.5 DSU)*, WT/DS58/AB/RW, adopted on 21 November 2001.

83. It is recalled that the WTO sub-system has been drafted in specific terms and that human rights provisions do not find direct application into the WTO law and cannot be enforced by WTO panels.

84. Appellate Body Report on *Argentina – Measures Affecting Imports of Footwear, Textiles, Apparel*, WT/DS56/AB/R, (*Argentina – Textiles*), adopted on 22 April 1998, at para. 69.

85. *Encyclopedia of Public International Law* (North-Holland 1984), p. 468. See also Wilfred Jenks, "The Conflict of Law-Making Treaties," *The British Yearbook of International Law* (BYIL) 1953, at p. 425 *et seq.* For, in such a case, it is possible for a state which is a signatory of both treaties to comply with both treaties at the same time. The presumption against conflict is especially reinforced in cases where separate agreements are concluded between the same parties, since it can be presumed that they are meant to be consistent with each other, failing any evidence to the contrary. See also E. W. Vierdag, "The Time of the 'Conclusion' of a Multilateral Treaty: Article 30 of the Vienna Convention on the Law of Treaties and Related Provisions," *BYIL*, 1988, at p. 100; Sir Robert Jennings/Sir Arthur Watts (ed.), *Oppenheim's International Law,* Vol. I., Parts 2 to 4, 1992, at p. 1280; Sir Gerald Fitzmaurice, "The Law and Procedure of the International Court of Justice," *BYIL*, 1957, at p. 237; and Sir Ian Sinclair, *The Vienna Convention on the Law of Treaties*, 1984, at p. 97.

86. Jenks, Op. cit.

87. Appellate Body Report on *Guatemala – Anti-Dumping Investigation Regarding Portland Cement from Mexico*, WT/DS60/AB/R, adopted on 25 November 1998, para. 65. The same narrow definition was also used by the panel in *Indonesia – Certain Measures Affecting the Automobile Industry* (WT/DS54, 55, 59 and 64/R), (*Indonesia – Automobiles*) adopted on 23 July 1998, paras. 14.29-14.36 and 14.97 to 14.99.

88. Appellate Body Report on *US- Hot-Rolled Steel*, at paras. 55 and 62.

89. In an exchange of email Milton Churche has suggested that the following argument could be made: Panels and the Appellate Body are required to follow customary rules of treaty interpretation. One could run an argument that panels and the Appellate Body are only applying customary rules of treaty interpretation in establishing that certain provisions of the WTO have been superseded by a non-WTO treaty? If so, then the panel and the WTO Members have to respect this interpretation. This is as much a part of Article 3.2 of the DSU as the requirement about not adding to or diminishing the rights and obligations in the covered agreements. Indeed, if this line of reasoning held, could one not argue that DSB recommendations based on an interpretation of WTO provisions consistent with customary rules of treaty interpretation cannot be seen as adding to or diminishing these rights and obligations (as the WTO provisions – and therefore these rights and obligations – cannot be read (and do not exist) in isolation from these rules).

90. See for instance Gabrielle Marceau and Alexandra Gonzalez, "The Relationship between the Settlement Systems of the WTO and MEAs," in *Trade and Environment, the WTO, and MEAs*, Heinrich Böll Foundation and Woodrow Wilson Center, 2001, at p. 71.

91. For Churche, ultimately, the existence of an irreconcilable conflict means a conflict between the approaches that the international community have taken to realize different policy objectives, and this will probably need to be addressed in a case-specific manner (e.g., by seeking to find new ways to achieve both sets of objectives). Dispute settlement processes may help to identify the issues, underscore the need to find a resolution, and galvanize governments to act but are unlikely to find a resolution (as essentially the conflict requires a rewriting of one or more of the treaties to reflect the new approaches that governments would hopefully find for realizing their objectives). From this perspective a failure of the dispute settlement processes to resolve a particular dispute may not necessarily be a bad thing, nor does it necessarily represent a "failure" on the part of the dispute settlement processes, but can be part of the way in which governments fumble their way through developing (new) international law. Points of political leverage may help to identify whether the issues raised by a dispute that involves an irreconcilable conflict are such that a solution is needed (through rewriting existing treaties) or whether no solution is yet needed (or, at least, that the international community wants to sweep the problem under the carpet at this stage and is not yet ready to confront it). Email exchange of 14 January 2002.

92. For a discussion of those principles as used in the WTO dispute settlement see Gabrielle Marceau, "Conflicts of Norms and Conflicts of Jurisdictions" Op. cit., p. 1086-1095.

93. M. Bos, "The Hierarchy among the Recognized Manifestations of International Law," in *Estudios de Derecho Internacional. Homenaje al Profesor Miaja de la Muela*, Madrid, 1979, p. 364-366; B. Simma, P. Alston, "The Sources of Human Rights Law: Custom, Jus Cogens, and General Principles," *Australian Yb. Int. Law*, 1982, p. 96; A. Cassese, *International Law in a Divided World*, 1986, p. 180; N. Kontou, "The termination and revision of treaties in the light of new customary international law," 1994, p. 24; M.E. Villiger, *Customary International Law and Treaties*, 1997, p. 59f.

94. M. Bos, "The Hierarchy among the Recognized Manifestations of International Law," in *Estudios de Derecho Internacional. Homenaje al Profesor Miaja de la Muela*, Madrid, 1979, p. 364-6; B. Simma, P. Alston, "The Sources of Human Rights Law: Custom, Jus Cogens, and General Principles," *Australian Yb. Int. Law*, 1982, p. 96; A. Cassese, *International Law in a Divided World*, 1986, p. 180; N. Kontou, "The termination and revision of treaties in the light of new customary international law," 1994, p. 24; M.E. Villiger, *Customary International Law and Treaties*, 1997, p. 59f.

95. Hungary was of the view that the Court had to decide the case on the basis of general principles of international law, among which it included the precautionary principle. Slovakia refuted the argument by making reference to the maxim *lex posterior generalis non derogat legi priori speciali*. The Court agreed with Slovakia when it concluded that: (...) since neither of the Parties contended that new peremptory norms of environmental law had emerged since the conclusion of the 1977 Treaty (...); "newly developed norms of environmental law" could be relevant as long as they are agreed on by the parties and incorporated into the treaty at issue." ICJ, rep. 1997.

96. In that dispute, the European Communities contended that Article 5.1 of the SPS Agreement should have been interpreted in light of the precautionary principle. The Appellate Body, as the panel before, did not took position about the status of the precautionary principle in international law. The Appellate Body considered it "unnecessary, and probably imprudent" to take position on such an important "but abstract" a question. It was of the view that aspects of this principle had been taken into account in the drafting of the SPS Agreement and in any case it concluded that "the principle has not been written into the *SPS Agreement* as a ground for justifying SPS measures that are otherwise inconsistent with the obligations of Members set out in particular provisions of that Agreement." Appellate Body report on *EC – Hormones*, paras. 126-127.

97. Article 41.2 of the Vienna Convention.

98. On *jus cogens* generally see for instance: A.G. Robledo, "Le ius cogens international: sa genèse, sa nature, ses fonctions," *Rec. Cours*, 1981, Vol. 172, p. 9; G. Gaja, "Jus cogens beyond the Vienna Convention," *Rec. Cours*, 1981, Vol. 172, p. 271/316; B. Simma, P. Alston, "The Sources of Human Rights Law: Custom, Jus Cogens, and General Principles," *Australian Yb. Int. Law*, 1982, p. 82/108; M. R. Saulle, "Jus Cogens and Human Rights," in *Studi in onore di R. Ago*, 1987; L. Hannikainen, *Peremptory Norms, Jus Cogens, in International Law*, 1988; G. Gaja, *Obligations erga omnes, international crimes and ius cogens*, 1989; B. Conforti, A. Labella, "Invalidity and Termination of Treaties: the Role of National Courts," *EJIL*, 1990; De Simone, *Jus cogens e diritti umani nelle relazioni internazionali*, 1994; N. Kontou, *The termination and revision of treaties in the light of new customary international law*, 1994; R. Kolb, *Théorie du ius cogens international*, 2001. On *jus cogens* and WTO law see for instance: Salman Bal, "International Free Trade Agreements and Human rights: reinterpreting Article XX of the GATT," 10 *Minn.J.Global Trade* 62; J. E. Alvarez, "Trade and environment: implications for global governance: how not to link: institutional conumdrums of an expanded trade regime," *Widener Law Symposium J.*, 2001; S. Charnovitz, "The moral exception in Trade Policy," *Virginia Journ. Int. Law*, 1998, p. 689; S. Charnovitz, "The globalization of economic human rights," *Brooklyn Journ. Int. Law*, 1999, p. 113/124; S. Charnovitz, "The WTO and the rights of the individual," *Intereconomics*, vol.36, n.2, 2001, p. 98/108; R. Howse, M. Mutua, *Protecting human rights in a global economy: challenges for the WTO*, 2000; J. Pauwelyn, "The Role of Public International Law in the WTO: How Far Can We Go?" *A.J.I.L.*, 2001, p. 535; E.-U. Petersmann, "From 'negative' to 'positive' integration in the WTO: time for 'mainstreaming human rights' into WTO law?" *CMLR*, 2001, p. 1363/1382; G. Schwarzenberger, "Economic world order? a basic problem of international economic law," 1970.

99. In its November 2001 issue.

100. Article 56 of the UN Charter provides: "All Members pledge themselves to take joint and separate action in co-operation with the Organization for the achievement of the purposes set forth in Article 55."

101. Article 55 of the UN Charter provides: "With a view to the creation of conditions of stability and well-being which are necessary for peaceful and friendly relations among nations based on respect for the principle of equal rights and self-determination of peoples, the United Nations shall promote:

(a) higher standards of living, full employment, and conditions of economic and social progress and development;

(b) solutions of international economic, social, health, and related problems; and international cultural and educational co-operation; and
(c) universal respect for, and observance of, human rights and fundamental freedoms for all without distinction as to race, sex, language, or religion."

102. On the question of hierarchy of the sources of international law with regard to *jus cogens*, see Alvarez, *Trade and environment: implications for global governance:* ... ; Howse and Mutua, *Protecting human rights in a global economy*, p. 9: "The UN Charter does not resolve the question of hierarchy of law, or put differently, whether human rights law has primacy over other domains of international law."

103. A/C.6/56/N.20, in A/RES/56/83, adopted on 12 December 2001 without a vote. On the new Rules on State responsibility see James Crawford, Jacqueline Peel, Simon Olleson, "The ILC's Articles on Responsibility of states for Internationally Wrongful Acts: Completion of the Second Reading" in *EJIL* (2001), Vol. 12, No. 5, 963 and James Crawford, *The International Law Commission's Articles on State Responsibility*, 2002, Cambridge.

104. Article 53 of the Vienna Convention provides that "a treaty is void if, at the time of its conclusion, it conflicts with a peremptory norm of general international law;" and Article 64 that "if a new peremptory norm of general international law emerges, any existing treaty which is in conflict with that norm becomes void and terminates." Article 44.5 prohibits the separability of the conflicting provision in the case of situations covered by Article 54. One could also assume that Articles 53 and 64 of the Vienna Convention are a non-derogable rule. As Kolb stated, (*Théorie du ius cogens international*, p. 139) rules of *jus cogens* exist at every level of the system of sources of international law: "le *jus cogens* est un phénomène hiérarchiquement relatif ou neutre." The kind of rules like that of Article 53 of the Vienna Convention are aimed at safeguarding a general interest of the legal system, namely the protection of its integrity against fragmentation or bilateralisation. (idem, p. 53).

105. In light of the sensitivity of human rights, a panel may do the same when faced with a conflict with any human rights provision.

106. Hélène Ruiz-Fabri, "Commentaire sur l'article 66 de la Convention de Vienne" et Michel Cosnard, "Commentaires sur l'article 65 de la Convention de Vienne," Corten et P. Klein (dir.), *Les Conventions de Vienne sur le droit des traités de 1969 et 1986 – Commentaire article par article*, Bruylant (forthcoming).

107. Article 65 of the same convention is entitled: *Procedure to be followed with respect to invalidity, termination, withdrawal from or suspension of the operation of a treaty.* It provides that "a party which, *under the provisions of the present Convention*, invokes either a defect in its consent to be bound by a treaty or a ground for impeaching the validity of a treaty, terminating it, withdrawing from it or suspending its operation, must notify the other parties of its claim. The notification shall indicate the measure proposed to be taken with respect to the treaty and the reasons therefor." If an "objection has been raised by any other party, the parties shall seek a solution through the means indicated in Article 33 of the Charter of the United Nations." Paragraph 4 of Article 65 states that "Nothing in the foregoing paragraphs shall affect the rights or obligations of the parties under any provisions in force binding the parties with regard to the settlement of disputes." Finally, Article 66 writes that "If, under paragraph 3 of Article 65, no solution has been reached within a pe-

riod of 12 months following the date on which the objection was raised, the following procedures shall be followed: (a) any one of the parties to a dispute concerning the application or the interpretation of Articles 53 or 64 may, by a written application, submit it to the International Court of Justice for a decision unless the parties by common consent agree to submit the dispute to arbitration."

108. Hélène Ruiz-Fabri, "L'ordre public en droit international" – Colloque de Caen, 11/12 mai 2000 M.-J. Rdor (dir.), *Ordre public et ordres publics: ordre public et droits fondamentaux*, Bruylant, 2001, p. 87 à 108. See also V. J. Combacau, "Le droit international: bric-à-brac ou système?" *Arch. Phil. Dr.*, 1986, pp. 85-105.

109. Article 44.5 of the Vienna Convention indicating the non-separability would not be customary.

110. On *non liquet* see: Bourgeois, J., WTO Dispute Settlement in the Field of Anti-Dumping Law, *J.I.E.L.* (1998) vol. 1, No. 1, 259 at 271, where the author argues that unregulated areas in the WTO could be considered as *non-liquet* allowing panels and the Appellate Body to refuse jurisdiction. See also Joel Trachtman, "The Domain of WTO Dispute Resolution," (1999) *Harvard International Law Journal*, vol. 40, No. 2, p. 333, at 337; Joost Pauwelyn "The Role of Public International Law in the WTO," Op. cit., at p. 559. On *non-liquet* generally see Peter Hulsroj, "Three sources – No River," *Zeitschrift für öffentliches Recht*, 1999, p. 219; Prosper Weil "The Court Cannot Conclude Definitively..." *Non liquet* resisted, 36 *Colum.J.Transn'l L.* 109 (1997).

111. Hélène Ruiz-Fabri, "L'ordre public en droit international," Op. cit.; Bruno Simma and Philip Alston, "The Sources of Human Rights Law," at p. 82; Jose Alvarez, "Comments on Howse and Makau's Paper," Op. cit.

112. For a discussion on the Rules on State responsibility see James Crawford, Jacqueline Peel, Simon Olleson, "The ILC's Articles on Responsibility of states for Internationally Wrongful Acts: Completion of the Second Reading" in *EJIL* (2001), Vol. 12, No. 5, p. 963 and James Crawford, *The International Law Commission's Articles on State Responsibility*, 2002, Cambridge.

113. Article 42 provides that: "Invocation of Responsibility by an Injured States": A State is entitled as an injured State to invoke the responsibility of another State if the obligation breached is owed to: (a) That State individually; or (b) A group of states including that state, or the international community as a whole, and the breach of the obligation: (i) Specially affects that State; or (ii) Is of such a character as radically to change the position of all the other States to which the obligation is owed with respect to the further performance of the obligation." In its first commentary the ILC wrote: Article 42 provides that the implementation of state responsibility is in the first place an entitlement of the "injured state." It defines this term in relatively narrow way, drawing a distinction between injury to an individual State or possibly a small number of states and the legal interests of several or all States in certain obligations established in the collective interest. The latter are dealt with in Article 48.

114. In the *Barcelona Traction* case the ICJ stated that there for some basic human rights "all States can held to have a legal interest in the fulfillment of these rights," ICJ Report 1970, p. 3, at p. 32, para. 33. This would mean that all States have a legal interest to ensure that these rights are respected and thus it can be argued that all states have a sufficient legal interest to initiate dispute settlement action against such violation. This right given to all States to complain about certain hu-

man rights violations is now recognized in Articles 28 and 42 of the ICL Draft on State Responsibility.

115. The directly injured States (whose individuals, for example, may have been the object of human rights violations) would be considered as injured States. Commentaries (12) and (13) distinguish between Art. 42(b)(I), under which a State may be "specially affected" by the violation of a collective obligation (the term "specially affected" is taken from Article 60(2)(b) of the Vienna Convention) and would cover a slightly wider group that the States directly injured, and Art. 42(b)(ii) under which a breach *per se* affects every other State to which the obligation is owed – that is, *erga omnes* obligations – for which all States can invoke the State responsibility of the concerned state.

116. Article 48 addresses the issue of "*erga omnes*" obligations, the violation of which entitles any State to assert the state responsibility of the violator, although the State injured and/or specifically affected may, in addition, use countermeasures against the violating state. It states: "Invocation of responsibility by a State other than an injured State. 1. Any State *other than an injured State* is entitled to invoke the State responsibility of another State in accordance with paragraph 2 if: (a) The obligation breached is owed to a group of states including that State, and is established for the protection of a collective interest of the group; or (b) The obligation breached is owed to the international community as a whole. 2. Any State entitled to invoke responsibility under paragraph 1 may claim from the responsible state: (a) Cessation of the internationally wrongful act, and assurances and guarantees of non-repetition in accordance with Article 30; and (b) Performance of the obligation of reparation in accordance with preceding articles, in the interest of the injured State or of the beneficiaries of the obligation breached."

117. This resembles the difficult situation of mutually exclusive and overlapping jurisdictions such as is the case between NAFTA and the WTO. When two for a claim to have exclusive jurisdiction, the use of one of them may lead to a violation of the other treaty. For further discussion of this issue of overlapping jurisdictions see Gabrielle Marceau "Conflicts of Norms and Conflicts of Jurisdictions" *JWT* (2001), Vol. 26 No. 5, p. 1081.

118. Could WTO Members or the WTO envisage the possibility of asking the International Court of Justice for an advisory opinion as to the direct application of *jus cogens* in all systems of laws?

119. For a discussion of the new WTO jurisprudence on Article XXIV, see Gabrielle Marceau and Cornelis Reiman, "When and How are Regional Trade Agreements Compatible with the WTO," *L.I.R.I.* (2001), No. 3.

120. This is to some extent a legal issue distinct from that where Member invokes a human rights provisions to refuse to comply with a WTO obligation – and when interpretation cannot reconcile both sets of norms – which calls for a discussion on conflicts between the WTO and human rights law discussed previously.

121. The human rights considerations *in the importing country* may also be invoked as a justification of regulatory distinction or preferences, in particular in the interpretation and application of the Agreement on Agriculture (right to food) or the SPS/TBT/III (right to health) or the TRIPS Agreement (right to health), GATS and the general and security exceptions.

122. See Steve Chartnovitz, "The Law of Environmental 'PPMs' in the World Trade Organization," *Yale Journal of International Law* (2002), Vol. 27, pp. 59-110.

123. GATT Panel report on *US – Measures Affecting Alcoholic and Malt Beverages*, (DS23/R), BISD 39S/206 (1992).

124. Panel report on *US – Restrictions on Imports of Tuna, complaint by Mexico*, (Tuna I) (DS21/R), report not adopted, circulated on 3 Sept. 1991; Panel report on *US – Restrictions on Imports of Tuna, complaint by EC*, (Tuna II) (DS29/R), report not adopted, circulated on 16 June 1994.

125. Panel report on *Tuna I*, at para. 5.11.

126. Panel report on *Tuna II*, para. 5.20.

127. Howse and Regan, however, argue that analyzing PPMs under Art. XI does not make sense, because PPMs which are enforced internally, even as against foreign products, will not be caught by quota-restrictions or border measure disciplines (Articles II or XI of GATT) and will therefore be undisciplined (Robert Howse and Donald Regan, "The Product/Process Distinction – An Illusory Basis for Disciplining 'Unilateralism' in Trade Policy" 11 *EJIL* 249 (2000)). If, as Howse and Regan suggest, PPMs ought to be evaluated under Art. III, then the like products test comes into play. They argue that likeness test should be interpreted as looking for the existence of differences between products that justify different regulation. Recently Howse and Tuerk have elsewhere suggested that the *EC – Asbestos* decision opens the door to consider distinctions based on PPMs in the context of the like products test (Robert Howse and Elizabeth Tuerk, The WTO Impact on Internal Regulations – A Case Study of the Canada-EC Asbestos Dispute, forthcoming in GRAINNE DE BURCA AND JOANNE SCOTT, EDS., THE EU AND THE WTO: LEGAL AND CONSTITUTIONAL ASPECTS (2001).On the other hand, Jackson, suggests that there is a textual basis for the product/process distinction, and if it is relaxed, how to insure that it is not abused (John H. Jackson, "Comments on Shrimp/Turtle and Product/Process Distinction," 11 *EJIL* 303 (2000)).

128. Appellate Body report on *EC – Asbestos*, para. 102.

129. Appellate Body report on *EC – Asbestos*, paras. 97-99.

130. Appellate Body report on *EC – Asbestos*, para. 117.

131. And even more so the dissenting member of the Appellate Body for whom the particularly different physical characteristics – toxicity – of the products at issue was irrebuttable evidence against their "likeness"; Ibid., paras. 151-153.

132. Appellate Body report on *EC – Asbestos*, paras. 102, 109, 111, 113, 139 and 140.

133. Appellate Body report on *EC – Asbestos*, para. 120.

134. Appellate Body report on *EC – Asbestos*, paras. 117 and 118.

135. Appellate Body report on *EC – Asbestos*, para. 117.

136. "… In reviewing this finding by the Panel, we note that neither the text of Article III:4 nor the practice of panels and the Appellate Body suggest that any evidence should be excluded *a priori* from a panel's examination of 'likeness.' Moreover, as we have said, in examining the 'likeness' of products, panels must evaluate *all* of the relevant evidence." Appellate Body report on *EC – Asbestos*, para. 113.

137. Brigitte Stern, "Can the United States set rules for the World? A French View," *JWT* (1997), Vol. 31, No. 4, p. 5, at 23.

138. BISD 1S/59 (1953).

139. Appellate Body Report on *US – Shrimp*, at para. 121.

140. See Appellate Body Reports on *US – Gasoline, US – Shrimp*.

141. "It is well to bear in mind that the policy of protecting and conserving the endangered see turtles here involved is shared by all participants in this appeal, indeed, by the vast majority of the Nations of the world." Appellate Body report on *US – Shrimp*, para. 135.

142. See, e.g., Philippe Sands, "Unilateralism, Values, and International Law," 11 *EJIL* 291 (2000).

143. Appellate Body Report on *EC – Asbestos*, at para. 178 referring to *EC – Hormones*.

144. I am grateful to Joel Trachtman whose discussions during the Bern Conference made me further aware of the important jurisdictional dimension surrounding the national treatment obligation and PPMs debate. See his discussion in "United States restrictions of Tuna," 86 *AJIL* 142 (1992). On the issue of the extraterritorial jurisdiction reach of measure enforcing human rights, Lorand Bartels is suggesting that Article XX is to be read consistently with the rules governing a WTO Member's right to exercise legislative jurisdiction over activities and things located outside of its territory, this provision should apply to save various trade measures designed to promote and protect human rights outside of the territory of the regulating Member. Lorand Bartels, "Article XX of GATT and the Problem of Extraterritorial Jurisdiction: the case of trade measures for the protection of human rights," *JWT* (2002), Vol. 36, No. 2, p. 353.

145. Howse and Regan suggest that in the PPM context, the extraterritoriality issue is not a problem at the core of the definition, because PPMs (including human rights policy based regulations) do not directly regulate any behaviour occurring outside the border. They recognize, however, that extraterritoriality concerns are raised in a loose way by an attempt to influence conduct in a foreign country. PPMs often deal with processes which effect the commons (and in the case of human rights policies, one could argue the moral commons, or the *jus cogens*) in which that country has a direct interest, and thus are not just an imposed policy preference (Turtles). But even if PPMs are aimed solely at preventing harm with no physical effects within the territory, one should also consider moral effects – do not want to be associated with that harm regardless of where the physical effects are felt.

146. Brigitte Stern, "Can the United States set Rules for the World," Op. cit., at p. 21; B. Stern, "Quelques observations sur les règles internationales relatives à l'application extraterritoriale du

droit," *A.F.D.I.*, 1986, p. 7-52; B. Stern, "Une tentative d'élucidation du concept d'application extraterritoriale," *Rev. Québécoise Dr. Int.*, 1986, p. 49-78; H. G. Maier, "Extraterritorial jurisdiction at a crossroads: an intersection between public and private international law," *A.J.I.L.*, 1982, p. 280-320.

147. DS29/R, para. 5.20.

148. *Tuna I*, DS21/R, para. 5.32.

149. *Tuna II*, DS29/R, para. 5.20.

150. Appellate Body Report on *US – Shrimp*, at para. 133.

151. Philippe Sands suggests that *US – Shrimp* made a great conceptual departure from *Tuna* by finding that a state could extend national conservation measures to activities beyond national jurisdiction – that is, assert jurisdiction over a producing country – if it showed a legitimate interest (this is the nexus between State and regulated resource/product), and also demonstrate that the policy is recognized as desirable. Phillipe Sands, Op. cit., at 299-300.

152. Appellate Body Report on *US – Gasoline*, at p. 17.

153. Appellate Body Report on *EC – Asbestos*, para. 103.

154. Brigitte Stern argues that the European view would limit jurisdiction to situations where the effect of an activity outside the territory is an element of the wrong without which there would be no wrong (she refers to the possibility of some extraterritorial jurisdiction in antitrust matters, if the distortion of competition which is a necessary element of the wrong is realized on the territory). For this author, the US view, however, requires only that the activity, wherever it takes place, have (or is intended to have) a substantial effect on the US territory, with some reasonableness requirement. Brigitte Stern, "Can the United States set Rules for the World?", Op. cit., at p. 13.

155. The codification of this principle in the ILC Rules on State Responsibility effectively dispenses with the need to run each problem through the effects test. See Art. 48 "Any State other than an injured State is entitled to invoke the responsibility of another State in accordance with paragraph 2 if: (a) The obligation breached is owed to a group of States including that State, and is established for the protection of a collective interest of the group; or (b) The obligation breached is owed to the international community as a whole." It does not, however, address the situation of secondary punishment of those sovereigns who refuse to join in the punishment of the violator.

156. Bernhard Jansen, "The Limits of Unilateralism from a European Perspective," 11 *EJIL* 309 (2000).

157. Brigitte Stern, "La compétence universelle en France: le cas des crimes commis en ex-Yougoslavie et au Rwanda," *German Yearbook of International Law,* Jahrbuch Für Internationales Recht, Vol. 40 (1997), p. 280.

158. Responsibility of States for internationally wrongful acts, adopted by the General Assembly as A/RES/56/83, on 12 Dec. 2001, without a vote. See the discussion in Part III:4 above.

159. Antonio Cassese, Ex iniuria ius oritur: Are We Moving toward International Legitimation of Forcible Humanitarian Countermeasures in the World Community?, *EJIL* 10 (1999) 23.

160. See the example of the NAFTA and the WTO which both contain exclusive jurisdiction clause for matters relating to SPS measures. Gabrielle Marceau "Conflicts of Norms and Conflicts of Jurisdictions," Op. cit., at p. 1116-1118.

161. On the issue of overlaps of jurisdictions see Gabrielle Marceau, "Conflicts of Norms and Conflicts of Jurisdictions," Op. cit., p. 1081.

162. The Commission on Human Rights is the general UN organ that meets annually for 6 weeks in Geneva. It has three procedures to address HR violations; the confidential 1503 procedure, the public debate under the 1235 procedure, and the designation of a thematic rapporteur. Individuals and NGOs may file complaints under these procedures. However, they deal with 'situations' rather than individual cases. The Human Rights Committee monitors the implementation of the International Covenant on Civil and Political Rights (CCPR). The First Optional Protocol to the Covenant authorises the Committee to receive and consider communications from individuals claiming to be victims of violations of the Covenant by States Parties to it, and to forward its views about these communications. As of March 2000, 95 of the 144 States Parties to the CCPR were parties to the First Optional Protocol. There is no provision stating that the Committee's views are binding, or providing what follow-up should take place if the Committee's views indicate that a State should take particular action and the state ignores them.

163. Article 6(2) and 7 of the Treaty on European Union.

164. As confirmed in Article 46(d) Treaty on European Union.

165. This has been further endorsed in United Nations General Assembly Resolution 53/14 of 1999.

166. The relevant provision states that "… everyone whose rights or freedoms are allegedly violated has the right, either in person or through legally authorized representation, to complain to and have that complaint promptly reviewed in a public hearing before an independent, impartial and competent judicial or other authority established by law and to obtain from such an authority a decision, in accordance with law, providing redress, including any compensation due, where there has been a violation of that person's rights or freedoms, as well as enforcement of the eventual decision and award, all without undue delay."

167. Which was subsequently endorsed by the United Nations General Assembly Resolutions 40/32 and 40/146 of 1985.

168. This important provision also makes a reference to due process in Article 14(3)(1) which states that "In the determination of any criminal charge against him, everyone shall be entitled to the following minimum guarantees, in full equality….(c) to be tried without undue delay."

169. The relevant portion of Article 4 states that "States Parties shall undertake all appropriate legislative, administrative, and other measures for the implementation of the rights recognized in the present Convention."

170. "[t]he GATT/WTO did not create a new legal order the subjects of which comprise both contracting parties or Members and their nationals. However, it would be entirely wrong to consider that the position of individuals is of no relevance to the GATT/WTO legal matrix. Many of the benefits to Members which are meant to flow as a result of the acceptance of various disciplines under the GATT/WTO depend on the activity of individual economic operators in the national and global market places. The purpose of many of these disciplines, indeed one of the primary objects of the GATT/WTO as a whole, is to produce certain market conditions which would allow this individual activity to flourish." *United States-Section 301*, WT/DS152/R, paras. 7.72-73.

171. See Gabrielle Marceau and Matthew Stilwell "Practical Suggestion for Amicus Curiae before WTO Adjudicating Bodies," *JIEL* (2001) Vol. 4, No. 1, at p. 155.

172. Appellate Body report on *US – Shrimp*, paras. 101-109.

173. Appellate Body report on *US – Hot-Rolled Steel*, para. 42, referring to Article 17.4 of the DSU and Rules 21 to 24 of the Working Procedures for Appellate Review.

174. Appellate Body Report in *EC – Bananas III*, para. 12.

175. "We conclude that it is for the Government of Indonesia to nominate the members of its delegation to meetings of this Panel, and we find no provision in the WTO Agreement or the DSU, including the standard rules of procedure included therein, which prevents a WTO Member from determining the composition of its delegation to WTO panel meetings. Nor does past practice in GATT and WTO dispute settlement point us to a different conclusion in this case." Panel report on *Indonesia- Automobiles*, para. 14.1.

176. On the issue of the rights of individuals see for instance Petros Mavroidis and Werner Zdouc, "Legal Means to Protect Private Parties' Interest in the WTO," *JIEL* (1998) Vol. 1, No. 3, p. 406; The panel discussion on "Is the WTO Dispute Settlement Mechanism Responsive to the Needs of the Traders?" 32 *JWT*, 2, p. 147.

177. See the Panel Report on *US – Section 301*: "[unilateral actions] may prompt economic operators to change their commercial behaviour in a way that distorts trade. Economic operators may be afraid, say, to continue ongoing trade with, or investment in, the industries or products threatened by unilateral measures. Existing trade may also be distorted because economic operators may feel a need to take out extra insurance to allow for the illegal possibility that the legislation contemplates, thus reducing the relative competitive opportunity of their products on the market. Other operators may be deterred from trading with such a Member altogether, distorting potential trade...." Panel Report on *US – Section 301*, para. 6.14.

178. Fur further reading on the publication, notification and transparency requirements and related rights of individuals under the WTO see Gabrielle Marceau and Peter Pedersen, "Is the WTO Open and Transparent," *JWT*, Vol. 33, No. 1 (1999), p. 5.

179. See the Appellate Body Reports on *EC-Bananas III*, para. 144, *India – Patents*, para. 95, *Argentina – Textiles*, para. 79, footnote 68.

180. Appellate Body Report on *EC-Hormones*, para. 152, footnote 138.

181. Appellate Body Report on *India – Patents*, para. 94.

182. Appellate Body Report on *Australia – Salmon*, paras. 272 and 278.

183. Appellate Body Reports on *EC – Hormones*, para. 133 and *US – Hot Rolled Steel*, para. 194.

184. WT/DSB/RC/1.

185. See Gabrielle Marceau, "Rules on Ethics for the New WTO Dispute Settlement Mechanism," *JWT* (1998), Vol. 32, No. 3, p. 57.

186. See http://www.itd.org.

187. Appellate Body report on *Chile – Alcoholic Beverages,* at para. 74. On the issue of the burden of proof see Joost Pauwelyn, "Evidence, Proof and Persuasion in WTO Dispute Settlement: Who bears the Burden?" *JIEL* (1998) Vol. 1, No. 2, p. 227.

188. Appellate Body Report on *Argentina-Textiles*, paras. 79-81.

189. Appellate Body Reports on *Argentina – Textiles*, paras. 79-81 and on *Australia-Salmon*, WT/DS18/AB/R, para. 272.

190. Appellate Body Report on *Canada – Aircraft*, WT/DS70/AB/R, adopted on 20 August 1999, para. 203.

191. Appellate Body Report on *US – Wheat Gluten*, WT/DS166/AB/R, adopted on 19 January 2001, para. 174.

192. "This authority embraces more than merely the choice and evaluation of the *source* of the information or advice which it may seek. A panel's authority includes the authority to decide *not to seek* such information or advice at all. We consider that a panel also has the authority to *accept or reject* any information or advice which it may have sought and received, or to *make some other appropriate disposition* thereof. It is particularly within the province and the authority of a panel to determine *the need for information and advice* in a specific case, to ascertain the *acceptability* and *relevancy* of information or advice received, and to decide *what weight to ascribe to that information or advice* or to conclude that no weight at all should be given to what has been received." Appellate Body report on *US – Shrimp,* para. 104.

193. See Patricio Grané, "Remedies under WTO Law," *JIEL* (2001) Vol. 4, No. 4, at p. 755.

194. At best it could be argued that the reasoning and findings by a panel and Appellate Body of this nature (a WTO provision has been superseded by a provision of another treaty) would be declaratory in nature. In *US – Certain EC Products*, the Appellate Body disagreed with the general recommendation of the Panel Report "that the US brings its measure into conformity" since the measure at issue was not longer in existence. The Appellate Body went on to consider fully the issue, recognized certain violations by the United States but did not make any recommendation for a measure no longer in existence. This conclusion by the Appellate Body may have all sorts of consequences on the types of remedies available to panels and the Appellate Body, but this is not the

relevant for this article. Although the political and legal context of this dispute is rather peculiar, this Appellate Body's conclusion confirms that it considers itself capable of issuing declaratory rulings.

195. Encouraged by the Appellate Body in *EC – Bananas III*, para. 144.

196. See WT/GC/W/162.

197. Appellate Body report on *EC – Bananas III*, para. 10.

198. Appellate Body Report on *US – Shrimp (21.5 DSU)*, paras. 135-149.

Part III

The Regional Experience of Human Rights and Trade

CHAPTER 11

Trade and Human Rights in European Union Law: Linkages in the Case-Law of the European Court of Justice

Piet Eeckhout

Introduction: an impressionistic landscape

There are considerable complexities involved in writing the story of the interrelationship between trade and human rights in EU law for the purpose of offering insights for the development of this interrelationship in international economic law generally, and in World Trade Organization (WTO) law in particular. For a start, the EU story itself is a long and convoluted one, recounted and narrated by so many, on so many occasions, and from so many perspectives. Next, there are fundamental differences between, on the one hand, the EU polity and its legal system, and, on the other hand, the international community, its World Trade Organization, and that organization's legal system. From a human rights perspective, one must raise the question whether those differences are so fundamental as to stand in the way of arriving at any meaningful insights. The EU polity is much smaller and cohesive than the international community, particularly with respect to human rights, where the European Convention on Human Rights (ECHR) has been the common denominator of human rights discourse for decades. The EU legal system has been constitutionalised, which sets it fundamentally apart from general international law. The very foundations of such constitutionalisation, namely, direct effect and supremacy,[1] are of central importance in fundamental rights protection, for they enable individuals to challenge violations in the courts. International economic law has not been constitutionalised as yet, and generally does not have those features of direct effect and supremacy. In the slipstream of EU constitutionalisation comes a complete system of remedies, with the European Court of Justice (ECJ) at the apex, leading to a constant flow of litigation in which individuals can make rights claims. Again this feature is lacking in international economic law.

Yet there are some analogies and similarities, which may tilt the balance in favour of making at least an attempt to engage in the comparative exercise.[2] There are, perhaps foremost, the substantive similarities and linkages between EU trade law and WTO law. The EU is a member of the WTO and thereby required to comply with WTO law and to implement it in areas such as anti-dumping and anti-subsidies, agriculture, intellectual property and government procurement. More importantly, the basic provisions and principles regarding free movement of goods and services in the EU's internal market are similar and comparable to the basic provisions and principles on free trade in GATT and GATS.[3] In so far as there are linkages between trade and human rights (and we have fortunately reached the stage that we are all most aware of those linkages), and in so far as these linkages raise substantive legal and policy issues, an analysis of EU law and practice may be useful.

Another similarity relates to the main trait of EU law fundamental rights protection, i.e., that such protection was developed, across a group of States, in the absence of any bill, charter, or list of rights, and was developed by the courts in the form of general principles of EC law. The position in WTO law is comparable, in that the WTO agreements do not contain a bill of rights, and in light of the fact that general principles of law are also a source of international law (and have been accepted as applicable in the WTO context by the appellate body).[4] One cannot here address the debate on the scope and reach of legal principles in WTO law,[5] but the analogy is worth exploring.

However, given the above complexities, and the current stage of the overall research project, this contribution will not attempt systematically to compare or bring together EU law and international economic law. What follows is a somewhat impressionistic depiction of the landscape of trade and human rights in EU law. The emphasis is on the case-law, and there is no analysis of the evolving EU human rights policy, as opposed to judicial enforcement and protection, even though here again there are obvious linkages with trade, particularly in the EU's external policies.[6] Nor is there any particular analysis of the novel EU Charter of Fundamental Rights,[7] which is the subject of another contribution to this volume. The focus of the inquiry is on the relationship between trade issues and fundamental rights protection as revealed in litigation, and the aim is to discuss their interaction in the judicial discourse. The first part of the paper looks at the broad horizon of EU fundamental rights protection, basic awareness of which is required for a proper understanding of the development of the case law. The subsequent sections investigate the extent to which general legal principles of free trade in the EU, both internally and externally, are properly understood as incorporating a fundamental rights dimension. The paper also examines challenges to trade restrictions based on fundamental rights. Then follows a section which looks at the role played by human rights in contexts of derogations from or exceptions to the rules of free trade. The paper subsequently addresses the interface between the administration of trade rules and policies, and human rights. In the concluding section some reflections are offered on the potential relevance of the EU experience for the WTO.

The horizon of EU fundamental rights protection

Most readers may be familiar with how EU fundamental rights protection has developed. As mentioned, the story is long and convoluted, and has so often been told. It is none the less worth recalling some of the basic features for the purpose of laying the foundations for the subsequent analysis.[8]

The original EC Treaties did not contain express references to human or fundamental rights. In the creation of European integration, human rights were located in the ECHR, and the economic integration launched through the EC was probably not perceived as requiring any particular focus on human rights. None the less, one cannot say that the EEC Treaty was completely foreign to fundamental rights.[9] The provisions on free movement of persons were centred around the prohibition of discrimination on grounds of nationality, clearly some type of fundamental right, and there was the principle of equal pay in Art 119 EEC (now Art 141 EC), which was developed into a general principle of non-discrimination on grounds of sex.

When the European Court of Justice (ECJ) invented and constructed the foundations of EC law – direct effect and supremacy – it was soon confronted with constitutional-type challenges to EC acts. After some initial reluctance, the Court famously established two principles in *Internationale Handelsgesellschaft.*[10] First, that the validity of EC acts could not be challenged on grounds of violation of national constitutional rules, even if such rules concerned fundamental rights. Second, that fundamental rights were to be protected within the framework of EC law in the legal form of general principles of EC law. That, in a sense, was the easy part of the exercise. Much more difficult was the determination of the content of fundamental rights qualifying for the general principles status. The Court attempted to find those rights in the constitutional traditions of the Member States, and in international human rights instruments to which the Member States are parties. With time, the emphasis came to lie on the second category for rather obvious reasons. It is particularly noteworthy that the reference to constitutional traditions of the Member States was clearly justified in theory, but was difficult to apply in practice. The ECHR conveniently embodies one single, minimum standard of human rights protection, binding on all Member States, and authoritatively interpreted by the European Court of Human Rights (ECtHR). Much has been made of the potential for conflict between the case-law of the ECJ and that of the ECtHR, but in general it is clear that the ECJ aims to respect and defer to the ECtHR's rulings, which are now *expressis verbis* referred to in the ECJ's judgments.[11] For all practical purposes, one can say that the ECJ (and the Court of First Instance, CFI) apply the ECHR as if the EC or EU were a party to it and as if the Convention had direct effect in the EC legal order. This is now confirmed by Art 6(2) TEU, according to which: "The Union shall respect fundamental rights, as guaranteed by the European Convention for the Protection of Human Rights and Fundamental Freedoms signed in Rome on 4 November 1950 and as they result from the constitutional traditions common to the Member States, as general principles of Community law".

However, the EC never actually joined the ECHR, and in 1996 the ECJ ruled that accession was, in the present state of EC law, *ultra vires*.[12] Perhaps partly as a result of that, the EU finally took up an idea which had been floating around for decades, namely to establish a bill of rights for the EU. In December 2000, the Charter of Fundamental Rights of the European Union was adopted as a solemn political declaration, signed by the EU's political institutions.[13] As this Charter is the subject of another contribution, it is not further analysed here, even though it will no doubt become central in the evolution of EU fundamental rights protection.

One word also on the scope of application of fundamental rights as general principles of EC law. Those rights are of course binding on the EU institutions; those institutions may not adopt acts which violate such rights.[14] However, they are also binding on Member States in so far as they act within the scope of EC law. More particularly, Member States are bound by those rights (a) when implementing EC acts,[15] and (b) when justifying measures which would otherwise be in breach of the EC Treaty provisions on free movement, on the basis of derogations available under that Treaty or under the ECJ's case law.[16] This type of effect of EU fundamental rights is particularly interesting from a WTO law perspective, as the functions of upholding the basic principles and the implementation of more detailed sets of rules are also present in the WTO system.

Fundamental rights are thus, in doctrinal terms, a well-defined category of EU law. It would be deceptive, however, to focus too closely on only those rights which come within that category. Fundamental rights are themselves only one limb of the broader category of general principles of EC law, which also contains principles such as non-discrimination, proportionality, legitimate expectations and legal certainty. Depending on the context and on the factual matrices of cases, these principles may also evoke fundamental rights tones. In addition, there are other rights conferred by EU law which may be part of a human rights discourse. In what follows this paper will therefore attempt not to take too narrow a view of what constitute fundamental rights. Nor does the paper distinguish between "fundamental" and "human" rights.

Free trade, free movement, and fundamental rights

The EC Treaty provisions on realising a single, internal market are of course central to European integration and to the functioning of the EU polity. The principles of free movement of goods, persons and capital are the cornerstones of EC substantive law, and they are very much the terrain of the ECJ, since that Court was given the opportunity to construct much of the EU law edifice, including its constitutionalisation. *Van Gend en Loos* was after all a case about the internal market,[17] and the direct effect of the free movement provisions was a vital tool in the building process. Direct effect generally entails the conferral of rights on individuals, enabling them to enforce the Treaty provisions directly before their domestic courts.

It is therefore not surprising that the ECJ has used the fundamental rights language when explicating the EC Treaty free movement principles. In *Procureur de la République* v *ADBHU* the Court said that "the principles of free movement of goods and freedom of competition, together with freedom of trade as a fundamental right, are general principles of Community law of which the Court ensures observance".[18] Similarly, in *UNECTEF* v *Heylens* the Court spoke of free access to employment as "a fundamental right which the Treaty confers individually on each worker in the Community".[19] In other cases, such as *Gebhard*, reference is made to the "fundamental freedoms".[20]

However, it would be wrong to conclude automatically and generally that free trade in goods and services (together with free movement of workers, right of establishment and free movement of capital) are regarded as fundamental human rights in the EC legal order.[21] The typical human rights discourse is certainly not omnipresent in the ECJ's case law on those internal market principles, and, contrary to what is sometimes suggested,[22] free trade in goods and services does not amount to a general principle of economic freedom. The case law on the free movement of goods is particularly instructive here. As is well known, in the evolution of that case law there was a period during which the ECJ adopted an overly broad approach to the scope of what is now Art 28 EC, inviting private parties to use that provision so as to challenge any form of domestic economic regulation which restricts economic freedom. This invitation was taken up in, for example,the Sunday Trading cases.[23] But the Court halted that development in *Keck and Mithouard*, referring to and rejecting "the increasing tendency of traders to invoke Article 30 of the Treaty [now 28] as a means of challenging any rules whose effect is to limit their commercial freedom even where such rules are not aimed at products from other Member States".[24] The principle of free movement of goods, broad and fundamental though it may be, remains functionally related to intra-Community trade and does not represent an individual right to general economic freedom. It is indeed very difficult to find a human rights, or even a mere rights, discourse in the relevant ECJ case law on this issue. Take, for example, a celebrated case such as Cassis de Dijon: there is, in the judgment, no emphasis whatsoever on the rights of the trader in question to import Cassis into Germany.[25] Or take *Keck and Mithouard.* One needs to read the facts of the case to be aware that it involved two managers of hypermarkets, *criminally* prosecuted for failing to observe French price legislation; in the Court's reasoning, however, there is no trace of any examination of the effects of the French legislation on those persons' rights, let alone their fundamental rights.

In the post-*Keck* era the discussion has centred around the concept of "market access", which in the view of some is the key to the interpretation of the EC Treaty's free trade principles.[26] In that connection, Advocate General Jacobs has spoken of the appropriate test being the "principle that all undertakings which engage in a legitimate economic activity in a Member State should have unfettered access to the whole of the Community market, unless there is a valid reason for denying them full access to a part of that market".[27] Those are formulations which go in the direction of rights language. The Court, however, did not take them up.

The case law on free movement of goods can be contrasted with that on free movement of workers and right of establishment. In respect of freedom of workers and right of establishment there is clearly more emphasis on rights, and more of a human-rights type discourse. That is understandable, as those freedoms are much more closely and structurally connected to the individual lives of real people than is the free movement of goods. As long ago as 1975, in *Rutili* v *Minister for the Interior*, a case involving an Italian national residing in France who had participated in the May 1968 contestation and was prohibited from residing in part of the French territory, the Court referred to Arts 8-11 ECHR as supporting its restrictive interpretation of the public policy exception.[28] A much more recent instance is *Angonese*, where the Court decided that Art 39 EC, the basic provision concerning the free movement of workers, has so-called horizontal direct effect, i.e., that it is not just binding on public authorities but also on private parties. The Court pointed out, among other things, that Art 39 lays down a fundamental freedom and that it constitutes a specific application of the general prohibition of discrimination on grounds of nationality contained in Art 12 EC. The Court concluded that, consequently, the prohibition of discrimination on grounds of nationality laid down in Art 39 EC must be regarded as applying to private persons as well.[29]

Free movement of workers and right of establishment are of course not concerned with trade as such. But the freedom to provide services, in current thinking, is indeed a trade issue. It is the ECJ's rights-oriented case law in that area which is interesting from the perspective of international economic law, and GATS in particular. The EC Treaty provisions on freedom to provide services are located between free movement of goods and free movement of persons (workers and establishment), and share features of both types of freedom. More particularly, the freedom to provide services shares the principle of non-discrimination on grounds of nationality (also embodied in Art 12 EC) with the free movement of persons, and it is in the application of that principle that the ECJ has delivered rights-oriented judgments. In *Cowan*, for example, the Court characterised a British tourist on a visit to Paris as a recipient of services, who came within the "scope of application of the Treaty" for the purpose of Art 12 EC. The fact that Mr Cowan was refused compensation for a criminal attack in the Paris *Métro* on grounds of his nationality was considered a violation of Art 12 EC, the only link with EC law being Mr Cowan's status as a tourist.[30] A similar case is that of *Bickel and Franz*, where a German lorry driver and an Austrian tourist were criminally prosecuted in Italy, and the issue of the use of German or Italian in court proceedings was subjected to the principle of non-discrimination on grounds of nationality. Again, the freedom to provide services was a convenient way of triggering the application of that principle, combined, in that case, with the EC Treaty provisions on European Union citizenship, which refer to the right to move to and reside freely in other Member States.[31] In cases of this kind, [32] the ECJ is clearly concerned with the rights of the individuals involved, and it is arguable that the broad approach towards the "scope of application of the Treaty" for the purpose of non-discrimination on grounds of nationality is fuelled by the judges' sympathy for the fate of the individuals concerned.

The above examples reveal that trade in services, as it involves and protects movement of persons across borders, may be inherently closer to human rights issues than trade in goods. This has particular relevance for the evolution of GATS, whose national treatment provision is analogous to the principle of non-discrimination on grounds of nationality.[33]

External trade and human rights

Given that the free movement of goods within the EU is not considered from a human rights perspective, it will come as no surprise that there is no case law on external trade which characterises the right to trade externally as being fundamental. The EC Treaty does not contain an express principle of free external trade, as the provision of rules on external trade is a function of the common commercial policy under Art 133 EC. It is true that Art 131 EC speaks of "the progressive abolition of restrictions on international trade", but that provision is programmatic, and it would be a rather forced interpretation to read it as referring to a fundamental freedom, let alone a human right.[34] The furthest the Court has gone is to give some force to the fact that the EU's basic export regulation speaks of a "principle" of freedom of trade. In *Centro-Com*, a case concerning the embargo on trade with Serbia and Montenegro, the Court considered that the relevant exception to the principle of freedom to export must be interpreted in a way that does not extend its effects beyond what is necessary for the protection of the interests which it is intended to guarantee.[35] But it is of course still a long way from that type of statement to a fundamental rights discourse.

The fact that there is at present no fundamental right to free external trade does not mean that there is no linkage with fundamental rights. Indeed challenges to EC measures imposing restrictions on imports or exports are often based on the right to property and on the freedom to pursue a trade or business. Both of those come within the category of fundamental rights as general principles of EC law. The right to property is protected in Art 1 of the First Protocol to the ECHR, and the freedom to conduct a trade or business is considered common to the constitutional traditions of the Member States. The seminal ECJ case concerning right to property is *Hauer*, on a prohibition of planting vines, where Advocate General Capotorti engaged in a comparative law exercise which resulted in clear and persuasive recommendations.[36] The subsequent case law has produced the following principle: neither the right to property nor the freedom to conduct a trade or business is absolute, and the ECJ emphasises that their exercise may be restricted, provided that those restrictions in fact correspond to objectives of general interest pursued by the EC and do not constitute an intolerable interference impairing the very substance of the rights guaranteed.[37]

It appears that, so far, no external trade measure has been struck down on grounds of breach of the right to property or the freedom to conduct a trade or business. Arguably, one of the hardest cases was *Bosphorus*, where a Turkish charter company challenged an Irish decision to impound one of its aircraft pursuant to an EC Regulation imposing a trade and transport embargo on the Federal Republic of Yugoslavia. The aircraft was owned by the Yugoslav national airline (JAT), but had been leased to Bosphorus Airways, which used the aircraft for charter flights in Europe and had no further links with the Yugoslav regime. Bosphorus Airways argued that the impounding was a violation of its right to property. The Irish High Court judge who referred the case to the ECJ showed some sympathy for that argument, considering that the purpose of the EC sanctions was to operate as a punishment, deterrent or sanction against the people of the FRY; that, conversely, the sanctions were not intended to punish or penalise peoples or countries who had not in any way caused or contributed to the tragic events; and that the impounding of the aircraft would constitute a wholly unwarranted intervention in the business of Bosphorus Airways.[38] However the ECJ, following the Opinion of the Advocate General, disagreed. It acknowledged the interference with the right to property, but considered it justified in the light of the aims of the sanctions. It pointed out that any measure imposing sanctions has, by definition, consequences which affect the right to property and the freedom to pursue a trade or business, thereby causing harm to persons who are in no way responsible for the situation which led to the adoption of the sanctions. The Court then considered that the importance of the aims pursued by the sanctions, namely, to stop the war in Bosnia-Herzegovina, was such as to justify negative consequences, even of a substantial nature, for some operators. The court concluded that "[a]s compared with an objective of general interest so fundamental for the international community, which consists in putting an end to the state of war in the region and to the massive violations of human rights and humanitarian law in the Republic of Bosnia-Herzegovina, the impounding of the aircraft in question, which is owned by an undertaking based in or operating from the Federal Republic of Yugoslavia, cannot be regarded as inappropriate or disproportionate".[39]

Violations of the right to property and the freedom to pursue a trade or business were also frequently alleged in the context of the infamous banana saga, particularly as regards the allocation of licences for importation of Latin American bananas. It is not possible to analyse the whole of the saga in these few pages. In *Germany* v *Council* (1994), the "mother" of all bananas judgments in so far as the original regime was concerned, the Court rejected the fundamental rights arguments. It pointed out that no economic operator can claim a right to property in a market share which he held at a time before the establishment of a common market organisation. Nor can an economic operator claim an acquired right or even a legitimate expectation that an existing situation which is capable of being altered by decisions taken by the EC institutions within the limits of their discretionary power will be maintained. The Court accepted that, as regards the freedom to pursue a trade or business, the regime did indeed alter the competitive position of economic operators on the German market in particular, but it also accepted that the regime corresponded to objectives of general EC interest and did not impair the very substance of that fundamental right.[40]

Whatever the merits of the ECJ's assessment of the legality of the banana regime, the saga is also important for broader constitutional reasons. Indeed, the banana regime was very badly received in Germany and was considered by many commentators to involve a breach of fundamental rights as protected by the German Constitution.[41] Cases were referred to the *Bundesverfassungsgericht* (the German Constitutional Court), and for a considerable period a possible negative ruling undermining the supremacy of EC law was hanging above the EC courts and the EC legal system, as a sword of Damocles. The threat did not materialise, as is now customary as regards the European case law of the *Bundesverfassungsgericht*.[42] Yet it may have had some effect on the ECJ which, in a later *Germany* v *Council* case, found that certain amendments to the banana regime infringed the general principle of non-discrimination.[43] If so, this would be another instance of the well-studied constitutional dialogue between the ECJ and national courts, which has been particularly important in the field of fundamental rights protection.[44] This dialogue is of course facilitated, or even simply enabled, by the formal dialogue between the ECJ and national courts through the preliminary rulings procedure (Art 234 EC). In international economic law, and particularly in the setting of the WTO, there is no such instrument, which, together with the much broader membership, is likely to render the development of any form of meaningful dialogue with national courts much more difficult.

Again without going too much into the substance of the banana litigation, the role of the general principle of non-discrimination, or equal treatment, is also worth considering for a moment. Art 34(2), second subparagraph, EC excludes, in the context of common market organisations, any discrimination between producers or consumers in the EC. It is established case law that this provision "is merely a specific enunciation of the general principle of equality, one of the fundamental principles of Community law".[45] The principle is frequently argued, and indeed sometimes successfully so, such as in the second *Germany* v *Council* case, where the alleged violations of the right to property and the freedom to pursue a trade or business were again rejected. Whether or not this betrays a preference on the part of the ECJ to apply the principle of equal treatment, an innate EC law fundamental right, rather than imported rights such as the right to property and the freedom to pursue a trade or business is not clear; the matter would require further analysis and reflection. But in any event, the importance in practice of the various non-discrimination principles in EC law is worth stressing. Reference was made above to the principle of non-discrimination on grounds of nationality, and EC directives adopted pursuant to the new Art 13 EC will greatly expand the territory of EU non-discrimination law.[46]

There is yet another general principle of EC law which, although not commonly regarded as a manifestation of a human-rights-based approach, may in some cases carry a human rights dimension: the principle of proportionality. There are a number of external trade cases, particularly concerning duties on imports of mushrooms from China, where the Court applied proportionality as a principle precluding measures which were more burdensome to traders than was required by the aim pursued. In the formulation by the Court, it follows from the principle of proportionality "that measures imposing financial charges on economic agents are lawful provided that the measures are appropriate and necessary for the objectives legitimately pursued by the legislation in question. Of course, where there is a choice between several appropriate measures, the least onerous measure must be used and the charges imposed must not be disproportionate to the aims pursued".[47] When proportionality is applied in this way, it can easily be regarded as a fundamental right prohibiting undue financial charges or excessive financial penalties.

Derogations and human rights

The above is not the end of the story of trade (internal and external), and human rights. Many of the "trade-and-..." linkages present themselves most forcefully in the field of exceptions to and derogations from the principles of free trade.[48] That is probably also the case with human rights. In any event, in EC free trade law, both internally and externally, human rights issues have also been raised as regards derogations.

As is mentioned above, the starting-point is that the ECJ will also safeguard the protection of fundamental rights as general principles of EC law where a Member State relies on a derogation from the principles of free trade and movement. That was firmly established in *ERT*, a case involving the Greek television monopoly, which was considered from the angle of the freedom to provide services. The Greek Government attempted to rely on Art 56 EC (now Art 46), which concerns justifications on grounds of public policy, public security or public health. The Court did not appear to accept such justification; but more importantly for our purposes, it pointed out that "where a Member State relies on the combined provisions of Articles 56 and 66 [now 46 and 56] in order to justify rules which are likely to obstruct the exercise of the freedom to provide services, such justification, provided for by Community law, must be interpreted in the light of the general principles of law and in particular of fundamental rights. Thus the national rules in question can fall under the exceptions provided for by the combined provisions of Articles 56 and 66 only if they are compatible with the fundamental rights the observance of which is ensured by the Court".[49] The Court subsequently identified the fundamental right in issue as the freedom of expression, embodied in Art 10 ECHR.

The ECJ decision in *ERT* merely established the principle; its application to the facts of the case was left to the Greek court which had referred it to the ECJ. Yet the implementation of the principle can give rise to difficult cases requiring intricate value judgments. This is illustrated by one of the hardest and most sensitive cases ever brought before the ECJ. In *Grogan* the Court was asked to rule in a case involving the distribution of information concerning the identity and location of abortion clinics in other Member States by officers of student associations in Ireland. Under the Irish Constitution, abortion is prohibited, and the Society for the Protection of Unborn Children brought a case against the students asking for an injunction restraining the said distribution. The question arose whether such an injunction would be contrary to the freedom to provide services, as abortion abroad could be considered as the receipt of a cross-border service. The Court, however, avoided ruling on the conflict between the freedom to provide and receive services and the prohibition on abortion, by stating that the link between the distribution of the information in issue and the actual provision of abortion services was too tenuous for a restriction on such distribution to be seen as a restriction on the freedom to provide services. There was therefore no EC law issue to begin with. The Court shied away from following the Opinion of Advocate General Van Gerven, who did analyse the human rights dimensions of the case, finding that there was a question of balancing two fundamental rights, namely the right to life and the freedom of expression.[50]

Another instance of the application of fundamental rights as general principles of EC law in a derogation context is in *Familiapress* v *Bauer Verlag*.[51] The case concerned the selling of a German magazine in Austria. Under Austrian legislation aimed at protecting small publishers and thus maintaining press diversity, it was prohibited for periodicals to contain prize puzzle competitions or games. The ECJ was asked whether this legislation operated as an import restriction caught by Art 28 EC. The Court ruled that the measure did indeed restrict trade, but that the maintenance of press diversity may constitute an overriding interest justifying the restriction. It referred to the requirement of proportionality, and pointed out that the justification had to be interpreted in the light of the general principles of law and in particular fundamental rights. The Court drew attention to Art 10 ECHR on freedom of expression, and considered that a prohibition on selling publications which offer the chance to take part in prize games or competitions may detract from freedom of expression. It then made reference to ECtHR case law, which accepts that Art 10 permits derogations for the purposes of maintaining press diversity, in so far as they are prescribed by law and are necessary in a democratic society. The Court's conclusion was that it had to be determined whether the Austrian prohibition was proportionate to the aim of maintaining press diversity and whether that objective might not be attained by measures less restrictive of both intra-Community trade and freedom of expression. The reader may wonder what the outcome was of that proportionality examination, but that was not something the Court engaged in; it referred the case back to the Austrian court for decision, instructing it to carry out the required examination on the basis of a study of the national press market- a truly daunting assignment!

Those are probably the most prominent cases, but it is clear that human rights issues, identified as such or not, are present in many derogation cases. It is beyond the scope of the present contribution to engage in a full-scale examination of those cases. However it may be worth touching upon the debate as to whether it is appropriate for the ECJ to engage in express review of the compatibility of national measures, benefiting from derogations, with human rights. Extra-judicially, Advocate General Jacobs recently argued against such review. In his view, once the ECJ has held that a particular derogation is in principle applicable, it should not address the further question whether the derogation is applied with respect for human rights. That, he argues, is not a question of EC law. Nor is the ECJ well placed to lay down, in such cases, the appropriate standard of fundamental rights protection.[52]

With respect, it is questionable whether the case which the Advocate General makes is entirely persuasive.[53] One can have sympathy for the basic argument, which is that EC law should not be all pervasive, and that the ECJ is not, and should not be, a general human rights court. But if fundamental rights are indeed general principles of EC law, and are to be taken seriously by the Court, they should be all pervasive in EC law. That must mean that where a Member State relies on an EC law derogation, the scope and contours of such a derogation have to be determined in line with the protection of fundamental rights. In some contexts, this is so obvious that it is not always clearly identified. For example, much of the case law on the public policy exception to the free movement of workers is concerned with fundamental rights type issues, such as the right to effective remedies, or the principle that sanctions be based on personal conduct.[54] In fact, attention and respect for the protection of fundamental rights in derogation cases could be seen as a mere instance of the principle that the Treaties need to be interpreted and applied in light of fundamental rights requirements. In this author's view, therefore, the Court cannot and should not leave fundamental rights issues in derogation cases unaddressed. The *Grogan* case is particularly illustrative in that respect. Suppose the Court had held that there was indeed an issue of free movement of services; the facts of the case could have been such that the Court would have been unable to say that the link with services was too tenuous. The Court would no doubt have found a restriction on the freedom to receive services, and would have had to consider the Irish Republic's defence based on the right to life. How could that be done without considering fundamental rights? Of course, the appropriate extent of consideration of human rights issues will differ depending upon the type of derogation, and Advocate General Jacobs is surely right to warn against consideration of fundamental rights in cases which do not properly call for that. Where there is no clear link between the restriction on cross-border movement and possible fundamental rights issues connected with the derogation or exception relied upon, it would not be appropriate for the ECJ to engage in full-scale review and impose a particular human rights standard. Conversely, however, where the fundamental rights issues are indeed more closely connected with the restriction on cross-border movement, the ECJ should not shy away from in-depth consideration of the fundamental rights issues.

The human rights dimension of derogations may also arise in the context of external trade. Many of the EC's basic external trade instruments have derogation clauses which are analogous to those that apply in internal trade. So far there appear to be no judgments in which the human rights dimension of derogations is expressly identified. What is perhaps noteworthy is an observation by Advocate General Jacobs in *Leifer and Others*. That case concerned German restrictions on exports of dual-use goods to Iraq at the time of the first Gulf War. At issue were exports of chemicals which, in the view of the German authorities, could be used for the production of chemical weapons. The German government argued that the restrictions were lawful under a provision of the EC's export rules permitting Member States to restrict exports on grounds of, *inter alia,* public security and the life and health of humans. As regards the latter, the German government argued that the restrictions served to prevent the use of chemical weapons in the Iran-Iraq war, and thus to protect the health and life of countless people. Counsel for Mr Leifer replied that the grounds on which the German authorities relied could only be invoked where there is a close link between the individuals whose health and life were being protected and the Member State relying on those grounds. Advocate General Jacobs disagreed. He argued that "where the health and life of humans is at stake that view must surely be wrong. When the Council adopted the Export Regulation it cannot have been its intention only to allow the Member States to protect the health and lives of their own nationals. As a rule, of course, a Member State will in the first place act so as to protect its own citizens. Where however a war is waged between certain third countries, entailing a great deal of bloodshed, it would be indefensible to interpret Art 11 of the Export Regulation as not allowing certain export restrictions aimed at not aggravating the loss of life".[55] Here the Advocate General addresses an important jurisdictional point, which also arises in WTO law as regards GATT exceptions, and it would seem that, depending on the circumstances, human rights considerations may be relevant in deciding that point.

The administration of trade and human rights

Human rights may also be relevant for the administration of trade. The ECJ and CFI have developed an extensive and sophisticated body of case law on due process and effective remedies requirements. It is beyond the scope of the present contribution to provide a survey of that case law, as it pervades nearly all areas of EC law and is relevant to both EC and Member State acts.[56] It is obvious, however, that the case law is also relevant for the administration of trade. An example in that area is *Al-Jubail Fertilizer* v *Council*, a case involving a challenge to an anti-dumping measure. The applicant argued that its right to a fair hearing had been violated. The ECJ referred to fundamental rights as general principles of EC law, and more particularly to the right to a fair hearing, "a principle whose fundamental character has been stressed on numerous occasions in the case-law of the Court". The Court pointed out that those requirements must be observed "not only in the course of proceedings which may result in the imposition of penalties, but also in investigative proceedings prior to the adoption of anti-dumping regulations which, despite their general scope, may directly and individually affect the undertakings concerned and entail adverse consequences for them". The Court also added that, "with regard to a fair hearing, any action taken by the Community institutions must be all the more scrupulous in view of the fact that, as they stand at present, the rules in question do not provide all the procedural guarantees for the protection of the individual which may exist in certain national legal systems". The Court then applied those principles to the facts of the case, and found that the EC institutions had not discharged their duty to place at the applicants' disposal all the information which would have enabled them effectively to defend their interests. It consequently annulled the regulation.[57]

Beyond due process and effective remedies the EU is developing a broad policy on good governance, including transparency. One of the most tangible and fast-moving developments in this area concerns access to documents, which is acquiring the status of a fundamental right. Again it is not possible to present a complete analysis of the relevant developments,[58] but some brief comments from a trade-and-human-rights perspective may be in order. Pressure on the EU institutions to open up and give broader access to documents has come from a wide variety of sources and is greatly aided by a fast-growing body of case-law from both the ECJ and the CFI. This has led the institutions to adopt clearer rules on access, and to the insertion of Art 255 EC by the Treaty of Amsterdam ("Any citizen of the Union, and any natural or legal person residing or having its registered office in a Member State, shall have a right of access to European Parliament, Council and Commission documents ..."). This provision is now implemented by a general Regulation, whose main aim is "to ensure the widest possible access to documents".[59] There are of course exceptions to the rule of general access, and it is those exceptions which determine the actual scope of the rule. Art 4 of the Regulation provides that the institutions shall refuse access where disclosure would undermine the protection of the public interest as regards public security, defence and military matters, international relations, and the financial, monetary or economic policy of the Community or a Member State. Further, there are exceptions relating to the protection of privacy and the integrity of the individual, commercial interests including intellectual property, court proceedings and legal advice, and inspections, investigations and audits.

It is obvious that some of those exceptions may be relevant in a trade context. From a trade-and-human-rights perspective, one of the most meaningful cases so far considered by the CFI and the ECJ is *Heidi Hautala.* Ms Hautala is a Member of the European Parliament, who had sought information from the Council concerning violations of human rights in non-member countries which were being assisted by arms exports from EU Member States. When learning that the Council's Political Committee had approved a report from a working group in which respect for human rights was mentioned as one of the eight criteria in arms exports decisions, she requested access to that report. Access was denied, however, in order to protect the public interest with regard to international relations. The Council felt that the report contained highly sensitive information, likely to jeopardise relations with non-member countries. Ms Hautala did not acquiesce, and challenged the refusal in the courts, which decided that the Council could not block access to the entire report when it admitted that only parts of it were sensitive from an international relations perspective. Partial access therefore had to be granted.[60]

The outcome of the case is not particularly remarkable, but a number of comments that were made in the course of deciding it are worth mentioning here. The CFI referred in its judgment[61] to the seminal Opinion of Advocate General Tesauro in the earlier *Netherlands* v *Council* case, where the AG considered that the basis for the right of access to documents should be sought in the democratic principle. It was, in the AG's view, the essential precondition for effective supervision by public opinion of the operations of the public authorities.[62] Those remarks were agreed with by Advocate General Léger in his Opinion on the appeal in *Hautala*. Mr Léger further explored the foundations of the right of access to documents, tracing its status in the laws of the EU Member States, and finding that thirteen of the fifteen Member States have a general rule that the public has a right of access, and that in nine Member States the right of access is a fundamental right. He thus concluded that the right of access is a fundamental right of EU law, coming within the category of general principles of EC law, in this case derived from the constitutional traditions of the Member States. He found support for that conclusion in the new Charter of Fundamental Rights, which contains the right of access in Art 42.[63] Whilst the ECJ did not expressly confirm that analysis, since it decided the case on narrower grounds, it is difficult to find any flaws in it.

The EU's experience with transparency and access to documents is surely interesting for other international organisations, including the WTO. One cannot here explore the further issues of democracy and legitimacy connected with the work of international organisations,[64] which raise fundamental questions beyond the scope of the present paper. It is clear, however, that the protection of human rights is an important, if not central, element of international democracy and legitimacy.

The EU and the WTO

This concluding section offers some thoughts on the potential relevance of the EU experience, as analysed above, for the WTO. These are no more than provisional reflections, which come nowhere near fully considered theses. It is hoped that they may inspire some further debate and reflection. The emphasis is on the role of the judiciary.

1. The ECJ has developed a clear human rights doctrine, consisting of the incorporation of fundamental rights in the judicially invented category of general principles of EC law. Such a doctrine has proved indispensable for the EU. Indeed, it was not in itself enough to lay to rest fears and criticisms pertaining to the level of fundamental rights protection in EU law, witness the case law of constitutional courts, the attempts to have the EC join the ECHR and the adoption of the Charter of Fundamental Rights. The WTO, too, may well be in need of some form of human rights doctrine, and there may be a role to be played by its judiciary, particularly the Appellate Body (AB). It is obvious that the AB currently does not enjoy the room for manoeuvre which the ECJ used to have through the assertion of the creation of a new legal order. The AB cannot there-

fore be as overtly creative as the ECJ has been. Its human rights doctrine would have to be located and embedded in more traditional categories of international law. Yet that is no doubt possible. Reference was made above to general principles as a source of international law. The AB could further draw on a number of international human rights instruments, taking up and developing its foundational dictum that WTO law does not exist in clinical isolation from international law.[65]

The road may be difficult, and the opportunities limited, yet there may be much to gain, not only from the perspective of harnassing the legitimacy of the WTO itself. There may also be gains in terms of strengthening international human rights law, substantively, through further judicial interpretations of international human rights norms, *and* formally, precisely by developing the linkages between such norms and other areas of international law.

2. The ECJ has been able to develop its human rights doctrine through judicial dialogue with national courts, and it is that constitutional dialogue which is one of the main contributors to EU fundamental rights protection. At WTO level, anything comparable appears to be excluded for the foreseeable future. There is nothing like the preliminary rulings system, and the WTO membership is much too broad and diverse for a general constitutional dialogue. Further, the WTO does not benefit from many of the mechanisms available in the ECJ context, such as that which allowed Advocate General Léger's analysis of the rules on access to documents in the Member States. Human rights will predominantly have to be found in general international law and in treaties and conventions, rather than in domestic legal systems. There is no dearth of material in those sources of law, but there is another disadvantage, namely the fact that the core of many human rights discourses continues to be located at domestic constitutional level. It is not clear how the AB could connect with that level.

3. It was argued above that the ECJ does not generally engage in a fundamental rights discourse when addressing free trade in goods and services. If free trade is not a fundamental right (in the sense, this time, of a human right) even within the EU, it is difficult to see how it could be characterised as such in the setting of the WTO. But perhaps it is worth distinguishing for a moment between adjective and noun. Indeed, a number of the free trade rules of the WTO agreements are clearly "fundamental". In the recent *US – Section 211* case for example, the AB speaks of the principles of national and most-favoured-nation treatment (NT and MFN) in terms of "cornerstone" and "fundamental principle of the world trading system", whose "significance can hardly be overstated".[66] It is at the level of "right" that problems arise. So far, the WTO is essentially concerned with rights of Members, and not of individu-

als.[67] That in itself of course removes much of the scope for a fundamental rights discourse. Yet, the fundamental principles just referred to do have a connection with the position of individuals: NT and MFN embody non-discrimination standards in the context of trade in goods directed at domestic and foreign goods (see Arts II and III GATT), but also in the context of trade in services and intellectual property rights directed at nationals and non-nationals (see Arts II and XVII GATS, and Arts 3 and 4 TRIPs). Thus, the recent *US – Section 211* case is, as regards NT and MFN, about differences in treatment at the level of trade mark protection between US nationals and non-nationals. Non-discrimination law is at the core of much human rights law. From this angle, therefore, there is bound to be pressure on the AB to develop discourses with a human rights dimension.

4. From a human rights perspective, there is one particularly noteworthy difference between the respective roles of the ECJ and the AB. The ECJ has jurisdiction to strike down EC acts other than the founding Treaties on the basis, *inter alia*, of a violation of fundamental rights. There are few examples of the exercise of that jurisdiction, but at least there is scope for those who are critical of certain legislative acts to seek recourse in the ECJ.[68] The AB does not appear to have jurisdiction to rule on whether provisions of WTO law are in conformity with fundamental rights. It is not possible, for example, to challenge the legality of TRIPs provisions on patents for medicines directly at WTO level. At most, it could be argued that there is a conflict between a WTO law provision and an international human rights instrument, and the conflict may have to be resolved by giving preference to the human rights norm. However, that is a much more tenuous connection with human rights principles than is inherent in the ECJ's capacity to annul EC legal acts.

If challenge at WTO level is not possible, there may well come a time when WTO law provisions are challenged at a domestic, constitutional level. The AB may then be faced with the same type of judicial contestation, based on fundamental rights, as was (and is) the ECJ.

5. One may expect that at the level of WTO dispute settlement, much like in ECJ case-law, the interaction between trade and human rights will present itself most forcefully where exceptions and derogations are relied upon. Particularly in the context of trade in goods, Art XX GATT may easily become a vehicle for arguments based on respect for human rights, much like it has become a vehicle for finding a balance between trade and environment.[69] A number of the Art XX exceptions clearly lend themselves to an interpretation in line with human rights. As the AB could hardly construct "general principles of WTO law", inspiration will have to be drawn from international human rights instruments. Again trade-and-environment offers a precedent, in that the AB has

been willing to refer to environmental protection treaties and conventions when interpreting, for example, the concept of exhaustible natural resources.[70]

Again the balancing act is likely to be a delicate one, as the AB may easily be accused of judicial activism when engaging in creative exercises of interpretation. It may also be accused of interpreting norms which do not come within its jurisdiction. However, to decline jurisdiction whenever human rights claims are made would seem an even less attractive route to take, for it will inevitably attract the criticism that human rights are disregarded by the WTO.

6. As regards transparency the WTO is already characterized by easy access to documents. However, the new Doha Round may none the less provide a test for openness when the really hard negotiations take place. Pressure for secrecy is likely to result from the reciprocity approach towards negotiations, with Members being concerned that final trade-offs may be easier to make away from public focus and attention. By contrast, those in favour of openness will argue that WTO negotiations have an impact on general public interests and thus require an open legislative process.

The Doha Round will also need to consider whether to give public access to the dispute settlement process. Given the (quasi-)judicial nature of WTO dispute settlement, as well as the type of interests at stake, the case for such access, under terms comparable with domestic judicial processes, is overwhelming. The argument that openness may interfere with negotiation and conciliation is clearly not persuasive. Domestic judicial processes also have a long history of encouraging out-of-court settlements, often with active participation of the judiciary, and manage to combine that perfectly with proceedings open to the general public.

Those are some initial reflections on the relationship between WTO law and human rights protection which come to mind after having analysed the EU experience. There is no doubt scope for a lot more detailed analysis of this topic, so central to the further development of both the EU and WTO political and legal systems.

NOTES

1. See recently P. Craig, "Constitutions, Constitutionalism and the European Union", *ELJ* (2001) at 128-135.

2. E. Stein, "International Integration and Democracy: No Love at First Sight", *AJIL* (2001) at 515.

3. For goods, see J.H.H. Weiler, "Epilogue: Towards a Common Law of International Trade", in Weiler (ed), *The EU, the WTO and the NAFTA – Towards a Common Law of International Trade* (OUP, 2000) at 201-232; for services, see P. Eeckhout, "Constitutional Concepts for Free Trade in

Services", in de Búrca and Scott (eds), *The EU and the WTO – Legal and Constitutional Issues* (Hart Publishing, 2001) 211-235.

4. See B. Brandtner and A. Rosas, "Trade Preferences and Human Rights", in P. Alston (ed), *The EU and Human Rights* (OUP, 1999) at 707-708.

5. M. Hilf, "Power, rules and principles – which orientation for WTO/GATT law?", *JIEL* (2001) 111-130.

6. See B. Brandtner and A. Rosas, "Human Rights and the External Relations of the European Community: An Analysis of Doctrine and Practice", *EJIL* (1998) 468-490.

7. OJ C 364/1 of 18 December 2000.

8. See e.g., P. Craig and G. de Búrca, *EU Law – Text, Cases and Materials* (OUP, 1998), chapter 7 and B. De Witte, "The Past and Future Role of the European Court of Justice in the Protection of Human Rights", in Alston, cited above, 859-897.

9. Fundamental rights, and not human rights, is the terminology generally used in EU law.

10. Case 11/70 [1970] ECR 1125. It must be noted that this was a trade case, involving exports of maize meal!

11. See, e.g., Case C-274/99 P *Bernard Connolly* v *Commission*, judgment of 6 March 2001, not yet reported, paras. 38-49.

12. Opinion 2/94 [1996] ECR I-1759.

13. Cited above.

14. I leave aside the issues raised by the extension of fundamental rights protection to the Second and Third Pillar.

15. Case 5/88 *Wachauf* [1989] ECR 2609.

16. Case C-260/89 *ERT* [1991] ECR I-2925.

17. Case 26/62 [1963] ECR 1.

18. Case 240/83 [1985] ECR 531, para. 9.

19. Case 222/86 [1987] ECR 4097, para. 14.

20. Case C-55/94 [1995] ECR I-4165, para. 37.

21. See also J.H.H. Weiler and N. Lockhart, " 'Taking rights seriously' seriously: the European Court and its fundamental rights jurisprudence", *CMLRev* (1995) at 593-596.

22. E.-U. Petersmann, "Proposals for a New Constitution for the European Union: Building-Blocks for a Constitutional Theory and Constitutional Law of the EU", *CMLRev* (1995) at 1153-1155.

23. E.g., Case 145/88 *Torfaen BC* v *B & Q* [1989] ECR 3851.

24. Joined Cases C-267/91 and C-268/91 [1993] ECR I-6097, para. 14.

25. Case 120/78 *Rewe* v *Bundesmonopolverwaltung für Branntwein* [1979] ECR 649.

26. See, e.g., S. Weatherill, "After *Keck*: Some Thoughts on How to Clarify the Clarification", *CMLRev* (1996) 885-906.

27. Case C-412/93 *Leclerc-Siplec* v *TF1 Publicité and M6 Publicité* [1995] ECR I-179, para. 41 of the Opinion.

28. Case 36/75 [1975] ECR 1219, para. 32.

29. Case C-281/98 *Roman Angonese* v *Cassa di Risparmio di Bolzano* [2000] ECR I-4139, paras. 35-36.

30. Case 186/87 [1989] ECR 195.

31. Case C-274/96 [1998] ECR I-7637.

32. See, e.g., Case C-85/96 *Martínez Sala* v *Freistaat Bayern* [1998] ECR I-2691 and Case C-184/99 *Grzelczyk* v *Centre public d'aide sociale d'Ottignies-Louvain-la-Neuve* [2001] ECR I-6193.

33. See P. Eeckhout, cited above, at 221-223.

34. In Case 5/73 *Balkan-Import-Export* v *Hauptzollamt Berlin-Packhof* [1973] ECR 1091, para. 27, the Court considered that Art 110 EEC (now Art 131 EC) conferred wide powers of assessment upon the Council in matters of commercial policy.

35. Case C-124/95 *The Queen, ex parte Centro-Com* v *HM Treasury and Bank of England* [1997] ECR I-81, para. 51.

36. Case 44/79 *Hauer* v *Land Rheinland-Pfalz* [1979] ECR 3727.

37. See, e.g., Case 265/87 *Schräder* v *Hauptzollamt Gronau* [1989] ECR 2237, para. 15; *Wachauf*, cited above, para. 18.

38. Case C-84/95 [1996] ECR I-3953, at paras. 37-38 of the Opinion of Advocate General Jacobs.

39. Paras. 22-26.

40. Case C-280/93 [1994] ECR I-4973, paras. 79-87.

41. See U. Everling, "Will Europe Slip on Bananas? The Bananas Judgment of the Court of Justice and National Courts", *CMLRev* (1996) 401-437.

42. See judgment of 7 June 2000, 2 BvL 1/97, available at http://www.bverfg.de.

43. Case C-122/95 [1998] ECR I-973; see also the near identical Joined Cases C-364/95 and C-365/95 *T.Port* v *Hauptzollamt Hamburg-Jonas* [1998] ECR I-1023. The effect is suggested by S. Peers, "Constitutional Principles and International Trade", *ELR* (1999) at 9-10.

44. See A.-M. Slaughter, A. Stone Sweet and J.H.H. Weiler (eds), *The European Court and National Courts - Doctrine and Jurisprudence* (Hart Publishing, 1998).

45. See, e.g., Joined Cases 117/76 and 16/77 *Ruckdeschel* v *Hauptzollamt Hamburg-St Annen* [1977] ECR 1753, para 7. See further T. Tridimas, *The General Principles of EC Law* (OUP, 1999), chapter 2.

46. Council Directive 2000/43 implementing the principle of equal treatment between persons irrespective of racial or ethnic origin, OJ [2000] L180/22 and Council Directive 2000/78 establishing a general framework for equal treatment in employment and occupation, OJ [2000] L303/16.

47. Case C-24/90 *Werner Faust* [1991] ECR I-4905, para. 12.

48. E.g., trade and environment, and trade and labour rights, see for an introduction regarding both M. Trebilcock and R. Howse, *The Regulation of International Trade* (2nd ed, Routledge 1999), chapters 15 and 16.

49. Cited above, para. 43.

50. Case C-159/90 *SPUC* v *Grogan* [1991] ECR I-4685.

51. Case C-368/95 [1997] ECR I-3689.

52. F.G. Jacobs, "Human Rights in the European Union: the role of the Court of Justice", *ELRev* (2001) at 336-339. See also J. Coppell and A. O'Neill, "The European Court of Justice: Taking Rights Seriously?", *CMLRev* (1992), at 680-681. It may be noted that the principle is not contained in the new Charter of Fundamental Rights, see Article 51(1).

53. See also Weiler and Lockhart, cited above, at 80.

54. See *inter alia* Case 41/74 *Van Duyn* v *Home Office* [1974] ECR 1337; Case 36/75 *Rutili* v *Minister for the Interior* [1975] ECR 1219; Case 30/77 *Regina* v *Bouchereau* [1977] ECR 1999; Joined Cases 115 and 116/81 *Adoui and Cornuaille* v *Belgium* [1982] ECR 1665; Case C-348/96 *Calfa* [1999] ECR I-11.

55. Case C-83/94 [1995] ECR I-3231, paras. 58-59 of the Opinion.

56. For an overview see, e.g., M. Brealey and M. Hoskins, *Remedies in EC Law* (2nd ed, Sweet & Maxwell 1998) ch. 6; K. Lenaerts and D. Arts, *Procedural Law of the European Union* (Sweet & Maxwell 1999) ch. 3.

57. Case C-49/88 [1991] ECR I-3187.

58. See, e.g., A. Tomkins, "Transparency and the Emergence of a European Administrative Law", *YEL* (1999-2000) 217-256; Stein, cited above, at 521-524.

59. Art 1(a) of Regulation 1049/2001 of the European Parliament and of the Council regarding public access to European Parliament, Council and Commission documents, OJ (2001) L 145/43.

60. Case T-14/98 *Hautala* v *Council* [1999] ECR II-2489 and Case C-353/99 P *Council* v *Hautala* [2001] ECR I-9565.

61. At para. 82.

62. Case C-58/94 *Netherlands* v *Council* [1996] ECR I-2169, para. 19 of the Opinion.

63. Opinion of 10 July 2001 in Case C-353/99 P [2001] ECR I-9565, paras. 52-87.

64. See Stein, cited above.

65. *US - Gasoline*, WT/DS2/AB/R of 29 April 1996.

66. *US - Section 211 Omnibus Appropriations Act*, WT/DS176/AB/R of 2 January 2002, paras. 233, 241-242 and 297.

67. See the Panel Report in *US - Sections 301-310 Trade Act*, WT/DS152/R of 22 Dec 1999.

68. See, e.g., Case C-377/98 *Netherlands* v *EP and Council* [2001] ECR I-7079. In this case the Netherlands challenged a directive on the legal protection of biotechnological inventions, arguing, inter alia, that the directive violated fundamental rights. The Court rejected the argument.

69. Cf. *US - Shrimp*, WT/DS158/AB/R of 12 Oct 1998 and WT/DS158/AB/RW of 22 October 2001.

70. Idem, WT/DS/158/AB/R, paras. 127-134.

CHAPTER 12

Comments on the European Union: Transparency and Human Rights

*Eric Stein**

I should like to add two points to the discussion on the European experience.

The first relates to the issue of transparency in the working of the EU institutions, which Professor Eeckhout expressly left aside in his excellent paper. Professor Cottier in his contribution on governance stressed the relevance of the issue for the WTO.

Until relatively recently, the European Community functioned under the principle that everything was secret except what was expressly stated to be made public. The proceedings in the executive Commission were secret, and the Council with its pyramid of committees was dubbed "the Kremlin of the West." It is estimated that nine-tenths of all decisions are still made in innumerable closed committees of national and Union officials and only rubberstamped by the Council. Secrecy has strengthened the tendency to shift the balance from national parliaments to the executive power and facilitated the privilege of one interest group over another. As in a modern administrative state, transparency in the Union is essential not only to inform member state parliaments and electorates, but also to help form an all-European debate and public opinion that are required to sustain advanced integration. Consequently, it has been argued that the veil of secrecy must be lifted beyond the indispensable confidential area.

The turning point in this debate was the conclusion of the Maastricht Treaty of 1992, which required the Council to lay down general principles on the right of access to public documents. In response, the Council adopted in 1993 the Code of Conduct declaring that, "[t]he public will have the widest possible access to documents held by the Commission and the Council," subject to specified exceptions designed to protect interests ranging from public security and international relations to confidentiality of the Council proceedings. Those whose requests for information had been refused had to be informed of the possible recourse to the ombudsman or the Court of First Instance.[1]

In its 1999 Rules of Procedure, although preserving "the obligation of professional secrecy" in its deliberations, the Council mandated the publication of

* This contribution was completed in June 2001.

results, explanation of votes, minutes, and statements entered in minutes when it acts in its *legislative* capacity. Finally, in March 2001, the Council adopted a decision introducing publication on the Internet of preparatory texts produced by the working groups.

Since 1996, the Court of First Instance has entertained some dozen complaints against the denial of access to information. In most cases the Court reversed in full or in part the decisions denying access to documents, either on procedural grounds (such as the institution's failure to state reasons) or on substantive grounds, and it has interpreted strictly the exceptions to the duty to disclose.[2]

Regarding confidentiality in the interest of the institutions, only documents relating to current or possible court proceedings and internal legal opinions are viewed as "confidential," the latter on the ground that disclosure could give rise to uncertainty about the legality of a Community measure, impairing "the public interest in the stability of Community law and the proper functioning of the institutions." This sweeping exclusion of legal opinions has been criticized.

Giuseppe Tesauro, an Advocate General at the Court of Justice, observes that openness is directly linked with the democratic nature of the institutions and appropriate publicity is required for effective supervision, thus emphasizing that the right of access to official documents is part of the democratic principle.

My second comment is intended as an addendum to the papers dealing with the European Union approach to the protection of fundamental human rights, which has become part of the Union's constitutional canon. The current Union system has been criticized as ambiguous, inconsistent and placing excessive reliance on the Court of Justice. In fact, most of the Community law in the field has originated in the Court case law. In the emergent debate, some observers call for a comprehensive and coherent human rights policy, consisting of a separate member of the executive Commission, a Directorate General within the Commission and a special agency with a monitoring function.[3]

Such proposals are opposed as both unrealistic and over-intrusive because of the existential difference (both in the definition and the mode of enforcement) between the "negative" civil and political rights on one hand and the economic and social rights on the other.[4]

From the WTO perspective, the controversy over the role of the Community judiciary within the Union system in relation to the protection of human rights may be of some interest when considering the function of the dispute settlement mechanism in the WTO institutional framework.

In a more general way, the Community judiciary, that is the Court of First Instance and the Court of Justice, sit in public sessions with reasonably free access to documents, while in the WTO dispute settlement mechanisms lack of transparency has been criticized. But that is a story for another day.

NOTES

1. For citations supporting this comment, see Eric Stein, *International Integration and Democracy: No Love at First Sight*, 95 AJIL 489, 522-523 (2001).

2. In addition to the cases and literature listed in Stein, supra note 1 at 522-23, see Claire-Francoise Durand et al., *Jurisprudence*, 37 Cah. de droit Eur. 441, 447-454 (2001) and most recently Case T-191/99 David Petrie et al. v. Commission, Court of First Instance, Dec. 11, 2001.

3. Philip Alston and J.H.H. Weiler, *An 'Ever Closer Union' in Need of a Human Rights Policy: The European Human Rights in* The EU and Human Rights, 3, 21-22 and *passim* (Philip Alston ed., 1999), Philip Alston, *Leading Example: A Human Rights Agenda for the European Union for the Year 2000, id.* at 919.

4. Armin von Bogdandy, *The European Union as a Human Rights Organization? Human Rights and the Core of the European Union*, 37 Common Mkt. L. Rev. 1307, 1310-1316 (2000).

CHAPTER 13

Trade and the European Convention on Human Rights

*Walter Kälin**

The European Convention on Human Rights[1] (hereinafter the ECHR) is the oldest of the regional human rights conventions and has been ratified by all members of the Council of Europe. The Convention has attained a degree of practical relevance for everyone in Europe today that was hardly expected at the time of its formulation. Individuals are the primary beneficiaries of its protection, but it has also become highly significant for corporate bodies. While it is true that the European Court of Human Rights (hereinafter the Court) has considered only a few cases dealing with international trade as such, there is a substantial number of cases related to transnational economic activities of some kind. A more important number of cases deals with economic activities inside a State party to the ECHR without an international dimension. However, it is likely that many of these cases would have been decided in the same way had a foreign economic actor been involved, and to this extent may offer some insights relevant to international trade issues.

As it is mainly companies and not individuals that are involved in international trade, this article first examines the extent to which corporate bodies can invoke the guarantees of the ECHR when faced with an interference by an authority of one of the States parties to the Convention (below, section 1). It then provides a short description of how these rights may be limited in certain cases (section 2). The overview ends with an analysis of how the caselaw of the European Court of Human Rights has created indirect human rights obligations on companies, by imposing a duty on States parties to the Convention to protect individuals whose human rights have been affected by private parties (section 3).

* I would like to thank lic. iur. Mirjam Baldegger, attorney at law, for her valuable assistance in the preparation of this article.

1. Human Rights Entitlements of Companies

1.1. The Principle

Article 1 ECHR obliges States parties to the Convention to "secure to *everyone* within their jurisdiction the rights and freedoms guaranteed by this instrument."[2] According to Article 34 ECHR, individual applications can be received not only "from any person" but, *inter alia*, also from any "non-governmental organisation ... claiming to be the victim of a violation" of ECHR rights by one of the States parties. Thus, private companies and other corporate bodies of a non-governmental character are entitled to invoke the protection of those Convention rights whose ambit is not limited to individuals only[3] and to lodge complaints regarding their violation.

This is not self-evident. According to the tradition of natural law that has so strongly influenced human rights thinking, not only during the age of enlightenment[4] but also in the development of modern international law at the universal level, individuals are the only bearers of human rights. Article 1 of the 1948 Universal Declaration of Human Rights,[5] for example emphasises that "[a]ll *human beings* are born free and equal in dignity and rights."[6] Similarly, Article 2(1) of the 1966 UN Covenant on Civil and Political Rights[7] obliges State parties "to respect and to ensure *to all individuals*"[8] under their jurisdiction the guarantees of the Covenant. It does not mention an equivalent duty vis-à-vis organizations, companies or legal persons. As a consequence, only individuals are entitled, according to Article 1 of the First Optional Protocol to the Covenant,[9] to submit communications to the Human Rights Committee if they claim to be victims of a violation of rights guaranteed by the Covenant.

In contrast, the drafters of the European Convention were clear about the need for human rights protection for companies. During the 1st session of the Consultative Assembly preparing the Convention the Rapporteur asked the question as to whom should be entitled to "appeal to the Court when a guaranteed right or liberty has been violated? Each of the Member States? *Corporate bodies*? Minorities? Individuals?"[10] The answer given was that "[a]ll persons or collective bodies who are victims of a violation of the Convention" should be entitled to submit their complaints,[11] that is, "that the victim, whether an individual, a society or association could bring the case directly" to the enforcement mechanism created by the Convention.[12] Draft Article 12 approved by the Consultative Assembly during its first session[13] thus gave the right to submit petitions to the then created European Commission on Human Rights[14] to "any person, or *corporate body*, which claims to have been the victim of a violation of the Convention by one of the signatory States."[15] In order to clarify that governmental bodies could never invoke human rights protection, the notion of corporate bodies was later replaced with "non-governmental organizations,"[16] but is was never contested that companies would fall within this definition. The drafting history does not reveal the reasons for this openness vis-à-vis the corporate world. However, the strong European constitutional tradition[17] of extending human rights protection to all activities undertaken by free citizens regardless of the legal form chosen was probably so present in the minds of the drafters that they felt no need for further discussion.

In a similar vein, the former European Commission of Human Rights early on decided, without any further explanation, that the right to make an individual application was not only granted by the ECHR to individuals but also to private organizations established according to the applicable domestic law.[18] Thus, for example, the Commission declared in 1975 that "a legal person under English law, a company with corporate capacity ... falls clearly within one of the categories of petitioners set out ... in the Convention as a 'non-governmental organisation.'"[19] Since then, numerous companies have brought their cases to Strasbourg and their right to petition (the former Commission and) the Court has never been disputed, at least as long as they do not exercise governmental functions.

Of course, companies cannot invoke those human rights which, by their very essence, protect individuals only. For obvious reasons, companies cannot claim violations of the right to life, the prohibition of torture and inhuman treatment or the right to marry. Legal persons active in the area of religion are protected by the guarantee of freedom of religion but not freedom of conscience.[20] Other rights, such as the right to a fair trial in the determination of civil rights (Article 6 ECHR), the freedom of expression (Article 10 ECHR), the right to an effective remedy (Article 13) and the right to property (Article 1 First Protocol to the ECHR) are equally important for individuals and for companies.

1.2. Relevance for International Trade

It is the personal scope of application of the ECHR that makes the Convention highly relevant for international trade. According to its Article 1, States parties to the Convention must secure its guarantees to "everyone within their jurisdiction." Therefore, companies from outside Europe can invoke ECHR protection if the authorities of a State party to the Convention allegedly violate their rights while they are operating on the territory of such State. Thus, for example, Air Canada was able to take its case without difficulty to Strasbourg when it felt that the seizure of one of its aircrafts by the British Customs and Excise at

Heathrow Airport violated its property rights.[21] Similarly, in Pressos Compania Naviera S.A. and others, not only European but also Liberian, Malaysian, Japanese, Brazilian and other Non-European ship owners whose ships were involved in accidents in Belgian territorial waters were able successfully to challenge, on the basis of Article 1 Protocol 1 on the protection of property, Belgian legislation barring domestic procedures for damages against both the allegedly responsible pilots and the Belgian State.[22] More generally, both European and non-European importers and exporters operating on the territory of any of the State parties to the ECHR are protected against any kind of interference with their business activities by authorities of such States, regardless of their national origin.

In addition, the ECHR also has a certain extraterritorial application. In the Loizidou case, the Court recalled "that, although Article 1 sets limits on the reach of the Convention, the concept of 'jurisdiction' under this provision is not restricted to the national territory of the High Contracting Parties. [...] In addition, the responsibility of Contracting Parties can be involved because of acts of their authorities, whether performed within or outside national boundaries, which produce effects outside their own territory."[23] This means that State parties must respect the ECHR even when they regulate the behavior of companies abroad, for example because the activities of companies operating abroad have an impact on their own territory. Thus, in the Radio Groppera case[24] a private radio station in Northern Italy was able to challenge the decision by Swiss authorities to prevent the dissemination of its programs in Switzerland. The court has also "accepted that the responsibility of Contracting Parties (...) could, in principle, be engaged because of acts of their authorities (...) which produced effects or were performed outside their own territory,"[25] for example if ships or premises of a foreign company were to be illegally searched abroad by police officers of a State party to the ECHR.[26]

1.3. Relevant Guarantees

The ECHR does not contain a guarantee of free movement of goods, services and capital across borders. Nevertheless, the Convention protects economic actors including companies engaged in international trade in several respects.

Even a cursory look at the case law of the European Court of Human Rights reveals that most cases brought to Strasbourg by economic actors concern alleged violations of procedural rights as guaranteed by *Article 6 ECHR*. This provision grants "a fair and public hearing within a reasonable time by an independent and impartial tribunal" in cases involving a determination of an applicant's "civil rights and obligations or of any criminal charges." Most of these cases concern matters where the judiciary, for example by delaying cases unreasonably or denying equal rights to produce evidence to one of the parties, does not properly fulfil its task to decide and resolve *conflicts among business partners* regarding matters such as non-fulfillment of contracts, torts, protection of property (including patents[27]) against infringements by private actors, or labor related conflicts. Other cases deal with criminal charges in the area of taxes or, more relevant for international trade, of custom duties. For example, in Garyfallou Aebe v. Greece[28] the applicant claimed (although without success) that his case was not heard "within a reasonable time" when he challenged the imposition of a penalty for violation of a prohibition to import certain goods and of his obligation to pay custom duties.[29] Protection under Article 6 is also available to companies doing *business with governments.* Although it has no international dimension, the case of Stran Greek Refineries[30] concerning the violation of procedural rights in a dispute about a contract with the Greek government regarding the construction of an oil refinery, is particularly interesting.

The notion of "civil rights and obligations," as embodied in Article 6 ECHR, does not only encompass "private law" matters in the (continental European) civil law tradition, but extends to administrative law issues pertaining to and affecting the property of private actors and their freedom of contract.[31] This means that even in countries with a strong tradition of purely administrative adjudication,[32] companies have in many cases a right to obtain access to an independent court if an administrative decision affects their business interests. They thus profit from the rule of law and its positive impact on the economy, not only when involved in procedures between private parties about contracts, torts etc., but also when dealing with national authorities who supervise companies,[33] for example by granting, withholding or revoking licenses, imposing prohibitions or penal sanctions and, by doing so, restrict economic activities related to the exercise of "civil rights" in the sense of this provision. In Traktörer Aktiebolag v. Sweden,[34] for example, the Court found a violation of the right to have access to a court for the determination of one's own civil rights (Article 6 para. 1 ECHR) because the legality of the revocation of a license to serve alcoholic beverages could not be examined by a proper court. Article 6 would also have been violated in such a case had the issue been the withholding or revocation of a license to export or import goods or to sell such goods.

Apart from Article 6, some other guarantees of the European Convention have become relevant for corporate bodies. Among these Convention rights, the right to property (Art. 1 Protocol No. 1 to the ECHR[35]) and freedom of expression (Art. 10 ECHR) have become particularly important in the Strasbourg case law. Companies are protected, by Article 1 of Protocol No. 1, *against unlawful taking of property or other infringements of the peaceful enjoyment of their possessions*. This right not only protects "ownership of physical goods" but also "certain other rights and interests constituting assets."[36] Thus, in the case of Beyeler v. Italy,[37] the Court ruled in favor of the applicant, a Swiss arts dealer who could not sell a painting he had acquired in Italy because the Italian State exercised its right of pre-emption in the sale of artistic works of historical and artistic interest in an unlawful manner. In the Pressos Compania Naviera S.A. and Others v. Belgium case,[38] the Court regarded the adoption of a Belgian law, which retroactively limited the liability of a private company offering pilot services, to be a violation of the property rights of several ship owners and mutual insurance companies who had sued the company after its pilots had allegedly caused a series of accidents in Belgian and Dutch territorial waters.

Companies are especially well protected if they belong to the media sector as they can invoke *the guarantee of freedom of expression*. Article 10 (1) ECHR guarantees the right "to receive and impart information and ideas ... regardless of frontiers," and can be invoked by those having purely economic interests in distributing or receiving information or radio or TV programs of any kind.[39] The Court protected, for example, the right of the Swiss company Autronic to receive programs from a Soviet telecommunications satellite by means of a dish aerial during a telecommunications fair by declaring a prohibition by relevant Swiss authorities to be in violation of Article 10. The Swiss authorities argued without success that the broadcasting State had not given its consent, which would have been necessary even though the broadcasts were uncoded and could be received by anyone having the necessary satellite dish.[40] Although such cases concern cross-border services and not international trade, they show the relevance of the ECHR for companies doing business with products that, like books, journals,[41] CDs, films and videos, disseminate communications protected by Article 10.

While these guarantees are important, they protect international trade to a limited extent only. Experiences with implementing the common market in the EU and the liberalization of world trade within the framework of the WTO have shown that discrimination is the main legal problem that economic actors are facing when trying to do business abroad. Until recently, the anti-discrimination provisions of the ECHR were of little avail to them. This is because the primary provision, Article 14, has no independent but only an accessory meaning; that is, it can only be invoked if one of the other human rights guarantees of the Convention is applied in a discriminatory manner. However, this might change in the future since Article 1 of Protocol No. 12 to the ECHR[42] provides that "[t]he enjoyment of any right set forth by law shall be secured without discrimination on any ground such as sex, race, colour, language, religion, political or other opinion, national or social origin, association with a national minority, property, birth or other status." While many of the reasons mentioned in this provision apply to individuals only, national origin[43] and property could also be invoked by corporate bodies.[44] It remains to be seen whether and to what extent this new guarantee becomes relevant for international trade in the near future.

2. Limitations on the Human Rights of Companies

With few exceptions not relevant here, human rights guarantees do not provide absolute protection but may be limited for reasons generally accepted as legitimate in democratic societies. The very idea of granting (the same) human rights to everyone makes it necessary to limit the exercise of these rights at least in situations where their exercise would collide with the rights and protected interests of others. Therefore, Article 29(1) of the Universal Declaration of Human Rights correctly stresses that "[e]veryone has duties to the community in which alone the free and full development of his personality is possible," and allows for limitations that "are determined by law solely for the purpose of securing due recognition and respect for the rights and freedoms of others and of meeting the just requirements of morality, public order and the general welfare in a democratic society."

In the case of companies involved in international trade or services, their economic activities may be restricted especially on the basis of limitations on their right to property. This guarantee can be limited, according to Article 1(2) Protocol No. 1, to the extent necessary "to control the use of property in accordance with the general interest or to secure the payment of taxes or other contributions or penalties." In the Agosi case[45] the Court came to the conclusion that the property rights of a firm trading in gold and silver coins were not violated when the United Kingdom refused to return 1,500 Kruegerrand gold coins minted in South Africa, which had been smuggled into the UK by two men who had defrauded the company. The coins had been seized by customs authorities on the basis of a governmental prohibition on the importation of gold coins from South Africa to the UK. The UK authorities had duly taken into account the degree of fault and carelessness displayed by Agosi and thus had "struck a fair balance between the interests of the State and those of the company."[46] Another application to the Court that was unsuccessful was by the German Gasus Dosier- und Fördertechnik GmbH, a case concerning the seizure by Dutch tax authorities of a concrete-mixer exported to the Netherlands, in the circumstance that the buyer, a Dutch company, had declared bankruptcy at a time when Gasus still was the owner of the mixer according to the applicable law. The Court came to the conclusion that the retention of the concrete-mixer could be justified with valid reasons and, therefore, did not violate the company's right to property.[47] The Court justified the seizure of the concrete mixer with the argument that "a legislature may in principle resort to that device to ensure, in the general interest, that taxation yields as much as possible and that tax debts are recovered as expeditiously as possible."[48]

For economic actors engaged in areas of cross-border communication and mass media, limitations on the freedom of expression are especially relevant. Such restrictions are lawful if "necessary in a democratic society, in the interests of national security, territorial integrity or public safety, for the prevention of disorder or crime, for the protection of health or morals, for the protection of the reputation or rights of others, for preventing the disclosure of information received in confidence, or for maintaining the authority and impartiality of the judiciary" (Art. 10 para. 2 ECHR). In the Radio Groppera case, for example, the Court came to the conclusion that the prohibition on distributing radio programs by cable on Swiss territory was lawful, as Groppera Radio SA had installed itself just across the border in Northern Italy in order to circumvent the Swiss legal provision[49] which, at that time, made it impossible to grant a license to broadcast in Switzerland. The Court held that this prohibition was necessary "for the prevention of disorder" and the protection of the "rights of others."[50] The Court also stressed the relevance of the fact that Radio Groppera's desire to broadcast from Italy into Switzerland without a license was not compatible with the international broadcast regime in force at that time.[51] This last argument shows a certain willingness by the Court to take into account other international law obligations of States parties when assessing ECHR cases and in particular, to consider whether human rights law and principles are being invoked in relation to activities that are not permissible under international treaty law. It should be noted, however, that in cases of a direct conflict between the ECHR and other international treaties, including those on international trade, the Court must accord priority to the Convention. The Court has justified this with the argument that a State party to the ECHR that has also ratified another treaty "is responsible, *ratione materiae* under Article 1 of the Convention [...] for the consequences" of that treaty,[52] if it has "entered into treaty commitments subsequent" to the ratification of the ECHR.[53]

3. Indirect Human Rights Obligations of Companies

Probably the most interesting aspect of the ECHR and the corresponding case law refers to the question whether corporations have any obligation to respect the human rights of third parties in cases where their behavior could have a negative impact upon such rights. This is highly relevant for companies engaged in international trade as some of them may be accused of aiding and abetting human rights violations committed by governmental authorities abroad or even of committing human rights violations themselves.

Of course, according to Article 1 ECHR it is only the "High Contracting Parties" and not private actors that are bound by the Convention. This reflects the traditional European understanding of human rights entitlements that create obligations of the State as holder of the monopoly of power. At the same time, however, Article 1 is not limited to the duty of States to abstain from interfering with the rights and freedoms of the persons under their jurisdiction, but is supplemented by the positive obligation on the State to provide protection to persons whose human rights are violated by other private parties. As the European Court of Human Rights has consistently held, "the responsibility of a State is engaged if a violation of one of the rights and freedoms defined in the Convention is the result of non-observance by that State of its obligation under Article 1 to secure those rights and freedoms in its domestic law to everyone within its jurisdiction."[54] This involves, in principle, a duty to "take measures designed to ensure that individuals within their jurisdiction are not subjected" to human rights violations "administered by private individuals."[55] This creates, in effect, an indirect obligation on private business actors to respect the human rights of others.

In the area of business activities, Article 8 ECHR, which guarantees to everyone "the right to respect for his private and family life," has become especially relevant as the European Court of Human Rights has derived from this provision a duty on States to ensure that private actors refrain from polluting or otherwise negatively impacting upon the environment in a way that harms the health and physical well-being of individuals. In the Lopez-Ostra case, the Court found a violation of Article 8 on the basis that the competent Spanish authorities had failed to intervene when a plant started to treat wastes from animal hide tanneries in a way that produced fumes negatively affecting the health of Ms. Lopez-Ostra and her family. The Court considered that, by remaining passive, the State "did not succeed in striking a fair balance between the interest of the town's economic well-being – that of having a waste-treatment plant – and the applicant's effective enjoyment of her right to respect for her home and her private and family life."[56] Similarly, in Guerra v. Italy, the Court found a violation of Article 8 ECHR because the local authorities had done nothing to assess and reduce the risks of producing certain fertilizers in the vicinity of the town of Manfredonia, even though those risks had been classified as "high" by the central government. The Court stressed "that severe environmental pollution may affect individuals' well-being and prevent them from enjoying their homes in such a way as to affect their private and family life adversely" and that the competent authorities violated the rights of the applicants by not providing them "essential information that would have enabled them to assess the risks they and their families might run if they continued to live at Manfredonia, a town particularly exposed to danger in the event of an accident at the factory."[57] Finally, in the Hatton case, a Chamber of the Court came to the conclusion that the UK was in violation of its duty "to take reasonable and appropriate measures to secure the applicants' rights under Article 8 § 1 of the Convention"[58] when it allowed (the privatized) Heathrow Airport to operate large numbers of night flights without having carefully examined and evaluated the impact of the noise produced by these flights on the sleep patterns of those living nearby.

The case law of the Court regarding such issues is still evolving and leaves many questions unanswered. In the context of international trade, it can be safely assumed that the Court would not tolerate the inaction of State parties if goods were imported from outside Europe that were known to be dangerous for the life, physical integrity and health of individuals using or consuming these goods on the territory of any of these States, or if goods designated for exportation to non-European countries were produced on the territory of a State party to the ECHR in a manner that affected the rights of individuals residing there. It is also clear that the obligations of States are not absolute in this regard. As the reference to the duty "to take reasonable and appropriate measures"[59] shows, the obligation to protect is not absolute; it depends on the knowledge and ability of the authorities concerned to act when the behavior of private actors results in an infringement of the human rights of individuals under their jurisdiction.[60] In contrast, it is doubtful whether the Court would be ready to oblige State parties to provide protection if the goods in question were produced outside of Europe in violation of human rights there. Its case law regarding the issue of extra-territorial application of the ECHR discussed above[61] requires that persons abroad who invoke protection must be under the jurisdiction of the State party concerned. This would not be the case if imported goods were produced in a non-European country, for example, under conditions of slave or forced labor or by prisoners who are victims of political or religious persecution.

4. Conclusion

This short analysis of the case law of the European Court of Human Rights shows that the European Convention on Human Rights is relevant to companies involved in international trade in three respects.

First, companies are protected, in all Member States of the Council of Europe, against violations of those guarantees of the ECHR that, like the procedural rights of Article 6 ECHR or the protection of property in accordance with Article 1 of Protocol No. 1 to the Convention, are applicable not only to individuals but also to corporate bodies. This is true regardless of the national origin of the company concerned as long as it is operating on the territory of a State party to the Convention and thus subject to its jurisdiction. Human rights protection for companies involved in international trade strengthens their position vis-à-vis authorities interfering with their economic activities and incorporates a crucial element of the rule of law into the area of trade across national frontiers. In this regard, human rights and economic interests go hand in hand, and the application of the ECHR strengthens international trade.

Second, companies may be restricted in the exercise of their rights because of limitations that are required to be imposed on them by legitimate public interests or to protect the rights of others. Depending on the case in question, such limitations may either be detrimental to economic interests or promote them by striking a balance between the interests of different participants in the market. One particularly interesting aspect of the case law of the Court is its willingness to accommodate obligations under the ECHR with other international law obligations of States parties by not allowing companies to invoke human rights in order to escape obligations under other international treaties as long as they do not violate such rights.

Third, companies may be indirectly bound by human rights guarantees insofar as the authorities in the country concerned are obliged to protect individuals under their jurisdiction against infringements of their rights by corporate behavior. States have such a duty to protect to the extent that they have or ought to have knowledge of such behavior and can be reasonably expected to take appropriate measures. Regarding trade, this means that companies are not permitted to produce products in a way that violates human rights if the place of production is in one of the States parties to the Convention, nor to import into one of these countries products harming the rights of users or consumers. This duty, in contrast, does not exist, according to current case law, if the victims reside outside Europe, because the obligation of States parties to secure the Convention guarantees does not reach persons that are not under their jurisdiction (Article 1 ECHR). This case law provides an interesting approach to the hotly debated issue of the human rights accountability of corporate actors, as it rests on the sound and uncontested premise that those who have rights have also duties, that is, that the exercise of a right reaches its limits when it violates the rights of others. This approach may contribute to a more objective discussion of this issue as it considers the obligations of companies not as additional duties but as something inherent in their position as bearers of rights. At the same time, the ECHR as a regional convention with a limited geographical scope of application cannot deal with the problem of human rights accountability in cases where products are imported that have been produced outside Europe in ways incompatible with human rights requirements. Such global problems must be solved at the global level.

NOTES

1. Convention for the Protection of Human Rights and Fundamental Freedoms of 4 November 1950 (ETS No. 005), as amended by Protocol No. 11 to the Convention for the Protection of Human Rights and Fundamental Freedoms, restructuring the control machinery established thereby (ETS No. 155).

2. Emphasis added.

3. See below at 1.3.

4. See, e.g., the language of the Virginia Bill of Rights of 12 June 1776: "... all men are by nature equally free and independent, and have certain inherent rights."

5. Universal Declaration of Human Rights of December 10, 1948, GAOR 3rd session, res. 219A.

6. Emphasis added.

7. International Covenant on Civil and Political Rights of December 16, 1966, UNTS, Vol, 999, p. 171.

8. Emphasis added.

9. Article 1 of the First Optional Protocol to the International Covenant on Civil and Political Rights of December 16, 1966 (UNTS Vol. 999, p. 302) empowers the Human Rights Committee "to receive and consider communications from individuals [...] who claim to be victims of a violation [...] of any of the rights set forth in the Covenant."

10. Collected Edition of the "Travaux Préparatoires," Vol. I, The Hague 1975, p. 162, para. 7 [Emphasis added].

11. Id., p. 202, para. 20.

12. Id. 286.

13. 11 May – 8 September 1949.

14. Until the entry into force of Protocol No. 11 to the ECHR on 1 November 1998, victims of an alleged violation of ECHR had to submit their application to the European Commission on Human Rights. The case could only be brought to the European Court on Human Rights after the Commission had declared the application admissible and issued a report about the facts and the law.

15. Article 12 of the draft approved by the Consultative Assembly during the first session, in: Collected Edition of the "Travaux Préparatoires," Vol. VII, The Hague 1985, p. 162 [emphasis added].

16. See the collection of the several draft versions in Collected Edition of the "Travaux Préparatoires," Vol. VII, The Hague 1985, pp. 162–166.

17. See, e.g., the national reports in: Albrecht Weber (ed.), Fundamental Rights in Europe and North America, Part A – Basic Work, The Hague/London/New York 2001.

18. Yearbook of the European Convention on Human Rights 1974, Sixteen Austrian Communes and some of their Councillors against Austria, Decision of May 1974, YB XVII[1974], p. 338 (352).

19. European Commission on Human Rights, Decision on Admissibility, Application 6538/74, 21 March 1975, Yearbook XVIII, p. 202 (230) and Decisions & Reports 2, p. 90 (95).

20. See, e.g., P. van Dijk/G.J.H. van Hoof, Theory and Practice of the European Convention on Human Rights, The Hague/London/Boston 1998, p. 46, referring to European Commission on Human Rights, Application 8282/78, Church of Scientology v. Sweden, Decisions & Reports 21 (1981), p. 109 (110), and Application 11921/86, Verein Kontakt Information Therapie and Hagen v. Austria, Decisions & Reports 57 (1988), p. 81 (88).

21. European Court of Human Rights, Judgment of 26 April 1995, Air Canada v. United Kingdom, Series A 316-A. The Court came to the conclusion that there was no violation.

22. European Court of Human Rights, Judgment of 20 November 1995, Pressos Compania Naviera S.A. and Others v. Belgium, Series A no. 332.

23. European Court of Human Rights, Loizidou v. Turkey judgment of 23 March 1995 (preliminary objections), Series A no. 310, § 62. In Decision on Admissibility by the Grand Chamber of 12 December 2001, Application no. 52207/99 by Vlastimir and Borka Bankovic et. al. against Belgium, the Czech Republic, Denmark, France, Germany, Greece, Hungary, Iceland, Italy, Luxembourg, the Netherlands, Norway, Poland, Portugal, Spain, Turkey and the United Kingdom, Reports and Decisions 2001-XII; the Court clarified that "acts of authorities" have to be understood as governmental acts in the classical sense and, therefore, the responsibility of State parties was not involved when they participated in the bombing campaign against the Republic of Serbia during the 1999 Kosovo crisis.

24. European Court of Human Rights, Judgment of 28 March 1990; Groppera Radio SA and Others v. Switzerland, Series A no. 173.

25. Bankovic case (supra note 23), § 69 referring to Drozd and Janousek v. France and Spain, judgment of 26 June 1992, Series A no. 240, § 91.

26. On the protection of business rooms against searches by Article 8 ECHR see, e.g., European Court of Human Rights, Judgment of 30 March 1989, Chappell v. UK, Series A no. 152-A.

27. See, e.g., European Court of Human Rights, Judgment of 20 November 1995, British-American Tobacco Company Ltd. V. The Netherlands, Series A no. 331.

28. European Court of Human Rights, Judgment of 24 September 1997, Garyfallou Aebe v. Greece, Reports of Judgments and Decisions 1997-V.

29. For another case regarding an alleged violation of procedural rights in the context of penal proceedings for evasion of custom duties see European Court of Human Rights, Judgment of 24 February 1994, Benedoun v. France, Series A no. 284.

30. European Court of Human Rights, Judgment of 9 December 1994, Stran Greek Refineries and Stratis Andreadis v. Greece, Series A no. 301-B.

31. The case law is very rich. For an overview see, e.g., van Dijk/G.J.H. van Hoof (supra note 20), pp. 392 – 406.

32. Traditionally Austria, Switzerland and the Scandinavian countries.

33. Cases regarding alleged unlawful behavior of supervisory administrative bodies include European Court of Human Rights, Judgment of 21 September 1994, Fayed v. UK, Series A no. 294-B; Judgment of 28 August 1991, Brandstetter v. Austria, Series A no. 211; and Judgment of 26 February 1998, Pafitis v. Greece, Reports of Judgments and Decisions 1998-I.

34. European Court of Human Rights, Judgment of 7 July 1989, Traktörer Aktiebolag v. Sweden, Series A no. 159, §§ 47 - 50. Similar, European Court of Human Rights, Judgment of 27 October 1987, Pudas v. Sweden, Series A no. 125-A.

35. Protocol to the Convention for the Protection of Human Rights and Fundamental Freedoms of March 20, 1952, ETS No. 9.

36. European Court of Human Rights, Judgment of 5 January 2000, Beyeler v. Italy, Reports of Judgments and Decisions 2000-I, § 100.

37. Supra note 36.

38. Pressos Compania Naviera S.A. case, supra note 22.

39. European Court of Human Rights, Judgment of 22 May 1990, Autronic v. Switzerland, Series A no. 178, § 47, and Groppera case (supra note 24), §§ 54 - 55.

40. Autronic case (supra note 39), § 63.

41. Cases without cross-border aspects include European Court of Human Rights, Judgment of 11 January 2000, News Verlags GmbH & Co. KG v. Austria, Reports of Judgments and Decisions 2000-I (publication of a picture of a suspected terrorist); Judgment of 26 February 2002, Dichand and Others v. Austria, Application no. 29271/95 (unpublished), (article criticizing a politician); Judgment of 26 February 2002, Krone Verlag GmbH & Co. KG v. Austria, Application no. 34315/96 (unpublished), (publication of a photograph of a member of parliament who allegedly was involved in unlawful conduct).

42. Protocol No. 12 to the Convention for the Protection of Human Rights and Fundamental Freedoms of 4 September 2002, ETS 177.

43. Regarding national origin, the Explanatory Report to Protocol No. 12 stresses, in paragraph 19, that distinctions based on national origin do not constitute discrimination if they are based on "an objective and reasonable justification."

44. The preamble of Protocol refers to "the fundamental principle according to which all persons are equal before the law and are entitled to the equal protection of the law," i.e., a right that can be invoked by corporate bodies, too. The Explanatory Report to Protocol No. 12 does not mention any limitation of the personal scope of application of the Protocol to individuals.

45. European Court of Human Rights, Judgment of 24 October 1986, Agosi v. UK, Series A no. 108, §§ 47 - 62.

46. Id., § 54.

47. European Court of Human Rights, Judgment of 23 March 1995, Gasus Dosier- und Fördertechnik GmbH v. the Netherlands, Series A no. 306-B, §§ 50 - 74.

48. Id., § 66.

49. Radio Groppera's programs were in (Swiss) German with commercials aimed at the Swiss market.

50. Groppera Radio case (supra note 24), §§ 69 - 73.

51. Id., § 70.

52. European Court of Human Rights, Judgment of 18 February 1999, Matthews v. UK, Reports of Judgments and Decisions 1999-I, § 33 regarding the ratification of the Maastricht treaty.

53. Id., § 34.

54. European Court of Human Rights, Judgment of 25 March 1993, Costello-Roberts v. UK, Series A no. 247-C, § 26.

55. European Court of Human Rights, Judgment of 10 May 2001, Z and Others v. UK, Reports and Decisions 2001-V; § 72 referring to the A. v. the United Kingdom judgment of 23 September 1998, Reports of Judgments and Decisions 1998-VI, § 22.

56. European Court of Human Rights, Judgment of 9 Dec. 1994, Lopez-Ostra v. Spain, Series A No.303C, § 58.

57. European Court of Human Rights, Judgment of 19 February 1998, Guerra and Others v. Italy, Reports of Judgments and Decisions 1998-I, § 60.

58. European Court of Human Rights, Judgment of 2 October 2001, Hatton and Others v. UK, § 95. The decision had been appealed to the Grand Chamber of the Court (Art. 43 ECHR) at the time of this writing. On 8 July 2003 the Grand Chamber confirmed the principle but concluded that the UK had not violated its duty to protect (Judgement of 8 July 2003, Hatton and Others v. UK, Application no. 36022/97, ECHR-VIII).

59. Hatton case, (supra note 58), § 95.

60. Very clear in this regard is the case law regarding the duty to protect the right to life. See European Court of Human Rights, Judgment of 28 October 1998, Osman v. United Kingdom, Reports 1998-VIII, §§ 115.

61. Supra, text accompanying note 23.

CHAPTER 14

The Use of Trade Instruments in the Pursuit of Human Rights: European Foreign Policy

Krista Nadakavukaren Schefer

Introduction

Although there is not much that one can say definitively about the relationship between trade and human rights, it is safe to assume that it is highly complex. I want to assert this apparent banality merely to bring to the forefront of our consciousness something that scholars presumably know, but often tend to repress when writing about this topic. It would be folly simply to *conclude* that the trade-human rights relationship is based on the two elements of reduction of trade barriers and protection of human rights, and proceed to debate whether or not human rights protection will "lead to" or "follow from" liberalized trade. The implications of a multi-faceted trade-human rights relationship cannot be understood without extending our horizons beyond those of trade law or human rights law, or perhaps even of international law altogether. As a result, I think the important question to discuss is how can we pursue the goal of ensuring that the protection of human rights accompanies a trade regime. The broader implications of this topic are profound, extending to the questions of:

- how trade instruments can be used to increase the protection of human rights;
- how the elements of liberalized trade relationships and the protection of human rights work together; and
- whether the relationship between the liberalization of trade and the protection of human rights can rationally be studied in isolation from deeper cultural/sociological studies. This may in turn require an examination of political, philosophical, geographic, economic, and cultural factors in any specific case – something the legal community will need to look outside itself to do.

While the present paper is essentially limited to the first of these questions, the other implications remain as background to inform the chosen approach. Specifically, the goal of the following is to identify the instruments used by the European Community and its Member States to try to secure the protection of individual rights outside European territory, while taking into account the political and structural constraints of the Community's legal framework.

Growth of the Protection of Human Rights as a Policy within Europe

Treaty of Rome 1957

In reviewing the foreign policy instruments of the European Community (EC) in the realm of trade and human rights, it is important to emphasize the extent to which the EC itself has *evolved* into a community committed to the protection of human rights within its own territory – a commitment that is not solely connected with the economic aspects of the Common Market. The Treaty of Rome, establishing the European Economic Communities (EEC) in 1957, made only indirect reference to human rights.[1] These can be found in its substantive Articles – first in Article 7 (non-discrimination on account of nationality)[2] and also in Article 119 (equal pay for equal work by men and women).[3]

More important than the treaty's failure specifically to identify non-discrimination as a human right is the treaty's lack of *intention* to set out the non-discrimination principle as a human right. The Treaty of Rome, as a legal instrument establishing a common market and progressively approximating the economic policies of Member States,[4] was distinctly focussed on economics and the elimination of market-distorting measures. Discrimination that was not based on grounds specific to a particular type of employment was seen in that context, quite simply, as inefficient. It is true that Article 2 of the 1957 Treaty provided:

> "The Community shall have as its task, by establishing a common market ..., an accelerated raising of the standard of living and closer relations between the States belonging to it ..."[5]

However, the goal of a higher standard of living was more directed at ensuring an adequate food supply in Post-War Europe than at the protection of second- much less third-generation human rights.[6] Indeed, the provision regarding the maintenance of labor standards is explicit in its reason for existence:

> "Member States agree upon the need to promote improved working conditions and an improved standard of living for workers, *so as to make possible their harmonization* while the improvement is being maintained."[7]

Thus, like the GATT 1947, the Prologue of which contains the statement that the Contracting Parties agree to the obligations "[r]ecognizing that their [trade] relations ... should be conducted with a view to raising the standards of living," the Treaty of Rome as originally in effect was little more than a trade agreement, either in fact or in aim.

Maastricht 1992

By the 1990s, however, the value the Member States placed on human rights had increased greatly. Not suprisingly, the agenda on trade liberalization both inside the Community and externally with third countries was influenced by this development.[8] When the EEC Member States and heads of government met in Maastricht in late 1991 through early 1992, the result was an elaborate new structure for European integration. Emerging from Maastricht was a dual treaty superstructure composed of the Treaty on European Union and the Treaty Establishing the European Community. Together these agreements paved the way for the ever-closer bonding of foreign economic policy to the pursuance of international protection of human rights based on an ethical conviction of the worth of the individual.[9]

The Maastricht Treaty contains an Article 2 that is slightly different from Article 2 of the Treaty of Rome as originally in effect. While there are only four additional words in the Maastricht version, they are noteworthy, as they offer a significantly different perception of the scope of the aims of the European Community. The current provision states:

> "The Community shall have as its task, by establishing a common market ..., the raising of the standard of living *and quality of life*, and economic and social cohesion ..."[10]

This text clearly distinguishes not just the means-end relationship of the common market and collective well-being (which the original text did as well), but it recognizes that quality of life – as well as the standard of living – must be enhanced through the economic integration. This perception of what organizational success means is at least a part of what in the long run has allowed the EC external trade regime to develop so differently from the World Trade Organization's regime. While the latter is concerned with an *objective and quantitative* measuring of its Member states' economic indicators (such as standard of living) to judge its success, the EC has to make a *qualitative* assessment, determining whether the lives of individuals are becoming *subjectively* better, that is, whether they are *more enjoyable* than before. The seemingly slight shift of focus from standard of living to quality of life that the EC Treaty makes prevents freer trade from being mistaken as an end in itself – trade is instead more clearly seen as the instrument that it is, capable of being exchanged, in full or in part, if it is discovered not to be achieving its given goals.

This recognition of economic integration as a goal towards subjectively better quality of life is much more important than any claims of cultural homogeneity within Europe or the more complete disappearance of trade barriers within the EC for the analysis of the differences between EC and World Trade Organization (WTO) views on the trade-human rights problematic. Of course (and this goes back to implication no. 3 above), the EC (and particularly the EU) does strive to create a community while the WTO does not. And membership to the European Union is explicitly founded on the protection of and respect for human rights,[11] while WTO membership is not.[12] Certainly, within the EC there are policy-practice discrepencies with the Community's (as well as among the Member States' individual) committment to the protection of human rights. However, regardless of what the EC *actually does* in relation to human rights violators,[13] there is still a textual legal basis that provides internally for what the EC's externalization of human rights protection does in its relations with third countries.

European Community Legal Instruments for the Protection of Human Rights

In the annex, there are excerpts from several different instruments framing European human rights law as well as several conditioning EU economic relations with third states on the third states' human rights practices.

Membership Qualifications

One of the most effective instruments possessed by the EU to further human rights externally is the use of human rights protection as a qualification for membership.[14] The Treaty on European Union[15] itself bases membership on adherence to the common principles of liberty, democracy, respect for human rights and fundamental freedoms, and the rule of law.[16] Thus, for all potential accessor states, these qualifications must be fulfilled before membership can be granted (and, once granted, violations of these principles can be grounds for a revocation of the privileges of membership).[17] The common principles are, in turn, incorporated as political conditions in the Accession Partnership agreements concluded between the EU and accession candidates. Known as the Copenhagen Criteria (after the Copenhagen European Council of 1993 where they were set forth as official policy), membership requires that accessors have

> "achieved stability of institutions guaranteeing democracy, the rule of law, human rights, and respect for and protection of minorities, … a functioning market economy … [and] presupposes the … ability to take on the obligations of membership …"[18]

Moreover, the common principles provide that "[t]he European Council will continue to follow closely progress in each associated country towards fulfilling the conditions of accession to the Union and draw the appropriate conclusions."[19]

The accession partnership agreements[20] set forth as Principles the Copenhagen criteria, and then determine short, medium and long-term objectives (based on the country's specific needs and internal conditions) to bring the country into fulfillment of the criteria. The EU promises financial and advisory assistance in implementing the necessary changes, but, importantly, there is also a Conditionality provision, requiring the accessor to fulfill its commitments under the Agreement in order to ensure its remaining a receiver of EU financial assistance.[21]

Conditionality in Partnership and Cooperation Agreements

At almost the same time as Maastricht codified attention to the individual's welfare within the Community, commitment to human rights became an explicit basis for EC cooperation with non-accession third countries. As of 1992, human rights provisions stating, for example, that the respect for democratic principles is an essential element of the agreement, appear in all of the European general[22] economic partnership agreements. While conditionality already appeared in the Lomé IV Convention of December 1989,[23] and although individual treaties in the early 1990s also referred to democracy and human rights protection, it was not until a couple of years later that the use of human rights clauses in external agreements became a condition of the agreement. In addition, the provisions' text became (more or less) standardized. EU bilateral and regional trade treaties contain clauses both in the Preamble and in the introductory substantive provisions (usually as Article 1) emphasizing respect for democracy and for the protection of human rights. This is true for Agreements with states in the *MEDA* programme (see, for example the Association Agreement between the EC and Morocco),[24] the *Phare* project (see, for example, the proposed Stabilization and Association Agreement with Macedonia),[25] and the

Tacis programme (see, for example, the Interim Agreement on Trade and Trade-Related Matters between the EC et al. and Uzbekistan);[26] programs for financial assistance as well as for EC-non-European country partners (see the various agreements between the EC and Latin American countries. The Economic Partnership, Political Coordination and Cooperation Agreement between the EC and Mexico is a typical example of this kind of agreement.[27] While the essential goal of the Agreement is to strengthen commercial and economic relations by means of the liberalisation of trade,[28] political dialogue based on the principles of democracy and human rights is an integral part of those strengthened relations.[29] Here, in contrast to NAFTA, for example, is the connection between trade and individual rights recognized and the agreement made firmly to rest on *both* trade *and* human rights principles.

In addition to such bilateral or regional agreements, the EU has a range of economic policy instruments which it can use to threaten, reprimand, or sanction human rights violators. There is, for example, the African, Caribbean and Pacific Group of States Partnership Agreement (Cotonou Agreement) of June 2000, and its satellite Partnership Agreements.[30] The Cotonou Agreement is unlike the other trade agreements in that its goals are poverty eradication, sustainable development, and the establishment of a stable and democratic political environment[31] rather than those of establishing a market economy or of deepening economic relations, although the latter set of goals are to be supported within the framework of the Partnership. Within the ACP Partnership Agreements the promotion and protection of human rights and democracy are explicitly set forth as both goals and bases of the agreement, with the Partnership conditioned on the active and demonstrable pursuit of these goals by the partner government (the text reads, for example, in the Council Common Position on Nigeria, "The EU considers the following as key areas for future EU support: (a) Development of a democratic culture: ...").[32]

Preferential Trade Agreements

Another tool for reconciling trade and human rights goals is the Generalized Tariff Preferences Regulation of 1998 (for preferences through the end of 2001).[33] This scheme, in place in various forms since 1971, is considered a part of the EC's development policy, offering tariff-free or low-tariff entry of different types of goods for low-income countries.[34] Of particular note is the Special Incentive Arrangements Concerning Labour Rights contained in Title II, Section 2 of the Regulation[35] (there is a parallel Special Incentive Arrangement Concerning Environmental Protection in Section 4 of the same Title[36]). These arrangements permit countries to benefit from further reductions in tariffs when the officials of those countries can prove that they (1) have domestic legislation providing for the right to organize and for collective bargaining and for a minimum working age; (2) have attempted to enforce such legislation and punish violators; and (3) take responsibility for administering the special arrangement.

The proposal for the 2002-2004 GSP scheme would alter the special incentive arrangement programs, among others.[37] In essence, the proposed changes would simplify and increase the general preferential benefits as well as grant duty-free access to nearly all products from least developed countries; ease the present requirement that a beneficiary country certify that all inputs of eligible products stem from labor-friendly processes; and increase the labor protection requirements to an adherence to ILO Conventions Nos. 29 (Forced Labor), 100 (Equal Remuneration for Men and Women), 105 (Prohibition of Forced Labor), 111 (Sex/Race/Religious/Political Opinion/Social Origin Discrimination in Hiring or Occupation), and 182 (Worst Forms of Child Labor) as well as to the previously imposed requirement of compliance with ILO Convention Nos. 87, 98, and 138.

Policy Instruments

While not related to trade, several further foreign policy instruments are worthy of mention, as they are often invoked in support of human rights.[38] These include three types of joint protest tools employed in pursuit of the Common Foreign and Security Policy (CFSP).[39] One of the tools of joint protest is that of the Public Statement made by the CFSP. These statements are simply condemnations of human rights abuses in other countries or expressions of praise regarding improvements in the human rights conditions in other countries.[40] A second instrument is that of the Public Démarches, a public, collective submission by Member States to a government expressing concern about a specific occurrence or condition in a third country, often accompanied by a call for action by the respective government.[41] The third instrument is the Private Démarche. This type of démarche remains confidential between governments and is consequently often the protest tool of choice for the CFSP, which claims that the confidentiality prevents the target government from hardening its position to protect its honor.[42] Critics counter that the privacy of such communications prevents the international community from learning about the issue and joining in the protest.[43] The European Parliament in particular is sceptical of private démarches, because it is unable to monitor the CFSP's actions in pursuance of human rights when such actions are kept secret.[44]

Economic and Diplomatic Sanctions

Finally, there is the possibility of imposing economic and diplomatic sanctions on countries that violate human rights.[45] In the EC, the use of economic sanctions is complicated by the duality of the Community/Member State authority structure. For trade embargos, as opposed to other economic sanctions, the Community itself must impose the relevant measures. For less severe/serious economic measures (such as arms embargos) or diplomatic sanctions (such as a refrain from military cooperation, the revocation of diplomatic visas, freezing of financial assets, or the suspension of cultural and technical cooperation), Member State measures are required. Although the Treaty on European Union created two instruments to harmonize Member State foreign policy with the Union's foreign and security policy (itself explicitly dedicated to furthering democracy, the rule of law, and the protection of human rights), Joint Actions[46] and Common Positions[47] do not change the legal structure of the Member State-Union relationship. Thus, conflicts in interest remain a stumbling block for forging a unified sanctions approach. The main difference brought about by the Joint Action/Common Position approach is that now conflicts are played out in the decision whether or not to enact a sanctions policy at all rather than allowing each Member State to choose for itself whether or not to impose sanctions.

Weaknesses in the EC's Use of Trade Instruments to Protect Human Rights

The strength of the European commitment to the protection of human rights outside of as well as within the Union is commendable and has many adherents. Yet, it would be incomplete to neglect to mention some of the weaknesses of the EC's instruments for tying economic relations to the establishment of democracy and the protection of human rights, as these weaknesses are exploitable by those with an interest in avoiding overly-strong attention to the human rights practices of certain governments. The partnership agreements and other bilateral or regional trade relations agreements, for example, can only be used to ensure the protection of human rights if there is the political will to invoke the conditionality clauses. This will is often absent, whether for economic reasons (for example because of the need to maintain oil supplies from Africa or the Mid-East) or for political reasons. Moreover, as Philip Alston and J. H. Weiler note, the emphasis on the promotion of democracy and rule of law, while praiseworthy in itself, is often the sole area of attention in such agreements.[48] Protection of other rights, particularly economic and social rights, by partnership members is too often ignored by the EU.[49] Finally, the multiplicity of bilateral partnership and trade agreements has resulted in a multiplicity of programs devoted to the development of democratic governance. This plethora of obligations and initiatives itself endangers the EU's ability actively to pursue a committed policy on human rights protection.[50]

Under preferential trade arrangements the weaknesses are similar. In addition, it is particularly significant that, while the EC Special Incentives Arrangement for labor rights is explicitly tied to ILO Conventions 87, 98, and 138, the EC itself retains the sole authority to decide if the Conventions are being implemented in the beneficiary country.[51] Thus, it is within the EC's political discretion to grant or withhold, or extend or cancel the benefits of this program. This would be different if the ILO itself were requested to make this decision, or at least to offer guidance to the EC in evaluating the evidence in question. However leaving the decision on whether to continue aid to a country that is, for example, violating (albeit not flagrantly) the Minimum Age Convention (ILO Conv. 138) to the EC opens the possibility that one of the Member States with an influential import lobby will block any critique of that country.

On the use of policy instruments, the use of private démarches, as already mentioned, has the disadvantage of not offering anything upon which to evaluate the intensity, frequency, or success of pursuing human rights violators.[52] Indeed, the CFSP's Annual Memorandum to Parliament, recording the use of statements and démarches, lends credence to the worst fears of the Parliamentarians by not mentioning several human rights violators at all nor giving the details of actions taken, or the results achieved in several other cases.[53]

It is in the area of sanctions that the EC's foreign policy in pursuit of human rights is most open to criticism. Certainly, if one advocates the effectiveness of using sanctions to achieve policy goals,[54] the history of European Community sanctioning sheds a different light on the European pursuit of human rights than does its economic agreements. As one commentator writes:

> "In a handful of cases between 1970 and 1993, the Twelve were able to agree that a violation of human rights was so serious that it called for a response going beyond the submission of a *démarche* or condemnation at the United Nations. However, the Twelve agreed on sanctions only in response to a handful of atypical cases; the vast majority of human rights abuses, no matter how egregious, attracted no more than criticism."[55]

While the EC has obediently implemented the collective sanctions programs required by the UN Security Council under Chapter VII of the UN Charter, the implementation of unilateral sanctions has more often than not been blocked at the Community level by individual Member States or, when implemented, have been either too late[56] or in a form so weak[57] that no appreciable changes could have been expected. The introduction of the joint action and the common position instruments have had little effect in hastening or strengthening the resolve to use economic sanctions, as each requires a unanimous acceptance by the Member States to come into effect,[58] and in the absence of a Common Position, the Member States act independently within both the Community and in the UN system.

Conclusion

Rectifying the theory and practice of the European Community/Union on the universal protection of human rights must become a priority if the commitment of Europe is to remain a model for the rest of the international community. Yet, despite the practical failure of the Community to enforce its externalization provisions, the model is one to emulate, if only because it offers an explicit text on which to build.

NOTES

1. Treaty Establishing the European Economic Community, opened for signature March 25, 1957, (found in *Office for Official Publications of the European Communities,* 115 [3d abr. ed. 1987]) (entered into force January 1, 1958) [hereinafter "Treaty Establishing the EEC (1957)" or "Treaty of Rome as originally in effect"].

2. Id., Article 7. Article 7 of the Treaty Establishing the EEC (1957) reads, in relevant part, "Within the scope of this Treaty, … any discrimination on grounds of nationality shall be prohibited. …"

3. Id. Article 119. Article 119 of the Treaty of Rome reads, in relevant part, "Each Member State shall … maintain the application of the principle that men and women should receive equal pay for equal work."

4. Id. Article 2.

5. Id.

6. Discussion with Eric Evtimov, LL.M, July, 2001.

7. Treaty Establishing the EEC (1957), Article 117 (Emphasis supplied).

8. Note that Philip Alston and Joseph Weiler regard the strong emphasis on human rights in the EU foreign policy area as a "paradox", contrasting sharply with the near "abdication" of responsibility for the strengthening of human rights within the Union. Philip Alson and J. H. H. Weiler, "An

'Ever Close Union' in Need of a Human Rights Policy: The European Union and Human Rights" in Philip Alson, ed., The EU and Human Rights 3-66, 6-7 (Oxford: Oxford Univ. Press, 1999).

9. See The Treaty on European Union, containing the Treaty Establishing the European Community, (in effect as of November 1, 1993). The Treaty Establishing the European Community [hereinafter "Maastricht Treaty"] changed the EEC to the EC, altering numerous procedural norms and deepening integration within the Community. The Treaty on European Union [hereinafter "TEU (Maastricht)"], created a "union among the peoples of Europe," by establishing common political goals and competences external to the EC in the areas of Foreign and Security Policy and Justice and Home Affairs. Stephen Weatherill and Paul Beaumont, EC Law: The Essential Guide to the Legal Workings of the European Community, 2d ed. 10-11 (London: Penguin Books, 1995).

10. Maastricht Treaty, Article 2.

11. Article 7, Treaty on European Union (Amsterdam version). See also Article 7, Treaty on European Union (Nice version, unratified) (amending TEU Article 7, Amsterdam, easing the threshhold for determining the existence of a serious and persistent breach by a Member State from unanimity to a four-fifths majority of the Council).

12. The Marrakesh Agreement Establishing the World Trade Organization ("Marrakesh Agreement"), Article XII sets out the membership criteria for accessionary members of the WTO: "Any State or separate customs territory possessing full autonomy in the conduct of its external commercial relations and of the other matters provided for in this Agreement and the Multilateral Trade Agreements may accede to this Agreement, on terms to be agreed between it and the WTO. ..." (Marrakesh Agreement, Article XI:1). There is the additional condition that two-thirds of the existing Member States accept the application for accession. Id., Article XI:2. The original Members of the WTO were simply taken over from the GATT Contracting Parties (with the addition of the European Communities), with the sole condition of acceptance of all the agreements and schedules. Id., Article XI.

13. Here I am not intending to belittle discrepancies between words and actions in pursuit of human rights, but rather I merely want to establish a framework for analyzing EC-WTO differences. The discrepancies become very important when one begins to try to incorporate human rights protections within the WTO.

14. See generally, Manfred Nowak, "Human Rights 'Conditionality' in Relation to Entry to, and Full Participation in, the EU" in Philip Alston, ed., The EU and Human Rights 687-698 (Oxford Univ. Press: Oxford, 1999).

15. References to the Treaty on European Union hereinafter refer to the consolidated version accepted after the 1996 intergovernmental conference in Amsterdam, unless indicated otherwise. See Treaty of Amsterdam Amending the Treaty on European Union, the Treaties establishing the European Communities and Certain Related Acts, Oct. 2, 1997, O.J. (C 340) 145 (consolidated version).For more on the changes wrought at Amsterdam, see Paul Craig and Gráinne de Búrca, EU Law: Text, Cases, and Materials, 2d ed. 32-46 (Oxford: Oxford University Press 1998).

At time of writing, the TEU version resulting from the meetings in Nice (2000) was not valid.

16. TEU Art. 6(1), incorporated by reference into Art. 49.

17. TEU Art. 7. See also footnote 3, supra.

18. iii, The Copenhagen Criteria – Presidency Conclusions, European Council, Copenhagen, 21-22 June 1993.

19. Id.

20. See, e.g., the Annex to Council Decision of 30 March 1998 on the principles, priorities, intermediate objectives and conditions contained in the accession partnership with the Republic of Slovenia, 98/268/EC; OJ L 121, 23/04/1998 p. 0046-0050.

21. Id., Annex, 5:

"*Conditionality*. Community assistance will be conditional on respect by Slovenia of its commitments under the Europe Agreement, further steps towards satisfying the Copenhagen process in implementing this accession partnership. Failure to respect these general conditions could lead to a decision by the Council on the suspension of financial assistance on the basis of Article 4 of Regulation (EC) No 622/98."

22. Commodity-specific trade agreements do not have such provisions.

23. Fourth ACP-EEC Convention, Lomé, December 15, 1989.

24. Euro-Mediterranean Agreement establishing an association between the European Communities and their Member States, of the one part, and the Kingdom of Morocco, of the other part, Art. 2 ("Respect for the democratic principles and fundamental human rights established by the Universal Declaration of Human Rights shall inspire the domestic and external policies of the Community and of Morocco and shall constitute an essential element of this Agreement").

25. Stabilizations and Association Agreement with Macedonia, Article 2:

"Respect for the democratic principles and human rights as proclaimed in the Universal Declaration of Human Rights and as defined in the Helsinki Final Act and the Charter of Paris for a New Europe, respect for international law principles and the rule of law as well as the principles of market economy as reflected in the Document of the CSCE Bonn Conference on Economic Co-operation, shall form the basis of the domestic and external policies of the Parties and constitute essential elements of this Agreement."

26. Interim Agreement on trade and trade-related matters between the European Community, the European Coal and Steel Community and the European Atomic Energy Community, of the one part, and the Republic of Uzbekistan, of the other part, OJ L 043, 14/02/1998 p. 0002-0019, Art. 1:

"Respect for democracy, principles of international law and human rights as defined in particular in the United Nations Charter, the Helsinki Final Act and the Charter of Paris for a New Europe, as well as the principles of market economy, including those enunciated in the documents of the CSCE Bonn Conference, underpin the internal and external policies of the Parties and constitute an essential element of this Agreement."

27. OJ L 276, 28/10/2000 p. 0045-0079.

28. Id., Article 2.

29. Id., Article 3.

30. Partnership Agreement between the Members of the African, Caribbean and Pacific Group of States and the European Community and its Member States, Cotonou, June 23, 2000.

31. Id., Article 1.

32. See also Council Decision of 25 June 2001, wherein Partnership Agreement consultations with Côte d'Ivoire were concluded because of a "lack of openness" of elections and "acts of violence carried out against civilians throughout the period of democratic transition."

33. EC No 2820/98 of 21 December 1998; OJ L 357/1 (30 December 1998). See also EC No 416/2001 of 28 February 2001, amending the GSP system so as to allow duty-free access without quantitative restrictions to least developing countries; OJ L 60/43 (1 March 2001).

34. See generally, Barbara Brandtner and Allan Rosas, "Trade Preferences and Human Rights" in Philip Alston, ed., The EU and Human Rights 699-723 (Oxford Univ. Press: Oxford, 1999).

35. OJ L 357/7.

36. OJ L 357/8-9.

37. Proposal for a Council Regulation applying a scheme of generalised tariff preferences for the period 1 January 2002 to 31 December 2004, COM(2001)293 final; 2001/0131(ACC).

38. The following discussion on the three "joint-protest" policy instruments is based on the description found in an excellent article by Toby King, "Human Rights in European Foreign Policy: Success or Failure for Post-modern Diplomacy?" 10:2 Europ. J. Int'l L. 313 (1999). See particularly id. at 316-318.

39. The CFSP is the successor to the former European Political Cooperation (EPC), which ended as of the coming into effect of the Treaty on European Union. See generally, TEU Title V. The TEU Articles 11 and 12 set out the goals of the CFSP:

"*Article 11* – 1. The Union shall define and implement a common foreign and security policy covering all areas of foreign and security policy, the objectives of which shall be:

- to safeguard the common values, fundamental interests, independence and integrity of the Union in conformity with the principles of the United Nations Charter;
- to strengthen the security of the Union in all ways;
- to preserve peace and strengthen international security, in accordance with the principles of the United Nations Charter, as well as the principles of the Helsinki Final Act and the objectives of the Paris Charter, including those on external borders;
- to promote international cooperation;
- to develop and consolidate democracy and the rule of law, and respect for human rights and fundamental freedoms.

2. The Member States shall support the Union's external and security policy actively and unreservedly in a spirit of loyalty and mutual solidarity.

The Member States shall work together to enhance and develop their mutual political solidarity. They shall refrain from any action which is contrary to the interests of the Union or likely to impair its effectiveness as a cohesive force in international relations.

The Council shall ensure that these principles are complied with.

Article 12 – The Union shall pursue the objectives set out in Article 11 by:

- defining the principles of and general guidelines for the common foreign and security policy;
- deciding on common strategies;
- adopting joint actions;
- adopting common positions;
- strengthening systematic cooperation between Member States in the conduct of policy."

For more on the CFSP, see Andrew Clapham, "Where is the EU's Human Rights Common Foreign Policy, and How is it Manifested in Multilateral Fora?" in Philip Alston, ed., The EU and Human Rights 627-683 (Oxford Univ. Press: Oxford, 1999) (including a description, history, practical effect, and critique of the various foreign policy instruments of the CFSP).

40. King, supra note 38 at 317.

41. Id.

42. Id. at 318.

43. Id.

44. Id.

45. See also discussion in King, supra note 38, at 322-324.

46. TEU Article 14:

"1. The Council shall adopt joint actions. Joint actions shall address specific situations where operational action by the Union is deemed to be required. They shall lay down their objectives, scope, the means to be made available to the Union, if necessary their duration, and the conditions for their implementation.

...

3. Joint actions shall commit the Member States in the positions they adopt and in the conduct of their activity."

47. TEU Article 15:

"The Council shall adopt common positions. Common positions shall define the approach of the Union to a particular matter of a geographical or thematic nature. Member States shall ensure that their national policies conform to the common positions."

48. Alston and Weiler, supra note – at 36-37; Bruno Simma, Jo Beatrix Aschenbrenner, and Constanze Schulte, "Human Rights Considerations in the Development of Co-operation Activities of the EC" in: Philip Alston, ed., The EU and Human Rights 571-577 (Oxford Univ. Press: Oxford, 1999).

49. Id. at 37.

50. Id.

51. EC No 2820/98, Article 13.1, OJ L 357/7:

"The Commission shall decide ... either to grant the special incentive arrangements ... or, if it considers that the requesting country's legislative, implementing and monitoring provisions do not ensure effective application of ILO Conventions No 87, No 98 and No 138, not to grant them."

52. See supra, notes 42-43 and accompanying text.

53. See, generally CFSC Annual Report 1999-2000, Section 3.1 ("EU Instruments and Initiatives in Relations with Third Countries"); see particularly id. at Section 3.1.4 ("Démarches/Declarations"):

"During the period covered by this report, besides the démarches on the death penalty (see section 1.5), démarches concerning human rights have been made inter alia in *Afghanistan, Algeria, Angola,* to the *Palestinian Authority,* in *Belarus, China, Columbia, India, Indonesia, Iran, Laos, Malaysia, Pakistan, Russia, Tanzania, Turkmenistan, Turkey, Uzbekistan* and *Vietnam.*"

54. Admittedly, many authors are not of this opinion. See, e.g., Richard N. Haass, Sanctioning Madness, Foreign Affairs 1996/1997, contained on the USA Engage website (www.usaengage.org) (Haass does not dispute that sanctions are sometimes effective, but disagrees with the frequency and manner in which they are being used); Robert A. Pape, Why Economic Sanctions Do Not Work, 22 Int'l Sec., Fall 1997, at 90; Abram Chayes & Antonia Chayes, The New Sovereignty: Compliance with International Regulatory Agreements (1995); Philip Alston, "International Trade as an Instrument of Positive Human Rights Policy" 4 Human Rights Q. 155 (1982); Simma, Aschenbrenner, and Schulte, supra note 48 at 578-582.

55. King, supra note 38 at 324.

56. Notable is the tardiness of Community sanctions against South Africa – it was not until September 1986 that the economic measures (ban on new investment, import prohibition on Krugerrands, iron, and steel) were put into effect on the Community level. King, supra note 38 at 322-323.

57. E.g., sanctions against China following the 1989 Tiananmen Square incident were limited in scope (Member States agreed to take measures to end military cooperation and impose an arms embargo, and to suspend cultural exchange programs, extend student visas for Chinese students in the Member States, and not support new World Bank credits) and lifespan (the sanctions were being phased out by Autumn 1990). King, supra note 38 at 323. See also Council Common Position of 29 October 2001 extending and amending Common Position 96/635/CFSP on Burma/Myanmar, OJ L 286/1 (2001/757/CFSP), Article 1 (banning the issuance of visas to officials and relatives of the Burmese executive, military, and tourism administration, with an exception for attendance at UN meetings and providing for waiver for the Minister for Foreign Affairs through an unanimous decision of the Member States that such waiver "is in the interests of the European Union").

58. TEU Article 23.1 ("Decisions under this Title shall be taken by the Council acting unanimously ...").

CHAPTER 15

International Trade and Human Rights in Africa: A Comment on Conceptual Linkages

Sisule Fredrick Musungu[*]

I. Introduction

Globalisation has meant different things to different people. To some it means increased growth, opportunity and prosperity, while to others it denotes an orgy of greed and inequality. In the context of human rights, globalisation has been seen by some as promoting human rights while others see it as negatively affecting efforts at the promotion and protection of human rights. Both human rights and trade rules set limitations on what states can do. However, trade rules and the idea of economic liberalization may also mean that the rules set limitations on what states can do in terms of welfare policies which are inextricably linked to socio-economic rights. From this perspective, globalisation has been seen as promoting what have been called "market friendly human rights while negatively affecting rights related to distributive justice. Inherently, civil and political rights are critical in ensuring the rule of law and in imposing checks on governmental power in relation to administrative and judicial activities that affect trade.

African governments and people are today more resolute about regional and continental goals of economic co-operation and integration in a quest to benefit from the processes of globalisation. In the last two decades or so there has been a marked expansion in regional economic blocks in Africa. At the same time, botha normative framework and institutions for human rights protection have been established. This comment focuses on how the legal developments in economic law and practice have taken into account developments in human rights and vice versa. The comment reviews particular conceptual linkages between the rules and operations of the regional economic institutions in Africa and human rights, primarily as conceptualized under the African Charter on Human and Peoples' Rights (the African Charter). In particular, the comment examines whether there are tensions and convergences between re-

* The views expressed in this comment are the personal views of the writer and do not necessarily reflect the views of the South Centre, its Member states or developing countries.

gional economic law and human rights law in the various instruments that form the normative framework of these two legal regimes.

II. An Overview of the African Human Rights and Economic Integration Regimes

A. The African Human Rights Regime

In the main, human rights norms have developed at three levels; international, regional and municipal. In Africa, under the auspices of the Organization of African Unity (OAU), various regional instruments have been devised to meet the challenges of promoting and protecting human rights. The main regional instrument is the African Charter. There are three other basic instruments which, together with the African Charter, comprise the normative framework of the African Human rights system: the Protocol to the African Charter on the Establishment of an African Court on Human and Peoples' Rights; the African Charter on the Rights and Welfare of the Child; and the OAU Convention Governing the Specific Aspects of Refugee Problems in Africa. There is also a draft Protocol to the African Charter on the Rights of Women. The comment will however concentrate on the African Charter as the primary human rights instrument in Africa.

The African human rights regime became a reality in 1981[1] when the Assembly of Heads of State and Government of the OAU adopted the African Charter, making Africa the third region after Europe and the Americas to put in place a regional intergovernmental system for human rights protection and the second after the 1966 UN conventions.[2] The African Charter recognizes the three generations of human rights but develops a rather novel concept by placing all of these rights on the same footing and, in particular, by treating the first and second generation rights as inseparable and equal. Essentially, the Charter departs from the general trend in international human rights instruments of providing for the first and second generation rights in separate instruments and thus makes a clear statement about the indivisibility of human rights by treating them side by side in a single document.[3] The obligation of the state parties to recognize the rights, duties and freedoms under the Charter therefore implies that the state parties recognize all three generations of rights as conceptualized under the Charter and not as separate and distinct rights.[4] In theory, therefore, the African human rights regime conceptualizes the three generations of rights as interdependent and indivisible.

Apart from the concept of indivisibility and interdependence, there are two other important features of the African Charter worth mentioning in the context of this comment. The first is the concept of individual duties and the second is the use of "clawback" clauses. In addition to guaranteeing rights, the African Charter imposes duties not only on the state but also on the individual.[5] However, it is not clear what sanctions are available for failure to fulfill the individual duties, a position which has led some human rights advocates and scholars to argue that the inclusion of duties only serves as an invitation to states to impose unlimited restrictions on the enjoyment of rights.[6] So far the jurisprudence of the African Commission on Human and Peoples' Rights (the Commission) does not shed any light on the effect of individual duties. It remains to be seen whether the African Court, once established, will take up this challenge.

The rights recognized under international human rights law are not absolute or enjoyable in all circumstances. In relation to some rights and in some circumstances limitations may be imposed. A distinguishing feature of the African Charter is however its use of "clawback" clauses as opposed to the more traditional derogation clauses. The distinction between the two is that derogation clauses set out the extent and conditions under which the right may be limited or its enjoyment restricted, whereas clawback clauses subject the rights to state discretion.[7] Essentially, the clawback clauses in the African Charter have the effect of subjecting the Charter's rights to limitations imposed by domestic law.[8] In the context of the present discussion, the clawback clauses may be used to enable trade considerations to supersede human rights rules, particularly where trade courts are called upon to apply human rights rules under the African Charter without a proper evaluation of the reasonableness of the measures pursuant to human rights rules.

B. Regional Economic Integration

In Africa regional economic integration has taken place both at the continental level and at the sub-regional level. At the continental level, under the auspices of the OAU and now the African Union (AU), there is the African Economic Community (AEC), which establishes a continental economic block.[9] At the sub-regional level, there are four main economic groupings, namely: the Common Market for Eastern and Southern Africa (COMESA); the Southern Africa Development Community (SADC); the Economic Community of West African States (ECOWAS); and the revived East African Community (EAC).[10] Several countries have overlapping memberships in the different arrangements. The sub-regional economic blocks are seen as the building blocks upon which the AEC will ultimately be based, in line with the 1980 Lagos Plan of Action and the Final Act of Lagos which envisaged African economic integration as an evolutionary and incremental process. The regional economic blocks generally share the common goals of economic transformation and development.

III. Trade and Human Rights in Africa: Conceptual Linkages

There are various instances where the African economic treaties make specific reference to human rights. Most of the instruments establishing the various economic groupings in Africa, particularly those created after the African Charter, explicitly refer to the promotion of human rights either as an objective or as a fundamental principle of the economic system. Apart from the direct references, there may also be other provisions that are closely linked to human rights concepts. For example, although at the time of the formation of the Organization of African Unity (OAU) there was no African human rights system, the OAU Charter makes reference to the Universal Declaration of Human Rights (UDHR) as an objective of the organization.[11]

The AEC treaty establishes the recognition, promotion and protection of human and peoples' rights in accordance with the African Charter as a fundamental principle of the economic system it establishes.[12] In similar fashion, the COMESA treaty also establishes the recognition, promotion and protection of fundamental human rights as a key principle of the system in addition to liberty, fundamental freedoms and rule of law.[13] The EAC treaty under Article 6 establishes good governance, democracy, rule of law, equality and the recognition, promotion and protection of human and peoples' rights, in accordance with the provisions of the African Charter, as fundamental principles. The EAC goes even further by requiring that any other states (apart from Kenya, Uganda and Tanzania) wishing to become a member must be seen to adhere to universally acceptable principles of good governance, democracy, rule of law and observance of human rights and social justice. The ECOWAS treaty follows the same approach as AEC, COMESA and EAC, and ordains the recognition, promotion and protection of human and peoples' rights in accordance with the provisions of the African Charter as a fundamental principle of the economic system.[14] The SADC treaty, although making no direct reference to the African Charter, also commits members to the fundamental principle of human rights, democracy and rule of law.

At the textual level, it is fair to conclude that the African economic groupings tacitly recognize human and peoples' rights as conceptualized under the African Charter as fundamental principles of the trade regimes. There is thus a clear conceptual linkage between the regional economic system and the human rights system. Specific reference to the provisions of the African Charter implies that all three generations of human rights are considered fundamental in the formulation and implementation of trade rules. This may diverge from the idea of developing a core category of rights that must be recognized in the trade rules and in their interpretation. There however remains a question whether the trade institutions are designed to address distributive justice.

All four sub-regional economic communities, together with the AEC, establish courts of justice along the lines of the European Court of Justice.[15] The sub-regional regimes also tacitly acknowledge the overarching principles and objectives of the AEC. Direct reference to the African Charter in the various economic treaties in Africa would, at least in theory, mean that the courts of Justice and tribunals are bound directly to apply human rights rules in determining trade disputes. In that sense, the African Charter could be seen as a kind of Bill of Rights for the African regional economic systems. Whether this potential is materialized will depend on the judges and lawyers practicing in these courts, but one can clearly say that there exist very clear entry points for the application of human rights principles in trade matters. At the same time, the tacit reference to the African Charter should permit the African Human Rights Court and the African Commission to apply a human rights test to governmental economic decisions which fail to take into account human rights. In addition, with the power to interpret the African Charter reposed in the African Court of Human and Peoples' Rights and the African Commission, interpretations of the African Charter by the two bodies will bind the trade courts when faced with questions of interpreting economic principles in light of the African Charter.

IV. Human Rights and Bilateral Trade Arrangements in Africa

There are numerous bilateral and multilateral economic initiatives, particularly with donor countries, that also provide useful insights into the relationship between international trade and human rights in Africa. The major initiatives in the recent past include the Cotonou Agreement, the African Growth and Opportunity Act (AGOA)[16] and the New Partnership for Africa's Development (NEPAD). These documents, along similar lines as the World Bank and IMF conditionality, refer in one way or another to human rights concepts and have significantly affected the relationship between human rights and trade in the African context. A detailed analysis of human rights in the context of bilateral trade arrangements in Africa is beyond the scope of this comment. For present purposes the question is whether reference to human rights in bilateral trade agreements corresponds to the concept of human rights in the African Charter.

The United States (US) and the European Union (EU) in particular have adopted a system of conditioning economic aid on improvements in human rights and also conditioning trade privileges on human rights practices. In some cases trade sanctions have been applied as a mechanism to ensure observance of human rights.[17] However, the concepts most commonly referred to are the rule of law and democratic governance, concepts that are more related to the first generation of human rights. The basic theory has been that where human rights are protected, open markets will flourish, as stability and rule of law are ensured. In particular, protection of civil and political rights has been seen as a necessary prerequisite for democratic governance which promotes trade and market access. It is therefore fair to say that in bilateral trade Agreements human rights have been approached from the context of their relevance to the administration of trade. A brief overview of the various arrangements bears out the point.

The Cotonou Agreement: In its preamble, the Agreement refers literally to all the main UN human rights instruments including the Covenant on Economic, Social and Cultural Rights, to the European Convention on Human Rights, the African Charter and the American Convention. Its predecessor, Lomé IV, also referred to human rights and democracy. Good governance, respect for human rights, democratic principles and the rule of law are singled out as essential elements of the partnership. By expressly acknowledging the rights in the UN Covenant on Economic, Social and Cultural Rights and the African Charter, the Cotonou Agreement can be said to approximate the general approach of the African regional economic groupings. In reality however, there remains a pervading categorization particularly when one examines the substantive provisions of the Agreement.

The African Growth and Opportunity Act: AGOA is part of the US Trade and Development Act 2000. The Act contains AGOA and the US-Caribbean Basin Trade Enhancement Act. The legislation establishes a framework that will govern future negotiations between the US and African Countries. The approach here is related to broader participation in political process and political freedom and the typical rule of law notion.[18] A better picture of the approach can be gleaned from an examination of the eligibility requirements.[19] African countries will be eligible to participate in the programme if they ensure the protection of private property rights, the rule of law, political pluralism, due process, and recognition of workers' rights. In the area of private property in particular there would be an inevitable clash if African governments insisted on the application of human rights as conceptualized under the African Charter. For example, the tensions that exist between the protection of intellectual property rights and health would be resolved in favour of the right to health since the African Charter recognizes the right to health but does not explicitly recognize intellectual property rights.

NEPAD: This initiative is intended to help in the eradication of poverty and promote sustainable growth and development to ensure the full participation of Africa in the world economy. As has been the case on many occasions, the African leadership undertook to promote democracy and human rights. However, in specific terms the undertaking is to develop standards of transparency, accountability and participation, a concept based on the traditional view of human rights in the market economy.

V. Conclusion

African economic treaties overwhelmingly recognize and acknowledge the promotion and protection of human and peoples' rights, as conceptualized under the African Charter, as fundamental principles of continental trade relations. In that context, it can be concluded that there exist clear conceptual linkages between regional economic trade rules and human rights rules in Africa. It will be critical to observe how seriously the regional trade courts take human rights considerations into account in the adjudication of trade disputes and in the interpretation of the economic treaties. Bilateral trade arrangements also clearly recognize the interlinkages between trade rules and human rights, although the approach in these arrangements is at variance with the concept of human rights embodied in the African Charter. The predominance of civil and political rights in the bilateral arrangements may run counter to the approach under African economic rules, especially where economic, social and cultural rights come into play and balancing is required, as in the case of intellectual property rights and health. While more work and research will be needed to establish the exact interrelation between trade rules and human rights in Africa, especially in practical terms, there exist very clear and promising entry points for integrating human rights into the economic rules, institutions and practices.

NOTES

1. The Charter was adopted on 17th June 1981 at Nairobi. See OAU document OAU/CAB/LEG/67/3/Rev. 5. The text of the Charter is reprinted in 3 I.L.M. (1964) p. 1116. The OAU had earlier in 1969 adopted the Convention on the specific Aspect of the Refugee problem in Africa 8 I.L.M 1288(1969).

2. The International Covenant on Civil and Political Rights (ICCPR) and International Covenant on Economic Social and Cultural Rights (ICESCR). Both Covenants were adopted by Resolution A/RES/2200A.

3. See F.J. Viljoen, "Review of the African Commission 1986-1997" vol. 2, p. 50 (unpublished). It is important to note however that the African Charter does not contain the full catalogue of civil and political rights and socio-economic rights as set out under the 1966 UN Conventions.

4. Art. 1 of the Charter.

5. See Article 29. While the African Charter is the first human rights document to meaningfully articulate the concept of combining individual rights and duties in the same instrument the idea is not entirely without precedent; see for example M. wa Mutua, "The Banjul Charter and African Cultural Fingerprint: An Evaluation of the Language of Duties" 35 *Virginia Journal International Law* (1995) p. 364.

6. See M. wa Mutua supra.

7. R. Gittleman, "The Banjul Charter on Human and People's Rights: A Legal Analysis." C.E. Welch and R. Melzer, eds., *Human Rights and Development in Africa* (1984) p. 154.

8. Viljoen op. cit. n. 3. The phraseology of the clawback clauses includes phrases such as except for reasons and conditions previously laid down by the law – within the law – provided one abides by the law – in accordance with the law.

9. The African Union is the successor of the OAU. The AEC treaty was signed in Abuja in 1991.

10. Other regional economic initiatives designated as pillars of the AEC are the Economic Community of Central African States (ECCAS) and the Arab Maghreb Union (AMU).

11. See Article 2(1) c.

12. Article 3(g) & (h).

13. See Article 6.

14. Article 4.

15. Only SADC has a tribunal which is not christened a court of justice.

16. Trade and Development Act of 2000. H. R. 434.

17. The latest example is the sanctions against Zimbabwe.

18. See Section 102(7), 103(5) and 103(7).

19. Section 104.

CHAPTER 16

Integrating Trade and Human Rights in the Americas

*Frank J. Garcia**

I. Introduction

This paper analyzes the relationship between the OAS Inter-American human rights system and several regional integration systems including NAFTA, MERCOSUR and the proposed Free Trade Area of the Americas (FTAA). Broadly speaking, there are two models for the relationship between integration systems and human rights protection: the leverage model and the incorporation model. The leverage model involves making effective participation in extrinsic human rights systems a legal or political condition of integration system membership.[1] The incorporation model focuses on the juridical interpenetration of the two systems at many levels. The degree of such interpenetration can range from the simple recognition that trade agreements already include "economic" human rights such as the protection of rights to capital and intellectual property,[2] to the inclusion of a full-blown human rights protocol within the integration treaty system itself.[3]

This paper will focus on the leverage model, as it applies or may apply to the American hemisphere. Such inquiry involves addressing two questions: first, to what extent has membership in hemispheric integration systems been used to leverage more effective human rights protection; and second, to what extent *should* such leverage be developed as part of the evolution of hemispheric integration. The paper concludes, first, that the existing relationship between trade and human rights in the Americas follows the leverage model, but only to a limited extent, and primarily between trade and democracy, rather than human rights more broadly conceived. The operative assumption seems to be that linking trade privileges, either legally or politically, to the maintenance of democratic forms of government, is tantamount to addressing the human rights aspect of trade. For linkage to have occurred even at this level, the economic and political pressure of a major market power such as the US or the EU has been necessary. Moreover, this approach has been carried forward into the FTAA

* The author would like to thank Professor Jo Pasqualucci and the 2001 World Trade Forum participants for their valuable comments. The paper has been updated through January 2004.

negotiations, which have tended to focus on democracy more than traditional human rights.

Linking trade to formal democracy, while desirable and to some extent successful in the hemisphere as this paper will show, is not adequate to address the range of human rights challenges facing the hemisphere.[4] In view of the fact that the OAS Inter-American system exists as a promising *legal* venue for human rights protection, this paper also concludes that hemispheric efforts to strengthen the relationship between trade and human rights should focus instead on linking membership in the emerging FTAA system with effective participation in the OAS system.[5] Since the U.S. does not even *participate* in the OAS system, further integration between trade and human rights in this hemisphere will therefore require strategies for overcoming U.S. resistance to the OAS system.

II. The OAS Human Rights System: A Framework for the Americas

A. OAS Texts and Institutions

The protection of human rights in the American hemisphere is part of the mission of the Organization of American States, the world's oldest regional organization.[6] The core of the human rights system is set out in three texts: the OAS Charter (hereafter the Charter),[7] the American Convention on Human Rights, adopted in 1969 under the auspices of the OAS (hereafter the Convention),[8] and the American Declaration on the Rights and Duties of Man, adopted in 1948 (hereafter the Declaration).[9]

The Charter itself does not include the protection of human rights *per se* as one of the purposes of the OAS, which is largely static and non-interventionist in character. OAS Member States do, however, proclaim "the fundamental rights of the individual without distinction as to race, nationality, creed or sex" to be a principle of their cooperation.[10] Although OAS Member States retain the right to develop their own cultural, political and economic life "freely and naturally," they remain bound in doing so to "respect the rights of the individual and the principles of universal morality."[11]

Specific human rights provisions are brought within the ambit of the Charter by the Declaration, a resolution adopted in 1948 by the Ninth International Conference of American States. The Declaration is a catalogue of human rights guarantees resembling in style the Universal Declaration, which it predates. The Declaration was brought into the OAS system through the Protocol of Buenos Aires and the Statute of the Commission, which establish the Declaration as an authoritative interpretation of the nature of human rights obligations attendant to OAS membership.[12] As such, it is of particular importance in determining the human rights obligations of OAS members not parties to the Convention.[13]

The Inter-American Convention is the core of the human rights protection system in the Americas. The Convention sets forth an extensive system of civil and political rights, enforced through the operation of two bodies, the Inter-American Commission on Human Rights (hereafter the Commission), and the Inter-American Court of Human Rights (hereafter the Court).[14]

The Commission is both an organ of the OAS and a treaty body of the Convention.[15] The principal function of the Commission is to promote the observance and protection of human rights throughout the OAS membership, and it is the consultative body of the OAS for these purposes. The Commission principally discharges this function in two ways: by preparing country reports on the status of human rights in each of the member countries, and by the examination of individual petitions. The reports, while not binding, do serve to organize public opinion and create political pressure. More importantly, the fact that individual petitions against States party to the Convention can be referred to the Court for binding decisions gives this aspect of the Commission's work increasing prominence.

The Court is the judicial organ of the OAS with authority to interpret and apply the Convention in both contentious and advisory cases.[16] Although the Court is young[17] and its non-advisory jurisdiction limited to cases referred by the Commission involving states-parties which have accepted the Court's contentious jurisdiction,[18] the Court has played an increasingly active role in hemispheric human rights matters, and has issued some important judgments.[19]

If the Court determines that a right protected under the Convention has been violated, the Court may order that the violation be remedied, and can order a range of remedies including both specific injunctive relief and compensation for the victim.[20] Such decisions are final and binding, and are enforceable through the OAS General Assembly.

B. Human Rights Protection as a Function of OAS Membership

All of the American states are members of the OAS. As such, they are all subject to the basic obligation to respect human rights set forth in the Charter, although this is minimal at best. OAS membership does, however, subject states to the Declaration, being an authoritative interpretation of their human rights obligations as parties to the OAS charter. This is not as promising as it seems, since the Declaration itself is not accompanied by an effective enforcement mechanism.

The primary vehicle for human rights protection through the OAS is the Commission and Court system established to enforce the Convention. Considering its well-documented limitations,[21] the Court has achieved significant successes.[22] Nevertheless, despite the promise of the basic system, Convention membership is not a condition for OAS membership.[23] In fact, only 25 of 34 hemispheric states have ratified the Convention,[24] and only 17 of these have accepted the compulsory jurisdiction of the Court.[25] Among the signatories that have not ratified, the United States stands out, since it is the undisputed leader of the American hemisphere and has been a strong advocate of Convention ratification on the part of other hemispheric states.[26] However, this opposition is unfortunately not an aberration. As Smith chronicles, the U.S. has a long history of resistance to participation in multilateral human rights systems,[27] most recently displayed in its failure to support creation of the International Criminal Court.

Turning from the question of human rights protection to the broader issue of democratic governance, membership in the OAS does commit states to the OAS' mandate to "promote and consolidate representative democracy," but of course "with due respect for the principle of non-intervention."[28] Recently, this commitment has been strengthened by adoption of the Inter-American Democratic Charter, which permits OAS Member States to suspend any state found to have undergone an "unconstitutional interruption of the democratic order."[29] The Democratic Charter follows a series of political initiatives in the OAS linking membership with democratic governance, most notably the Protocol of Washington and the Santiago Declaration committing OAS states to democratic principles,[30] and Resolution 1080 calling for an emergency meeting of the OAS foreign ministers to decide upon a collective response to any interruptions of democratic governance among the membership.[31]

Due to U.S. non-participation and the lack of widespread acceptance of the Court's jurisdiction, the OAS system remains a work-in-progress. However, with respect to multilateral human rights systems in the Americas, it is the only game in town. For these reasons, efforts to increase effective human rights protection in this hemisphere should focus on strengthening the OAS system, in particular by increasing its membership and the degree of acceptance of the Court's compulsory jurisdiction.[32] Contemporary developments in regional economic integration may offer opportunities in this respect.

III. Human Rights and Hemispheric Trading Systems

In assessing the status of human rights in this hemisphere's regional trading systems, this paper will focus on NAFTA and MERCOSUR. Since their collective membership includes the United States, Canada, Mexico, Argentina, Brazil, and Chile, these two systems together include the bulk of the hemisphere's GDP and the states most active in the FTAA hemispheric integration process.

It should also be recalled that this paper is evaluating the trade-human rights relationship according to the leverage model only. Thus, while both NAFTA and MERCOSUR contain numerous trade-related provisions which could also be construed as provisions protecting economic human rights, this aspect of the agreements will not be addressed.[33] Similarly, this paper will also not address the allegations that trade agreements such as NAFTA in fact /themselves *contribute* to human rights problems, such as the immigration and environmental degradation problems at the U.S. – Mexico border.[34]

A. NAFTA

As hemispheric leaders and, in the case of the U.S. and Canada, advanced liberal democracies, one would hope that the NAFTA states would also lead in the process of linking trade with human rights. At a minimum, one must accept that whatever stance these states do in fact adopt with respect to the issue will exert a strong influence throughout the hemisphere. Unfortunately, leadership on the issue of human rights and trade on the part of the U.S., Canada and Mexico has not been strong, in particular in the case of the United States. The relationship between NAFTA and human rights is in many respects a lost opportunity.[35]

1. Formal Links

The text of NAFTA does not establish any formal linkages between free trade and human rights or democracy. Workers' rights are mentioned in the preamble, and are the subject of a related agreement (discussed below), but no formal links are established in the treaty for existing members. With respect to new members, NAFTA's accession provision makes it clear that the terms of any NAFTA accessions, and therefore the inclusion of any human rights conditions, are political matters to be worked out between the parties at the time of accession.[36] The text does not impose human rights obligations, or formal conditions of any kind.[37]

a. Trade and Human Rights

Formally speaking, participation in the OAS human rights system is not a requirement of NAFTA membership, although as a practical matter all current NAFTA members are also parties to the OAS Charter. Given the roster of OAS members, this will be true for any forseeable NAFTA accession. However, as discussed above, Charter party status only entails the minimal level of human rights protection required by the Charter and Declaration.

Turning to the more substantive protections offered through the OAS Convention, there is certainly no formal requirement that NAFTA members be parties to the OAS Convention. On the contrary, the U.S. is probably the most notorious of the OAS members *not* to ratify the Convention, although Canada is also not a party. Curiously, of the three NAFTA states, only Mexico is a party to the Convention, although it does not accept the Court's contentious jurisdiction.[38]

All three NAFTA parties are also parties to the so-called "Labor Side Agreement," the North American Agreement on Labor Cooperation, or NAALC.[39] By subjecting the protection of certain domestic labor rights to international enforcement, the NAALC does to some extent link trade and human rights. However, the link is a weak one.[40] The NAALC essentially obligates each party only to the enforcement of its own domestic labor laws.[41] Moreover, only a subset of those domestic rules (minimum wage, child labor and workplace safety rules) can be the subject of an international enforcement action, and such an action is capable of resulting in trade sanctions only in extreme cases.[42]

2. Political Conditionality

a. Trade and Human Rights

There is no stated political expectation that current or future NAFTA members maintain any minimum levels of human rights protection as a condition of their good standing in or admission into the NAFTA system. Informally, the US is active in monitoring Mexico's human rights record, but this has not been stated publicly as a condition of Mexico's NAFTA membership.

b. Trade and Democratic Governance

With respect to the broader question of "democratic governance," there is likewise no stated political expectation that NAFTA parties maintain democratic forms of government.[43] Nevertheless, it can be inferred from the stance taken by the U.S. with respect to the FTAA process that maintaining a formally democratic system would be a requirement for future NAFTA membership. It must be remembered, however, that this is formal democracy only – Mexico's negotiation of the NAFTA at a time when it could be called democratic only in a strictly formalist sense is evidence of the wide latitude with which this requirement has been and may well be imposed.

The clearest example of political conditionality is the current U.S. policy towards Cuba, which has not been included in FTAA negotiations. Therefore, to the extent that one can associate communist states with human rights abuse, and the link is far from straightforward and unproblematic, this approach can be viewed as a human rights condition.[44]

B. MERCOSUR

The relationship between trade and human rights/democracy in MERCOSUR is closely linked with two issues: political instability within Paraguay, and MERCOSUR's ambitions with respect to partnership with the European Union. Both factors, together with broader participation in the OAS system among MERCOSUR states, have led to a stronger formal relationship between trade and human rights in MERCOSUR than in NAFTA, despite the poorer human rights record among MERCOSUR members.

1. Formal Links

The principal text of the MERCOSUR system, the Treaty of Asuncion,[45] does not establish any formal links between party status and human rights/democracy, either for MERCOSUR members or for new parties. However, the Protocol of Ushuaia, discussed below, does establish a formal link between MERCOSUR trade benefits and democratic governance.

a. Trade and Human Rights

OAS membership is not a prerequisite for MERCOSUR membership. However, as is the case with NAFTA, all current MERCOSUR members are OAS members, and that will continue to hold true as MERCOSUR expands. As discussed above, however, the human rights protection this entails is minimal, subjecting MERCOSUR parties only to the Charter and Declaration.

As with NAFTA, Convention membership is not a formal requirement of MERCOSUR membership. However, in contrast to NAFTA, all MERCOSUR members (Argentina, Brazil, Paraguay and Uruguay) are parties to the American Convention, as are associates Chile and Bolivia. More importantly, Argentina, Paraguay, Uruguay, Chile and Bolivia all accept the jurisdiction of the Court, Brazil being the only (but significant) exception.[46] Thus, a clear *de facto* link between MERCOSUR membership and effective participation in the OAS system is established.

b. Trade and Democratic Governance

With respect to the broader link between trade and democratic governance, MERCOSUR states have adopted a democracy clause as part of the MERCOSUR treaty system. In the "Protocol of Ushuaia" of 24 July 1998, the MERCOSUR states, as well as Bolivia and Chile, agreed that the maintenance of democratic institutions is a fundamental condition of MERCOSUR integration.[47] The protocol sets out a consultation framework to be followed whenever there is a breach of democratic order (not defined) in a MERCOSUR state, and envisions the imposition of sanctions upon the breaching state ranging from suspension of participation in MERCOSUR organs to suspension of MERCOSUR membership itself.[48] Full rights and privileges are to be restored when the sanctioning states are satisfied that democratic order has been re-established.

The Protocol grows out of a tradition of political linkage related to Paraguayan instability, discussed below. However, the Protocol goes farther than its predecessors, both in institutionalizing the political consultation mechanism as part of the Treaty of Asuncion, and in clarifying that the democracy clause is to be part of any future integration agreements between MERCOSUR and Chile and Bolivia, thus making adherence to the democracy clause a condition of future accessions.

The level of commitment to the Protocol on the part of the MERCOSUR states was recently put to the test. In 1999 Paraguay again plunged into political turmoil with the assassination of vice president Luis Maria Argana, rumored to have been the work of then-president Raul Cubas and his political master, General Oviedo.[49] MERCOSUR leaders immediately reminded Paraguay, and the world, that should the assassination lead to a full-scale coup, Paraguay would be suspended from MERCOSUR pursuant to the Protocol of Ushuaia.[50]

Instability continued, and a subsequent coup attempt in May of 2000 against the care-taker government of Luis Gonzalez Macchi prompted strong condemnation by MERCOSUR officials.[51] The coup failed, and MERCOSUR action was once again credited with helping to foil the coup attempt.[52] MERCOSUR heads of state reaffirmed their commitment to the Protocol of Ushuaia at their next summit, the December 2000 meeting in Florianopolis, Brazil.[53]

2. Political Conditionality as Background to Formal Linkage

The Protocol is the latest in a series of MERCOSUR actions expressing political commitment to democracy. The Protocol builds on earlier expressions of a political nature, most importantly the 1992 and 1996 presidential declarations highlighting democracy as an essential condition of MERCOSUR integration.[54]

A key motivating force behind these expressions of support for democracy has been the chronic political instability in Paraguay. In April of 1996, Paraguayan president Juan Carlos Wasmosy survived a coup attempt on the part of the Paraguayan military, also led by General Oviedo. A key factor in the military's stand-down was the statement by MERCOSUR heads of state that such a coup would lead to a suspension of Paraguay's rights as a MERCOSUR country, and a total embargo by MERCOSUR states of land-locked Paraguay's imports and exports.[55]

It was in response to this situation that the MERCOSUR presidents made the San Luis Declaration at their June 1996 annual summit, which affirmed the bloc's commitment to democracy and announced that sanctions would follow any breach of democratic order.[56]

3. Role of MERCOSUR-EU Negotiations

The second major factor in MERCOSUR's process of political and formal linkage between trade and democracy/human rights has been the evolution of MERCOSUR-EU relations. On the part of the EU, its role in conditioning cooperation with MERCOSUR on democracy and human rights is consistent with its overall commitment to democracy and human rights as an aspect of its program of bilateral and regional cooperation agreements.[57]

It is interesting that Paraguay, of all states, should also have attained early prominence in EU-MERCOSUR relations, since Paraguay has been such a "stimulant" to the development of MERCOSUR's own trade and democracy/human rights policy. In February 1992 the EC and Paraguay entered into the first MERCOSUR-EU cooperation agreement, grounding mutual cooperation in the continued observance of democratic principles and human rights.[58] Later that same year the Commission of the EC signed an agreement for institutional cooperation with the MERCOSUR states as a whole, but this agreement was limited to technical economic and institutional matters.[59]

In April of 1995 the EC and MERCOSUR agreed to begin negotiations towards formulation of an agreement on trade and cooperation.[60] On the part of the EC, approval of the negotiating mandate was expressly conditioned on respect for human rights and democratic principles, and on the condition that any accord would be suspended in the event those principles were compromised.[61] This same linkage was expressed in the EU's own commitment to broader political cooperation with MERCOSUR, issued later that year,[62] a commitment which led to the negotiation of a framework agreement in September of 1995 establishing an inter-regional association between the EU and MERCOSUR.[63] Uruguayan officials, speaking for MERCOSUR, noted that the agreement was "based on the respect for human rights, democratic principles and the rule of law within MERCOSUR…"[64] When this agreement was formally adopted by MERCOSUR and EU heads of state in Madrid in December, 1995, both sides highlighted the centrality of MERCOSUR's commitment to human rights and democratic principles as a cornerstone of the agreement.[65]

The preamble to the MERCOSUR-EU treaty of cooperation cites their common commitment to democratic values, the rule of law, and the promotion of human rights.[66] More importantly, Article 1 of the treaty clearly establishes respect for democratic principles and fundamental human rights, as set forth in the UDHR, as the basis for their cooperation.[67]

The treaty does not refer to participation in the OAS system, nor does it directly subject MERCOSUR member states to European human rights obligations. However, it does affirm the centrality of human rights to MERCOSUR's economic cooperation with Europe, and obligates MERCOSUR states to maintain democratic governments and pursue domestic and international policies in keeping with fundamental human rights. Otherwise, Article 35 makes clear that a separate, distinct ground for termination of the agreement is "a violation of those essential elements of the agreement referenced in Article 1 [democracy and human rights]."[68]

The Cooperation Agreement would quickly play an important role in stabilizing MERCOSUR politics. In 1996, four months after the signing of the Cooperation Agreement, the first of the two Paraguayan coup attempts occurred, and the MERCOSUR parties quickly warned Paraguay that it would be suspended from MERCOSUR unless democratic governance was restored, an act which not incidentally would also preserve the future economic benefits of EC cooperation. The possibility that a successful coup in Paraguay would endanger MERCOSUR's much sought-after economic cooperation with the EC was definitely a factor motivating the other MERCOSUR governments in their decisive response to the Paraguayan crisis.[69]

Attempts at managing the Paraguayan situation with an eye to European cooperation continued even after the risk of the coup had passed. The EU-MERCOSUR ministerial the following year highlighted MERCOSUR's San Luis Declaration on Democratic Commitment, issued in June 1996 in response to the Paraguayan crisis. The EU's official press release following the ministerial lauded the San Luis Declaration as reaffirming the centrality of human rights and democracy as the basis for the EU-MERCOSUR accord.[70]

Since that time, MERCOSUR has continued to conduct a regular public relations campaign to bolster the impression in European eyes of the central importance of democracy and human rights in its integration system.[71] In doing so, MERCOSUR officials used several other regional and international challenges to democracy as a platform/occasion on which to adopt statements affirming the centrality of democracy and human rights to MERCOSUR. Within the hemisphere, for example, the end of the Fujimori regime in Peru and the constitutional crisis it initiated was carefully and publicly monitored by Argentina and other MERCOSUR states,[72] which together cited with approval the election of President Valentin Paniagua Corazao as a step towards "Peru's full return to democratic stability and normalcy."[73]

Outside the hemisphere, the controversy in Europe over the formation of the Heider government in Austria offered another opportunity for MERCOSUR states to articulate their stance on the relationship between trade and democracy/human rights. In February of 2000 the MERCOSUR states, together with Bolivia and Chile, issued a statement under the leadership of Argentina which reaffirmed their view that democratic institutions and the protection of human rights are essential conditions for the development of any integration process.[74] MERCOSUR's statement with respect to European integration is particularly ironic given the role which the EU has played in the development of MERCOSUR's own position.

Despite these public statements and formal links, it is fair to say that the MERCOSUR approach to trade and human rights keeps the issue somewhat at arm's length from the core of the integration process as a domestic matter. For example, in December of 1999 a group of relatives of "disappeared" Argentinean human rights victims proposed the creation of an "Office of Human Rights" in MERCOSUR to investigate past human rights abuses by member states, thereby expressly linking human rights with the MERCOSUR institutional apparatus.[75] However, the proposal was not acted upon.

Recognizing that human rights in the MERCOSUR states continue to be at risk, and that the MERCOSUR trade/human rights linkage, while significant, remains underdeveloped, interested parties within MERCOSUR and the EU have pressed for more aggressive leverage.[76] In connection with ongoing EU-MERCOSUR negotiations on further trade liberalization, international and Latin American human rights NGOs have called upon the EU to include explicit human rights proposals in the negotiations, which might translate the general statements of political support into concrete action programs.[77] Also in connection with these negotiations, the European Parliament has called for an agreement which makes reference to specific mechanisms to guarantee strict observance of human rights and democratic principles as essential elements of the new relationship,[78] a development that suggests a similar impatience on the part of this progressive body to see rhetoric translated into accountability and action at this next level.

C. Other Regional Trading Systems

MERCOSUR's own course of development has taken place in a larger regional context, with the formation of new formal and political linkages involving many of the region's other trading systems such as the Central American Common Market (CACM) and the Andean Common Market (ANCOM), also in several cases with EU involvement.

1. Formal Links

At the treaty level, in June 2000 the heads of state of the five ANCOM members adopted the Act of Lima, a measure intended to establish a broad work program to revitalize Andean integration and implement the Andean common market.[79] Most importantly for the purposes of this paper, the Act of Lima also includes human rights and democracy as elements of the Community's common foreign policy.[80] As with MERCOSUR, inclusion of human rights and democracy in this work program may be a response to EU conditionality, as a result of the 1998 EU-ANCOM cooperation agreement.

Specifically, Article 13 directs the council of foreign ministers to develop policy guidelines and identify specific actions for cooperation among ANCOM states in furtherance of "effective protection of human rights and the practice of democracy in the Andean subregion."[81] Article 14 pledges the ANCOM states to protect their nationals from human rights violations throughout the region. Both provisions are to an extent aspirational, since Article 13 requests a plan of action which must first, of course, be negotiated, and then implemented; and Article 14 is in the form of a mere pledge, having more concrete relevance only when raised in the context of an ANCOM dispute,[82] or invoked as the basis for some form of political or economic pressure by ANCOM states against an offending member. The fact that the pledge is contained in an article of a treaty rather than merely in preambulatory language might lend it additional weight, although ultimately enforcement will depend upon many factors.

2. Political Conditionality

There have also been several developments at the political level. With respect to the CACM, a meeting in late 2000 between Argentinean President de la Rua and CACM heads of state resulted in a joint declaration containing a "democracy clause." This took the form of a political commitment among the relevant states to suspend the participation in any integration system of any state which violates the constitutional order.[83]

Most importantly, at a 2000 summit of 12 Latin American states, heads of state adopted a democracy clause as part of their pledge to create a South

American FTA by uniting ANCOM and MERCOSUR. Further, it was determined that the heads of state of any South American nation in which democracy or the rule of law had been compromised would be barred from participating in future summits.[84] Moreover, the preamble to the related framework agreement between ANCOM and MERCOSUR makes reference to the maintenance of democratic institutions as central to the integration process.[85] While this commitment reflects political developments within both systems, it is worth noting again that both systems are involved in EU cooperation agreements, which place a premium on such commitments.[86]

D. FTAA

1. Formal Links

As the FTAA is suspended in the negotiation stage as of this writing, it is premature to conclude what formal links, if any, between trade and human rights or democracy might be established in an eventual treaty system.[87] However, the FTAA process has produced a variety of documents from its various summits and ministerials, in which one can see progress towards a more explicit political linkage.

2. Political Conditionality

At the level of political statements, the FTAA negotiating parties seem to be adopting increasingly progressive positions with respect to the visibility of human rights, particularly in view of the fact that the FTAA process has been overwhelmingly trade-oriented to date.

The 1994 Miami Summit Declaration endorses the centrality of democratic governance to the FTAA process, and cites the preservation and strengthening of democracy in the Americas as one of the four principal goals of the FTAA. Indeed, Cuba was not invited ostensibly for this reason. However, the only direct mention of human rights is in reference to the role of democracy as the sole system "guarantee[ing]" human rights, thus reflecting the general approach taken by the U.S. towards this issue, namely that promoting formal democracy is tantamount to promoting human rights. By itself this would not be objectionable, except that human rights are not mentioned anywhere else in the Miami Declaration; in particular human rights are not referenced in the sections dealing with the FTAA itself.

The Miami Plan of Action does contain a separate heading on human rights. Interestingly enough, the first item in that section states that "governments will give serious consideration to adherence to international human rights instruments to which they are not already party." It is not clear if this provision was specifically aimed at the US failure to ratify the Convention, but it certainly draws attention to this fact. Moreover, in the second paragraph the hemisphere's governments pledge to "cooperate fully" with all inter-American human rights bodies. This might or might not be read as an impetus to states to accept the jurisdiction of the Court – after all, full cooperation without submission to jurisdiction is a hollow concept indeed. The final element in the list is a committment to strengthen further both the Court and the Commission, although without elaboration as to what this might involve.

The section of the Plan of Action devoted to the FTAA itself does not mention human rights, beyond the reference to observance and promotion of workers' rights as an aspect of the further integration of the hemisphere. However, the approach taken mirrors the WTO approach, in that such rights are to be defined by other bodies, not the FTAA itself. It is also left unclear as to whether the FTAA would follow the NAFTA model and seek enforcement of domestic labor laws only, but that would seem most likely.[88]

The 1998 Santiago Summit Declaration improves on the Miami Declaration with respect to the visibility of human rights, which were mentioned more extensively in the text of the Santiago Declaration itself:

> "Respect for and promotion of human rights and the fundamental freedoms of all individuals is a primary concern of our governments. In commemorating the fiftieth anniversary of the American Declaration of the Rights and Duties of Man and the Universal Declaration of Human Rights, we agree on the need to promote the ratification and implementation of the international agreements aimed at preserving them and to continue strengthening the pertinent national and international institutions."

Although the Convention is not mentioned by name, the Declaration is, and the word "ratification" does appear. Moreover, in the Santiago Plan of Action, the FTAA parties further pledged to "strengthen the inter-American human rights system through concrete initiatives and measures which aim to reinforce its institutional structure and promote its links with national systems and regional entities that promote human rights."

Such language could form the basis for continued pressure on the U.S. to ratify the American Convention if the politics so allowed. However, there is no mention of any specific *link* between increased human rights protection, and participation in the economic benefits of the FTAA. The two are mentioned side by side, but not with any conditionality.

The Santiago Summit and its aftermath do, however, signal an important development in the relationship between trade and human rights in the FTAA process, and between the FTAA and the OAS. Even though the 1994 Miami Plan of Action made reference to strengthening the OAS system, this aspect of the FTAA process did not really fully develop until the Santiago Summit, in which the FTAA parties pledged to formulate "concrete initiatives" for OAS reform. The OAS itself thereafter became the designated forum for this development, but at a superficial level, as existing internal self-study and reform initiatives were repositioned as steps in fulfillment of the Santiago mandate. Thus, for example, the preamble to the 1999 General Assembly resolution adopting the OAS Inter- American Program for the Promotion of Human Rights[89] cites the Santiago Declaration and Plan of Action as part of the rationale for the Program, even though the Program itself had already been under development prior to the Santiago Summit as an internal matter.[90]

This process of OAS implementation of FTAA human rights commitments was accelerated by the Quebec Summit of April 2001. In the Quebec Declaration, the FTAA negotiating parties further raised the visibility of the OAS system, referring once again to the goal of strengthening the Commission and Court, and directing the OAS to consider increased funding to the system:

> "We support strengthening and enhancing the effectiveness of the inter-American human rights system, which includes the Inter-American Commission on Human Rights and the Inter-American Court of Human Rights. We mandate the thirty-first regular session of the General Assembly of the OAS to consider an adequate increase in resources for the activities of the Commission and the Court in order to improve human rights mechanisms and to promote the observance of the recommendations of the Commission and compliance with the judgments of the Court."[91]

Further, the Quebec Plan of Action contains the most extensive human rights agenda of any of the FTAA process documents, addressing treaty implementation, reforming the OAS system, migration, women's rights, children's rights and freedom of expression.

Two aspects of the Quebec Summit are particularly noteworthy, as they may signal a fundamental step closer to formally linking trade and human rights in the Americas. First, as part of the measures identified for strengthening the OAS system in the Plan of Action, the FTAA negotiating parties publicly state the goal of hemispheric adherence to the OAS Convention as an element of the FTAA process.[92] Although resolutions calling for universal adherence to the Convention are a regular staple in the OAS agenda,[93] this is the first time that the issue of universal Convention membership has been raised so explicitly in the FTAA documents. While the general idea of increased ratification does surface in the Santiago Declaration as consensus on "the need to promote the ratification...of international [human rights] agreements," this sentiment has evolved into a more specific reference to universal adherence as a concrete measure in the Quebec Plan of Action. Moreover, the OAS has followed this up in resolutions adopted in June of 2001, which direct the OAS Permanent Council to initiate substantive and technical meetings on the issue of universal adherence to the Convention, with specific reference to the Quebec mandate.[94]

The second noteworthy aspect of the Quebec Summit is that the Declaration actually contains a democracy clause:

> "We [the democratically elected Heads of State and Government of the Americas] acknowledge that the values and practices of democracy are fundamental to the advancement of all our objectives. The maintenance and strengthening of the rule of law and strict respect for the democratic system are, at the same time, a goal and a shared commitment and are an essential condition of our presence at this and future Summits. Consequently, any unconstitutional alteration or interruption of the democratic order in a state of the Hemisphere constitutes an insurmountable obstacle to the participation of that State's government in the Summit of the Americas process. Having due regard for existing hemispheric, regional and subregional mechanisms, we agree to conduct consultations in the event of a disruption of the democratic system of a country that participates in the Summit process."[95]

This clause is similar in approach to the democracy clause adopted by Latin American trading systems, and one can speculate as to the degree to which this current effort is also the result of continued overtures to Europe. The Quebec Summit's inclusion of this democracy clause was an important stage in the process leading to the Inter-American Democratic Charter.[96] However, there is no indication of any decision on the part of the FTAA states as to whether to include a democracy clause in the final treaty, and the U.S. in particular has expressed resistance to this idea behind the scenes.[97]

The fourth Summit, referred to as the "Special Summit of the Americas," was called early at Canada's behest January 12-13, 2004, in response to flagging energy in the Summit process, as well as the need to involve newly-elected leaders of Summit countries, comprising one-third of the Summit membership.[98] This Summit added little to the FTAA negotiations with respect to human rights and democracy, overshadowed as it was by the Bush Administration's anti-terrorism agenda.[99] Whereas the Quebec Summit Declaration incorporated a democracy clause and explicit reference to the OAS human rights system, the Special Summit's Declaration of Nuevo Leon referred only minimally to the Inter-American Democratic Charter[100] and not at all to the OAS human rights system, focusing instead on the Inter-American Convention against Terrorism and related UN terrorism-related instruments.[101]

IV. Conclusions, Options and Recommendations

Currently there are two strands of development with respect to the linkage between trade and human rights in this hemisphere: regional efforts focusing on formal treaty links between trade and democratic governance, and hemispheric political statements linking trade with democracy and with human rights in a general sense. When compared to the gold standard of EU integration, this level of human rights integration is embryonic. While one can point to the concerted response to the Paraguayan crises as a notable success at the regional level with respect to trade and democratic governance, and to the increasingly progressive nature of the FTAA declarations with respect to both democracy and human rights, the hemisphere's major trading states and systems have stopped well short of formulating an explicit formal requirement of effective human rights protection as a condition of trade liberalization benefits.

At the regional level, there is an emerging consensus as to the necessity of maintaining a democratic form of government as a condition of trade benefits. MERCOSUR's history with respect to the various Paraguayan coup attempts, as influenced by the involvement of the EU, have been paramount in this process. The Paraguayan case illustrates that the leverage model can be successful in strengthening democracy and human rights in the hemisphere, when potential authoritarian regimes face the credible risk of crippling economic losses within their trading system and, if in partnership with a major economic bloc like the EU, in their external relations as well.

Throughout the rest of the region one finds some legal and many political statements linking trade and democratic governance. It is encouraging to note in this respect that MERCOSUR's own democracy protocol originated in a series of similar political commitments to democracy. This suggests an evolutionary dynamic, in which parties move from political linkages to formal treaty obligations. This could form a significant pattern if repeated at the hemispheric level.

With respect to hemispheric developments, the FTAA parties have not to date made effective participation in the OAS system a legal or political *condition* of FTAA participation. Democracy is a legal condition of OAS membership for states accepting the Protocol of Washington, and democracy has been established as a *political* condition of participation in the FTAA process through the Quebec Declaration. Strengthening and improving the OAS system has been mentioned as *one* of the goals of the FTAA process in its broad form, but *not* with respect to the FTAA treaty itself. Rather, development of the human rights component of the FTAA process has been delegated to the OAS. Functionally this may be a prudent use of resources, but strategically it represents a decision not to link the FTAA with human rights in the strong sense, similar to the WTO's decision with respect to labor rights and the ILO. Nevertheless, the various summit declarations and OAS actions together suggest that the FTAA process as a whole is having some positive effect on the efforts to strengthen the OAS system. That, in itself, is a form of linkage, in that the political statements made in a trade negotiation context are leading to proposals to strengthen human rights protections in a related human rights forum.

In summary, current FTAA statements and regional developments together suggest a hemispheric consensus on democracy as a formal requirement of FTAA membership, and on a stronger Inter-American system as political commitment of FTAA process. This is certainly a valuable base, but by itself this position fails fully to capitalize on the leverage opportunities which hemispheric integration presents.

If FTAA negotiating parties are truly prepared to strengthen human rights protection as an aspect of their economic integration, then the logical next step would be for FTAA negotiating parties to require effective participation in the Inter-American system as a condition of FTAA membership.[102] In European integration, this linkage has been one of the chief factors in the success of the European Convention system for the protection of human rights.[103] In the Americas, the chief obstacle to this step is US opposition to Convention ratification.[104] For an explicit link between trade and human rights to become part of hemispheric integration, US intransigence with respect to the Convention must be overcome. This is principally a matter of domestic U.S. politics, and the current administration does not seem likely to move this issue forward.

Outside of domestic US politics, the regional level could offer opportunities for near-term progress on this front if regional declarations supporting a trade-human rights linkage continue to develop. For example, as was discussed above, all MERCOSUR states are parties to the Convention, and all but Brazil (an important exception) have accepted the Court's contentious jurisdiction. Therefore, it might not be too difficult for MERCOSUR to adopt a formal requirement (should it be able to convince Brazil) that MERCOSUR states must be Convention parties and accept the court's jurisdiction, and to require this of prospective members in any MERCOSUR expansion. Under current conditions the EU continues to have the best opportunity to push this because of its active leadership on this issue, coupled with the perceived value that increased EU trade has for Latin America, particularly while the FTAA remains only a future possibility.

The next step would be for the rest of the hemisphere to then unite in requiring US agreement to incorporating such an approach into the FTAA and formally linking FTAA membership with full Convention participation, perhaps coupled with reforms of the OAS system to address US concerns.[105] Politically, this step seems unlikely, as the chief goal of the rest of the hemisphere in the FTAA is securing favorable access into US markets and investment. The rest of the hemisphere would be unlikely to put this on the line for a change in the US position with regard to the Convention.

If such a linkage is not politically feasible, a more modest step would be to carry over into the FTAA treaty itself the existing political link in the FTAA process between trade and democracy and trade and human rights. The FTAA parties, including the US, already agree on the importance of democratic governance as a *political* condition of FTAA participation, despite the U.S. opposition to an explicit democracy clause in the treaty. An initial negotiating objective for the rest of this hemisphere might then be to secure U.S. consent to incorporation of the Quebec Declaration's democracy clause into the FTAA treaty. If the U.S. continues to oppose a democracy clause in the FTAA treaty itself, it might be feasible to incorporate the Quebec Declaration's democracy clause into the preamble as a recital on the importance of democratic governance for a just and effective FTAA system. Similarly, with respect to human rights more broadly, it might be possible to secure U.S. consent to incorporation of human rights language, such as that found in the Santiago or Quebec Declarations, into the preamble to the FTAA treaty. The preamble (heavily bracketed) to the current FTAA Draft Agreement dated November 21, 2003 contains only one reference to strengthening "democratic values and institutions, [and] protecting fundamental human rights," and no references to the Inter-American Democratic Charter ot the OAS human rights system at all.

If some linkage between hemispheric free trade and democracy/human rights can be established even in the FTAA treaty preamble, this would be a significant, if modest, step. When compared with the opportunity to link the FTAA to effective participation in the OAS system, the preamble approach is disappointing. When compared to the very limited link between trade and democracy/human rights in NAFTA, an FTAA with a human rights-sensitive preamble would still represent an important advance. Failure to build on the existing NAFTA level of linkage would represent yet another lost opportunity.

NOTES

1. Within the leverage model, one can distinguish between making human rights protection a condition of membership as a matter of law, or as a matter of politics. In the former, adherence is a condition by virtue of the constitutive treaties, which require human rights treaty membership as a part of integration system membership. In the political case, while adherence is not formalized as a legal obligation, member states exert political pressure on one another to maintain democratic systems and human rights standards expressly or implicitly as a condition of continuing membership in good standing, and expect such adherence as a political condition of new membership. The two forms of conditionality are not completely distinct, of course, since even legalized conditionality requires political will for its enforcement. See Krista Schefer, The Use of Trade Instruments in the Pursuit of Human Rights: European Foreign Policy, page 5 (conference paper version) (enforcement of legal conditionality regime established by the EU accession and partnership agreements weakened by absence of political will).

2. This aspect of trade agreements has been highlighted in the constitutionalism literature. See generally Ernst Ulrich Petersmann, *Constitutionalism and International Organizations*, 17 NW J Int'l L & Bus. 398 (1996-97).

3. Such as, for example, the Draft Charter of Fundamental Rights of the European Union. See Werner Meng, Charter of Fundamental Rights of the European Union: Human Rights and the Four Freedoms (conference paper).

4. Sadly, the human rights records of many Latin American and African states suggest that while democracy may be a necessary condition of full human rights protection (and that itself is hotly debated), democracy by itself, and in particular formal democracy alone, is not a sufficient condition to guarantee effective human rights protection. See Bruno Simma et al., *Human Rights Considerations in the Development of Co-operation Activities of the EC*, in THE EU AND HUMAN RIGHTS 591 (Philip Alston, ed. 1999) (noting limits of promoting democratic processes as method of guaranteeing human rights); see generally Ellen L. Lutz, *Strengthening Core Values in the Americas: Regional Commitment to Democracy and the Protection of Human Rights*, 19 Hous. J. Int'l L. 643 1997 (summarizing role of democracy in official posture of American states, and noting difficulties in Mexican democracy and human rights record).

5. In so arguing, the paper makes two related empirical assumptions: first, that incorporation is legally, politically and socially a more complex and difficult human rights enforcement strategy than leverage; and second, that a leverage strategy is a natural preliminary stage to an incorporation strategy, i.e., one must walk before one can run. The human rights experience of the European Union lends some plausibility to these assumptions. This paper also relies upon a further, explicitly normative, assumption that strengthening human rights protection is a desirable end and an appropriate one for integration systems to pursue. For some of the moral arguments underlying this view, see Frank J. Garcia, *Building a Just Trade Order for a New Millennium*, 33 Geo. Wash. Int'l L. Rev 1015 (2001).

6. The roots of the Organization of American States (OAS) extend back to the International Union of American Republics, established in 1890 by the First International Conference of American States.

7. OAS Charter, 30 Apr. 1948, 33 I.L.M. 981 (entered into force 13 Dec. 1951).

8. The American Convention on Human Rights, Nov. 22, 1969, 9 I.L.M. 693, OEA/ser.K/XVI/1.1/ Doc. 65 (English) Rev. 1. Corr. 2 (1970) (entered into force Jul. 18, 1978).

9. American Declaration on the Rights and Duties of Man, OEA/Ser. L/V/I.4 Rev. (1965). Over the time these core instruments have been supplemented by two protocols to the American Convention (the "Protocol of San Salvador" on economic, social and cultural rights, and the Protocol to Abolish the Death Penalty); the Inter-American Convention to Prevent and Punish Torture; the Inter-American Convention on the Forced Disappearance of Persons; the Inter-American Convention on the Prevention, Punishment, and Eradication of Violence Against Women; and the Inter-American Convention on the Elimination of All Forms of Discrimination Against Persons with Disabilities. See generally JO PASQUALUCCI, THE PRACTICE AND PROCEDURES OF THE INTER-AMERICAN COURT OF HUMAN RIGHTS 2-4 (2003) [hereinafter PASQUALUCCI, PRACTICE].

10. See OAS Charter art. II(k).

11. Id. art. 16.

12. Thomas Buergenthal, *The Advisory Practice of the Inter-American Human Rights Court*, 79 Amer. J. Int'l L. 7, 1-27 (1985) [hereinafter, Advisory Practice].

13. The Commission does rely on the Declaration when considering individual petitions against OAS Member States that are not Convention parties. Moreover, while holding that the Declaration is not a treaty *per se*, the Court has issued an advisory opinion concluding that the Declaration is an authoritative interpretation of the Charter and the Convention. See generally PASQUALUCCI, PRACTICE, supra note 9 at 57.

14. Although the OAS General Assembly plays a role in human rights protection through the adoption of resolutions and through the enforcement of the Court's decisions, its role is secondary.

15. The current Commission was established by the Convention as the successor to the 1959 Commission, which was an organ of the OAS, with additional duties as set forth in the Convention.

16. On the advisory practice of the Court, see generally Buergenthal, Advisory Practice supra note 12.

17. The court heard its first case in 1981.

18. See Buergenthal, Advisory Practice supra note 12. Of the 24 states parties to the Convention, only 21 accept the contentious jurisdiction of the Court. Those are Argentina, Barbados, Bolivia, Brazil, Chile, Colombia, Costa Rica, Dominican Republic, Ecuador, El Salvador, Guatemala, Haiti, Honduras, Mexico, Nicaragua, Panama, Paraguay, Peru, Suriname, Uruguay and Venezuela; Pasqualucci, Practice, supra note 9 at 11.

19. For example, Velasquez Rodriguez Case, Inter-Am. C.H.R., Ser. C, No. 4, (1988) (Honduras was found responsible for the disappearance of the named party).

20. See generally Pasqualucci, supra note 9, at 230-90.

21. See , e.g., Jo M. Pasqualucci, *Victim Reparations in the Inter-American Human Rights System: a Critical Assessment of Current Practice and Procedure*, 18 MICH. J. INT'L. I, 6-7 (1996) [hereinafter Pasqualucci, Victim Reparations]; Jo M. Pasqualucci, *The Inter-American Human Rights System: establishing Precedents and Procedure in Human Rights Law*, 26 U. MIAMI INTER-AM. L. Rev. 297, 307-322 (1994-95) [hereinafter Pasqualucci, *The Inter-American Human Rights System*].

22. See, e.g., David J. Harris, *Regional Protection of Human Rights: The Inter-American Achievement*, in THE INTER-AMERICAN SYSTEM OF HUMAN RIGHTS 28-29 (David J. Harris and Stephen Livingstone eds. 1998) (Inter-American system has achieved a great deal despite weak political support); Claudio Grossman, *Moving Toward Improved Human Rights Enforcement in the Americas*, 27-Sum. Hum. Rts. 16 (2000) (crediting Inter-American system with primary role in improved democracy and human rights record in the Americas); Pasqualucci, *The Inter-American Human Rights System,* supra note 21 at 361 (concluding that Inter-American system effectively promotes human rights protection despite its limitations).

23. In contrast, it is an obligation of membership in the Council of Europe that states ratify the European Convention. Harris, supra note 22 at 1.

24. Ratifiers include Argentina, Barbados, Bolivia, Brazil, Chile, Colombia, Costa Rica, Dominica, Dominican Republic, Ecuador, El Salvador, Grenada, Guatemala, Haiti, Honduras, Jamaica, Mexico, Nicaragua, Panama, Paraguay, Peru, Suriname, Trinidad/Tobago, Uruguay and Venezuela.

25. Pasqualucci, *The Inter-American Human Rights System,* supra note 21 at 307 n. 53.

26. James F. Smith, *NAFTA and Human Rights: A Necessary Linkage*, 27 UC Davis L. Rev 793, n. 65-66 (1994). [hereinafter Smith, *NAFTA*].

27. See generally id.

28. Article 2(b), OAS Charter, supra note 7.

29. Inter-American Democratic Charter, AG/doc.8 (XXVIII-E/01), 6 September 2001, resolution adopted at Lima, Peru, September 11, 2001, www.oas.org/main/main.asp?sLang=E&sLink=http://www.upd.oas.org.

30. Protocol of Washington, 14 Dec. 1992, 1-E OEA/Ser. A/2 Add. 3 (SEPF), entered into force 25 Sept. 1997). Only 24 of the 34 OAS members have ratified the protocol and are thereby bound by the new Article 9. The Santiago Commitment to Democracy and the Renewal of the Inter-American System, OAS 3d plenary sess., June 4, 1991, discussed in Stephen J. Schnably, *The Santiago Commitment as a Call to Democracy in the U.S.: Evaluations of the OAS Role in Haiti, Peru and Guatemala*, 25 U. Miami Inter-Am. L. Rev. 393 (1994).

31. AG/Res. 1080 (XXI-O/91), available at www.oas.org/juridico/english/agres1080.htm. These measures were successful with respect to the 1993 coup in Guatemala. Following the Santiago

Declaration process, OAS members threatened trade sanctions against Guatemala, including the loss of U.S. GSP benefits, which was an important factor in the coup's failure. See generally Ellen L. Lutz and Kathyrn Sikkink, International Human Rights Law and Practice in Latin America, 54 Int'l. Org. 633 (2000)). While this episode supports the general thesis of this paper, it did not involve linkage to a trade agreement *per se*, so is not further analyzed here.

32. See Harris, supra note 22 at 28-29 (ratification of Convention by remaining states would supply necessary political support for increased effectiveness of OAS system); Grossman, supra note 22 at 18 (adherence to Inter-American system is essential for full compliance with human rights norms in the Americas).

33. For example, NAFTA and MERCOSUR both contain provisions mandating specific levels of protection for capital and intellectual property, as well as limited rights of freedom of movement and establishment.

34. See generally Roberto L. Martinez, *NAFTA's Effect on Human Rights at the Border*, 27 U.C. Davis L. Rev. 979 (1994); Alejandro Sobarzo, *NAFTA and Human Rights in Mexico*, 27 U.C. Davis L. Rev. 865 (1994).

35. See Smith, NAFTA supra note 26.

36. NAFTA art. 2204 reads as follows: "Any country or group of countries may accede to this Agreement subject to such terms and conditions as may be agreed between such country or countries and the Commission and following approval in accordance with the applicable legal procedures of each country."

37. The accession provision as written does not even require new parties to accede to the labor or environmental side agreements. See Robert F. Housman, *The Treatment of Labor and Environmental Issues in Future Western Hemisphere Trade Liberalization Efforts*, 10 Conn. J. Int'l L. 301, 303-304 (1995). [thereinafter, Housman, *The Treatment*].

38. The fact that, of the three NAFTA parties, Mexico is both the only OAS Convention party and the state with the worst human rights record, does raise an apparent challenge to the thesis of this paper that mandatory participation in the OAS system would contribute to increased human rights protection in this hemisphere. In fact, this pattern suggests the narrower point that OAS Convention party status *alone*, and outside any trade-based leverage system, does not guarantee human rights protection, particularly when one's trade partners are not even Convention parties and therefore not in a position to utilize the OAS system to apply pressure. This paper suggests that if *all three* NAFTA states were OAS Convention parties, and all three accepted the contentious jurisdiction of the Court as a condition of NAFTA membership, the situation in Mexico could very well be different.

39. North American Agreement on Labor Cooperation (NAALC), opened for signature Sept. 8, 1993, 32 I.L.M. 1499 (entered into force Jan. 1, 1994). [hereinafter, NAALC].

40. But see David P. Kelly, *Trading Indigenous Rights: The NAFTA Side Agreements as an Impetus for Human Rights Enforcement*, 6 Buff. Hum. Rts. L. Rev. 113, 132 (2000) (arguing that the

compliance approach adopted by the side agreements may be more effective than imposition of external standards).

41. NAALC art. 3 (1). The NAALC does contain a list of labor rights under its definition of the term in art. 49, but this list really only defines the scope of the term, not its substantive content. Moreover, the list of labor principles in the Annex specifically rejects any reading of those principles as establishing any "common minimum standards."

42. See Housman, *The Treatment*, supra note 36, at 308. (discussing sanctions process); see generally Lance Compa, *Going Multilateral: The Evolution of U.S. Hemispheric Labor Rights Policy under GSP and NAFTA*, 10 Conn. J. Int'l L. 337 (1995).

43. Although as an OAS member Mexico is bound by the general obligation to support democracy in Article 2 of the OAS Charter, it is interesting to note that Mexico did not ratify the Protocol of Washington.

44. Moreover, given the fact that the U.S. normalized trade relations with China and accepted China's WTO accession, this condition should more accurately be considered an artifact of history, regional geopolitics, and domestic U.S. politics. In any event, nominally democratic states in this hemisphere have been so chronically linked to serious human rights abuses that it is disingenuous to single out Cuba on the basis of political ideology alone.

45. MERCOSUR was formed among Argentina, Brazil, Paraguay and Uruguay through negotiation of the Treaty of Asuncion Mar. 26, 1991, 30 ILM 1041 (1991).

46. Pasqualucci, The Inter-American Human Rights System supra note 25, n. 53.

47. Protocol of Ushuaia concerning the commitment to democracy in MERCOSUR (Bolivia and Chile).

48. Id. art. 5.

49. *President under Siege Following Argana Murder,* The Irish Times, Mar. 26, 1999.

50. *Paraguayan Membership would be Frozen in Event of Coup,* (AFX News Mar. 26, 1999).

51. *South American Countries Condemn Paraguay Coup Attempt* (BBC Summary of World Broadcasts, May 22, 2000).

52. Honorable Chris Patten, EC Commissioner, speech at The Right for Union, External Relations *Why Brazil Matters to the European* (Nov. 8, 2000).

53. *Communiqué Issued at End of MERCOSUR-Bolivia-Chile Summit in Florianopolis,* (BBC Summary of World Broadcasts, Dec. 19, 2000).

54. See infra note 53 and accompanying text.

55. From jail, where he was awaiting trial in connection with his role in the aborted coup, General Oviedo acknowledged that no coup in Paraguay could succeed in the face of such action. *Paraguay Tests Bloc's Democratic Clause*, (Inter Press Service, Mar. 6, 1998).

56. Declaracion Presidencial Sobre Compromiso Democratico en el MERCOSUR, (Jun. 25, 1996), *available at* http://www.mercosur.org.uy/espanol/snor/normativa/cdem196.htm.

57. See Schefer, supra note 1.

58. EC Press Release, President of Paraguay Visits Commission, (Apr. 18, 1994) (Such linkages between trade and democracy/human rights have been a consistent element in the EC's program of framework and association agreements). See Garcia, *"Americas Agreements"- An Interim Stage in Building the Free Trade Area of the Americas,* 35 Colum. J. Transnat'l L. 63, 92-93 (1997).

59. MARIA ANGELES BENITEZ, RELACIONES ENTRE la UE y el MERCOSUR, Del MERCOSUR 50-51 (Miguel Angel Ciuro Caldani, ed. 1996) (1996).

60. *MERCOSUR, Brussels Link-up Gets Green Light,* (Inter Press Service, April 4, 1995).

61. Id; Schefer, supra note 1 (Dr. Schefer does note that the enforcement of this condition is highly dependent on the political will of the EU states).

62. *Joint Declaration Strengthens Political Dialogue with MERCOSUR*, (Agence Europe, Jun. 15, 1995) (EU and MERCOSUR jointly affirm "the value of human dignity and the promotion of human rights as the founding of democratic societies, as well as the essential role of democratic institutions founded on the state of law.").

63. *Historic EU-MERCOSUR cooperation agreement signed in Montevideo*, (BBC Summary of World Broadcasts, Oct. 2, 1995).

64. Id.

65. *EU Signs South American Agreement*, The Irish Times, Dec. 16, 1995 (Agreement commits MERCOSUR to respect human rights and democratic values); *European Parliament Welcomes MERCOSUR Deal*, European Report, May 25, 1996 (European Parliament welcomes Cooperation Agreement with MERCOSUR; MEP cites democracy and human rights provisions in particular).

66. Preamble, Interregional Cooperation Framework Agreement between the EU and MERCOSUR, Dec. 15, 1995.

67. Id. art. 1.

68. Id. art. 35.

69. Conversation between the author and Dr. Belter Garre-Copelo, Universidad de la Republica, Montevideo, Uruguay, (Apr. 1997).

70. Press Release, Council of Ministers, EU-MERCOSUR Noordwijk Ministerial Meeting, (Apr. 17, 1997).

71. For example, in response to an article on EU-Latin American relations published in The Irish Times, the ambassadors of Argentina and Brazil to the EU wrote a letter to the editor reiterating that "democracy and human rights are MERCOSUR's institutional framework chosen by the associating countries which believe that no integration process can grow and prosper without honouring fundamental political and social values. It will be useful to recall that the democratic clause is a clausula petrea within MERCOSUR's constitutional structure." *MERCOSUR and the EU*, The Irish Times, Jan. 8, 1999 at Editorial Page.

72. *MERCOSUR, Argentine President Hope for Return to Democracy in Peru*, (BBC Summary of World Broadcasts, Nov. 23, 2000).

73. *Communiqué Issued at End of MERCOSUR-Bolivia-Chile Summit in Florianopolis*, (BBC Summary of World Broadcasts, Dec. 19, 2000).

74. *MERCOSUR, Chile y Bolivia Apoyan Democracia y Derechos Humanos*, (EFE News Service, Feb. 8, 2000).

75. *Familiares Desaparecidos Proponen Oranismo Humanitario MERCOSUR*, (EFE News Service, Dec. 1, 1999).

76. *EU-MERCOSUR/Chile: Piden Incluir a la Sociedad Civil y los Derechos Humanos*, (Agence France Presse, Nov. 9, 2000).

77. Id.

78. *Europarlamentarios Piden Disvincular Negociacion UE-MERCOSUR/Chile de OMC*, (Agence France Presse, Feb. 6, 2001).

79. Act of Lima, 10 June 2000, available at www.comunidadandina.org/ingles/document/act10-6-00.htm

80. Id.

81. Id. art. 13.

82. It is not clear of this provision could be the basis for an action within the ANCOM tribunal.

83. *De la Rua Concluye Visita y Ratifica su Acercamiento a Centroamerica*, (Agence France Press, Dec. 6, 2000).

84. *South American Presidents Unite in Pledges to Form Economic Bloc*, (UPI Sept. 1, 2000).

85. Preamble, Framework Agreement for the Creation of an FTA between ANCOM and MERCOSUR (translation by author).

86. Smith, NAFTA supra note 26 at 817. EU has linked trade and human rights in part to foster democratic values.

87. The current draft text (heavily bracketed), dated 13 November 2003, is completely silent on the issue of human rights or democratic governance other than a brief mention in the preamble. http://www.ftaa-alca.org/FTAADraft03/Index_e.asp.

88. See Housman, *The Treatment*, supra note 36, at 314-326. (discussing various approaches to labor issues in NAFTA accession and concluding current model is most politically feasible and therefore most likely).

89. Inter-American Program for the Promotion of Human Rights, Jun. 7, 1999, OEA/Ser. P/AG/Res 1663 (XXIX-O/00).

90. The Program began as part of the Commission's 1997 Annual Report to the General Assembly, in response to an earlier General Assembly Resolution calling for such a program.

91. Third Summit of the Americas, Declaration of Quebec City, April 22, 2001, available at www.sice.oas.org/ftaa/quebec/declara_e.asp.

92. In the Plan of Action, the FTAA negotiating parties commit to "concrete measures to strengthen and improve the inter-American human rights system, in particular the functioning of the Inter-American Court of Human Rights and the Inter-American Commission on Human Rights (IACHR), focusing on: *the universalization of the inter-American human rights system*, increasing adherence to its founding instruments, complying with the decisions of the Inter-American Court and following up on the recommendations of the Commission, facilitating the access of persons to this protection mechanism and substantially increasing resources to maintain ongoing operations, including the encouragement of voluntary contributions, and examining the possibility that the Court and the IACHR will function permanently." (Italics added.)

93. Letter from Professor Pascualucci, Aug. 8, 2001 (on file with author). Such resolutions have been an annual matter in the OAS, without apparent effect on the U.S. position.

94. Evaluation of the Workings of the Inter-American System of the Protection and Promotion of Human Rights with a View to its Improvement and Strengthening, OEA/Ser. P/AAG/Rees. 1828 (XXXI-O/01), 5 Jun. 2001; Support for Inter-American Human Rights Instruments, OEA/Ser. P/AG/Res 1829 (XXXI-O/01), 5 Jun. 2001.

95. Quebec Summit Declaration, supra note 91.

96. See supra note 29 and accompanying text.

97. "Bush Links Trade with Democracy at Quebec Talks," The New York Times, April 22, 2001, A1, at A4.

98. John W. Graham, *The Special Summit of the Americas*, 3 FOCAL POINT 1 (JANUARY 2004).

99. Id., at 2; *Divided Leaders of the Americas to Hold Summit, Strains Evident*, AGENCE FRANCE PRESSE (11 JANUARY 2004).

100. See supra note 29 and accompanying text.

101. Declaration of Nuevo Leon, January 13, 2004, www.summit-americas.org/SpecialSummit/Declarations/Declaration%20of%20Nuevo%20Leon%20-%20final.pdf, last visited 11/03/04.

102. See Smith, supra note 26 at 839-840 (widespread ratification of Inter-American system and acceptance of Court's jurisdiction through linkage with regional integration is missing step in increasing effective human rights protection).

103. Smith, supra note 26 at 817-823.

104. Id., at 840-841.

105. US reluctance involves the Convention's pro-life stance, and its prohibition on the execution of minors. There may be some support among OAS members to accept reservations to the conception-based approach to the right to life, which could open the door to US and Canadian participation. Letter from Professor Pasqualucci, Aug. 8, 2001 (on file with author).

CHAPTER 17

Unilateralism and Multilateralism in U.S. Human Rights Laws Affecting International Trade

*Joel P. Trachtman**

1. Introduction

The United States has been an active advocate of human rights in other countries. While in some cases the U.S. motives may be characterized as politically self-serving, sometimes catering to a particular ethnic interest group or engaging in "selective enforcement," in at least some cases the motives seem to be altruistic. The human rights addressed are of varying types, including labor rights, rights to be free of torture and genocide and rights against expropriation. The universe of human rights can be very broad, including, perhaps paradoxically, the right to trade freely without being subject to human rights enforcement-based limits.[1] For example, an embargo that restricts the trade of private persons in response to human rights transgressions of their government may infringe the human rights of those private persons. Indeed, from a (perhaps absurdly) reductionist Coasean perspective, which is not too far removed from a strong cultural relativist perspective, each right accorded one person is a "right" denied another.[2]

This chapter is intended to offer a brief, and incomplete, taxonomy of U.S. human rights measures affecting international trade. Its motivation is to seek to evaluate several of these measures in terms of the relationship between unilateral action and multilateral rules and institutions, and specifically to suggest the issues that they may raise under WTO law. I suggest that unilateralism has an important role in a global system, even in a multilateral system.

This chapter's theoretical perspective sets up four related dichotomies: (i) sovereignty and international law; (ii) unilateralism and multilateralism; (iii) the market and the firm; and (iv) natural law and positive law. States are autonomous to the extent that they are not bound by international law, leaving them free to engage in unilateral action. Unilateralism can be compared to unconstrained operations in a market. According to Coase's theory of the firm, individual operators may enter into a firm – an institution – when doing so

* The author expresses his appreciation to participants at the 2001 Berne World Trade Institute conference on Trade and Human Rights, and especially to Hurst Hannum, Robert Hudec, Alfred Rubin and Gabrielle Marceau, for comments and suggestions.

improves their ability to transact – in our case, to engage in the kinds of transactions in authority, such as reciprocal agreements to respect certain human rights, that they would like, at reduced transaction costs. International law is an artifact of multilateralism (or at least plurilateralism) – it constrains individual state action. International law has varying binding force. Certain human rights may be characterized as natural law: they have not been legislated by the operation of custom or by treaty. While there is much positive human rights law, it often lacks positive law enforcement mechanisms: mandatory independent dispute settlement, backed up by the ability to impose effective sanctions.

This is the main reason human rights advocates are interested in the trade system: as a source of effective sanctions. It is also one of the reasons opponents of unilateral U.S. action are interested in the trade law system: as a source of effective constraints on unilateral action. We thus may observe an emergent struggle over the application of the tools of trade: between forces promoting human rights through unilateral action and forces opposed to such unilateral action.

a. Sovereignty and International Law

In every case where the U.S. advocates a change of policy in another country, the U.S. action may be characterized as an attack on the target's national sovereignty. However, this characterization has important limits. First, to the extent that the rights advocated are protected by positive international law, another state is estopped from claiming that the matter is within its *domain réservé*. Second, so long as the U.S. measures are not attacks on territorial sovereignty, but, as in the cases discussed here, are measures such as primary boycotts and trade restrictions that are within the territorial sovereignty of the U.S., they often do not violate customary international law or the U.N. Charter. On the other hand, where the measures violate a particular substantive provision of WTO law, the fact of their non-trade motivation may not always provide an exemption. Finally, from a moral or natural law standpoint, many may view intervention in cases of violation of at least certain human rights as a responsibility of states; certainly states have been embarrassed by their inaction in the past. Obviously, the type of human right at stake, and the magnitude of its violation, are material factors.

Article 2(4) of the U.N. Charter prohibits "threat or use of force against the territorial integrity or political independence of any state..." This provision seems to permit the use of economic sanctions, although some have argued that these are prohibited as well.[3] There is also an emerging norm of humanitarian intervention that may authorize intervention in certain cases to promote human rights. Furthermore, Article 56 of the U.N. Charter obligates states to take "separate action" to promote human rights. Nor does customary international law provide general limitations, beyond those referenced above relating to territorial sovereignty, on the rights of states to take unilateral action to promote human rights.[4] The general public international law norms of sovereignty, non-intervention, territorial jurisdiction and sovereign equality have substantial limits. For one, they are limited to the extent that the relevant states have taken on international legal obligations, or have permitted intervention. For another, these norms are generally limited to protecting the territory of states from physical intervention.

b. Unilateralism and Multilateralism

All multilateral systems, in accordance with subsidiarity, and in accordance with institutional economic theory, are complementary – "subsidiary" – to unilateral action.[5] We may understand unilateralism as the "market" of international relations, and multilateralism as the "firm."[6] In today's international legal context, there are various entities that together may be viewed, loosely, as the "firm" or as a complex of "firms," in connection with international human rights. There are various human rights treaties. Outside of the jurisdiction of the Inter-American Court of Human Rights and the European Court of Human Rights, these often lack substantial judicial enforcement mechanisms. However, the Optional Protocol of the International Covenant on Civil and Political Rights provides for non-judicial enforcement, and we might also refer to the international tribunals relating to Rwanda and Yugoslavia.

On the other hand, it is for states, acting according to their own interests and views, to act unilaterally. Obviously, sometimes they act for better and sometimes for worse. Sometimes, when they act unilaterally, they violate international law, and sometimes they do not. States acting unilaterally can influence the behavior of other states believed to be violating human rights in a variety of ways. They can provide positive or negative incentives: carrots or sticks. They can even engage in secondary or tertiary boycotts, putting pressure on third states to join in their action. Target states and third states can respond in a variety of ways, from retaliation to submission.[7]

c. The Market and the Firm

Interestingly and importantly for this essay, target states may alternatively respond by proposing a multilateral solution – the transfer of authority to an international institution, a "firm." This could simply be a treaty, or it could be an international organization. It would have the advantages of independence and, perhaps, greater predictability. We have seen the U.S. in the role of *demandeur* in the trade arena, where aggressive unilateralism in trade dispute resolution generally, and in intellectual property in particular, precipitated a multilateral response in the Uruguay Round. In institutional economic theory, the reason for creating an international institution would be to achieve states' goals at lower cost; it may be, for example, that the creation of an international institution could reduce future bargaining costs.

d. Natural Law and Positive Law

In the human rights area in particular (but certain other areas, such as environmental protection, are not so different), we might understand much of the law as belonging to the natural law order. While much of the law is positive, either in the form of customary international law or conventional international law, the fact that it lacks effective enforcement devices relegates it to at least a world of natural law *enforcement*:[8] shaming, or reputational sanctions, lobbying or sometimes litigation in foreign domestic courts to "bootstrap" this law into a positive law enforcement mechanism. It will thus be useful in this paper to distinguish between the following three types of circumstances: (i) those in which there is no positive international law and no positive international law enforcement, (ii) those in which there is positive international human rights law, but no positive international law enforcement, and (iii) those in which there is both positive international human rights law and positive international law enforcement. In case (iii), which may indeed be a null set outside of the European context and perhaps the Inter-American system, there might be interesting choice of law and choice of forum issues where a conflict with WTO law arises.

One might argue that the more important distinction, rather than that between natural law and positive law, is between less binding law and more binding law.

e. Natural Law and Positive Law; Unilateralism and Multilateralism

Unilateral action by other states may be understood, at the international level, as part of the natural law enforcement mechanism. Where this natural law enforcement mechanism has binding force, it may, as suggested above, drive the target state to propose or accept positive law enforcement mechanisms. This would be especially true where the natural law enforcement mechanism fails to accord the target guarantees of due process or proportionality of response. Thus, developing or smaller states may be concerned that "human rights"-denominated measures may be used for protectionist purposes, and their fears are not wholly unfounded.

In the case of positive law agreements with weak positive enforcement mechanisms, in the context of GATT and commercial policy under section 301 of the U.S. Trade Act of 1974, Sykes has stated that, "[w]hen concern for reputation is not enough to induce nations to honor their commitments and when ... agreements do not provide effective third-party dispute resolution with the power to coerce compliance, a powerful argument can be made for unilateral or "self-help" measures to penalize a breach of promise."[9]

Hudec goes even further, arguing that "not all disobedience to GATT law is necessarily wrong."[10] He asserts that there may be instances in which a kind of "civil disobedience" makes a constructive contribution to breaking deadlocks or improving GATT law. If this is true in connection with commercial policy, could it *a fortiori* be true in connection with human rights?[11] Hudec notes the utility of U.S. unilateralism to push forward the "new issues" in the Uruguay Round agenda.[12] We might imagine that if human rights is to appear on the WTO's agenda in the future, unilateralism will be a precipitating factor. Of course, one might well ask, if disobedience is indeed "justified," why did not the parties to GATT or the WTO agree to allow these kinds of action as exceptions to the treaties' obligations? Here, we might move to a debate regarding the content of the exceptional provisions of GATT: Articles XX and XXI.

Hudec suggests that "justifiable disobedience" must be predicated on five substantive guidelines: (i) the objective must be consistent with the general objectives of the GATT, (ii) disobedience must be preceded by a good faith effort to negotiate, (iii) disobedience must be accompanied by an offer to continue to negotiate in good faith, (iv) the disobedience must be limited to that which is necessary to achieve a negotiated legal reform, and (v) governments must respect GATT law as fully as possible in their action, even if it includes accepting counter-retaliation.[13] Although item (i) seems more relevant to commercial policy matters than to human rights matters, Hudec did a reasonable job, in 1990, of anticipating what the Appellate Body has done in the *Shrimp* case in determining what is "justifiable disobedience" under Article XX of GATT for environmental purposes. The fifth item may have been added in the *Asbestos* case.

We cannot readily transfer Sykes' and Hudec's observations to the world of human rights. There is an important difference between the world of human rights and the world of commercial market access that section 301 inhabits. In the world of market access, the welfare implications of foreign liberalization under threat are generally positive, even for the target state. In the world of human rights, it will not always be true that foreign enhancement of human rights will be beneficial to the target state. For example, tragic as child labor often is, a coerced rule against child labor may, under some circumstances, diminish welfare for children and others. So in welfare economics terms unilateralism is less clearly benign in human rights than it is in market access.

Thus, a core question is that of the incentives of the target government. If the target government is already maximizing the welfare of its citizens, including a locally optimal combination of wealth and human rights, we might ask when it would be efficient for foreign governments or international organizations to interfere. The propriety of interference would depend on the "accountability" of the foreign government to its citizens, but also on the degree of externalization – the degree to which the sensibilities or other values of foreign persons are affected. However, there is an important circular aspect to this analysis. If the local government is already maximizing local welfare, foreign sensibilities *should* not be substantially offended.[14] Thus, it may be more important to provide a broader margin of appreciation of domestic arrangements in the field of human rights than in the field of commercial policy, where there is greater danger of external effects. This margin of appreciation might assess first the degree to which target country policies are reflective of national preferences, presumably giving appropriate weight to the preferences of the dispossessed. This kind of analysis quickly becomes extremely interventionist in domestic affairs.

We have so far assumed nothing but good intentions on the part of the interfering state. Of course, in unilateral sanctions, there is a further danger of opportunism,[15] of protectionism veiled as high-minded human rights advocacy.[16] Mechanisms that may limit unilateral action to appropriate cases, for example by limiting unilateral action to cases where there is a violation of a multilaterally-agreed human right, or a multilateral determination of such violation, would tend to limit abuse. Furthermore, requirements of proportionality in response to violations would also tend to limit abuse. Certainly, as a reputational matter, these types of limitations may have some application.

f. Trade and Human Rights and Other Trade And ... Problems

I wish also to suggest that the trade and human rights problem is but a sub-category of a broader set of issues, of "trade and . . . problems," which should be viewed together as an integrated challenge to the present institutional structure of international relations. While each category of "trade and ... problem" has unique characteristics, they are strongly related to one another. Of course, human rights includes a well-known, and widely discussed, "trade and ... problem" – that of trade and labor rights. Labor rights differ from other human rights, however, to the extent that denial of other human rights would ordinarily not be expected to have positive competitive effects, whereas some argue that denial of labor rights may reduce production costs. Some cultural relativists may argue that denial of non-labor human rights also has positive competitive effects.

Furthermore, some suggest that denial of human rights can have negative *political* externalities: states that deny human rights reduce regional or global stability or produce refugees. This argument relates to Anne-Marie Slaughter's liberal states theory of international relations.[17] Under these circumstances, it is not just altruism that causes concern for human rights in other states. However, it is possible to discern circumstances where altruism alone promotes action.

Human rights, in this sense, is not terribly different from environmental protection as a linked issue with trade. There are both non-pecuniary externalities (cross-border pollution; regional instability) and pecuniary externalities (reduced costs of environmental compliance; cheaper labor due to denial of collective bargaining rights). There are both use values and non-use values. Both kinds implicate or may be considered preferences of individuals for purposes of economic analysis.[18] Both kinds may be expressed through the state, and/or through international action. Of course, the environment is specifically referenced in several places in WTO law, while human rights, *per se*, is not generally covered.

The critical point, though, is that linkages are neither natural nor unnatural: all linkages are constructed. There are no "natural" trade or commercial policy issues. While it may make sense to establish these categories and to populate them with particular issues for particular purposes, each categorization is a political act, with particular political ramifications. In the state of nature, states are not restricted in the kinds of linkages they may establish: they may assert that they will refuse to trade with other states that do not worship the same gods, or that they will, as a society, have no truck with tyrants and oppressors. Where does international law modify this state of nature?

2. U.S. Unilateral Measures Restricting Trade in Relation to Human Rights, and Issues of WTO Law

a. Jackson-Vanik: Sticks in the Form of Less-Than-MFN Treatment

With the accession of China to the WTO, there has been much recent discussion of the role of the Jackson-Vanik Amendment.[19] The Jackson-Vanik Amendment imposes a kind of conditionality on MFN[20] (most favoured nation) treatment by the U.S., with respect to "non-market economy" countries. The statutory condition is recognition of freedom to emigrate, but has been extended to include other human rights.[21] The President is authorized to waive the requirement of freedom of emigration, if he determines that the non-market economy country is making progress toward that goal.

Thus, the operation of the Jackson-Vanik Amendment required China (and the U.S. executive) to undergo annual reviews in order to obtain an annual waiver to preserve MFN status.

The U.S. denies MFN status/treatment to only a handful of countries, such as Cuba, North Korea and Laos. However, the threat of MFN denial is a big stick, especially for countries like China for which the U.S. is an important export market. Some countries, such as Russia, are deemed to be in compliance with the Jackson-Vanik Amendment, while other countries, such as China, were until recently subject to continuing requirements to obtain waivers. For other countries, like Iran, Iraq and Libya, while they retain theoretical MFN treatment, the U.S. market is closed to them due to overall embargoes.

As a condition to granting the President the authority to accord permanent MFN treatment to China upon its accession to the WTO, the U.S. Congress set up a number of mechanisms to address issues of forced or prison labor in China, compliance with international human rights norms, and the development of "the rule of law" in commercial and labor fields.

The U.S. appears unconstrained by legal rules that prevent it from imposing this kind of conditionality with respect to states that are not members of the WTO.

b. GSP and Other Preferences: Carrots in the Form of Better-Than-MFN Treatment

The U.S. has several programs providing tariff preferences to developing countries. As tariff reduction progresses through successive tariff-reducing rounds, and as further regional integration takes place, these preferences become less valuable. On the other hand, the U.S. Generalized System of Preferences ("USGSP")[22] has imposed substantial conditions on access to these preferences.

i. Generalized System of Preferences

The USGSP provides tariff preferences for certain developing countries. The USGSP includes a series of policy-based conditions, including a requirement to respect "internationally recognized labor rights."[23] These include (i) freedom of association, (ii) the right to bargain collectively, (iii) prohibition of forced labor, (iv) prohibition of child labor under a certain age, (v) minimum acceptable employment conditions regarding wages, hours, and occupational safety and health, and (vi) prohibition of the worst forms of child labor. In 2000, the law was amended to include the requirement, referenced in item (vi), to implement commitments to eliminate the worst forms of child labor, as defined.[24] The USGSP is actively used as an incentive to promote labor rights, with many countries having their USGSP status reviewed, and some having their status suspended or removed under this program.[25] For example, in 1988, the Reagan Administration suspended Chile's beneficiary developing country status because of suppression of labor rights under the Pinochet government.[26] It is worth noting that India recently challenged the European Community's use of conditions relating to drug enforcement as a predicate for availability of its GSP program.[27] In that case, the WTO Appellate Body found the EC's program to violate the requirement of non-discrimination in the Enabling Clause. Although there may be substantial bases for distinguishing the EC's drug enforcement program from human rights conditionality, this decision must be understood as a threat to any policy-based conditions for GSP.

The U.S. use of USGSP may be viewed as an incentive–a carrot–for respect for labor rights. It is a "carrot" insofar as beneficiary countries receive a benefit "in exchange" for compliance. However, when one recalls that most developing countries are eligible for these benefits, and compete with one another in exporting certain types of goods, the GSP, from a market competition standpoint, may begin to seem like more of a stick.[28] That is, denial of USGSP removes a fundamental predicate for the competitiveness of the target country's exports.

This raises the theoretical question of the difference between a carrot and a stick.[29] The more important question appears to be the potential effect on behavior of the particular policy.

Thus, it is necessary to ask in any particular context, is there a realistic risk, in connection with carrots, that states will demean their human rights protections in order to become eligible for receipt of incentives. In the context of the USGSP program this is not a serious risk. The U.S. does not seek out human rights violators and offer them consideration to improve their policies; rather, the U.S. establishes a baseline and states that the USGSP will only be available to those states that satisfy the baseline. On the other hand, it is at least theoretically possible that if a request-offer style of negotiations were extended to place domestic human rights policies on the table, there could, theoretically, be a risk that states would demean their human rights protections in order to earn a bargaining chip. In other GATT/WTO contexts, rules of standstill and rollback have been used to avoid states seeking rewards for bad behavior.

ii. WTO Legality

The U.S. imposition of various types of conditionality, including human rights conditionality, in connection with the USGSP may arguably violate WTO law. The original GSP waiver required that preferences be made generally available to all developing countries on a non-discriminatory basis.[30] The 1979 "Enabling Clause" reiterated this requirement.[31] Of course, the meaning of "non-discriminatory" raises some issues. It is not clear whether it means that no conditions are permitted: that all developing countries must unconditionally be accorded GSP rights, or whether it permits conditions so long as they themselves are applied on a non-discriminatory basis. This issue was recently raised, and dropped, in dispute settlement proceedings by Brazil against the EU. As noted above, it has recently been raised again in litigation brought by India, and decided against the EC's drug enforcement program at the panel level. The Appellate Body reversed this decision.[32]

c. Massachusetts-Burma: State Sticks for Cooptation

In 1996, Massachusetts passed a law, similar to an earlier law that it had enacted to restrict procurement from companies that did business with South Africa, imposing sanctions on Burma. The basic thrust of the law, the Massachusetts Burma Statute,[33] was to impose a 10% negative preference on bidders for state business that also engaged in business with Burma. In this sense, it was in the nature of a secondary boycott, providing incentives for both U.S. and foreign firms to avoid doing business with Burma. This law was invalidated in 2000 by the U.S. Supreme Court, on narrow statutory pre-emption grounds.[34] This left in continued uncertainty the legality under the U.S. federal constitutional structure of the many state and local international "sanctions" laws. Constitutional issues that were not addressed by the Supreme Court include those relating to the Commerce Clause and to an asserted "exclusive foreign affairs power."

The European Union and Japan sought consultations under the WTO Government Procurement Agreement, and a panel was established in 1998 to review their claims.[35] As the U.S. Supreme Court invalidated the law, the European Union and Japan dropped the case.[36] Finally, while Myanmar (Burma) is a WTO member, it is not party to the GPA.

In order to understand some of the types of issues that may arise in future cases of this kind , and as an example of some of the interpretative issues that may arise under WTO law, I review some of the WTO legal issues surrounding this case. The following discussion briefly addresses the major claims brought by the European Union and Japan.

i. Article III

Article III(1) of the GPA requires national treatment and MFN non-discrimination to be accorded to the products, services and suppliers of other parties to the GPA. Although the EU did not bring a claim under Article III, Japan did so.

Article III of the GPA, unlike the national treatment requirement of GATT, explicitly authorizes regulation of suppliers. Thus, the Massachusetts Burma Law should be analyzed in terms of whether it discriminates among similarly-situated foreign suppliers, as suppliers.

With respect to suppliers, the Burma Law is non-discriminatory in terms of nationality, as it treats all suppliers equally. It distinguishes between two categories of supplier: those that do business with Burma within its definition and those that do not. This method of distinction, like a distinction between a low bidder and a high bidder, may only be categorized as discrimination if it is an impermissible distinction. Nothing in the GPA or in WTO law seems to forbid this method of distinction.[37]

It cannot plausibly be argued that a procuring state is forbidden from distinguishing among goods by virtue of the identity of the supplier of the goods, given that GPA Articles VIII(b), X and XII specifically permit distinctions by virtue of the identity of the supplier. What is specifically forbidden by the clear language of GPA Article III is the application of "buy national" laws, which discriminate on the basis of nationality.

ii. Article VIII(b): Qualification of Suppliers

Article VIII was the principal provision relied upon by the EU. However, Article VIII deals with only a particular range of procurement issues: those concerning "qualification of suppliers" in the context of selective tendering procedures (see Article VII(3)(b)). As described in more detail below, while the GPA contains a prohibition on the application of "non-economic" criteria for *qualification* of bidders in selective tenders, the EU simply did not bargain for, or obtain, a commitment to avoid using non-economic factors in evaluating tenders. In fact, the GPA clearly permits the use of such factors.

From a functional or substantive standpoint, this charge of violation of Article VIII is inapposite, as the Burma Law does not deal at all with qualification of suppliers. Rather, in economic substance, the Burma Law merely imposes a 10% preference for suppliers that do not "do business with Burma." The Burma Law must be evaluated in terms of its substantive effects.

Thus, no part of Article VIII is applicable to the Burma Law, which merely imposes a preference, and does not affect the qualification of suppliers. More specifically, the EU relied on the first sentence of Article VIII(b). This sentence states that "any conditions for participation in tendering procedures shall be limited to those which are essential to ensure the firm's capability to fulfil the contract in question." Again, the Burma Law does not impose "conditions for participation"; it simply does not condition participation on any criterion. Rather, it sets a standard for evaluation.

iii. Article XIII

In relevant part, Article XIII(4)(b) requires procurement contracts to be awarded to the tenderer whose tender "is either the lowest tender or the tender which in terms of the specific evaluation criteria set forth in the notices or tender documentation is determined to be the most advantageous." As the Burma Law provides a preference, it does not comply with the first alternative prong. However, the Burma Law seems to comply with the second alternative prong of this provision: it includes the criterion of "doing business in Burma" as a specific evaluation criterion, and specifies the manner in which this criterion is factored into the bid evaluation, in order to determine which bid is most advantageous. Article XIII(4)(c) requires that awards be "made in accordance with the criteria and essential requirements specified in the tender documentation." It contains no restriction on the content of these criteria. We refer to Article XII for guidance as to the types of requirements that may be set forth in tender documentation.

Article XII(h) specifically contemplates non-price factors as permissible of consideration in respect of tenders. These "factors other than price" are specifically separated from price-affecting cost elements, such as transport, insurance and inspection costs. Moreover, Article XII(j) refers to "any other terms or conditions," refuting the EU's contention that Articles VIII, X and XIII somehow exclude non-price or non-economic factors.

iv. Article XXIII(2)

In the event that a panel were to find that the Burma Law otherwise violates the GPA, the U.S. would be likely to argue that the provisions of Article XXIII(2) protect the Burma Law. The relevant language states that, provided the measure is not an arbitrary or unjustifiable discrimination or a disguised restriction on trade, nothing in the GPA shall be construed to prevent any Party from imposing or enforcing measures *necessary* to protect public morals, order or safety, or human life. In order to satisfy these requirements, the Burma Law (i) must not be found to constitute unjustifiable discrimination, (ii) must not be found to constitute a disguised restriction on trade, (iii) must be found necessary in the sense that it is the least trade restrictive alternative available to achieve the permitted end, and (iv) must relate sufficiently to public morals, order or safety, or human health. Addressing this provision would raise the problem of interpretation of "public morals, order or safety" addressed elsewhere in this paper. Furthermore, a panel evaluating this measure would have to evaluate whether Article XXIII(2) encompasses the protection of human life, etc., outside the territory of the state taking the measure. Importantly, in the *Shrimp* case, the Appellate Body specifically declined to rule on whether there is a territorial or jurisdictional limitation in Article XX(g) – whether the "extraterritorial" nature of the U.S. measure removed it from eligibility for an exception under that provision.

v. Article XXIII(1): The Helms-Burton Manoeuvre

Of course, if the WTO dispute settlement proceedings had continued, it is possible the U.S. would have asserted a "non-reviewable" national security justification under Article XXIII(1) of the GPA, which is somewhat similar to Article XXI of GATT.[38] This would amount to an assertion that this measure is part of the "natural law" world, and not subject to WTO positive law. However, Article XXIII(1) of the GPA does not provide authorization that seems broad enough to include the Massachusetts Burma Law, as it refers to action which the party "considers necessary for the protection of its essential security interests relating to the procurement of arms, ammunition or war materials, or to procurement indispensable for national security or for national defense purposes."

vi. Positivism and Natural Law

A WTO panel, or the Appellate Body, could find ways to hold the Burma Law a violation of the GPA – there are certainly colorable arguments available. However, in order to do so, some violence would have to be done to the strict terms of the GPA. The Appellate Body has shown a good deal of respect for the strict terms of the WTO Agreements. Here, a positivist approach would seem to support the "human rights" position – the unilateralist position; while a natural law approach (the "natural law" of unencumbered trade) would support the restrictive view.

d. Helms-Burton: Federal Sticks for Cooptation

i. Helms Burton and the Reciprocal Nature of Human Rights

When discussing Helms-Burton, the first question we should ask is, is it a human rights statute? Of course, Helms-Burton has several components, which perhaps should be analyzed separately, but one of its express goals is to provide incentives for greater democracy and greater respect for human rights in Cuba. Even its provisions relating to restitution or compensation for expropriated property may be viewed as motivated by the goal of enhancing the human right of security in the ownership of private property. One person's pro-democracy, human rights-motivated statute may be another person's imperialist incursion on sovereign independence and territorial integrity. On the other hand, it is worthwhile to explore the link between human rights and national security, as national security benefits from a special exception under Article XXI of GATT. Here, the theory that liberal states do not go to war with one another, if true, could link human rights with national security.

The Helms-Burton Act, formally termed the "Cuban Liberty and Democratic Solidarity (LIBERTAD) Act of 1996,"[39] contains several measures against the Castro government. Of course, the U.S. has maintained a trade embargo against Cuban goods since 1962,[40] although the U.S. could not invoke Article XXXV of GATT or Article XIII of the WTO Charter, concerning non-application of the respective treaties, in relation to Cuba.[41] Cuba has been a member of the WTO since April 20, 1995. Under Title II of the Helms Burton Act, in order to terminate the U.S. embargo, Cuba must take certain steps in order to have its government considered "democratically elected." These include conducting internationally-supervised elections, displaying respect for internationally recognized human rights and making demonstrable progress toward returning or paying full compensation for property expropriated from persons currently U.S. citizens, including naturalized Cubans. Helms-Burton was challenged at the WTO,[42] but the EU and the U.S. reached a settlement.[43] The EU has said that it would request the re-establishment of a WTO panel against the US should any action be taken against EU companies or individuals under the Helms-Burton Act or the Iran-Libya Sanctions Act.

ii. Title I

Among other things, Title I of the Helms-Burton Act codified the existing U.S. trade embargo, and other sanctions, against Cuba. It is noteworthy that Cuba, a member of the WTO since 1995, has not brought a dispute settlement case regarding the U.S. embargo on Cuban goods.

Title I is vulnerable to attack under Articles I (MFN), III (national treatment), V (right of transit), XI (elimination of quantitative restrictions) and XIII (MFN administration of quantitative restrictions).[44] In a case brought by Cuba, these would be bases for invalidating the embargo provisions of Title I. However, from a political (as opposed to legal) standpoint, it should be noted that the embargo codified in Title I is composed of "settled" measures that were in place long before the advent of the WTO. Of course, generally speaking, the U.S. measures are not "grandfathered," and therefore enjoy no special exception due to the time that has passed without legal challenge.

Furthermore, section 110(a) of the Helms-Burton Act confirms long-standing regulations that bar entry into the U.S. of goods "made or derived in whole or in part of any article which is the growth, produce, or manufacture of Cuba." While raising questions about rules of origin, this provision can be viewed as a partial secondary boycott: those who purchase inputs from Cuba will not be permitted to send goods incorporating those inputs to the U.S. In a case brought by a third country, such as the EU, this provision might be attacked under Articles III, XI or XIII. Whether this case would be successful would hinge on the analytical approach taken by the panel or Appellate Body. On the one hand, the Helms-Burton Act might be viewed as a legitimate domestic regulation, enforced at the border, and subject to Article III, excluding the application of Article XI. Provided that the focus is on the question of discrimination between U.S. manufacturers, prohibited from using Cuban ingredients, and foreign manufacturers, similarly restricted, this measure could be found legal under Article III. On the other hand, if the U.S. measure is understood as regulation of a production process, and found on that basis to be in violation of, or outside the coverage of Article III, and also subject to the stricter scrutiny of Article XI, it might be invalidated (subject to the exceptional provisions discussed below). Alternatively, if the U.S. measure is understood to be purely a border measure, it would simply violate Articles XI and XIII.

iii. Title III

Title III provides a private right of action for U.S. nationals whose property was expropriated by the Cuban government, against persons who "traffic" in the expropriated property. Title III has been suspended since its enactment, including most recently by President George W. Bush. Its suspension may or may not insulate it from review under WTO law, especially as liability of "traffickers" under Title III began to accrue as of November 1, 1996.[45] However, it is not clear what grounds for attack exist under WTO law. While this provision may certainly be argued to be "extraterritorial," WTO law does not proscribe extraterritoriality *per se*. It might be argued that the U.S. was improperly burdening the import or export of such expropriated property, perhaps in violation of Articles II, III or XI, or perhaps resulting in non-violation nullification or impairment. However, the linkage of this measure to trade in goods might not be direct or strong enough to establish a violation.

iv. Title IV

Title IV provides for denial of entry visas to any foreign person who has confiscated property or trafficked in confiscated property. While this provision may raise issues under GATS, it is not clear that an attack based on GATS would be successful, as GATS contains no obligation to allow free access to all individuals from other member states.[46] The EU might have argued that Title IV is *de facto* a violation of MFN, or results in a non-violation nullification or impairment of the EU's GATS rights.

v. The Article XXI Defense

One of the most dangerous defensive tactics in international legal disputes is to decline to attend the relevant procedure at which the dispute is to be adjudicated. The U.S. threatened to do so in connection with the WTO proceedings brought by the EU.[47] The U.S. based its defense on Article XXI(b), arguing that the availability of this defense is self-judging, and hence non-justiciable.[48] In relevant part, Article XXI(b) provides that nothing in the GATT shall be construed to prevent any contracting party from taking any action *which it considers* necessary for the protection of its essential security interests taken in time of war or other emergency in international relations. It is also worth considering Article XXI(c), which allows action in pursuance of obligations under the United Nations Charter for the maintenance of international peace and security. In the GATT Panel Report: United States-Trade Measures Affecting Nicaragua,[49] the Panel notes its terms of reference: "To examine [the U.S. measures], in the light of the relevant GATT provisions [and] of the understanding reached at the Council on 10 October 1985 that the Panel cannot examine or judge the validity of or motivation for the invocation of Article XXI(b)(iii) by the United States ..." Thus, the GATT Council reached an understanding in that particular case that the availability of the Article XXI(b)(iii) exception was "self-judging." However, these terms of reference would not bind a WTO panel. Textually, while the "necessity" of action appears to be self-judging, the determination of whether a "war or other emergency in international relations" exists appears to be subject to an objective standard.

vi. The Helms-Burton Settlement

Given the limited possibility for recourse at the WTO against the Helms-Burton Act, one might simply recognize that this is a problem that lacks a forum, and perhaps rules. However, it is open to states to negotiate conventional limitations on these activities, and indeed, the U.S. and EU have begun to do so, in connection with the failed negotiations for a Multilateral Agreement on Investment.

Such a negotiation has the character of exchange of unilateral power for multilateral power, not unlike the negotiation of the DSU: the U.S., as *demandeur*, says that it cannot give up its unilateral weapons unless the international community agrees on an acceptable multilateral weapon. States negotiate an international legal rule, and a method for enforcement of the rule. Notably, in 1998, the U.S. and the EU came to a bilateral political agreement to refrain from coercive extraterritorial sanctions.[50]

In the EU-U.S. Declaration on Political Cooperation, dated May 22, 1998, the parties agree to make a "maximum effort to ensure that economic sanctions are multilateral." Most saliently, they agree that "a partner will not seek or propose, and will resist, the passage of new economic sanctions legislation based on foreign policy grounds which is designed to make economic operators of the other behave in a manner similar to that required of its own economic operators." This type of political agreement begins to divide up prescriptive jurisdiction in ways designed to limit future unilateral action. It begins to develop a "firm."

vii. No Hard Law Forum for Violations of Non-WTO International Law

One observation prompted by a review of the Massachusetts Burma Law, as well as the Helms-Burton and Iran-Libya Sanctions[51] Acts, is that these unilateral measures, and the responses to them by the U.S.' trading partners,[52] are suggestive of a gap in international law. Customary international law lacks clear norms regarding the legality of "extraterritorial" measures and quasi-secondary boycotts, such as those used by the U.S. in these cases. States are thus left to their own devices to act and react to particular events. While the Inter-American Juridical Committee found the Helms-Burton Act to violate customary international law,[53] this finding did not have the positive law enforcement capability definitively to resolve this dispute. Given this gap in enforcement capability, states have referred some of these matters to the WTO. However, while WTO law may set some limits on these measures, to the extent that they are characterized as for "political" or "national security" purposes, the U.S. may deny the jurisdiction of the WTO dispute settlement system over these matters.

e. Trade Act of 1974 Section 301: More Sticks

Section 301 of the Trade Act of 1974 is the provision of U.S. law by which the U.S. acts to assert its rights under WTO law and in other trade contexts. Section 301(d)(3)(B)(iii) includes in the definition of "unreasonable" acts which constitute a persistent pattern of conduct that (i) denies workers the right of association, (ii) denies workers the right to organize and bargain collectively, (iii) permits any form of forced or compulsory labor, (iv) fails to provide a minimum age for the employment of children, or (v) fails to provide standards for minimum wages, hours of work, and occupational safety and health of workers.

This provision gives rise to the possibility of *discretionary* action by the USTR under section 301(b), <u>if it burdens or restricts United States commerce</u>. The latter restriction may be interpreted as a requirement for a real externality in the form of a restriction on trade, as opposed to a moral externality. It appears that this provision has never been applied to promote worker rights.[54]

Presumably, U.S. determinations under this provision are unrestricted under WTO law, as human rights use does not fall under Article 23 of the DSU, although the sanctions available to the U.S. are restricted under WTO law. Article 23 permits unilateralism *outside* the area of obligations, and non-violation nullification or impairment, under the covered agreements, provided, of course, that a quota or tariff modification or other action that violates another part of WTO law would not be permitted. Thus, while the U.S. seems free to review and make determinations regarding foreign states' workers' rights practices, at least in relation to WTO members the sanctions available to the U.S. under this law are restricted.

International law permits what it does not prohibit.[55] The U.S. has retained sovereignty to act to promote workers' rights, so long as it does not use sanctions prohibited under WTO (or other) law. While U.S. sovereignty may infringe the sovereignty of other states, and may even violate international law, these issues do not serve as a basis for claims in WTO dispute resolution, unless they also violate WTO law. In this particular context, the limitations of WTO dispute resolution may be pleasing to NGOs promoting human rights.

f. Tariff Act § 307, 19 U.S.C. § 1307 and Child Labor

Section 307 of the Tariff Act[56] prohibits the import of goods made using prison or forced labor. It has been invoked with respect to Mexico[57] and China.[58] Child labor *per se* is not covered, but in 1998, amendments provided for the exclusion from the U.S. of goods produced by forced or indentured child labor.[59] By a 1999 executive order, President Clinton defined "forced or indentured child labor" to include work "(1) exacted from any person under the age of 18 under the menace of any penalty for its nonperformance and for which the worker does not offer himself voluntarily; or (2) performed by any person under the age of 18 pursuant to a contract the enforcement of which can be accomplished by process or penalties." This is a rather broad definition.[60] Clinton also established procurement regulations that require contractors to certify the absence of forced or indentured child labor. Interestingly, these regulations exclude from their coverage procurement from countries party to the GPA or NAFTA, where the procurement is above the applicable thresholds.

Article XX(e) of GATT permits an exception for measures "relating to the products of prison labor." While there is no specific exception for other categories of forced or indentured labor, it may be that Article XX(b), relating to human health, would provide a justification for some types of barriers. Perhaps more importantly, states may be reluctant to raise complaints regarding these types of barriers.

From time to time during the past 10 years, varying bills have been proposed in the U.S. Congress to impose an embargo on goods produced using child labor generally.[61] Such an embargo would be likely to violate Article XI of GATT, and would require justification pursuant to Article XX of GATT.[62] There are arguments that Article XX(a)[63] or XX(b) might apply. Article XX(a) relates to "public morals." There is little guidance on the content of the term "public morals."[64] An argument under Article XX(b) might be more availing, but the embargo would be required to be justified as "necessary" to protect human health.

Some have argued that *jus cogens* norms should be a basis for interpretation, or revision, of GATT obligations.[65] There are substantial questions regarding the content of *jus cogens*.[66] It appears unlikely for example that uncoerced child labor could be viewed as prohibited by *jus cogens*. There are also substantial questions about the role of *jus cogens* in WTO dispute settlement. While of course all states would be bound by true *jus cogens*, and must conduct themselves accordingly, the WTO Dispute Settlement Understanding does not authorize panels or the Appellate Body to apply directly *jus cogens*, or other customary international law.[67] Through its reference to the customary rules of *interpretation* of public international law, it does authorize them to "take into account" non-WTO law in their task of interpreting WTO law.[68]

g. International Emergency Economic Powers Act

Under the International Emergency Economic Powers Act (IEEPA),[69] Congress has granted the President broad authority to impose certain types of economic sanctions for foreign policy and national security purposes. This authority has been used for human rights purposes, as, for example, when President Reagan imposed sanctions on South Africa in 1985.[70] Reagan was seeking to preempt stronger sanctions legislation then pending in Congress. In 1986, Congress overruled Reagan's veto to pass the Comprehensive Anti-Apartheid Act, which was supported by U.N. declarations, and which, *inter alia*, restricted trade in goods between the U.S. and South Africa.

IEEPA has also been used to impose sanctions for human rights purposes on Nicaragua, Libya, Panama, Iraq, Haiti, Yugoslavia, Ethiopia, Eritrea and Burma.[71]

To the extent that the President uses the national security authority under the IEEPA, it may be that these actions would qualify for exemption under Article XXI of GATT and similar national security provisions in other WTO agreements. Where the President instead uses the foreign policy authority, the WTO case may be undermined.

h. A Foray into Bilateralism in Labor Rights: Cambodia, Jordan and NAFTA

The U.S. has had notorious domestic disagreement in determining whether to seek labor rights requirements in international trade agreements: whether to seek to establish formal linkage between trade norms and labor rights norms. The general expectation has been that these linkages would be fairly general, such as requiring partners to adhere to certain international labor rights conventions, or particular groups of standards. Another alternative approach in addressing these types of issues would be more particular: using a "request-offer" system to negotiate specific reforms with particular other states.[72] This would have the advantage of predictability for other states, as well as providing an occasion for other states to negotiate compensation for the requested reforms.

The U.S. has established a prototype agreement that contains some characteristics of this type of specific arrangement in its recent agreement with Cambodia. The 1999 U.S.-Cambodia Textiles Agreement is the first bilateral textiles agreement to contain a provision regarding labor rights, and incorporates a kind of continuing labor rights conditionality, expanding Cambodia's textiles quota by 14% each year it is judged by the U.S. to be in "substantial compliance" with core labor rights.[73]

The 2000 Jordan-U.S. Free Trade Agreement contains a more standard labor rights provision.[74] It requires that each country enforce its own labor laws and that those laws reflect "internationally-recognized worker rights" as defined by the U.S. Trade Act of 1974, as well as "core labor standards" defined by the ILO.

3. Sovereignty and International Law; Unilateralism and Multilateralism; Market and Firm; Natural Law and Positive Law

The unilateral actions of states are dynamic acts that build or diminish particular customary international law rules. Where there is no positive law requiring other states to protect certain human rights, or the existing positive law is not enforceable through positive law mechanisms, coercive acts of "officious intermeddlers" may be part of the "natural law" system of legislation and enforcement. However, states must approach these unilateral acts with care, and they may be restricted by international law.

Perhaps more importantly, unilateral acts by states may be the only way to get the attention of other states, in order to begin a serious dialogue toward institutionalization, toward movement from the market to the firm. There is an important relationship between unilateral acts and multilateral development of conventional law. Just as establishing a firm is not always appropriate, so establishing international institutions is not necessarily the best response to international concerns.

Finally, it is important to recognize that there is weak and strong international law. Often, international law that relies on natural law enforcement may be characterized as weak. It is open to lobbyists and commentators to seek stronger enforcement of this type of international law, but it is not open to scholars to simply assume that international law designed with limited binding force should be accorded greater binding force.

NOTES

1. For a recent example of this point of view, see John O. McGinnis, *No, Free Trade Needs a Free Rein*, L.A. Times, July 30, 2001: "Lower tariffs overseas actually increase liberty by freeing U.S. producers from restrictions that reduce their exports. And reducing tariffs at home leaves our consumers free to choose better goods at lower prices."

2. These perspectives present a challenge to a deontological approach to human rights, such as that expressed in Frank Garcia, *The Global Market and Human Rights: Trading Away the Human Rights Principle*, 25 BROOKLYN J. INT'L L. 51 (1999). Any disagreement regarding the priorities and weighting among human rights gives rise to a need to compromise some or all of them. In a liberal world, the existential task of public policy is to do so.

3. Sarah H. Cleveland, *Norm Internalization and U.S. Economic Sanctions*, 26 YALE J. INT'L L. 1, 51, n. 303 (2001).

4. See Military and Paramilitary Activities (Nicar. V. U.S.), 1986 I.C.J. 14, 126 (June 27); Lori Fisler Damrosch, *Politics Across Borders: Nonintervention and Nonforcible Influence over Domestic Affairs*, 83 AM. J. INT'L L. 39 (1989); Cleveland, supra note 3, at 52-56.

5. One may take the reverse view, that it is the domestic, or the unilateral, that is complementary to the multilateral, or the global. However, if one focuses on people, and their wishes, as the fount of authority, then, at least at the present historical moment, the unilateral seems to have greater access to their wishes than the multilateral.

6. For a more extensive discussion of this perspective, see Joel P. Trachtman, *The Theory of the Firm and the Theory of the International Economic Organization: Toward Comparative Institutional Analysis*, 17 NORTHW. J. INT'L L. & BUS. 470 (1997).

7. Target states may argue that the world trade system – the underlying market – should not be jeopardized in order to engage in these types of coercive acts. This is the argument of the *Le Louis* case, holding international commerce paramount, regardless of applicable legal rules against slavery. In order to accept this argument, utilitarians would have to know more about the value of unimpeded commerce, and compare it to the value of engaging in conduct to influence the behavior of others. It is an argument that we have not accepted within domestic society. While the contribution of unimpeded trade is indeed important, we must remain free to make decisions, through governmental processes, that may regulate or even curtail the operation of the market.

8. I thank my colleague Al Rubin for introducing me to this distinction.

9. Alan O. Sykes, *Constructive Unilateral Threats in International Commercial Relations: The Limited Case for Section 301*, 23 L. & POL'Y INT'L BUS. 263, 267 (1992) (discussing trade commitments). Sykes concludes that "[t]he case for unilateral threat strategies ultimately rests on the existence of important aspects of commercial relations that are outside the scope of international compacts, or that are subject to compacts without effective third-party dispute resolution." Id. at 269. See also Alan O. Sykes, *"Mandatory Retaliation" for Breach of Trade Agreements: Some Thoughts on the Strategic Design of Section 301*, 8 B.U. INT'L L.J. 301 (1990); John McMillan, *Strategic Bargaining and Section 301*, in AGGRESSIVE UNILATERALISM 203 (Jagdish Bhagwati & Hugh T. Patrick (eds.), 1990).

10. Robert E. Hudec, *Thinking About the New Section 301: Beyond Good and Evil*, in AGGRESSIVE UNILATERALISM 113, 116 (Jagdish Bhagwati & Hugh T. Patrick eds., 1990). Obviously, Hudec wrote before the advent of the WTO, and so refers to GATT.

11. For this argument, see James P. Kelleher, *The Child Labor Deterrence Act: American Unilateralism and the GATT*, 3 MINN. J. GLOBAL TRADE 161 (1994).

12. Hudec, supra note 10, at 130-31.

13. Id. at 137-38.

14. This raises an interesting public relations, or public diplomacy, concern. Of course, much depends on whose welfare is being maximized – on the distribution of wealth. One might argue that it is not sufficient for the aggregate social welfare to be maximized; rather, in accordance with something like Rawls' maximin principle, outsiders might demand that the wealth of the poorest segment be maximized. JOHN RAWLS, A THEORY OF JUSTICE 152-57 (Harvard Univ. Press 1972).

15. See Sykes, Constructive Unilateral Threats, supra note 9, at 283.

16. See Robert Howse, *The World Trade Organization and the Protection of Workers' Rights*, 3 J. SMALL & EMERGING BUS. L. 131, 162 (1999).

17. See Anne-Marie Burley, *Toward an Age of Liberal Nations*, 33 HARV. INT'L L.J. 393 (1992). See also José E. Alvarez, *Do Liberal States Behave Better? A Critique of Slaughter's Liberal Theory*, 12 EUR. J. INT'L L. 183 (2001).

18. See Lynn Stout, *Other-Regarding Preferences and Social Norms*, Georgetown University Law Center, Public Law and Legal Theory Working Paper No. 265902, March 2, 2001, available at http://papers.ssrn.com/sol3/papers.cfm?abstract_id=265902.

19. Jackson-Vanik Amendment of the Trade Act of 1974, § 402, 19 U.S.C. § 2432 (1994 & Supp. V 2000). U.S.-China Relations Act of 2000, Pub. L. No. 106-286, 114 Stat. 880.

20. Although since 1998, for evident public relations purposes, the U.S. has termed this "normal trade relations," we will continue to use MFN.

21. See Statement on Most-Favored Nation Trade Status for China, 29 Weekly Comp. Pres. Doc. 981, 982 (May 31, 1993); Cleveland, supra note 3, at 35. See also DANIEL F. WILHELM, MOST-FAVORED-NATION CERTIFICATION AND HUMAN RIGHTS: A CASE STUDY OF CHINA AND THE UNITED STATES (1996).

22. 19 U.S.C. § 2462(c)(7) (Supp. V 2000).

23. Similar labor rights-based conditionality is contained in the Caribbean Basin Economic Recovery Expansion Act, 19 U.S.C. § 2702(c)(8) (1994); the Andean Trade Preference Act, 19 U.S.C. § 3202(c)(7) (Supp. V 2000); and the African Growth and Opportunity Act, 19 U.S.C.A. § 3703(a)(1)(F) (West 2001).

24. Trade and Development Act of 2000, Pub. L. No. 106-200, § 412, 114 Stat. 251 (2000) (amending definition of forced or indentured labor to include forced or indentured child labor).

25. Those countries that have undergone a review, suspension or removal include Romania, Nicaragua, Paraguay, Chile, Burma, Central African Republic, Liberia, Yugoslavia, Sudan, Syria, Mauritania, the Maldives, Pakistan, North Korea, El Salvador, Guatemala, Indonesia, Thailand, Malawi, Oman, Belarus and Swaziland. Cleveland, supra note 3, at 45.

26. Proclamation No. 5758, 52 Fed. Reg. 49,129 (Dec. 24, 1987).

27. Appellate Body Report, European Communities – Conditions for the Granting of Tariff Preferences to Developing Countries, WT/DS246/AB/R (April 20, 2004).

28. For an explicit statement about similar characteristics of the African Growth and Opportunity Act, see Jagdish Bhagwati & Arvind Panagariya, *A Trojan Horse for Africa: The Africa Act Offers More to U.S. Lobby Groups Than to Participant Countries*, Financial Times, June 30, 2000, at 13.

29. For an analysis of unilateral measures relating to environmental protection in terms of "carrots" and "sticks," see Howard F. Chang, *An Economic Analysis of Trade Measures to Protect the Global Environment*, 83 GEO. L.J. 2131 (1995).

30. GATT, BISD, 18S/24 (1972).

31. Differential and More Favourable Treatment, Reciprocity and Fuller Participation of Developing Countries , L/4903 (Nov. 28, 1979) ("Enabling Clause"), GATT, BISD 26S/203. Footnote 3 to the Enabling Clause, referring to the Generalized System of Preferences, states as follows: "As described in the Decision of the Contracting Parties of 25 June 1971, relating to the establishment of 'generalized, non-reciprocal and non-discriminatory preferences beneficial to the developing countries.' (BISD 18S/24)."

32. Request for Consultations by Brazil, European Communities – Measures Affecting Soluble Coffee, WT/DS209/1, 19 October 2000. European Communities – Conditions for Granting of Tariff Preferences to Developing Countries, Report of the Appellate Body, WT/DS246/AB/R, 20 April 2004.

33. MASS. GEN. LAWS ch. 7, § 22 (2000).

34. Crosby v. National Foreign Trade Council, 530 U.S. 363 (2000). The Court found that the Massachusetts Burma Statute was pre-empted by federal legislation imposing sanctions on Burma, but avoided a broader holding to the effect that U.S. states are always prohibited from interfering with international commerce or interfering in foreign relations in this way. See Robert J. Delahunty, *Federalism Beyond the Water's Edge: State Procurement Sanctions and Foreign Affairs*, 37 STANFORD J. INT'L L. 1 (2001).

35. United States-Measures Affecting Government Procurement; Request for Consultations by the European Communities, WT/DS88/1 (June 26, 1997); United States– Measures Affecting Government Procurement; Request for Consultations by Japan, WT/DS95/1 (July 21, 1997). See also Christopher McCrudden, *International Economic Law and the Pursuit of Human Rights: A Framework for Discussion of the Legality of 'Selective Purchasing' Laws under the WTO Government Procurement Agreement*, 2 J. INT'L ECON. L. 3 (1999). The present author served as an adviser to the Commonwealth of Massachusetts in connection with this dispute. However, the statements made herein are the author's sole responsibility, and are not intended to represent the views of the Commonwealth.

36. WTO, United States-Measure Affecting Government Procurement: Lapse of Authority for Establishment of the Panel: Note by the Secretariat, WT/DS88/6, WT/DS95/6 (Feb. 14, 2000).

37. The second recital of the GPA confirms the intent to address discrimination on the basis of nationality, not differential treatment of the type provided under the Burma Law.

38. See the discussion of Article XXI of GATT in connection with Helms-Burton below.

39. Pub. L. No. 104-114, 110 Stat. 785.

40. Imposed by regulation pursuant to the Foreign Assistance Act of 1961, Pub. L. No. 87-195, § 620(a), 75 Stat. 424, 444-45, codified at 22 U.S.C. § 2370(a), and the Trading with the Enemy Act, 50 U.S.C. app. § 5(b) (1994 & Supp. V 2000).

41. Cuba was an original member of the GATT in 1947, and so the U.S. had no opportunity to invoke Article XXXV of GATT as to the Castro regime, and Article XIII of the WTO Charter is only available where Article XXXV of GATT 1947 was previously invoked.

42. See John A. Spanogle, *Can Helms-Burton be Challenged Under WTO?*, 27 STETSON L. REV. 1313 (1998); Raj Bhala, *National Security and International Trade Law: What the GATT Says, and What the United States Does*, 19 U. PA. J. INT'L ECON. L N 263 (1998).

43. Memorandum of Understanding Concerning the U.S. Helms-Burton Act and the U.S. Iran and Libya Sanctions Act, Apr. 11 1997, EU-U.S., *reprinted in* 36 I.L.M 529 (1997), 91 AM. J. INT'L L. 498 (1997); http://www.eurunion.org/legislat/extrel/cuba/understd.htm. This was followed up in 1998 with several additional agreements. 1998 Understanding with Respect to Disciplines for the Strengthening of Investment Protection (May 18, 1998) and the Understanding on Conflicting Requirements, at http://www.eurunion.org/partner/summit/Summit9805/invest.htm. See Stefaan Smis & Kim Van der Borght, *The EU-U.S. Compromise on the Helms- Burton and D'Amato Acts*, 93 AM. J. INT'L L. 227 (1999).

44. See Spanogle, supra note 42, at 1318-1328.

45. See 22 U.S.C. §§ 6082(a)(1), 6085(a) (Supp. V 2000).

46. See Spanogle, supra note 42, at 1326.

47. Paul Blustein & Anne Swardson, U.S. Vows to Boycott WTO Panel, Wash. Post, Feb. 21, 1997, at A12.

48. See John H. Jackson & Andreas F. Lowenfeld, *Helms-Burton, the U.S., & the WTO*, ASIL Insight (Mar. 1997), available at http://www.asil.org/insight7.htm; Bhala, supra note 42; Rene E. Browne, *Revisiting "National Security" in an Interdependent World*, 86 GEO. L.J. 405 (1997). See also GATT Panel Report, U.S-Trade Measures Affecting Nicaragua, GATT Doc. L/ 6053, Oct. 13, 1986.

49. L/6053, 13 October 1986 (not adopted). See Richard S. Whitt, *The Politics of Procedure: An Examination of the GATT Dispute Settlement Panel and the Article XXI Defense in the Context of the U.S. Embargo of Nicaragua,* 19 L. & POL'Y INT'L BUS. 603 (1987).

50. Transatlantic Partnership on Political Cooperation, May 18, 1998, P 2(h), reprinted in EU-U.S. Declaration on Political Cooperation, Inside U.S. Trade, May 22, 1998, at 23-27.

51. The 1996 Iran and Libya Sanctions Act, recently renewed for a five-year period, requires a secondary boycott against foreign companies that make substantial oil investment in Iran or Libya. Some of the issues that it raises are similar to some of the issues raised by Helms-Burton.

52. See Canadian Foreign Extraterritorial Measures Act Incorporating the Amendments Countering the U.S. Helms-Burton Act, 36 I.L.M. 111 (1997); the European Union Council Regulation (EC) No. 2271/96, blocking the Helms-Burton Act, 36 I.L.M. 125 (1997); and the Mexican Act to Protect Trade and Investment from Foreign Norms that Contravene International Law, 36 I.L.M. 133 (1997).

53. OAS Inter-American Juridical Committee Opinion Examining the U.S. Helms-Burton Act, 35 ILM 1322 (1996). The Committee found that the Helms-Burton Act violated international law for a number of reasons, including by extending U.S. jurisdiction "extraterritorially," by improperly

assigning domestic courts to deal with state-to-state claims, by espousing claims of persons who were not nationals at the time of injury, and by attributing liability to third-state nationals for claims against a foreign state.

54. Cleveland, supra note 3, at 33, n 175.

55. See, e.g., Military and Paramilitary Activities (Nicar. v. U.S.), 1991 I.C.J. 47 (Sept. 1986); The Case of the S.S. Lotus (Fr. V. Turk.), 1927 P.C.I.J. (Ser. A) No. 10, at 19.

56. Tariff Act of 1930, ch. 497, 46 Stat. 590, 689-90 (codified as amended at 19 U.S.C.A. § 1307 (West 1999 & Supp. 2001)). This provision is the successor to § 51 of the McKinley Tariff Act of 1890, ch. 1244, 26 Stat. 567, 624.

57. Merchandise Produced by Convict, Forced, or Indentured Labor, 19 C.F.R. § 12.42(h) (2001).

58. Determination that Merchandise Imported from the People's Republic of China Is Being Produced with Convict, Forced or Indentured Labor by the Qinghai Hide and Garment Factory, 58 Fed. Reg. 32,746 (June 11, 1993); Determination that Merchandise Imported from the People's Republic of China Is Produced Using Convict, Forced, or Indentured Labor by the Tianjin Malleable Iron Factory, 61 Fed. Reg. 17,956 (Apr. 23, 1996). See also China Diesel Imports v. United States, 870 F.Supp. 347 (Ct. Int'l Trade 1994).

59. Treasury and General Government Appropriations Act, Pub. L. No. 105-61, § 634, 111 Stat. 1272, 1316 (1997) (the "Sanders Law"). See Donna L. Bade, *Corporate Responsibility and U.S. Import Regulations Against Forced Labor*, 8 TULSA J. COMP. & INT'L L. 5, 9 (2000). See also § 411 of the Trade and Development Act of 2000, Pub. L. 106-200, 114 Stat. 251 (amending definition of forced or indentured labor to include forced or indentured child labor).

60. Exec. Order No. 13,126, 64 Fed. Reg. 32,383 (June 12, 1999).

61. See generally, Kelleher, supra note 11.

62. This statement is true under current interpretations of Article III of GATT. If the product-process distinction were abrogated, and if Article III continues to be interpreted to insulate measures thereunder from Article XI scrutiny, no Article XX justification would be required.

63. See Steve Charnovitz, *The Moral Exception in Trade Policy*, 38 VA. J. INT'L L. 689 (1998).

64. Id., at 729-730.

65. Janelle M. Diller & David A. Levy, *Child Labor, Trade and Investment: Toward the Harmonization of International Law*, 91 AM. J. INT'L L. 663 (1997).

66. The following areas are included under the RESTATEMENT (THIRD) OF FOREIGN RELATIONS LAW OF THE UNITED STATES § 702 (1987): genocide, slavery, summary execution or disappearance, torture or other cruel, inhuman or degrading treatment or punishment, prolonged arbitrary detention, systematic racial discrimination and a consistent pattern of gross violations of

internationally recognized human rights. Rights of association, uncoerced child labor and other more general labor rights do not seem to be included.

67. But see Joost Pauwelyn, *The Role of Public International Law in the WTO: How Far Can We Go?*, 95 AM. J. INT'L L. 535 (2001).

68. Vienna Convention on the Law of Treaties, Article 31(3)(c).

69. Pub. L. No. 95-223, tit. II, 91 Stat. 1625, 1626-29 (1977) (codified as amended at 50 U.S.C. §§ 1701-1706 (1994 & Supp. V 2000)).

70. Exec. Order No. 12,532, 50 Fed. Reg. 36,861 (Sept. 9, 1985).

71. Cleveland, supra note 3, at 41-42, *citing* notes following 50 U.S.C. § 1701 (1994).

72. See Joel P. Trachtman, *International Trade as a Vector in Domestic Regulatory Reform: Discrimination, Cost-Benefit Analysis and Negotiations*, 24 FORDHAM INT'L L.J. 726, 741-42 (2000).

73. See Adjustment of Import Limits for Certain Cotton, Wool and Man-Made Fiber Textile Products Produced or Manufactured in Cambodia, 65 Fed. Reg. 56,537 (Sept. 19, 2000); see also Cambodia Unlikely to Get Full Hike of Labor-Linked Textile Quotas, Inside U.S. Trade, Dec. 15, 2000, at 3.

74. Agreement Between the United States of America and the Hashemite Kingdom of Jordan on the Establishment of a Free Trade Area, Article 6.4(a).